GERMAN BLOOD, SLAVIC SOIL

A volume in the series

Battlegrounds: Cornell Studies in Military History

Edited by David J. Silbey

Editorial Board: Petra Goedde, Wayne E. Lee, Brian McAllister Linn, and Lien-Hang T. Nguyen

A list of titles in this series is available at cornellpress.cornell.edu.

GERMAN BLOOD, SLAVIC SOIL

HOW NAZI KÖNIGSBERG BECAME SOVIET KALININGRAD

NICOLE EATON

CORNELL UNIVERSITY PRESS
Ithaca and London

First published 2023 by Cornell University Press

Library of Congress Cataloging-in-Publication Data
Names: Eaton, Nicole, 1979– author.
Title: German blood, Slavic soil : how Nazi Königsberg
    became Soviet Kaliningrad / Nicole Eaton.
Description: Ithaca [New York] : Cornell University
    Press, 2023. | Series: Battlegrounds : Cornell studies
    in military history | Includes bibliographical
    references and index.
Identifiers: LCCN 2022025594 (print) | LCCN
    2022025595 (ebook) | ISBN 9781501767364
    (hardcover) | ISBN 9781501767371 (epub) |
    ISBN 9781501767388 (pdf)
Subjects: LCSH: World War, 1939-1945—Russia
    (Federation)—Kaliningrad (Kaliningradskaia oblast') |
    World War, 1939-1945—Prussia, East (Poland and
    Russia) | Kaliningrad (Kaliningradskaia oblast',
    Russia)—History—20th century. | Kaliningrad
    (Kaliningradskaia oblast', Russia)—Ethnic relations.
Classification: LCC DK651.K1213 E28 2023 (print) |
    LCC DK651.K1213 (ebook) |
    DDC 947/.24084—dc23/eng/20220622
LC record available at https://lccn.loc.gov/2022025594
LC ebook record available at https://lccn.loc.
    gov/2022025595

CONTENTS

Acknowledgments

A whole city's worth of people and institutions helped make this book possible. The research was supported by generous grants from the Fulbright-Hays Doctoral Dissertation Research Abroad Program, the German Academic Exchange Service, the Mabelle McLeod Lewis Memorial Fund, the University of California, Berkeley Institute for International Studies John Simpson Memorial Fellowship, the Charlotte W. Newcombe Doctoral Dissertation Fellowship, the Social Sciences Research Council Eurasia Dissertation Fellowship, the Berlin Program for Advanced German and European Studies Fellowship, the United States Holocaust Memorial Museum (USHMM) Research Fellowship, the Harriman Institute at Columbia University, and the Kennan Institute of the Woodrow Wilson Center for Scholars. The Department of History, Institute for Slavic, Eastern European, and Eurasian Studies, and the Program in Soviet, Eastern European, and Eurasian Studies at Berkeley helped a midwestern émigré feel at home.

During research trips to Russia, Germany, Poland, and Ukraine, I received excellent guidance from numerous institutions. The archivists at the State Archive of Kaliningrad Oblast (GAKO) and the State Archive of Contemporary History of Kaliningrad Oblast provided exceptional support, especially Varvara Ivanovna Egorova and Anatolii Bakhtin at GAKO. Karin Goihl at the Berlin Program facilitated scholarly camaraderie and guided me through German bureaucracy. Conversations in three languages and on two continents with scholars of the region, including Yury Kostyashov, Markus Podehl, Bert Hoppe, Per Brodersen, Katja Grupp, Natalia Palamarchuk, Holt Meyer, and David Bridges ignited my passion for Kaliningrad and people who have lived there.

In the early stages of research and writing, Victoria Bonnell got me to think about the practices of everyday life, and John Connelly helped me think outside the German and Soviet microcosm. Stephen Brain, Christine Evans, Victoria Frede-Montemayor, Alice Goff, Faith Hillis, Stefan-Ludwig Hoffmann, Filippo Marsili, Martina Nguyen, Alina

Polyakova, Ned Richardson-Little, Kevin Rothrock, Tehila Sasson, Erik Scott, James Skee, Victoria Smolkin, Jarrod Tanny, and Ned Walker encouraged me to think about pictures big and small. Peggy Anderson and Reggie Zelnik deserve special thanks for encouraging me to put Russia and Germany together in the first place.

Many people, including members of the working groups at Berkeley, the Free University of Berlin, Ludwig Maximilian University of Munich, USHMM, Georgetown University, Columbia University, the Harvard Davis Center, Brown University, and Boston College, helped refine the manuscript through conversation or by commenting on the written text in part or as a whole. Numerous colleagues provided valuable feedback, including Rachel Applebaum, Jadwiga Biskupska, Johanna Conterio, Bathsheba Demuth, Rhiannon Dowling, Steven Feldman, Anna Ivanova, Emil Kerenji, Nataliia Laas, Vojin Majstorović, Terry Martin, Jürgen Matthäus, Erina Megowan, Alexis Peri, Serhii Plokhii, Steven Sage, Yana Skorobogatova, and Alan Timberlake. At Boston College, I was inspired by conversations with Julian Bourg, Thomas Dodman, Robin Fleming, Penelope Ismay, Marilynn Johnson, Stacie Kent, Lynn Lyerly, Yajun Mo, Prasannan Parthasarathi, Devin Pendas, Virginia Reinburg, Sarah Ross, Sylvia Sellers-Garcia, Franziska Seraphim (whose relative once lived in Königsberg), and Conevery Bolton Valencius (who got me thinking about bodies and places more broadly). Yuri Slezkine, a friend and mentor in matters of form and content, helped give shape to the first draft and polished the final one.

This book, despite its lingering flaws and omissions, has been much improved thanks to constructive feedback from Brandon Schechter and Michael David-Fox. Series editor, David Silbey, and outstanding editors at Cornell, Emily Andrew, Bethany Wasik, and Karen Laun, shepherded the manuscript from submission to publication. Andrei Nesterov navigated Russian archives to secure image permissions, Irina Burns made my prose shine, and Gregory T. Woolston produced beautiful maps.

For steadfast support and intellectual engagement, I could wish for no better a friend than Ryan Calder. Erika Hughes continues to inspire me with her wisdom, joy, and poignant understanding of all things sacred and profane. Diane Cordeiro would certainly never read a book like this, but she is perhaps the person who most greatly facilitated its completion. Finally, this book is for Srdjan Smajić, for companionship and long-suffering patience, for Charley, who never lost faith, and for Sonja, who was not there at the start but made it all worth it in the end.

ARCHIVAL ABBREVIATIONS

AA	Archiv des Auswärtigen Amtes, Berlin
AP-Olsztyn	Archiwum Państwowe w Olsztynie, Olsztyn
BA-Berlin	Bundesarchiv-Berlin Lichterfelde, Berlin
BA-Freiburg	Bundesarchiv-Freiburg, Militär-Abteilung, Freiburg
BA-Ludwigsburg	Bundesarchiv-Ludwigsburg, Ludwigsburg
GAKO	Gosudarstvennyi Arkhiv Kaliningradskoi Oblasti, Kaliningrad
GANIKO	Gosudarstvennyi Arkhiv Noveishei Istorii Kaliningradskoi Oblasti, Kaliningrad
GARF	Gosudarstvennyi Arkhiv Rossiiskii Federatsii, Moscow
GStPK	Geheimes Staatsarchiv Preußischer Kulturbesitz, Berlin
HIA	The Hoover Institution Archives, Palo Alto
MVS	Tsentral'nyi Muzei Vooruzhennykh Sil, Moscow
RGAKFD	Rossiiskii Gosudarstvennyi Arkhiv Kinofotodokumentov, Krasnogorsk
RGASPI	Rossiiskii Gosudarstvennyi Arkhiv Sotsial'no-Politicheskoi Istorii, Moscow
RGVA	Rossiiskii Gosudarstvennyi Voennyi Arkhiv, Moscow
TsAMO	Tsentral'nyi Arkhiv Ministerstva Oborony, Moscow
TsDAVOU	Tsentral'nyi derzhavnyi arkhiv vyshchykh orhaniv vlady Ukrainy, Kyiv

Baltic Sea

LITHUANIA

Memel / Klaipėda

ceded to Lithuania, 1923 to 1939

Tilsit

Memel River

Free City of Danzig / Gdańsk

Polish Corridor

Cranz

Königsberg

Gumbinnen

Pillau

Insterburg

East Prussia

Area of 1920 Plebiscite

Marienwerder

Allenstein

GERMANY

Vistula River

POLAND

ceded to Poland

--- 1914 borders —— interwar borders

SWEDEN

SOVIET UNION

GERMANY

POLAND

FRANCE

ROMANIA

YUGOSLAVIA

MAP 1. East Prussia in the interwar period.

MAP 2. East Prussia during the Second World War, showing annexed territories along the province's borders and Reichskommissar Erich Koch's dominion in Ukraine.

MAP 3. Kaliningrad Oblast after the Second World War. The Memel/Klaipėda region was granted to the Lithuanian SSR and the Masurian region to Poland. Kaliningrad Oblast became part of the Russian Soviet Federative Socialist Republic in 1946.

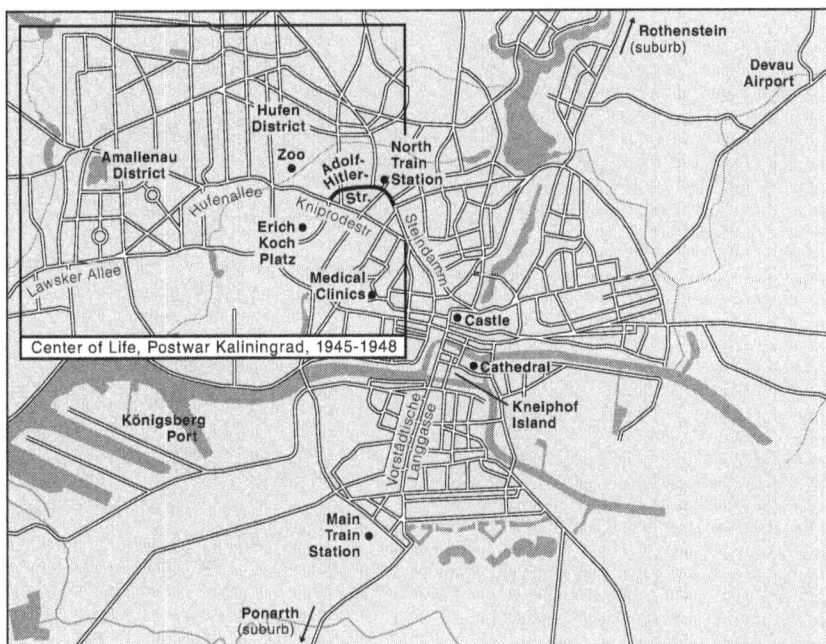

Map of Königsberg showing districts and landmarks including: Rothenstein (suburb), Devau Airport, Hufen District, Zoo, Amalienau District, Adolf-Hitler-Str., North Train Station, Hufenallee, Kniprodestr, Erich Koch Platz, Lawsker Allee, Steindamm, Medical Clinics, Center of Life, Postwar Kaliningrad, 1945-1948, Castle, Cathedral, Königsberg Port, Vorstädtische Langgasse, Kneiphof Island, Main Train Station, Ponarth (suburb).

MAP 4. Map of Königsberg, circa 1938. The wartime destruction of the historic city center led to the shift of postwar urban life in Kaliningrad to the turn-of-the-century suburbs northwest of the former city walls.

Introduction

Königsberg/Kaliningrad is the only city to have been ruled by both Hitler and Stalin as their own domain—not only in wartime occupation, but also as an integral part of their empires. As a borderland of both the Third Reich and the Soviet Union, the city became a battleground of revolutionary politics, radical upheaval, and extended encounters between the two regimes and their more or less willing representatives. This book is about how Königsberg became Kaliningrad—how modern Europe's two most violent revolutionary regimes battled over one city and the people who lived there. It offers a microcosm of the Nazi-Soviet conflict in the decade surrounding the Second World War. It explores how two states sought to refashion the same city and reveals how local inhabitants became proponents of radical transformation, perpetrators of exclusionary violence, beneficiaries of social advancement, and victims of oppression. The book focuses especially on the period from 1944 to 1948, when Germans and Soviets lived and died together, first under Nazi and then under Soviet rule, as they tried to make sense of the war that had drawn them together.

Königsberg, a port city on the Baltic Sea, was founded in the thirteenth century by the Teutonic Knights and grew to be the easternmost major city in the German lands, a vibrant trading port and cultural capital of the German Enlightenment. After the First World War, the city and the surrounding territory of East Prussia became "orphans of Versailles," cut off from the mainland of the Reich by the Polish Corridor, a twenty-to-seventy-mile strip of land designed to grant the new Polish state access to the Baltic Sea.[1] East Prussia became an exclave: a symbol of the "severed body" of the Reich. Trapped behind the Corridor, with its inhabitants fearing invasion by hostile neighbors or the infiltration of Bolshevik communism, Königsberg became a breeding ground for radical German nationalism. By 1933, East Prussia became the territory with the highest Nazi vote and a stage for local National Socialist leaders to carry out their plans for German national renewal.[2] During the Second World War, East Prussia became an epicenter for the apocalyptic encounter between two opposing ideologies, states, armies, and peoples. The region played an outsized role in the war as a launching point for Germany's genocidal campaigns in the East, and Königsberg's Nazi leaders enriched themselves by incorporating large swaths of neighboring Polish territory into East Prussia and dominating the Nazi civilian administration of German-occupied Soviet Ukraine.[3] East Prussia was also the place where the war first returned to German soil. The Soviet invasion of East Prussia in the spring of 1945 began one of the largest offensives of the Second World War, triggered one of the greatest civilian exoduses in human history, and produced the most violent encounter between the Soviet army and a civilian population, as invading soldiers looted and pillaged the towns, raped tens of thousands of German women, and executed German men in bloody revenge for the years of Nazi occupation.[4]

At the end of the war, East Prussia was divided into three parts, as the Allies resolved to strip the far-flung province from the postwar German state. Königsberg and the surrounding countryside of northern East Prussia were granted to the Soviet Union as part of the agreement between Stalin and the Western Allies over postwar borders in Eastern Europe, and the remainder of the province was divided between Poland and Lithuania.[5] The territory and its capital were renamed Kaliningrad in 1946 and were eventually incorporated as the westernmost oblast (district) of the Russian Soviet Federative Socialist Republic. Kaliningrad was among the most devastated territories in Eastern Europe, nearly razed by British bombing raids in August 1944, a scorched-earth Wehrmacht retreat and months-long futile defense, and the exceptionally violent and prolonged Red Army occupation in the spring of 1945.[6] The remaining population, between 150,000 and 200,000 German civilians in the spring of 1945, were primarily women, children, and the elderly, as most able-bodied German men had been killed, interned, or deported as forced laborers.[7] They were joined by Red Army soldiers and officers who served in the initial military administration and over 10,000 former Soviet forced laborers.[8] Over the course of 1945–46, Soviet citizens, primarily from Russia, Belorussia, and Ukraine, arrived to rebuild the region's decimated industry and agriculture.[9] For over three years, German and Soviet civilians, sworn wartime enemies and chosen peoples of mutually antagonistic regimes, lived together in the ruins of Kaliningrad.[10] Soviet officials, unsure of what to do with the fascist population they had inherited, planned alternately for the Sovietization of their German neighbors (with antifascist clubs, collective work brigades, and the promise of full citizenship) and their eradication (through starvation wages, imprisonment, execution, and increasing marginalization). By the time the Soviets expelled the remaining Germans in late 1948, nearly half of the original population had died.[11]

The impulse to compare the Third Reich and Stalin's Soviet Union is almost as old as the regimes themselves. Hannah Arendt, who had grown up in Königsberg and had first witnessed there the rise of radical revolutionary movements in the wake of the First World War, argued that the two states constituted novel forms of government—not just authoritarian dictatorships, but totalitarian regimes that systematically terrorized their populations to subject them to complete domination.[12] During the Cold War, Western politicians used the specter of totalitarianism to cast Soviet communism as fundamentally opposed to the moral values of the liberal-democratic "free world." A subsequent generation of historians rejected the totalitarianism model as grossly oversimplified and sought to analyze the Third Reich and the Soviet Union through more historically informed structural comparisons.[13] Such works compared various claims, practices, and institutions of the two societies and revealed that there were indeed striking similarities: both were authoritarian dictatorships built around the cult of the leader; both used an ideological party apparatus to dominate the activities of the state; both fabricated emergencies to break down the rule of law and resorted to terror in the name of security against perceived enemies, internal and external; both relied on imprisonment and encampment to eliminate political, social, and racial or ethnic enemies.[14]

But along with similarities, these comparative histories revealed some fundamental differences. Hitler, the undisciplined firebrand artist, left much of the implementation of his vision to his loyal henchmen, whereas Stalin, the didactic bureaucrat, spent long hours at his desk micromanaging fine points of policy.[15] There were crucial differences in all spheres, including government structures, approaches to the economy, attitudes toward culture and religious expression, and conceptions of the place of women and the family in revolutionary society.[16] In both cases, "totalitarian control" over society was a mirage—the two regimes suffered from widespread bureaucratic inefficiency, and it was often this political disorder, rather than the leader's total grip on power, that escalated violence over time.[17] But for all the nuance and insight of these comparative histories, such rule and system comparisons often replicated the top-down, theory-driven framework of the old totalitarian paradigm. They also tended to present the two regimes in an analytical bubble, depicting the two as deviations from normal European democratic development.[18]

The Third Reich and the Soviet Union were radically transformative and violent revolutionary regimes. The idea of revolution conjures up images of the masses rising up to overthrow tyrannical rule, but revolutions are also about long-term transformative projects carried out by the state. Both the Third Reich and the Soviet Union aimed to solve the seemingly intractable problems of their age—the tensions of urbanization, industrialization, widening economic inequality, nationalism, and the inefficiencies of parliamentary democracy—by envisioning the total refashioning of politics, the economy, society, culture, and geopolitical space. Both aspired to transcend the ills of modernity and bring about the end of history; both aimed to end pettiness and competition by eliminating the middleman between the individual and the state. Both rejected free-market capitalism and turned from bourgeois individualism and the divisiveness of parliamentary politics toward dictatorships that promised to carry out the will of the people, foster collective unity, and heal the wounds of war losses and social divisions.

The Soviet Union has long been considered a revolutionary state. Lenin and the Bolsheviks, proclaiming themselves to be a revolutionary vanguard, fused Karl Marx's critique of capitalism with the nineteenth-century Russian intelligentsia's fervent mission to liberate the empire's peasants and workers from oppression. Even as the shape of the revolution changed once the Bolsheviks assumed power, the transformative urge remained—the drive to civilize and uplift the former victims of oppression from backwardness and to reshape the natural and built environments in service of the future communist society.[19]

Nazi Germany, by contrast, has been more often presented as an authoritarian conservative regime. Yet the Nazis also had radically transformative revolutionary visions for the state, politics, economy, and society.[20] Although they rejected Marx's logic of class struggle, they were decidedly anticapitalist and sought to break the German economy free from international finance capital. Although they embraced ethnic nationalism and biological racism to maintain presumed German racial purity, Nazi eugenic programs attempted to improve the German race through euthanasia and scientific breeding, and social programs sought to reshape German people into conscious National Socialists who would build a new collective culture around the values of the state. Their most ambitious transformative project was the genocidal impulse to reconfigure the multiethnic "land and peoples" of Eastern Europe into "spaces and races" under German control.[21] When it came to the eastern territories of Prussia, the Nazi movement had an especially strong focus on revolution. East Prussia's Nazis, in particular, as self-proclaimed "conservative revolutionaries" and "Prussian socialists," shared with the Bolsheviks a strong emphasis on overcoming economic backwardness without succumbing to the social ills and economic inequality of capitalism.[22]

Both states were revolutionary responses to the tensions of the "age of the masses"; however, the representatives of these two revolutions felt that what fundamentally divided them were their radically different terms for inclusion into the new societies they were forging. The Nazis sought to unify the German people through blood, excluding all those they deemed to be racial outsiders. The Soviets, rejecting such biological racism on principle, sought to unify the entire world around the value of labor, excluding all those they considered actual or potential exploiters. The two regimes ultimately emphasized these distinctions, and by the mid-1930s, they became so preoccupied with the danger presented by the other that each increasingly defined its revolutions in opposition to its nemesis. Nazism pitted itself against Bolshevism, and Soviet communism defined itself against European fascism, in general, and the Third Reich, in particular.[23]

At early points in their revolutionary trajectories, the two regimes saw themselves as a rejection of the legacies of European civilization. During the war, however, both changed their tune, each side claiming to be defending European civilization against the other. The Nazis, downplaying attacks against Western capitalism, emphasized Germany's mission to defend all of Western Europe against Bolshevism. By 1944, when the Soviet invasion seemed inevitable, the Nazis in Königsberg attempted to rally the population for defense by casting Königsberg—the city of Kant's enlightenment—as Europe's greatest hope and most willing martyr against the Red Slavic tide about to wash over the continent. The Soviet Union also claimed that the war was about the defense of Western civilization, in this case against German racism and imperialism. Wartime journalists propagated a form of "socialist humanism," tied to the old internationalist mission of global communism—the idea that workers of the world could unite in a society open to all peoples of the world, including, in theory, the Germans. Yet tied together with socialist humanism was the idea that this was a "Great Patriotic War," a triumph of the Russian people over the Germans. Building on Stalin's official reintroduction of Russian nationalism in the 1930s (including patriotic history textbooks, celebration of prerevolutionary Russian military heroes, and a cult of Russia's national poet, Alexander Pushkin), the idea of a sacred war had a profound influence on Russian mass culture. The war was cast as the battle of the Russian Ivan, who was good, strong, and pure, against the technologically capable but depraved German Fritz. Both of these ideas—the defense of European civilization and the triumph of the Russian people—were central to Soviet citizens' understanding of their mission. Both the Nazis and the Soviets claimed to be defending the Europe of Shakespeare and Goethe, but only the Soviets raised their guns to defend Heinrich Heine, a German Jew.

This book moves away from structural comparisons by presenting Königsberg and Kaliningrad as an entangled history of these two regimes, showing how they not only grew out of a common historical context, but also competed for the same geographical space and understood each other to be mortal enemies and competitors for the future of humanity.[24] Whereas structural comparisons tend to treat the two regimes as separate entities, this book shows how the two were in constant dialogue, reacting and responding to each other over time. They did so not only in the world of ideas—imagining the fascist or Judeo-Bolshevik enemy—but also in the world of real-life encounters. Königsberg and Kaliningrad show how the ideologies of Nazism and Stalinism responded and adapted to local context, and what happened to these ideologies as their torchbearers and victims encountered each other on dramatically shifting terms. While each side claimed to be defending the values of European civilization against the barbarians, their wartime encounter forced both Germans and Soviets to question their adherence to these values. On the eve of the Red Army's siege of Königsberg, German civilians first confronted their complicity in geno-cide as the Nazi leadership involved them in the murder of thousands of Jews from the liquidated Stutthof concentration camp. In seeking eye-for-an-eye punishment for the crimes of the fascist beasts, Red Army soldiers raped and murdered tens of thousands of German civil-ians, forcing Soviet officers, propagandists, and ordinary soldiers to wonder about a fitting retribution for the Germans' crimes that would preserve socialism's moral superiority over fascism.

Königsberg and Kaliningrad assumed special importance as a bor-derland of each empire, and, as witnesses saw it, between competing civilizations and ways of life. East Prussia had long played a large role in German life and imagination. After the partitions of Poland in the late eighteenth and early nineteenth centuries, the province served as a border between the German lands and the Russian Empire. Königsberg, as Prussia's easternmost major seaport, served as a nexus for commerce and cultural exchange between Germans and Poles, Lithuanians, and Russians in the Baltic realm. The myth of "the German East" strongly shaped German perceptions of the far-flung city and territory. As Vejas Gabriel Liulevicius writes, for Germans, the East denoted not only a location, but also a state of being—an alleged condition of disorgani-zation or underdevelopment. The East meant not just some faraway land, but a condition that endured within Prussia's borders and even within Germans themselves.[25] East Prussia, as an agrarian, relatively unindustrialized region of Germany, was often cast as uncivilized, even half Russian, and its rural population caricatured as reactionary Junker landlords ruling over backward peasant yokels.[26] Local inhabitants, by contrast, emphasized Königsberg's Enlightenment heritage and East Prussian values of simplicity and discipline, which they imagined to be shaped by the harsh climate of the Baltic East.

Myths of the German East assumed the superiority of German cul-tural development (*Kultur*) over that of Germans' eastern neighbors. Germans, in this view, were destined by geography to uplift or rule over inferior populations. During the Third Reich, such visions gave way to exclusionary biological racism, as Nazi leaders sought to subjugate Eastern Europe as a colonial space for the German race and enslave or annihilate its populations. But these views of the East were not mono-lithic.[27] In Königsberg, especially, the region's peculiar economic and geopolitical context led many Germans, despite their assumption of cultural superiority and fear of hostile neighbors, to strive for partnerships and economic exchange. Remarkably, such orientations survived into the Nazi period; the region's geopolitical isolation led Königsberg's Nazis to seek economic and political cooperation with their neighbors, including Poland and the Soviet Union, two states that Berlin considered to be open enemies. After the outbreak of the war, however, these visions of a revived trade nexus in the East under German leadership gave way to fantasies of colonial extraction, and Königsberg's Nazi leadership pivoted to embrace Hitler's plans for domination, helping to shape the power networks of the civilian occupation administrations in German-occupied northern Poland, Białystok, and Ukraine.[28]

After the war, Kaliningrad's transformation was part of the larger dramatic expansion of the Soviet empire. The new western borderlands of the Soviet Union, distant geographically, culturally, and linguistically from Moscow, were subjected to Sovietization, that is, incorporation into the Soviet Union's political system, social order, and imperial national imaginary. Early Bolshevik leaders had used the term "sovietization" to describe the revolutionary transformations they sought to bring about in the imperial fringes of the Soviet Union—they imagined Sovietization to be a modernizing, industrializing force and a civilizing mission to uplift less-developed cultures from backwardness. The term disappeared from Soviet usage by the late 1930s, but this implicit template remained: the idea that the Soviet revolutionary project would transform new territories and peoples as they came under Soviet influence, using predetermined methods and achieving the same outcome in each case.[29] Sovietization at the end of the war meant the transfer of the Soviet project that had fully shaped society at home. Sovietization, in this period, entailed the nationalization of private property and creation of a command economy, the elimination of social and political opposition through mass purges, and the establishment of one-party rule. It also involved sweeping demographic transformations, often through violence, and industrialization and modernization according to Soviet prescriptions.[30]

During the Cold War, Western scholars described Sovietization in terms of the top-down imposition of Stalinist totalitarian control. Early works focused primarily on the countries of Eastern Europe that fell behind the Iron Curtain, whereas works since the early 2000s have turned attention to European territories incorporated into the Soviet Union directly, including, in addition to the Königsberg region, the Baltic republics of Estonia, Latvia, and Lithuania, the border region of

Petsamo/Pechenga and Karelia, territories in eastern Poland, the Carpathian region of Western Ukraine, and Bessarabia.[31] In both contexts, it turns out, Sovietization was neither completely predetermined nor monolithic. Sovietization in the Soviet western borderlands was shaped dramatically by the context in which it was carried out—in the wake of overlapping Nazi and Soviet wartime occupations, wartime violence, genocide, forced migrations, and population transfers.[32] Kaliningrad presents an evocative case of Sovietization, as its experience shared many features with other territories coming into the Soviet Union directly, including dramatic wartime devastation, an uprooted civilian population, and radical political and economic transformation. But the circumstances were exceptional in a number of ways, including the late and especially violent wartime occupation and the fact that most Soviet accounts represented the local population not as people liberated from fascism but as fascists themselves.[33]

Königsberg and Kaliningrad show how both revolutionary ideologies and lived experience were shaped profoundly not only by encounter but also by isolation. For much of the twentieth century, the city's leaders and their inhabitants lived in semi-closed territories distant both geographically and administratively from their respective capitals. Conditions in the borderlands of Nazism and Stalinism differed dramatically from those in Berlin and Moscow, leading the revolutionaries to create local versions of their utopias in response to the complex cultural inheritances and economic conditions on the ground. In both Königsberg and Kaliningrad, extended isolation made for peculiar manifestations of the two revolutionary projects. But it is precisely these exceptional cases that reveal how the two regimes worked not just on paper but in practice. They do so by making explicit the cultural assumptions and underpinnings of national ideologies, with all their internal tensions and contradictions, and by showing the processes by which they adapted and responded to conditions on the ground, in dialogue with their beneficiaries and victims.

Because of interwar East Prussia's geographic isolation, Königsberg's Nazi leaders amassed significant power and were able to carry out their plans for most of the 1930s with far greater autonomy than was the case elsewhere in the Reich.[34] Regional peculiarities also profoundly shaped Soviet rule. In the first years after the war, the newest Soviet city grew up in the wild western borderlands of socialism in conditions of extreme privation and without consistent direction from Moscow. Most day-to-day decisions in Kaliningrad were left up to local Soviet administrators, most of whom were young and undereducated, having been inducted into the party because of their bravery in battle, not for their understanding of Marxism-Leninism. They brought with them an intuitive understanding of communism that combined the old goals of socialist internationalism ("workers of the world, unite") with newer currents of Soviet Russian nationalism (the victory of the Great Russian people over the German fascists).

Königsberg/Kaliningrad's relative isolation also led its inhabitants to suspect that the territory was at high risk of incursion and sabotage. Throughout the first half of the twentieth century, siege mentalities developed around fears of foreign incursions, both tangible and intangible, including the threat of hostile armies, ideological corruption, bodily contamination, and disease. Nazi racial ideals prohibited physical intermixing out of fear that German blood might be contaminated by lesser races. Nazi propagandists likewise waged war against the ideology of communism, which, through its elevation of class over race, threatened the foundations of the Nazi regime. In Kaliningrad, new Soviet leaders found both the German people and the East Prussian landscape to be sick—physically contaminated with lice and epidemic diseases and ideologically contaminated with foreign influence and lingering fascist sentiment. In both Königsberg and Kaliningrad, fears of contamination from hostile forces outside the territory's vulnerable borders and from suspected subversives within them led leaders as well as common citizens to pursue increasingly radical politics of exclusion. Successive periods of Nazi and Soviet civilian and military rule led to the breakdown of legal restrictions and the escalation of mass violence. Without legal rights or recourse, minority populations under Nazi and Soviet rule were reduced to poverty and starvation. The growing differences in the living standards between masters and slaves forced each side to rationalize the reasons for the inequality on different terms.

Radically transformative ideological projects are based on inclusion and exclusion—in order to save its chosen people, the state prioritizes beneficiaries and oppresses those it deems outsiders.[35] But the process of determining the difference between us and them became especially complex in the borderlands of these two empires. Efforts to unify Germans by blood met with great difficulties when applied to the multiethnic, polyglot population of East Prussia. Up to one-half of the inhabitants in the southern two-thirds of the province identified strongly with Protestantism and with the state of Prussia but spoke the Masurian dialect of Polish; a significant number of East Prussians living in the northern and eastern regions had until the turn of the century mostly spoken Lithuanian at home. In order to incorporate these populations, East Prussia's Nazi leaders posited that "German blood" could actually be a matter of will—the desire to belong to the German nation—though they denied that opportunity to even ardent German patriots of Jewish ancestry.[36] Polish and Lithuanian nationalists in the interwar period argued, by contrast, that these parts of East Prussia were rooted in ancient Slavic and Lithuanian soil.

Contradictions in the terms for belonging also became manifest in Kaliningrad. Because of the extraordinary nature of the encounter—the longest and largest-scale cohabitation between Soviet and German civilians after the war—new Soviet settlers, in their attempts to make the city Soviet, had to grapple more explicitly than leaders in Moscow with the contents of postwar socialism's understanding of liberation and rehabilitation. After wartime filtrations led to the arrest of suspected Nazi party members, Wehrmacht soldiers, and would-be saboteurs, the remaining Germans became de facto a stateless population: not considered prisoners of war or charged with war crimes, but also not immediately designated Soviet citizens by virtue of living on Soviet territory, in contrast to the populations in neighboring Lithuania, Latvia, and Estonia.[37] Elsewhere in Eastern Europe, German minorities began to be expelled in the summer of 1945; Moscow made no plans to expel Königsberg's Germans or to grant them some form of German Soviet Socialist Republic.[38] Soviet overseers came to see the Germans as not fully redeemed from fascism and in need of further rehabilitation before becoming full members of the socialist community. For over three years, the practitioners of socialism in Kaliningrad paired the wartime trend of Great Russian nationalism with a persistent internationalism and, along with it, the earnest belief that fascism was a condition that could be treated and that those who suffered from it could be cured. Amid failures of rebuilding, fears of ideological and material contamination became a point of fixation for the new administration and led to a local drive to expel the German population. Fascism, it turned out, was not just a recent aberration that had led the Germans astray but an intrinsic quality of their very blood.

The chapters of this book are organized chronologically. They trace the rise of German Königsberg as a bastion of the Third Reich in the East, its downfall in 1944–45 as Red Army soldiers invaded East Prussia and captured Königsberg after months of siege, and its resurrection as Soviet Kaliningrad in the early years after the war, as the new Soviet occupiers attempted to bring the Soviet revolution to the formerly German city and its people.

Chapter 1 explores how inhabitants of Königsberg created myths about their history and destiny in relation to the changing political climate following the First World War. It presents an overview of Königsberg's history from its origins in the medieval period through the Nazi seizure of power and focuses on the myths Königsberg's inhabitants constructed about the city and the province of East Prussia as they found themselves cut off from the mainland of the German Reich by the Polish Corridor. Amid rising fears of economic and political isolation, Königsbergers sought radical political solutions to the political and economic problems of Weimar. By 1933, the Nazis became the party most successful in mobilizing East Prussians' fears of incursion, leading them to win an absolute majority of votes in the province, their strongest showing in the entire Reich.

Chapter 2 follows the rise and fall of the Nazi revolution in Königsberg, showing how Nazi leaders in the city developed an agrarian populist variant of National Socialism within Germany's borders and then extended it into the border regions of Poland and Lithuania at the start of the Second World War and to Nazi-occupied Ukraine in 1941. Königsberg's Nazis asserted East Prussia's central role as a vanguard in the Nazi experiment to transform the German national community and to create *Lebensraum* for German settlers in the East. The contours of the national community became ambiguous, however, as Germans encountered their neighbors and victims: Nazi racial scholars struggled to determine who among East Prussia's polyglot population was a German, a Lithuanian, or a Pole. At the start of the Second World War, Königsberg's Nazis extended their rule to the wartime German occupations of Eastern Europe and exported their rule to a vast stretch of territory from the Baltic to the Black Sea.

By the fall of 1944, the Red Army had reached the East Prussian border. Chapter 3 shows how East Prussia became the first German territory to experience "total war" as Königsberg's leaders mobilized the entire population for the defense of Germany's borders. Königsberg became one of Hitler's "fortress cities" in the last months of the war. The Nazis presented the city's defense not just as a matter of political survival for the Nazi regime but as an effort to stem the tide of barbarism that was threatening to extinguish European civilization itself. Yet as the Red Army closed off the city in the spring of 1945, Königsberg's

Nazi leaders used the barbaric tools of mass violence they had developed during the Nazi occupations of the Soviet Union to oppress their citizens and subjects inside Fortress Königsberg and to carry out one of the tragic final episodes of the Holocaust: the murder of over 7,000 Jewish prisoners from the Stutthof concentration camp. Both memoirists and historians of East Prussia tell the story of East Prussia's demise in the mode of tragedy in order to emphasize the victimhood of ordinary German civilians at the hands of the Nazi party. This chapter shows how these narratives of East Prussian victimhood, by focusing only on the German tragedy at the end of the war, omit discussions of ordinary citizens' participation in the Nazi war machine and ignore the tragedy of Jews and other non-German victims.

Chapter 4 shifts to the perspective of the Soviet soldiers who invaded East Prussia in the fall of 1944 and the spring of 1945. As East Prussia became the first territory that the Red Army invaded during the war, soldiers sought vengeance for the German occupation by looting and pillaging East Prussian villages and raping and murdering tens of thousands of German civilians. This chapter shows how ordinary Soviet soldiers, officers, and propagandists reacted to their first encounter with German territory and how they justified, rationalized, or condemned the mass violence against German civilians. Red Army soldiers sought to carry out their revenge against fascist Germans while maintaining the values of socialist humanism and refusing to stoop to the level of Hitler's criminals. But the Soviets' violent encounter with the German civilian population in East Prussia in the spring of 1945 exposed the internal tensions between the strands of Great Russian exclusionary nationalism and socialist internationalism within Soviet ideology. As the Red Army invaders became occupiers, they incorporated these same overlapping ideals when dealing with the ruins and the peoples of Königsberg.

During the first year of Soviet rule, the Red Army occupation government set out to build socialism on the ruins of fascism. Chapter 5 shows how Soviet Königsberg in 1945 developed in conditions of isolation with little funding or direction from Moscow, as the new occupiers raced against the clock to save over 150,000 Germans from starvation and epidemic disease. Far from being monolithic, the process of postwar Sovietization in Eastern Europe and the Soviet Union adapted to local conditions. In Soviet Königsberg, especially, geographic and administrative isolation, material hardship, and the local administration's inability to make crucial decisions about the fate of the territory and the German population had a profound effect on the city's development. The most significant consequence of the decision-making vacuum was the prolonged ambiguity about the status of the German population, who were charged with building the new socialist society but were not yet designated as its beneficiaries. Ongoing hardship in the city led to an economy of shortages based around a de facto ethnic hierarchy, as Germans became second-tier inhabitants without formalized rights or legal recourse.

Beginning in the summer of 1946, the Soviet civilian administration attempted to end the military government's arbitrary rule and transform Kaliningrad into a genuine Soviet city. Chapter 6 shows how German civilians and new Soviet settlers navigated living and working together after the war. In the wake of the improvised military occupation, Kaliningrad's Soviet civilian government sought to rebuild the city according to socialist principles and to integrate and rehabilitate the German population through education and social welfare. Despite increasing efforts to convert the Germans to socialism and the Soviets' ostensible commitment to antiracism, internal contradictions in these efforts—both ideological and practical—further entrenched the ethnic divide between Soviets and Germans.

Chapter 7 shows how ongoing material hardship, a winter famine in 1946-47, and mounting pressures from new Soviet settlers and institutions in Moscow to rebuild more quickly led local Soviet leaders, especially Communist Party leaders, to scapegoat the Germans and initiate a campaign to expel them from Kaliningrad. Even as tens of thousands of Germans starved to death because the Soviet government was unable to provide them with sufficient food, Kaliningrad's party leaders blamed the Germans for the terrible conditions in the city. They presented the Germans as incurable contaminants and saboteurs who were preventing Kaliningrad from being rebuilt, and demanded that the Germans be expelled so that Kaliningrad could become a real Soviet city. As the Germans left Kaliningrad for the future East Germany, the city's Soviet leaders and new settlers created new founding myths about Kaliningrad's history and its landscape in order to assert ideological, moral, and ethnic arguments for socialism's superiority over fascism.

Chapter 1

The Bridge and the Bulwark

In the early eighteenth century, residents of the Baltic German city of Königsberg frequently strolled through the narrow streets of the old town, crossing bridges over the Pregel River to and from the Kneiphof Island, which formed the center of the old town. Seven bridges connected the north and south banks of the city to the island, and Königsbergers entertained themselves by trying to chart a course through the city center that crossed each of these bridges exactly once. By the 1730s, no one had yet succeeded in seeing the whole city this way, and the conundrum gave rise to a famous episode in the history of mathematics. As legend has it, the mayor of the neighboring city of Danzig first alerted the Swiss mathematician Leonhard Euler to the problem. Euler, then working in the Saint Petersburg Academy of Sciences, initially expressed his indifference, writing in 1736 that the problem had little to do with mathematics, and that its solution would be based "on reason alone."[1] Soon, however, Euler became intrigued, precisely because the bridge problem did not fit comfortably within any existing mathematical framework. Euler discovered that although the Königsberg bridge problem seemed geometrical, what mattered was only the relative position of the bridges, not the distances between them. In other words, one needed only to visualize Königsberg and its many bridges abstractly, from a bird's-eye view, in order to work out the solution.[2] To do so, Euler produced diagrams, plotted trajectories, and distilled them into a simple formula, thereby creating the forerunner to the modern field of topology. He demonstrated—to the delight of Europe's mathematicians but the dismay of Königsberg's inhabitants— that the Königsberg bridge problem had only a negative solution. It was impossible to cross each of the city's bridges only once.

The bridge problem became famous as a mathematical puzzle, but it emerged out of the real-life desires of Königsberg's inhabitants to walk through their city and see it in its entirety—to create their own mental maps of Königsberg and its bridges. Immanuel Kant was the most famous of these Königsbergers for whom walking and knowing were inseparable; born in Königsberg in 1724, he famously never left during his lifetime. Kant's philosophy aspired to universal applicability, but it was through his daily strolls and conversations about politics, science, and commerce with the Scottish merchants trading in Königsberg's harbor that Kant learned about the world beyond the city walls. Kant is an example of the coexisting impulses among urban dwellers to stroll through their city and to experience its particularities, on the one hand, and to draw universal abstractions from it, on the other. Königsberg's less-famous residents, while not developing categorical imperatives or critiques of pure reason, combined this same desire to see the city and somehow capture its essence.[3]

From Königsberg's founding in the thirteenth century to its death and rebirth as Kaliningrad in the twentieth, the city's inhabitants sought to create meaningful pictures of the city to assert its identity. Over the centuries, lithographs, woodcuts, and maps provided geographic orientation for travelers, but they were also powerful conceptual objects that asserted political and social meanings—city autobiographies in picture form.[4] Medieval and Renaissance cartographers imagined Königsberg's cityscape from impossible bird's-eye views, drawing together individual buildings into larger architectural spaces and portraying the flurry of activity that took place within them. The earliest images depict a medieval ring set into a wide peninsula on the Baltic Sea, its architecture contained by dense fortification walls to protect it from foreign incursion—a legacy of Königsberg's origins as a fortress of the Teutonic Knights for their crusades into the pagan lands to the East.

But cutting through these bulwarks is a series of waterways, a visual reminder that Königsberg by the middle of the fourteenth century had become a port city of the Hanseatic League, a site for exchange. Two branches of the Pregel River penetrate the city's dense eastern walls,

FIGURE 1. Bird's-eye view of Königsberg. Copper engraving by Matthaeus Merian, circa 1650. Collection: AKG-Images.

form the Kneiphof Island at the center of town, then join and travel west from the city's harbor to the Frisches Haff Bay, the Baltic Sea, and the maritime expanse of northern Europe. In the earliest images of Königsberg, the southern sections of this ring city remain empty, filled with textured shrubs or grazing horses to depict marshlands. In maps from the early nineteenth century, the geometric structures of settlement encroach on the marshes, as the city expands to fill the container of the fortress walls. By the early twentieth century, when the city's population, then almost a quarter million, had outgrown the *Altstadt*, the thick fortress walls disappeared from the maps, though their outlines still mark the divide between the old city and the nineteenth-century suburbs that grew up around it. Train lines from all directions enter the city along the waterways, converging on the busy harbor.[5]

The maps of Königsberg, as they evolve over the course of centuries, show a city that was once styling itself as a bulwark, becoming instead a bridge: a fortress designed for defense against the East gradually took on the identity of a facilitator of exchange with it. After German unification, Königsberg built its identity primarily around connecting Germany and the East, particularly the Russian Empire, which until the First World War bordered East Prussia on three sides. Russia was

Königsberg's primary trading partner by land and by sea, and Königsberg's own prosperity was affected by the rise and fall of Russia's fortunes. When Russia waged wars, and especially if its Baltic Sea ports were closed, trade through Königsberg's harbor increased dramatically; when Germany and Russia waged tariff wars, Königsberg's trade dwindled.[6]

The First World War brought political revolutions and economic devastation to both Russia and Germany. Defeat in the war crippled Germany's economy, and the Bolshevik Revolution tore apart the Russian Empire, leaving a new revolutionary state ideologically hostile to private market trade. Königsberg and the province of East Prussia were surrounded by the Russian Empire's successor states: Poland in the east, south, and west, and Lithuania in the north. Poland became an independent state for the first time since the final partitions between Prussia and the Russian Empire in 1795, and in the interest of protecting the new state's economic independence from its German neighbor, the brokers of Versailles granted to Poland in 1920 a twenty- to seventy-mile wide strip of ethnically mixed, but majority Polish territory from Pomerania, part of the German province of West Prussia, and transformed Danzig into a Free State administered by the League of Nations.[7] The resulting Polish Corridor guaranteed Poland's access to the Baltic Sea and free use of Danzig's ports but severed Königsberg's and East Prussia's land routes to the rest of the fledgling Weimar Republic. Germany and Poland each accused the other of plotting an invasion (either to reclaim the lands of the Corridor for Germany or to claim all of East Prussia for Poland), and relations between the new neighbors swiftly turned hostile.

Cut off from the mainland of Germany by the Corridor, isolated from its former trade networks, and seemingly surrounded by enemies, Königsberg in the 1920s suffered from an altogether different sort of bridge problem: the self-styled bridge from West to East had become a bridge to nowhere. Over the next decade, Königsberg's inhabitants continued to visualize their city and continued to tell stories both to describe its identity and to shape it. They told these stories all the more frequently and all the more self-consciously, as cities do in times of great political and social upheaval.[8] They told them through highly politicized maps of the Corridor, of East Prussia's borders, of the ethnic and linguistic identities of populations on either side. But they also told them by other means: through travel guides and studies of the region's economic predicament and through polemical essays and political speeches. As the city's inhabitants created and reproduced myths about their city, they sought a solution to Königsberg's new bridge problem: could Königsberg become once again a bridge to the East, or must it become a bulwark against it?

Seeing the City: Königsberg, 1927

Despite the economic hardship brought about by Germany's defeat in the First World War, Germans traveled in the 1920s more than ever before. Strict passport and visa regulations imposed by other European countries led German tourists to eschew foreign travel and visit German regions closer to home. The interwar period became a golden age for German city tourism, in particular, and prompted the publication of a whole array of guidebooks for the demographic of lower-income German travelers entering the tourist market for the first time. These guidebooks, especially the famous Baedeker and Meyer guides, told Germans "what ought to be seen" to experience Germany. They were, in that sense, part of tourism's role in formulating a postwar German national identity.[9] The trouble was that visiting Königsberg in the 1920s felt more like traveling abroad: the trip from mainland Germany required a Polish transit visa or a cumbersome ferry connection over the Baltic Sea. The average German tourist spent a few days in Munich or Hamburg but never made it to Königsberg.[10] The city, it seemed, risked falling off the symbolic map of Germany.

Königsberg publishers continued to produce travel guides—not for far-flung vacationers from the Reich, but for local residents and travelers from nearby East Prussian towns who came to visit family, shop, drink and eat, go to concerts, or to take in the latest film at the cinema. Unlike the more famous Baedekers, which promise the traveler succinct advice marked by an aspiration to objectivity, these guides are defined by their emotive tone and distinctly local character.[11] While sometimes addressing the hypothetical long-distance traveler with general information about arrival, hotels, and transportation lines, they leave out important practical details—the maps in these guidebooks include only major streets with place markers that do not correspond with the sites noted in the text. By contrast, they devote extensive time to lecturing on favorite topics concerning the economy, architecture, city life, and history. Like Königsberg's historical panoramas, these guidebooks are an exercise in identity formation, affirming stories already familiar to local readers while cautiously trying out new narratives that would only come to make sense through repetition.

The rare long-distance traveler planning to visit Königsberg in the late 1920s might pick up a copy of one such guidebook, the 1927 edition of the *Travel Guide through Königsberg in Prussia*. The autobiographical nature of this guide is all the more explicit in that its author is listed only as "Regiomontanus," the Latin toponym for Königsberg. The guidebook's introduction, a self-described "general picture" that incorporates the familiar urges to capture the city's essence and see it in panorama, asserts that Königsberg in 1927 is "the capital of a colony, the only one that Germany possesses, at the same time, a bridge from West to East, perhaps more so than Breslau and Vienna; moreover, it is not a rich city. That makes itself unmistakable in its outward appearance. The vista from afar, with the arrival by water or by land, is not terrible: a vast sea of houses, dominated by a towering castle and crowned by numerous towers. The view is especially majestic when one arrives by airplane." The technologies of photography and flight made it possible for the first time truly to see the shape of the city—to view its contours, streets, and architecture in their totality—in ways the medieval map-makers had only imagined. The guidebook apologizes that these breath-taking vistas belie Königsberg's true essence. "As soon as you step closer," it warns, "you can't help but feel a slight sense of disappointment." The train station looks "unpleasant, almost a little Russian," and the rest of the city is also a bit dull, as it had been built partially on swamp land, decimated in the Napoleonic Wars and plagued by financial hardship, and "not always treated kindly by powerful rulers."[12] Throughout its pages, the guidebook combines pride in the city's cultural landmarks and history with lamentations about its current economic predicament and the toll it has taken on the city's appearance. The Königsberg of the traveler's guidebook is one attempting to come to terms with its newfound isolation: to balance its new identity as a colony detached from Germany with its former one as a bridge connecting Germany to the East.

Although the guidebook warns that the trip to Königsberg is "long, arduous, and expensive," our hypothetical traveler decides to brave the multiday journey. Departing from Berlin, the train crosses the Polish Corridor and arrives at the main train station. Nearing the city center, the visitor consults the guidebook for suitable accommodation. A list of a dozen hotels recalls the former territorial expanse of the now-defunct Prussian monarchy (the Berliner Hof, the Preußischer Hof, the Rheinischer Hof, the Schlesischer Hof, and Hotel Germania). The traveler may settle on a suitable hotel in the old town, perhaps the Preußischer

Hof, which lies directly on the embankment of the Pregel River and overlooks the Kneiphof Island. All of the notable eating establishments in the old town specialize in the regional delicacies: *Königsberger Klops* (meatballs in white sauce with capers), *Königsberger Fleck* (calf stomach), gray peas with bacon, *Schwarzsauer* (a blood soup made with poultry giblets), and *Schmand mit Glumse* (fresh farmer's cheese with chives). After dinner, the guidebook suggests a glass of wine at one of the wine taverns in the old town (though far from any growing region, the port city grew as a distribution hub for luxuries from warmer climes), perhaps at the beloved but chillingly named Blood Court (*Blutgericht*), housed inside the ancient cellar rooms of the Königsberg Castle. For dessert and coffee, the guidebook recommends relaxing and reading the newspaper in a café or enjoying a local treat made from Mediterranean almonds: Königsberg marzipan (a noble competitor to the more famous variety from Lübeck).[13]

The book suggests several walking tours, but as the first is the most comprehensive, our traveler chooses the path that meanders from the old town toward the northwest suburb of Hufen. The first stops on the tour, in the heart of the historic old town, are two childhood homes of Kant, each marked with a commemorative plaque. From there, crossing the Green Bridge, one of the city's many famed bridges over the Pregel, is the south entrance to the Kneiphof Island, and the inner harbor, the center of the city's commercial district. From first glance, the guidebook writes, "you notice the pulsing artery of Königsberg's trade," and our visitor is directed to watch the cargo ships, boats, countless seagulls, and the ceaseless work of loading and unloading of goods into red brick warehouses. The actual scene is more subdued, and the traveler realizes that the description of this bustling commercial life has carried over from the guidebook's previous edition. The guidebook laments that "harbor traffic has waned significantly" since the war, and the docks no longer brim with ships. Yet the evening view from the Green Bridge, the guidebook notes in compensation, is still one of the most beautiful in Germany: "which other major city offers, amid the center of commerce, such a magnificent sunset?"[14] To the right lies the Stock Market building, designed in the historicist style of an Italian Renaissance palace. The guidebook deems it perhaps the most beautiful building in Königsberg, bringing a "friendly, almost cheerful note to the earnestness" of the otherwise austere Prussian cityscape.

The Kneiphof Island features most of the old town's narrow streets and historic architecture. At its center is the cathedral, an austere

fourteenth-century brick Gothic church, which the guidebook remarks is "more notable for its ancientness than for its beauty"; after
the church's two parallel spires burned down in the sixteenth century,
only one was rebuilt, leaving a lopsided silhouette.[15] Although the cathedral's exterior is unassuming, it contains the city's most important
shrine: Kant's mausoleum, rebuilt in modern style in 1924 for the
200th anniversary of the philosopher's birth. The cathedral is dwarfed
by the larger and more stately New Synagogue (completed in 1896),
which stands directly to the east of the island on the former Pregel
River marshlands, a symbol (although the guidebook does not emphasize it) for the prominence that notable members of Königsberg's Jewish community (who comprised just under 2 percent of the population
before the war) played in the city's civic life.

Across the Krämer Bridge to the north of the island, the Königsberg Castle looms above, "a genuine patchwork of several centuries of
architectural forms"—Gothic, Renaissance, Baroque, Rococo, and Clas-
sicism. The guidebook laments that the castle, like the cathedral, is neither beautiful nor abundant with architectural detail, but it appreciates
its stateliness and the several museums contained within its walls. At
the base of the castle, Kaiser Wilhelm Square features statues of Otto
von Bismarck and Wilhelm I (crowned king of Prussia in Königsberg
in 1861, before more famously being crowned emperor at Versailles a
decade later). The original old town church once also stood here, now
marked by a memorial stone designating the burial place of Luther
(Hans Luther, the son of the more famous one), who rests under the location of the former altar—marking Königsberg's role in the Protestant
Reformation. Beyond the castle lies the Paradeplatz, a center for restaurants and shops, and the new campus of the Albertina, the affectionate
name given to the University of Königsberg, founded in 1544 and one
of the oldest universities in Germany.[16]

Beyond the castle, the road curves to the northwest and becomes
Kant Street. (The street's former name, Princess Street, was sacrificed
in 1924 to commemorate the philosopher's 200th birthday.) Past Gesekus Square begins the Steindamm, the broad commercial thorough-
fare connecting to the newer city districts in the northwest. On the
right, the guidebook points to the Steindamm Church, the oldest surviving medieval church in the city. (It omits that for almost 500 years,
until the turn of the twentieth century, it had been known colloquially
as the "Polish Church," where the city's Polish-speaking community,
especially Prussian soldiers stationed from the southern East Prussian

region of Masuria, heard Lutheran services in their local dialect.)[17] The Hufen district begins just outside the former fortress walls, and most of the province's administration buildings are located here, where space is more plentiful than in the dense, narrow streets of the historic center. Here, too, are the city's two newest ventures designed to reestablish Königsberg as a modern center for trade with the East: the German *Ostmesse* (Eastern Exhibition Grounds) and the House of Technology. Both pavilions were designed by the local architect Hanns Hopp, along with much of the rest of Königsberg's modernist architecture in the same neighborhood.[18] The guidebook displays great pride in the *Ostmesse*, while apologizing that its rather unimpressive entryway is only a temporary façade, "built in difficult times, soon after the World War." Across from the *Ostmesse* lies the large and "slightly cumbersome" city hall, and nearby are the Police Presidium, the Courthouse, the Main Postal Administration, and the New Dramatic Theater. The Hufen district also features numerous parks and green spaces, including the Zoological Garden, featuring not only live animals but also daily concerts and festivals. Nearby lies the well-manicured Park Luisenwahl, a walking park dedicated to the memory of Queen Louise, who negotiated with Napoleon to save Prussia, and a fifteen-minute walk farther leads to the city's outer reaches and the picturesque suburb of Amalienau.[19]

Beyond the walking tour, the guidebook dedicates the greatest space to recounting Königsberg's history, with a narrative that shows the traces of a well-rehearsed script. Königsberg, the guidebook proclaims, was founded in 1255 on "ancient German soil," when the Teutonic Knights defeated the indigenous Baltic Prussians to reclaim the territory that, it insists, had been inhabited even earlier by Germanic Goths. To defend themselves against the insurgent Prussians, the Teutonic Knights established their fortress on a hill overlooking the Pregel River, naming it Königsberg. The Knights launched crusades into Lithuania, earning them fame across Europe and bringing goods back to Königsberg; eventually, the city's wealth grew no longer from plunder but from trade. "Our city," the guidebook insists, "was at that time, as it remains today, the most important bridgehead of Germandom and of all of Western Europe to the wild Northeast."[20] As the Teutonic Order's influence waned (the guidebook likewise makes no mention of the Teutonic Knights' defeat and decades-long fealty to Poland), Duke Albrecht, then the Grand Master of the Teutonic Order, finally disbanded it in 1525. After the Reformation, Königsberg became the residence of the secular, Protestant Prussian dukes; in 1701, it became the coronation capital of the new Prussian monarchy. In this narrative, Königsberg, though a distant outlier in the geography of the Reich, emerges, through its ties to the origins of Prussia, as central to the history of the German Empire.

The walking tour already introduced the material traces of this history, prompting the visitor to behold the cultural artifacts that tie Königsberg strongly to the symbolic origins of the German nation. Monuments celebrate the deeds of important Prussian men through sculpture and plaque, while the castle museums celebrate Teutonic heritage and Prussian royal lineage. The museums of amber jewelry and decoration show East Prussia's prominent role in the manufacture of German luxury (the Baltic coast of the Samland Peninsula produces more amber than any other region in the world). The museums and objects surrounding Kant's life affirm Königsberg as an inheritor of the legacies of Enlightenment philosophy and scholarship, while frequent mentions of other famous musicians, poets, and scholars with even brief connections to Königsberg, including Johann Georg Hamann, Friedrich Bessel, E. T. A. Hoffmann, Heinrich von Kleist, Richard Wagner, and Simon Dach, assert Königsberg's place in the pantheon of German *Kultur*—that is, of German national culture and civilization.[21]

These celebrations of the city's history and material traces of its grandeur, however, reveal the unmistakable marks of a city coming to terms with its waning significance. The guidebook deems it more important to highlight Königsberg's contributions to the canonical events of German national history than to describe the city's own development. Accordingly, details about the previous sixty years, after the 1871 German unification asserted Berlin's dominance and rendered Königsberg merely a curiosity in the history of Prussia, are sparse. The guidebook laments how Königsberg, the beneficiary of ancient wars of expansion, became the victim of more recent ones: invasions by the Russians during the Seven Years' War and by the French during the Napoleonic Wars destroyed Königsberg's most picturesque architecture and left the city in an economic depression for much of the following century. Most of the guidebook's scenic sights are impressive mainly for evoking the feeling of being somewhere more spectacular: the port conjures images of Hamburg, the Stock Market tries to recreate an Italian Renaissance palace, the streets of the Kneiphof Island seem reminiscent of old Danzig. One gets the sense traveling through the guidebook that Königsberg is merely a poor reflection of other, more assuredly German cities.

Königsberg, in coming to terms with its isolation from the physical body of the Reich and from the symbolic heart of the German nation, has written itself a central role in not only Germany's past but also its future. If Königsberg's performance of German national identity was based in part on the legacy of castles, monarchs, and philosophers, it was also based on a strong appreciation for commercial exchange and technological advance.[22] Both of these were in short supply after the war, as Russian markets collapsed, the inland German trade network was truncated by the Corridor. Although gradually improving by the late 1920s, trade volume in the Königsberg harbor remained significantly below prewar levels; the total import of goods by train, sea, and canal in 1924 was only half of what it had been in 1913.[23] But Königsberg, the guidebook insists, remains at "at its core" a city designed for trade. As Germany's economic interests "point toward the East" more than ever before, Königsberg hopes that "the gradual resurgence of the German Reich and the awakening the dormant forces in the eastern states, especially in Russia," would fill the city's ports and warehouses once more.[24]

The guidebook captures a snapshot of Königsberg in 1927: a tour through the city, past monuments, architecture and historical artifacts, public spaces, commercial centers, restaurants, theaters, and parks. Even as this snapshot betrays the city's insecurity and uncertain future, it remains an idealized depiction: a modern panorama painting, portraying a city of royal lineage, culture, and scholarship, a port city filled with ships, bridges connecting it to Germany and to the lands to the East.

The Bridge between East and West

The *Travel Guide through Königsberg in Prussia* reveals a city oriented toward exchange with the East. Until the First World War and Bolshevik Revolution tore Eastern Europe apart, Königsberg based much of its economy—and its self-conception—around connecting Germany to the Russian Empire. East Prussia shared three-quarters of its prewar land border with Russia, and three-quarters of Königsberg's port trade was made up of goods of Russian origin or processed with Russian materials. Grains, legumes, wood, oil products, hemp, flax, and wool came in large quantities from Russia, while imports of herring, salt, fertilizer, machinery, and specialty industrial products traveled through

Königsberg's port in the other direction.[25] The city was also connected to the Russian Baltics through other cultural and commercial
networks: Königsbergers frequently studied and taught at prominent
universities in Dorpat, Riga, and St. Petersburg and traded in major
coastal urban centers, where ethnic Germans communities thrived, and
German remained a lingua franca into the twentieth century. Many
of Königsbergers' perceptions about the Russian Empire were based
on actual encounters; however, the eastern border also played an important symbolic role in the larger German imaginary as the divide
between Western civilization and eastern backwardness. Germans had
long viewed their Slavic neighbors as technologically and culturally inferior and defined their own cultural identity in opposition. They felt
this way especially strongly about their closest neighbors and most familiar strangers, the ethnic Poles who lived in Prussian lands within the
German Empire and in the neighboring Russian Empire after the final
partitions of Poland at the end of the eighteenth century.[26]

In the Russian imaginary, Königsberg played a similarly complex
role. The main route from Russia to western Europe traveled through
Königsberg, and from the seventeenth century into the twentieth,
thousands of diplomats, scholars, artists, soldiers, and revolutionaries
visited the city on their journey to Europe. Rather than seeming like a
pale reflection of more assuredly German cities, Königsberg, for many
of these travelers, stood as the very archetype of Germanness, and of
Western civilization at large. Crossing into East Prussia at the German
border towns of Eydtkuhnen or Memel, Russian travelers frequently
noted the sharp contrast between the East and West. Alexander Herzen
wrote in 1847 that "it is enough to travel for one hour to find oneself
in a completely different world," and that "cleanliness and orderliness
bear witness to a long history of civilization."[27] Although East Prussia's
relative level of industrialization lagged behind Western Europe in the
late nineteenth century, the border between the two empires nonetheless seemed to mark the divide between backwardness and progress; the
composer Peter Tchaikovsky insisted that the German train cars were
warmer and more inviting; in 1904, the traveler Nadezhda Vladimirovna
Iakovleva found the landscape to be more bountiful, with roads lined
with fruit trees and forests that looked like parks.[28] Königsberg also
held the reputation as a center for free expression and cultural capital
for oppressed minorities fleeing the Russian Empire. When the printing of books in Lithuanian became illegal after the violent suppression
of Lithuanian uprisings in 1863, Königsberg became a publishing hub

for contraband books and a center for the Lithuanian national renaissance.[29] Königsberg also became a destination for Jews fleeing pogroms in the Russian Pale of Settlement at the turn of the century: the city's strong bourgeois-liberal milieu and long-standing Prussian tradition of religious tolerance meant that Jews experienced less antisemitism than elsewhere in Germany.[30]

This seeming superiority of the West was highly subjective. For Russians visiting Königsberg from the imperial capitals of Moscow or Petersburg, views of the city depended to a large degree on these travelers' attitudes toward their own country. Russians applied reigning stereotypes about their ethnic German neighbors inside Russia similarly to Germans across the border: praise for German cultural norms of discipline, organization, and fastidiousness, alternating with disgust at the banality, soullessness, and middle-class merchant mentality of the German bourgeoisie. The writer Denis Ivanovich Fonvizin in 1784 derided Kant's Königsberg for being tragically common, with narrow streets, and "large houses filled with Germans with big dumb faces."[31] In 1893, the theater director and playwright Vasilii Ivanovich Nemirovich-Danchenko found Königsberg to be filled with all kinds of uncleanliness; not only did the houses and narrow streets seem "pathetic," but also there were "masses of Slavic types and a lot of Jews everywhere," raging drunkards, and taverns on every corner. "I can't think of a nastier place in Germany." At the border between Germany and Russia, he wrote, "Königsberg managed to unite the sins of both without assimilating their virtues."[32] The poet Sergei Esenin, arriving by plane from Moscow in 1922, remarked that Königsbergers seemed to have no civilizational aspirations besides dancing the foxtrot—although everything was rigidly straightened into perfection, to the point that the "birds shit with permission and sit down wherever they are told." Esenin, disenchanted with the pettiness of European postwar popular culture he saw in Königsberg, contrasted it with the devastation caused by the Russian Civil War, declaring that "we [Russians] may be beggars, we may have hunger, cold, and cannibalism, but we have a soul."[33]

Despite Soviet revolutionary culture's general disdain of petty philistinism and private market trade, the young Soviet Union, after abandoning hope in the mid-1920s for imminent world revolution, sought to reestablish bridges to Königsberg. Several German-Soviet friendship societies sprang up in the mid-1920s, some of them cultivated by the Soviet All-Union Society of Cultural Ties Abroad (VOKS).[34] Such friendship organizations also appeared in other German cities, but as the head of VOKS (and sister of Leon Trotsky) O'lga Kameneva reported in 1926, "Königsberg, besides Berlin, was the brightest corner" for German-Soviet relations because the region's economic crisis led the city to "turn its eyes reluctantly toward the USSR."[35] Although most of Königsberg's politicians and scholars were anti-Bolshevik, they believed that Germany's national interest lay in a strong alliance with Russia (no matter its political fates) as a counterbalance to Poland.[36] Soviet delegations regularly traveled to Königsberg, and the Soviet Union even occupied a permanent pavilion at the annual German Eastern Exhibition Fair, the *Ostmesse*.

Despite their hostility to Bolshevism, Königsberg politicians and economists also sought to strengthen ties, even forming a German-Russian Club, independent of Soviet oversight, in 1925. The club was a prominent fixture in Königsberg public life, where Soviet representatives mixed with liberal and conservative nationalist East Prussian politicians, industrial figures, and social scientists. The club sponsored many lectures about the Soviet economy and even hosted exchange visits to the USSR to strengthen trade relations. The city's architect and fellow traveler Hopp visited the Soviet Union's first Agricultural Exhibition in 1923, and Soviet officials invited twelve industrialists from Königsberg and East Prussia to Moscow to foster further exchange.[37] Attempts on both sides to strengthen ties were met with frequent obstacles, however, and increasingly so as the ideological divide between the Left and Right grew sharper in the late 1920s. Although Soviet Consulate members in Königsberg participated in the German-Russian Club's activities, their ideological commitments led them simultaneously to dismiss the club as "purely bourgeois" and to throw their support behind a competing society organized by German communists.[38] Soviet authorities sometimes blocked Königsberg tour groups from entering the Soviet Union, suspecting them to be provocateurs or spies, and tensions mounted in the German-Russian Club between Soviet diplomats and anticommunist Russian émigrés. In the late 1920s, the consulate threatened to sever ties entirely after speakers criticized the Soviet Union, but both sides, attempting to advance their own goals, continued the courtship until 1933.[39]

Bulwark Syndromes

Parallel to these efforts to rebuild bridges, the region's isolation also fostered competing symbolic geography—the image of East Prussia as a bulwark of Germandom in the East. Königsbergers depicted the province as anciently and inalienably German, a wellspring of German culture and civilization destined with the sacred historical mission to defend Germany from barbaric eastern hordes. But this German stronghold, Königsbergers insisted, itself needed protected and was in constant danger of attack, at risk of incursion by hostile armies and foreign influence. Over the course of the 1920s, the imagery of the vulnerable German East, particularly of embattled East Prussia, became critical to East Prussians' self-conception and transformed the way Germans across the Reich viewed Germany's eastern border.

Before the war, most Germans knew little about far-flung East Prussia. What they did know about it was usually informed by negative stereotypes of rich Junkers and their conservative, antidemocratic politics. As an article in the *Hamburger Nachrichten* explained in 1931, East Prussia "in our eyes was already halfway Russia," a backward land where peasants kissed the shoes of feudal lords who lived on grand estates and exercised nearly total power.[40] A travel guide to Königsberg printed in Leipzig in 1926 similarly admitted that Germans had held "a lot of prejudice" about the region because it had bordered Russia and even sought to correct the "common assumption" among would-be travelers that East Prussia suffered from "Russian-Siberian temperatures."[41]

With the outbreak of the First World War, East Prussia entered the German national consciousness as a martyr for the defense of the fatherland and a symbol of Germany's great heroism and undeserved suffering at the hands of the victors. East Prussia became the only major battle zone on German soil during the war, as the invading Russian Imperial Army advanced deep into the province in the summer of 1914, destroying farms and villages and stopping their advance only sixty kilometers from Königsberg.[42] An estimated 1,500 civilians died, 13,500 were deported to Russia, and another half-million became refugees before the Russian army was finally expelled in early 1915.[43] Immediately after the armistice, in December 1918, Polish national uprisings in West Prussia and Posen cut off the connection between East Prussia and the Reich, precipitating the creation of the Corridor in 1920; Polish military groups even planned to invade southern East Prussia to capture more territory for the new Polish state. Although their efforts were thwarted by the onset of the Polish-Soviet war, troops from both sides crossed into East Prussia during their campaigns.[44] After Germany's disastrous defeat in the winter of 1918, Königsberg became one of a number of German ports where soldiers and sailors seized control of large parts of the city, including the Königsberg Castle, declaring a communist revolution and establishing rule by workers' and military councils. The revolutionary groups in Königsberg even attempted to create a breakaway German Eastern State (*Oststaat*) under Bolshevik protection before the fledgling revolution was suppressed by German *Freikorps* paramilitary groups in March 1919.[45] Although the revolution was soon thwarted, to both the revolution's participants and opponents, the specter of communism continued to loom more largely there than elsewhere in Germany because of the region's close proximity to the Soviet Union.[46]

The Versailles Treaty, in addition to dictating that Germany pay harsh reparations to the victors, transferred a number of contested territories to Germany's neighbors and forced plebiscites in ethnically heterogeneous regions to determine the local population's national consciousness. East Prussia was among the German lands most strongly affected by these provisions, as it was not only isolated by the transfer of West Prussian territory to Poland (the lands that made up the Corridor), but also stripped of territory among its own borders to Poland and Lithuania. In addition, a forced plebiscite was held in 1920 for over half a million East Prussian registered voters in the southern two-thirds of the province, the Masuria region, where according to a 1910 census, 47.4 percent of the population spoke a dialect of Polish.[47] Germans across the Reich saw this plebiscite as proof that Western powers were working with Poland to dismantle East Prussia. The plebiscite campaign took on militaristic and nationalistic overtones; the battle for the border regions of East Prussia became nothing less than a battle for the German identity of the entire province.[48] Campaigners on both sides worked to convince the Masurians that they were definitively German or Polish. Each side accused the other of misinformation, obstruction of the voting process, the import of foreign voters, and fraud.[49] The results of the plebiscite, however, were virtually unanimous: almost 90 percent of the population participated, and nearly 98 percent voted to remain in East Prussia.[50] Although the Polish government insisted that voters in Masuria had been too intimidated to vote their conscience, the international oversight commission declared the results were valid. (Meanwhile, officials in both Berlin and Warsaw recognized that the ongoing Polish-Bolshevik War on Polish soil may also have influenced the outcome.)[51] By contrast, the ethnically heterogeneous Memel region (Klaipėda in Lithuanian) along East Prussia's northeastern border, with a population of 140,000, was detached from East Prussia and transformed into a "free state" under League of Nations protectorate status without an immediate plebiscite.[52] The main town, Memel/Klaipėda, had been East Prussia's second largest seaport, and both Poland and Lithuania sought to claim the valuable territory as their own. In January 1923, Lithuanian military bands claimed it for Lithuania outright, suppressing protests among the local population, and in 1924, Great Britain, France, Italy, and Japan agreed that the Memel/Klaipėda region could be integrated as a semi-autonomous territory into the Lithuanian state. Lithuanian authorities supported the annexation by claiming the territory was ancestrally Lithuanian, whereas German propaganda denounced it as the illegal hostage-taking of German citizens.[53]

The long-term economic consequences of the Polish Corridor even further bolstered the sense that East Prussia was under siege. The architects of the Versailles Treaty had argued that East Prussia's economic viability could be assured by allowing free transit across the Corridor, but in practice, geographic isolation, bureaucratic hurdles, and mutual hostilities discouraged both travel and trade.[54] Border towns were transformed into dead zones, and numerous highways, bridges, railway lines, and train stations were abandoned when traffic was diverted. East Prussia's rural population stagnated as young farmers were forced to leave for factory work in German industrial centers. Many of them came to Königsberg, whose population grew to almost 300,000 by 1925, but the city's industries could not support them all.[55] Königsbergers already made lower wages than Germans in other large cities, with tax receipts falling at a full 70 percent below the Reich average, yet Königsberg in the 1920s was one of the most expensive places in Germany to live.[56] High freight costs forced industries to slash prices to remain competitive, and in 1929, the ailing Schichau shipbuilding plant—one of Königsberg's premier industries—became one of a number of factories taken over by the Prussian state.[57] Many of these economic problems were compounded by structural factors present long before: East Prussia was one of the largest agricultural regions in Germany, second only to Bavaria, but the growing season was shorter and the soil less fertile than elsewhere, and the agricultural economy suffered from competition with growing world markets.[58] Although Königsberg hosted a few niche industries connected to agriculture, shipbuilding, and locomotive engines, its distance from major German industrial centers and natural resources such as coal and iron had caused industrialization to lag significantly behind other parts of Germany. Government officials in Berlin scrambled to bolster the region's failing economy with aid packages, but they did little to address the long-term crisis of agriculture, outmigration, and the collapse of trade.[59]

East Prussians responded to the growing sense of being under siege by proclaiming that the territory was anciently, inalienably, and unassailably German. A growing number of "Eastern research" (*Ostforschung*) institutes in Königsberg, Berlin, and other eastern German cities produced idealized histories of the land's Teutonic heritage, with increasingly nationalist and racist overtones, while political polemics warned that if borderland areas were depopulated, East Prussia would be vulnerable to Lithuanian and (especially) Polish onslaught.[60] Polish counterparts across the border, meanwhile, insisted that the Corridor was no long-term solution and that East Prussia's continued existence constituted a dire threat to Poland. Each side drew on competing charts and graphs citing population statistics and economic factors, and both referenced ancient texts to bolster their authority. Citing Ptolemy, Polish nationalists could claim that all territory East of the Elbe was inhabited by Slavonic tribes since the dawn of time, while German nationalists could argue with equal fervor that in the ancient period, no Poles had lived in either East or West Prussia. These arguments for historical and ancestral rights were as adamant as they were unprovable, as neither side agreed on the standard for determining East Prussia's natural inheritance.[61] In East Prussia, the bulwark rhetoric spread across the political spectrum and entered every sphere of daily life. At the annual German Lutheran Church Summit (*Kirchentag*) held in Königsberg in 1927, for example, church officials spoke at length about East Prussia's heroic sacrifice for Germany and its "special mission . . . to form a damn against the Slavic flood."[62]

Such imagery was not unique to East Prussia; other regions along Germany's eastern, northern, and western borders (and even the intra-German border with Austria) were cast as strongholds to defend German culture and territorial integrity. East Prussia's eastern location and geographic isolation elevated the siege mentality to a fever pitch. As East Prussia's *Oberpräsident* (governor), the national-liberal politician Ernst Siehr, warned in 1929, East Prussia, having "fulfilled its historical mission to be the bulwark of the German Reich in the East" during the war, would need to be further defended, for not only its own sake, but also Germany's as a whole. If East Prussia were lost, he explained, Germany's border would be pushed as far west as the Oder River, and "the whole 700-year-long cultural work of the German people in the East would have been in vain." "Try to imagine," Siehr warned ominously, "whether Berlin, lying unprotected so close to that border, would be able to maintain its position as the capital of the Reich."[63]

East Prussia's status as amputee gained it infamy as nationalist groups across Germany pointed to the province's "strangulation" as the greatest injustice of Versailles.[64] Although recreational travel to Königsberg and East Prussia plummeted after the war, nationalist pilgrimages grew precipitously, as programs offered youth and adults the chance to visit the fragile East Prussian border, witness the site of Field Marshall Paul von Hindenburg's World War I victory at Tannenburg, and be inculcated with the sense of the vulnerability and the intrinsic Germanness of the East. According to one estimate, 400,000 such travelers visited East Prussia in 1930 alone.[65] The trend continued unaltered after the Nazis' rise to power: in 1935, for example, thirty young women in the League of German Girls took a day trip along the East Prussian border near Marienwerder (the site of a major Teutonic fortress and place of the Knights' defeat to Poland) as part of their training as kindergarten teachers. As their guide, an official from the Reich Youth Leadership, commented, "we stopped at the main border sites, showed the girls the insanity of the border and the historic edifices of the Teutonic Order. Here they stood amazed—many were experiencing the border for the first time. For some this excursion had been decisive and I had moreover the chance of getting to know the girls, for the value of a person is revealed in the border experience."[66] These excursions were designed to remind visitors not only of the ancient German roots of the territory, but also its fundamental influence on the history and culture of the German nation.

But in emphasizing the region's ancient and inalienable German identity, these assertions revealed the often precarious basis on which they were founded. Königsberg could easily claim to be a German city, founded by Teutonic Knights 700 years before and populated overwhelmingly by German-speaking Lutherans.[67] But as one traveled in any direction, it became increasingly difficult to tell where German stopped and Polish or Lithuanian began. Because East Prussia had developed through hundreds of years of fluid settlement and cultural exchange, the region had been populated over the course of the millennium with speakers of old Prussian, German, Lithuanian, Polish, and Yiddish. Herbert Crüger, a Communist Party activist sent from Berlin in the early 1930s to agitate among East Prussian farmers in the Gumbinnen region, one hundred kilometers east of Königsberg, was surprised by this cultural palimpsest. Soon after his arrival, he began questioning the "ancient German character" everyone had been talking about. The place names, he realized, "came almost exclusively from Lithuanian origins: Karcziamupchen, Uszupönen, Wilpischen," while the farmers mostly had names "like Schlaugat, Nugat, etc., barely Germanized by dropping the Lithuanian ending -as or -is."[68] Much of what made up East Prussia's inalienable German identity was an admixture of many traditions from the Baltic region. The East Prussian dialect contained many Polish and Lithuanian loan words, and even Königsberg's quintessentially East Prussian German cuisine owed much to its non-German neighbors: Königsberger *Fleck* tripe soup came from the Polish word *flaki* (guts); *Schwarzsauer* blood soup was virtually identical to the Polish *czarnina*. Authentic East Prussian beet soup, or *Betenbartsch*, was just as authentically known as *barszch* (Polish), *botwinka* (Lithuanian), or *borshch* (Russian).[69]

East Prussia, more than any other region in the German-speaking world, was defined by the polyglot and heterogeneous characteristics of its inhabitants.[70] Lithuanian and Polish were the dominant languages throughout much of the province before German became the language of elementary instruction in the late nineteenth century. Even as Lithuanian mostly disappeared from public life by the 1920s, older East Prussians still spoke Lithuanian, and German speakers of Lithuanian ancestry maintained strong connections to Prussian-Lithuanian political and cultural traditions. This trend was even more pronounced in the Masurian region in the southern two-thirds of the province. Masurians fused Polish origins and customs with German political traditions, maintained the Polish dialect in public life but wrote in German, combined Polish surnames with (often) German first names, and wed Polish-Catholic religious traditions to a formal affiliation with a Prussian-Protestant church. While Masurians and inhabitants of "Lithuania Minor" (*Kleinlitauer*) did not consider themselves to be ethnically German, most of them also refused to identify as Poles or Lithuanians and demonstrated consistent loyalty to Germany. If they called themselves anything, it might be "Prussian," "Lutheran," or, in the case of the Masurians, even "Masurian-speaking Prusaki." (To most Masurians, being "Polish" meant being Catholic.)[71] In the 1920s, numerous towns in polyglot regions changed their names to more boldly assert their essential connection to Germany. The town Marggrabowa and the Oletzko region, for example, became Treuburg ("Mount Faithful"); despite having a significant Masurian-speaking population, it had the

highest percentage of vote to remain in all of East Prussia.[72] Hans Rothfels, a prominent German (and Jewish) nationalist conservative historian at the University of Königsberg, argued that East Prussia's ethnic
heterogeneity and its population's strong loyalty to the German state
demonstrated the greatest tension in the Wilsonian ideal of national
self-determination: namely the unclear relationship between language
and nationality.[73] As numerous East Prussian German nationalists insisted in the 1920s, it was not language that defined what it meant to
be German, but purely the will to belong.

But inclusion through voluntary association had its limits. Despite
the long-standing Prussian tradition of religious tolerance and the high
degree of assimilation of Königsberg's Jews, antisemitism became by
the 1920s a central feature of Königsberg's social and intellectual life.
As many German Jews in East Prussia had converted to Protestantism
or had moved to larger cities in the Reich, many of the observant Jews
living in East Prussia in the early twentieth century were more recent
immigrants from the Russian Empire, marked by their nonnative ac-
cents and visibly distinctive style of dress. Their expulsion (as foreign
nationals) at the start of the First World War heightened the sense
among non-Jewish East Prussians that Jews were inherently other.[74]
Antisemitism grew throughout Germany in the 1920s, fueled by the
stab-in-the-back myth that Germany's Jews had conspired to bring
about the country's defeat and the idea that the foreign, pernicious
influence of Judeo-Bolshevism was responsible for homegrown communist uprisings in Germany. The rise in antisemitism in East Prussia
was especially dramatic, in large part an exclusionary reaction to fears
of incursion and the region's deepening economic crisis.[75] With the
establishment of the Corridor in 1920, antidemocratic and nationalist student groups in Königsberg harassed Jewish students from Baltic countries and demanded that foreign Jewish students be expelled.
Soon thereafter, students and faculty even rallied to expel Jews who
were German citizens.[76] In 1923, a series of small-scale pogroms broke
out across the province, and by 1924, the explicitly antisemitic German
Völkisch Freedom Party (DVFP), a splinter party of the agrarian German National People's Party (DNVP), won over 10 percent of the East
Prussian vote.[77]

By the end of the decade, East Prussian bulwark rhetoric became
more hyperbolic, illiberal, and exclusionary, as East Prussians joined
Germans and Europeans across the continent in search of more radical
solutions to the growing crises of parliamentary democracy and the

global capitalist order. The image of the vulnerable German East proved especially powerful in shaping the political discourse, both among East Prussians, and increasingly among Germans across the Reich.

Mobilizing the Masses

The young farmer Willi Neuhöfer was one of the many East Prussians struggling to make ends meet after the war. Any unexpected tragedy, such as the death of a horse, could mean ruin for a farm. In the best-case scenario, a farmer would be allowed to stay while working to pay off debts to the tax collector, but sometimes farmers were forcibly evicted from their land. Neuhöfer remembers how he and his fellow farmers looked for radical political solutions for the growing agricultural crisis, and by the early 1930s, the answer seemed clear. "Yes, we voted for Hitler," Neuhöfer explains. "We hoped for more security for ourselves and an improvement of the catastrophic economic situation. . . . We had 32 parties to choose from, but for us there was only one choice: a party that promised us security and a path out of economic misery. The thought that this party would bring about a horrible war did not occur to us back then."[78] Neuhöfer's story shares familiar qualities with other Königsberg and East Prussian memoirs after the war—the insistence that by 1933, the Nazis seemed to be the only party capable of saving East Prussia from foreign incursion and economic collapse.

In 1933, 700,000 East Prussians voted for Hitler—an absolute majority in the province, and the highest percentage in the Reich. Remarkably, however, just five years before, the Nazis had their worst showing there, less than 1 percent of the vote. The party's meteoric rise in East Prussia owed to the Nazis' masterful mobilization of the region's siege mentality. And by the early 1930s, the Nazis' success across Germany came, in large part, from their ability to transform East Prussia's politics of fear into a party platform for the entire Reich.

Before the war, rural East Prussia was already a conservative and antidemocratic stronghold, but Königsberg itself was an island of red politics in a sea of black. The socialist Social Democratic Party of Germany (SPD) received an average of 50 percent of the vote in Königsberg from 1890 until after the First World War, well above the Reich average. Several famous SPD leaders made their start there before heading to Berlin, including Prussian minister president Otto Braun, and they were influential in shaping both the political climate of Königsberg and the national character of their party. The collapse of the monarchy led even more Königsbergers to turn to the left; the SPD won almost twice as many votes for the Weimar National Assembly as any other party. Even amid the city's close encounter with Bolshevism in 1918–19, the democratic SPD continued to enjoy the strongest showing in the city.[79] The establishment of the Corridor in 1920, however, completely transformed the political discourse. Although all major political parties (with the exception of the communists) favored some sort of border revision, Königsbergers and rural East Prussian voters flocked to the most strident opponents of Versailles, the conservative nationalist DNVP. In other parts of Prussia, socialist and liberal parties maintained their support in the 1920s almost without interruption, but in Königsberg, voters' support for the SPD dropped by half.[80]

The Nazis remained a small but vocal party on the fringe. Although a former soldier and bakery owner, Waldemar Magunia, established a National Socialist German Workers' Party (NSDAP) party cell in the Steindamm neighborhood already in 1921, the party struggled to gain a following, attracting only sixty people to a city-wide meeting in March 1926 and even losing members that year.[81] As late as 1928, there were only two hundred party members in all of East Prussia.[82] Initially, the Nazi platform in Königsberg differed little from the now-familiar tenets of Nazi ideology: party members focused on the failure of democracy, the lies of socialism, and the economic, social, and racial threat posed to the German nation from all sides. Königsberg police informants infiltrated early party meetings, noting how disgruntled young men, many of them veterans of the First World War, denounced global capitalism as a danger to the German people and called to "clean the German government out of the swamp of international Jewry and the market."[83] Despite the marked rise in antisemitism in East Prussia in the 1920s, this early rhetoric flopped with East Prussian voters. During the Reichstag elections in May 1928, the NSDAP received only 0.8 percent of the vote, the lowest showing in the entire Reich. The Nazis suffered an especially humiliating defeat in Königsberg, where leftist working-class parties, including the democratic SPD and Communist Party of Germany (KPD), were luring urban voters back from the conservative nationalist DNVP.

As an increasing number of Königsberg voters looked to more radical solutions to the problems of the postwar political and economic order, the communists were at first the only successful radical antidemocratic party to attract followers.[84] Nazi party members in Königsberg saw the communists as their greatest opponents, and recognized early on that the decisive battle for the future of the German nation would, as one party member put it, be "between the swastika and the Soviet star."[85] During a 1925 public debate between members of the NSDAP and KPD, speakers recognized that their ideologies actually had a great deal in common—both rejected liberal democracy and global capitalism in favor of authoritarian revolution and the salvation of the masses. The only difference, as one communist representative saw it, was that while the communists "looked to free the world's proletariat from international capitalism," the Nazis wanted "first to be national, and then to battle the international market." The Nazis' foolishness, the communist speaker insisted, was that their exclusionary nationalism shut them off from the rest of the world. (Hitler's crude early propagandist, Hermann Esser, who had traveled from Munich for the event, vehemently disagreed.)[86]

The Nazis first became contenders in late 1928, after Hitler gained increasing popularity on the national scene. As the Weimar government began to crumble, Hitler made a name for himself as a charismatic firebrand and vociferous opponent of the much-despised Young Plan, the US government's proposal to amend German reparations payments for its crushing war debt. Hitler joined forces with the DNVP (at that time the most popular party in East Prussia) to call for a "Liberty Law" to renounce all reparations payments and reinstate Germany's prewar borders. Although the campaign soon fizzled, Hitler gained popularity across Germany as the most vociferous opponent of Versailles. In 1929, the Nazis won 4.3 percent of the vote to the East Prussian Provincial Assembly (Landtag)—five times more than in the previous year.[87] The increase was also due to the arrival of a new Gauleiter (regional party leader), Erich Koch. Koch was a former railway clerk born in 1896 in Eberfeld, a town in the industrial Ruhr Valley in western Germany. Although he had early on been lured by socialism, his experience as a soldier radicalized him and led him to embrace National Socialism. Although Koch's accent betrayed his non-East-Prussian origins, Koch traveled tirelessly across the province, meeting with local inhabitants, hearing their concerns, and establishing local party cells. He delivered 723 speeches during his first year as Gauleiter, and within four months of his arrival, party membership quadrupled. Koch's reputation soon grew beyond Königsberg, and he became one of the most sought-after national speakers in the NSDAP.[88]

The Nazis' meteoric rise owed even more, however, to the party's switch in grassroots tactics. In the wake of the disastrous 1928 election,

Hitler instructed the party temporarily to abandon the battle for urban workers and shift its focus to rural areas. Regional party leaders were to act as "little Führers" and exercise significant influence over propaganda efforts, tailoring the Nazi message to local concerns. Although the Nazi party in Hamburg adapted its message to present the port city as a "gateway to the world," in Königsberg, Koch and visiting national speakers adapted their platform entirely to East Prussia's bulwark rhetoric.[89] In January 1929 at a speech in Königsberg City Hall, Heinrich Himmler, the newly appointed leader of the Nazi SS (Schutzstaffel) paramilitary organization, drew on the familiar script that East Prussia was "separated from the Reich and surrounded by enemies," but taking the rhetoric even further, he insisted that East Prussia's most "fatal struggle" was with Berlin. He blamed the German government for refusing to rescue East Prussian agriculture and for failing to prevent Poland from strangling East Prussia. He claimed that Berlin was allowing East Prussia to become depopulated of Germans, as farmers were forced to leave in search of factory jobs further west, while Poland was scheming with the League of Nations to parcel off the territory and claim the "sacred right" to settle it with ethnic Poles. Unlike any other party, Himmler explained, the Nazis had made it their mission to show East Prussia—and all of Germany—the imminent danger the region faced and to present the radical, but necessary solutions to defend East Prussia and the Reich.[90]

Gauleiter Koch took this rhetoric to even greater extremes in July 1932, at the height of the Depression. Broadcasting on Königsberg radio, Koch read passages from a sensationalist novel describing a Polish invasion of East Prussia, the horror scenario of every German living "on the other side of the Corridor."[91] "Warning! This is the Eastern Mark Radio Station! Polish troops have crossed the East Prussian border!" Koch proclaimed, "There lies East Prussia, ripped away from its Motherland; there two-and-a-quarter million German brothers are fighting in a heroic battle for their *national* self-determination against the Polish flood, a hard and bloody battle for their *economic* national self-determination against misery and hardship."[92] Koch quoted textbook statistics about East Prussia's population, demography, and economy for a broader German audience, while appealing to listeners to remember that "behind these dry statistics is hidden the horrific misery of hundreds of thousands of Germans, the desperate struggle for their own patch of soil [*Scholle*], for each bit of soil fertilized by the blood of the heroes of Tannenberg." Although Koch blamed the economic crisis of trade and agriculture on East Prussia's exclave status, he explained that the larger cause was capitalism. The politics of free trade and global markets forced agricultural prices to match the global prices, but Eastern Germany's poor soils and unfavorable climate could never hope to compete. Instead of another patch for a failing system, the Nazis called for a total economic revolution. In a national populist vein, Koch argued that Germany's social and economic problems were intricately bound with its national struggle. Such was true nowhere more so than East Prussia because "no corner of German soil is more endangered by enemy incursion."[93]

The Nazi embrace of East Prussia's bulwark rhetoric proved wildly successful. East Prussia went from being the place with the lowest turnout for the Nazis to the region with the strongest showing in all of Germany. By July 1932, the Nazis won 47.1 percent in the Reichstag elections, nearly an absolute majority.[94] The Depression also played a large role, as it did across Germany, in turning voters away from liberal democratic parties in search of more radical solutions to the crisis of capitalism. Poorer East Prussian farmers came to see the conservative nationalist DNVP, previously the dominant party in rural East Prussia, as too allied with Berlin and rich Junker estate owners, leading many to ally with the Nazis. In Königsberg, however, leftist parties still overshadowed the Nazis into 1932; the NSDAP had the best showing of any single party in the city with over a quarter of the vote, whereas the KPD and SPD won a combined 43 percent.[95]

Already with the onset of the Depression in 1929, the historian and Königsberg émigré Fritz Gause wrote decades later, "one could feel the thunderstorm brewing on the horizon."[96] Attendance at Königsberg's *Ostmesse* annual trade fair, once the city's greatest hope to reestablish itself as a trading port, was so low that long rows of empty exhibition spaces had to be covered up with a local art display and picturesque scenes of East Prussian village life. Young men who had earlier left the province in search of work returned in floods, almost 4,000 of them in 1931 alone, and had to be housed in temporary camps for the homeless and unemployed.[97] After the Reichstag elections of July 1932, Königsberg became an epicenter for Nazi paramilitary street terror in Germany, as many of the itinerant young men joined the Nazi SA (Sturmabteilung) and battled communists from other camps, shattered the shop windows of Jewish businesses, and set gas stations ablaze. Whole neighborhoods became Nazi or communist strongholds, including one street in the Hufen district, known by locals as "little Moscow." The

Nazis staged a large paramilitary parade at the *Ostmesse* with a crowd of 25,000. A week later, the democratic pro-Weimar coalition, the Iron Front, countered with an even larger demonstration in protest. Koch and the SA attempted to assassinate Königsberg leaders, wounding both Königsberg's district president (*Regierungspräsident*) and the chief editor of the social democratic *Volkszeitung* newspaper and murdering a city representative in his bed.[98]

The author Thomas Mann, horrified by "the bloody days of pillage" in Königsberg, wrote an impassioned critique to the *Berliner Tageblatt* newspaper from his East Prussian Baltic Sea retreat in Nidden on August 8, 1932. He called on the adorers of the "emotional movement that calls itself National Socialism" to finally open their eyes to the true nature of this "national disease, this jumble of hysteria and musty romanticism, and its megaphone-Germandom."[99] The violence only briefly deterred voters, however. After a slightly lower turnout in the elections of November 1932, the NSDAP came back with an unprecedented showing by January 1933, winning an absolute majority in East Prussia. By that time, 27,527 East Prussians had joined the party; within two years, that number tripled to 86,281.[100] Many of East Prussia's prominent figures and old landed aristocrats first switched to the NSDAP at this time, once the previously strong conservative nationalist DNVP party was sidelined into irrelevance. Although East Prussian elites had at first dismissed the Nazis as uncultured, and bristled at their incendiary rhetoric and overt violence, they agreed with most of the Nazis' platform—staunch anticommunism, illiberalism, and redress for the injustices of Versailles. As Alexander Prince of Dohna-Schlobitten later recalled, he and his wife "after some hesitation," chose to vote for Hitler in 1932. "We, too, succumbed to the mistaken belief that the political and economic situation would stabilize" if the NSDAP assumed control.[101]

Dohna-Schlobitten's belief soon came to an ironic realization. After the victory in January 1933, the Reichstag fire in Berlin provided Hitler the excuse to take over the government, with new elections called for March 5, 1933. Hitler came to Königsberg on the eve of that election, "cheered on like a demigod," as the social-democratic journalist Wilhelm Matull later recalled, by adoring crowds who did not realize "what kind of catastrophe, the complete loss of their homeland," this moment would bring.[102] After leading a torchlight procession through the city, Hitler thanked President Hindenburg for liberating East Prussia from Russia at the Battle of Tannenberg during the First World

War, and he called on Königsbergers to transform the nation through their own strength. The next day, East Prussian voters expressed their unprecedented support—56.5 percent for Hitler, the highest result in the Reich and a full 12.6 percent above the national average.[103] Arguing that the communists were planning a putsch, the Nazis swiftly passed an Enabling Act that granted emergency powers to Hitler. Civil liberties were suspended, the German Communist Party was banned, and its members arrested. Hitler, possessing the right to rule by decree, became a dictator. The Thousand-Year Reich had begun.

Königsberg 1938: Between Bridge and Bulwark

The hypothetical traveler revisiting Königsberg five years later, in late 1938, might pick up a new guidebook, the revised and updated *Travel Guide through Königsberg and Environs* (*Führer durch Königsberg und Umgebung*), to see how the city has changed.[104] The stroll through town presents a city that remains, at first glance, familiar. Sightseers are instructed to visit Königsberg's same canonical sites to see where Kant was born, where Kant lived, where Kant taught, and where Kant is buried. Königsberg restaurants still serve up tripe soup and marzipan; wine cellars and taverns still offer plenty to drink. Travelers must still transit through the Polish Corridor to reach Königsberg (though the guidebook chooses not to mention it). Yet the city does seem different from the way it was before, more picturesque—crossing into the old town, the traveler's gaze is no longer directed to the traces of damage wrought by the Napoleonic Wars but to the beautiful medieval streets that remain. The cathedral, while unchanged, is depicted as less austere, the castle more formidable.

As before, the historical narrative asserts this far eastern periphery's centrality to German history and culture. But the city of 1938 feels more self-assured about its place in the Reich. The narrative of the Teutonic conquest is triumphant, as is the depiction of the city's role in Prussian and German history. While the previous edition of this guidebook from 1934 informed the reader of the (long-accepted) fact that Königsberg was named after the Slavic-speaking King Ottokar II of Bohemia, this 1938 edition speculates instead that Königsberg earned its name from another German fortress.[105] Even the city's repeated suffering at the hands of foreign armies, the guidebook insists, has served the greater purpose of awakening in Königsberg the spirit of the German nation.

Königsberg i. Pr.   Am Pregel mit Fischmarkt

FIGURE 2. Postcard of Königsberg from 1943, depicting austere northern Prussian architecture and bustling commerce at the Fish Market on the Pregel River. The Königsberg Castle looms in the background. Collection: AKG-Images.

The city's symbolic geography has been updated for the new era. Monuments celebrate the young martyrs of the Nazi revolution, particularly those who died in the battle against communism: a bronze memorial for Fritz Tschierse, the Königsberg SA and SS member fatally stabbed in 1931 by a communist gang, now stands prominently on the former Gesekus Square (now Tschierse Square) near the castle. A park in the southern part of town honors the national SA martyr Horst Wessel, shot in the head by communists in 1930, and another street memorializes "Victims of the Uprising" at large. A number of Nazi leaders have already earned their place in the pantheon: among others, the former Hansa Ring and Hansa Square, the location of many important governmental buildings, have been renamed after Hitler, as has the former Friedrich Ebert School (once named for the Social Democrat and first Weimar president).[106] King's Street (Königstraße) is now the Street of the SA (Straße der SA).

The architectural face of the city has changed, but it owes less to National Socialist Gothic monumentalism than to Hopp's Bauhaus-inflected style, whose extensive public projects to facilitate Königsberg's role as a center for eastern trade—Devau Airport, the *Ostmesse*, the House of Technology, the Park Hotel—are now all complete. Although Hopp's politics and modernist architecture fell out of favor in 1933 (as a once-outspoken communist sympathizer, he has been banished to working only on residential projects), his public buildings have come to define the city's contemporary architectural style.[107] The other visual changes in the city appear mainly ornamental: swastikas and eagles flank the prominent commercial streets and adorn the façades of public offices. Although Königsberg was passed over for a list of five "Führer cities" designated for grand reconstruction, it is one of dozens of smaller cities slated for significant construction in the spirit of Nazi monumentalism, with large office buildings, stadiums, and squares to host mass demonstrations and spectacles for the German national community.[108] (Blueprints for Königsberg's reconstruction were finally drawn up in 1941, though the funding to realize them was immediately diverted to the war effort.)[109]

The new Nazi government appears only sporadically in the text, tacked on to the end of the history section to celebrate Koch's successful battle against unemployment. In late 1938, however, it is not the additions but the omissions—both from the guidebook and from the city's panorama—that speak most to Königsberg's transformation. The guidebook lists the Lutheran and Catholic churches but no synagogues; once numerous advertisements for Jewish-owned businesses have disappeared from the appendix. Plaques, street names, and monuments honoring notable members of the Königsberg Jewish community have been removed, including the bust of Johann Jacoby, the nineteenth-century Prussian proponent of Jewish emancipation, Bismarck opponent, and radical Social Democrat, and of Dr. Paul Stettiner, a city councilor for education, and in 1932–33, a member of the Prussian State Council. The name of Koch's monumental sports and recreation complex, the Erich-Koch-Platz, obscures its origins: it had been named in honor of the Jewish banker, philanthropist, and city council member Walter Simon, who granted the land for its construction. The traveler who walks past the Cathedral on Kneiphof Island looks across the Pregel River to see the ruins of the once formidable New Synagogue. Its absence is the most striking transformation of Königsberg's panorama; during *Kristallnacht* in November 1938, the Nazis set it ablaze.

Although the Nazis came to power with the imagery of Königsberg as a German bulwark, the city depicted by the guidebook still seeks to be a bridge. Despite Nazi political rhetoric's open antagonism toward Poland and the Soviet Union, Königsberg continues to orient itself toward the exchange of goods with the successor states of the

Russian Empire—Poland, Russia, and Lithuania. The guidebook insists that Königsberg's mission under National Socialism will be dictated by the city's geographical position as an "intermediary between Central Europe and the East."[110] Although it begins with the bold assertion that the Nazi ideal of "the bond between blood and soil" has set Germany's sights eastward, the guidebook still imagines that Königsberg's primary "role in raising Germany's commercial and cultural influence" will come not from Teutonic conquest but from Hanseatic trade.[111]

Only months later, in March 1939, East Prussia reclaimed the Memel territory of Lithuania at gunpoint. Less than a year later, in September 1939, Germany invaded Poland. The Nazis fulfilled their promise to the German people to eliminate the Polish Corridor. Königsberg was no longer separated from the Reich, but it also ceased to be a bridge. With the start of the Second World War, Königsberg shed its former identity to become the launching point for Hitler's war in the East and a capital of its imperial dominion.

CHAPTER 2

Empire in the East

In July 1931, Joseph Goebbels toured towns along the East Prussian border to draw attention to the unnatural boundaries dictated by the Treaty of Versailles. The most publicized of his stops was in Tilsit, along the Neman (Memel) River bordering Lithuania. The town had more than once gained infamy in the German national conscience. It had been the site where Prussia had been forced into humiliating concessions by Napoleon and Alexander I in 1807, leading to the loss of Prussia's eighteenth-century territorial gains from the partitions of Poland. It had also become a symbol of Germany's bleeding border, as the Memel region on the north side of the river from Tilsit was first occupied by the Western Allies and then forcibly annexed by Lithuania in 1923. In the nationalist conscience, Tilsit represented Germany's perennial struggle against hostile powers to maintain its eastern borders. With East Prussia once again threatened by enemies, Hitler's propagandist used this politically charged memory to assert the eastern borderland's central role in the project of German national renewal. As Goebbels proclaimed to the crowd in Tilsit, "the East Prussian problem is a question of German destiny in general and a good measure for the rise or fall of our nation [*Volkstums*], which draws its strength not from the big city, but from the broad plains. If the Germans manage, despite all political fates, to rebuild East Prussia and bring about its economic and cultural prosperity, then that proves that German strength is indefatigable and strong enough to defy all opposing forces. The politics of East Prussia is German destiny!"[1]

East Prussia, as an economically depressed rural borderland, was the region of Germany in most dire need of political and economic revival. Yet, as a land not ruined by excessive industrialization and urbanization, it was regarded by many Nazis as the seed for Germany's rebirth. Königsberg's local Nazi leadership embraced this idea that East Prussia's revival held the keys to German destiny and saw themselves as uniquely positioned to bring it about. Precisely because East Prussia was trapped behind the Polish Corridor, because it had long lagged in industrial development, because its agriculture suffered and its population had stagnated from outmigration, the region, they argued, would become the foremost site for the great Nazi experiment in full societal transformation.[2] As East Prussia's regional party boss, Gauleiter Erich Koch, proclaimed in 1934, Königsberg's Nazis were not simply the "representatives of east German interests or representatives of just our own land," but the "vanguard and pioneers of the German people in their way from the West to the East, from the big city to the land, from the tenement house to the homeland."[3] The farmlands of East Prussia would become the soil on which the new Third Reich would grow and first take shape.

Although Königsberg's Nazis asserted that their revolution would lead the way, their region's peculiarities also led them to develop a peculiarly local variant of Nazism. This variant was shaped by East Prussia's geopolitical isolation, its borderland geography, and the crisis of rural agriculture.[4] Their visions for the German national community also differed from elsewhere in the Reich, as they were forced to define German national and racial identity in dialogue with East Prussia's multiethnic and multilingual population. East Prussia's isolation allowed Königsberg's Nazis significant autonomy to carry out their rule, and by the late 1930s, Gauleiter Koch became the Reich's strongest party boss, with the Königsberg's Nazis forming the Reich's most powerful regional party. In the end, despite the regional peculiarities that shaped the Nazi revolution in East Prussia over the course of the 1930s, East Prussia indeed became a vanguard for the Reich—not as the soil on which Germany's agrarian paradise would be built, but as an exemplar of the contradictions and brutality of Nazi rule.

By the late 1930s, most of the peculiar economic and ethnic regional visions developed by Königsberg's Nazis gave way to the national priorities set by Berlin. But Königsberg's Nazis still held significant power at home in East Prussia. And with the start of the Second World War, they used that power to extend their influence over a vast expanse of Nazi-occupied Eastern Europe. In doing so, they transformed Königsberg, long the provincial backwater, into a capital of Germany's empire in the East.

The School of the Revolution

The popular image of revolution today is one of the masses rising up and overthrowing an oppressive dictatorship. But it could also be very much the opposite. While 'red' brigades stormed Königsberg in 1919 and homeless workers, disenchanted with Weimar, pitched paramilitary street battles a decade later, Königsberg's most successful revolutionaries were disillusioned aristocrats and bourgeoisie who dreamed of overcoming industrial modernity with visions of strong state leadership. For them, revolution did not mean the overthrow of the state or just dramatic rupture, but the gradual reforming of state and society that would unfold in the decades after. Their vision of revolution was decidedly in favor of the state, rather than against it.

Frustrated by the Weimar Republic's inability to rescue the German East from economic ruin, a group of young politicians, economists, scholars, and administrators known as the "Königsberg Circle" came together in the late 1920s to draft wide-ranging plans to transform the state, economy, and society of East Prussia as the first step toward transforming the Reich. Originally members of the conservative agrarian DNVP party, they joined forces with the Nazis as the party soared in popularity, and by 1933 they formed the inner circle of Gauleiter Koch's leadership team. With a few exceptions, these men came from well-heeled bourgeois or conservative aristocratic backgrounds. Among their ranks were young Prussian state administrators, such as Fritz-Dietlof von der Schulenburg, Hermann Bethke, and Klaus von der Groeben, as well as a few early Nazi party activists such as the university economist and political editor of the *Preußische Zeitung* (the local Nazi party newspaper) Hans-Bernhard von Grünberg, Koch's Deputy Gauleiter Ferdinand Großherr, and the Propaganda Leader Paul Dargel. Most of them came from relatively comfortable traditional conservative backgrounds, but the crisis of agriculture and the plight of downtrodden farmers after the First World War led them to turn their attentions toward the common man, and the geopolitical vulnerability of the

German East inspired them to become romantic nationalists in defense of the purity of rural German life. The members of the Königsberg Circle at first dismissed the vulgar mass politics and street brawls of National Socialism, but as the movement gained momentum, they saw in it—and in Koch's charismatic leadership—the opportunity to bring their plans to fruition. Meanwhile, Koch, as a newcomer to East Prussia, harnessed their local expertise to support his revolutionary plans.

Koch and his inner circle adhered to all the main tenets of Nazi ideology: they were radical German nationalists, racists, and antisemites; they rejected Versailles and parliamentary democracy; and they subscribed to the "leadership principle" (*Führerprinzip*), which called for absolute adherence to Hitler's will. But they were also proponents of an especially anticapitalist and socialist variant of National Socialism—the Nazi defector Hermann Rauschning once described Koch as "one of the sincere socialists in the movement."[5] Because of East Prussia's rural agricultural crisis, Königsberg's Nazis, unlike some other regional parties, focused less on racial purity and more on reviving agriculture and rectifying the economic inequality wrought by liberalism.[6] They considered themselves to be conservative revolutionaries and were inspired by the intellectual traditions of Prussian socialism, an interwar right-wing socialist movement that pit itself against English liberalism. As Prussian socialists, they maintained that the salvation of the entire German people would come through adherence to a truly German form of socialism based on Prussian cultural traditions of hard work, discipline, self-sacrifice, and concern for the greater good.[7]

Königsberg's Nazi leadership embraced socialism, but they strongly opposed Marxism, criticizing it as soulless and lacking an organic connection to national culture. Still, their Prussian socialism had much in common with Marxism, as both were preoccupied with solving the problems of inequality spawned by the industrial age. They embraced some similar language of class struggle: during his campaigns, Koch pitted small farmers against large-estate holders and pointed to unfettered capitalism as the source of East Prussia's ills. In addition, Königsberg's Nazis, like their neighbors in the Soviet Union, combined populist sentiments with faith in the transformative power of the state. Their common geographical and economic position—united by a lower rate of industrialization and urbanization, harsh climates, and less fertile soils—meant that both grappled with problems of relative backwardness—in East Prussia's case, vis-à-vis western Germany, and in Soviet Union's case, vis-à-vis Western Europe. While the Soviets looked to the global working classes and embraced urbanization and industrialization, Königsberg's Nazis, like their National Socialist contemporaries across the Reich, sought redemption through national unity. But at the same time, Königsberg's Nazis rejected the idea that their Prussian socialist revolution had anything in common with fascism. Fascism, they insisted, was a foreign ideology from the Catholic, Mediterranean world. Their Prussian socialism drew its inspirations instead from the German Northeast: from the communal values of the Teutonic Order, the discipline of northern Protestantism and Martin Luther, and state service of the "kings of Prussian socialism," Friedrich Wilhelm I and Friedrich the Great.[8]

Königsberg's Nazis were likewise remarkable for their aspirations to carry out their plans on the national stage. The two most comprehensive of these plans came from the civil servant Fritz-Dietlof Count von der Schulenburg, who sought to revolutionize the German state, and the political scientist Grünberg, who planned to revolutionize the German economy. Schulenburg and Grünberg, like the other members of the Königsberg Circle, looked to rural East Prussia as a site of relative cultural purity, and they sought to build a strong German state that could overcome the indecision of Weimar and rescue the East German countryside from economic ruin. Most important, they assumed that transformations in East Prussia would create the foundation for the spiritual rebirth of the German people and become a template for the rest of the Reich. In the words of Grünberg, East Prussia would become the "school of the revolution," in which "the new lifeways of the *Volk* would first take shape."[9]

Schulenburg, the most eloquent theorist of the Königsberg Circle, later became famous for his role in the German resistance—long before Claus Schenk von Stauffenberg, Schulenburg was a driving force in the wartime plot to kill Hitler. But in the early 1930s, Schulenburg was a fervent young National Socialist. He rejected the destructive influences of urban individualism, idealized rural living conditions, and distrusted large industrial companies. Although he came from an elite aristocratic background, he was particularly invested in helping poor rural farmers. His efforts to overcome class divisions and bring about social justice as a Prussian civil servant in the Ruhr had even earned him the nickname "the Red Count."[10] Schulenburg first transferred to a Prussian state service post in Königsberg in 1932, on the eve of the seizure of power; he hoped that East Prussia, rural and isolated by the Corridor, would be the ideal place to carry out his plans to refashion state and society for the common good. Schulenburg had witnessed how the structures of Weimar bureaucracy led to opportunism, the dominance of vested interests, and a parliamentary system that promoted conflict. As his colleague Klaus von der Groeben later wrote, Schulenburg was "fascinated with the vision of a strong state" in the tradition of the great Prussian kings, and drafted plans to replace the Weimar Republic with a popular authoritarian government supported by cadres of ascetic military and service elite, working single-mindedly to transform the directives of their Führer into governmental practice.[11] His plans corresponded with those of the Nazi Party apparatus to place all of state administration under its direct authority, a move which Schulenburg supported enthusiastically, seeing it as the first step in creating an orderly Nazi bureaucracy.[12] But Schulenburg also desired to balance strong central authority with increased power for localities: he sought to ensure that the government always remain in touch with the needs of the people, from the most rural eastern German village to Berlin. The party, he planned, would serve only as the temporary catalyst for the transformation: civil servants would ultimately owe their loyalty to the governmental institutions in which they served. At heart, Schulenburg wished to create a strong, rational state designed to provide for the social welfare of the population.[13]

Grünberg was similarly a populist but with even bolder technocratic fantasies. In 1932, at the age of twenty-nine, he published, with the assistance of the Königsberg civil servant Dr. Bethke, a sweeping socialist program for solving the crisis of German agriculture. The book was nothing less than revolutionary, as it called for the German state to dismantle political and economic liberalism in order to bring about "the inglorious end of capitalism."[14] After the seizure of power in 1933, Grünberg worked together with Gauleiter Koch to transform these visions into the East Prussia Plan, a bold economic blueprint that nonetheless toned down Grünberg's most radical proposals in order to get approval and funding from Berlin. The language surrounding the plan, as the historian Wolfgang Schivelbusch points out, shared common features with the "new deal" rhetoric of the early 1930s in the United States and Italy: "the desire to recultivate a landscape ravaged by liberalism; the establishment of a middle-class mixed economy in which light industry and agriculture would harmoniously coexist; the realization of the Landstadt concept [a back-to-the-land movement] on nearly virgin soil; the creation of a generally National Socialist form of culture from the wastelands of liberalism."[15] It provided tax breaks, subsidies, and debt repayment programs to protect small farms from foreclosure, and implemented programs to eliminate hyperinflation, eradicate unemployment, and increase the production of East Prussian consumer goods. In contrast to other "new deal" programs, the East Prussia Plan was also shaped by the region's borderland geography, seeking to reverse the long-standing problem of rural outmigration from the German East through agricultural incentives and carefully planned industrialization measures. By relocating small and medium-sized factories and their workers from western Germany to the East, East Prussia's population would grow from 2 to 3.5 million, German industrial workers would leave the overcrowded cities to become rural farmers cultivating the land, and a strongly repopulated East Prussia would serve as a bulwark against Polish incursion.[16]

Königsberg's Nazi elite rallied around Gauleiter Koch because they saw in him the charismatic leader they needed to carry out their revolution in East Prussia. They argued that the province's backwardness and isolation made it the ideal place to first bring about German national renewal. As proponents of "Prussian socialism," they had combined collectivist ideals to provide for the German people's social welfare with modern and technocratic plans for a strong state. In 1933, the Königsberg revolutionaries finally got their chance to carry out these visions. But within months, their revolution was plagued with the same corruption and inefficiencies that were rampant across Nazi-ruled Germany, and Gauleiter Koch, outmaneuvering his opponents, transformed himself into a quasi-dictator, a local version of Hitler.

Schulenburg's dream to create a well-ordered Prussian service state was put in jeopardy already before the seizure of power. In the fall of 1932, worrying that the party had become filled with opportunists and thugs, Schulenburg asked Gauleiter Koch to purge its ranks so that a leaner, ideologically committed party could assume power.[17] But with the takeover just months later, Schulenburg found himself trying to reform the party's motley rank and file, even as those party members were already seizing the reins of state power. Schulenburg became Koch's personal consultant, in charge of organizing the purges (*Gleichschaltung*) of Königsberg's local and provincial government to eliminate nepotism in favor of Prussian self-discipline and altruistic commitment to self-service.

In the wake of the Nazi victory, the purges immediately escaped Schulenburg's control. Koch and the rest of the party leadership flaunted their newfound power and ordered Nazi SA paramilitary squads to terrorize opposition leaders. Within months, hundreds of communists, socialists, liberals, conservatives, Jewish public figures, Freemasons, and members of Catholic opposition groups were arrested and tortured, and in some cases even murdered, as in the case of East Prussia's Communist Party leader, Walter Schulz.[18] These terror campaigns were personal and vindictive, as Koch sought to intimidate anyone who had opposed his rise to power. Yet, in contrast to Schulenburg's dream of state servants united by their ideological commitments, Koch preferred personal loyalty above commitment to the cause and allowed numerous long-term state and city officials to keep their posts so long as they accepted his command. The majority of Königsberg officials stayed in office, as did half of the regional district presidents (*Regierungspräsidenten*), making East Prussia second only to Saxony for the lowest personnel turnover in the Reich. Koch even appointed members of other parties to positions of expertise if they agreed to switch ranks, while others never joined at all.[19]

Schulenburg had hoped to fuse party and state organizations in order to streamline the bureaucracy and imbue it with ideological purpose. But in the rush to assume power, Koch and his inner circle simply grafted new offices on top of existing structures. The Nazi party-state in Königsberg by late 1933 became a behemoth of overlapping jurisdictions, internecine struggles, and bureaucratic self-enrichment. Power became based on personal connections to Koch, and his policy of appointing his loyal followers to multiple offices within the party administration and the state only created further nepotism. Schulenburg was horrified by these developments, but his calls for reform went unheard as other party members climbed into positions of power. Königsberg in this regard was no different from any other region in Germany, where bureaucratic morass became institutionalized in the new Nazi state. Königsberg's tangle of party and state institutions was, if anything, exemplary.

But Königsberg was outstanding in at least one important way: the power that Koch himself could amass. Koch was already the most powerful man in Königsberg; his appointment as East Prussia's governor (*Oberpräsident*) in June 1933 made him the most powerful regional party leader in the Reich. Although a few other Gauleiter were also appointed Prussian regional heads of state, most of them found their power limited by overlapping jurisdictions. East Prussia's geographic isolation, however, meant that Koch reigned supreme, ruling over the entire territory with no local checks on his power from either party or state.[20]

As Koch's power grew, so did his ego. He began styling a personality cult around himself as East Prussia's Führer, the embodiment of the leadership principle and East Prussia's local equivalent to Hitler. Koch's self-aggrandizing rule became infamous among a later generation of memoirists and scholars. The historian Dietrich Orlow, for example, went so far as to describe Koch as a "prototype of colonial viceroy" ruling over East Prussia as an imperial domain, and a popular biography of Koch described him as nothing less than "Hitler's brown Tsar." As the historian Christian Rohrer points out, however, Koch, while powerful, was never omnipotent. He remained limited both by his ability to curry favor with his patrons in Berlin and the need to maintain a loyal following among his cadres in Königsberg.[21]

Although Schulenburg had initially supported Koch's bid to become East Prussia's head of state, he soon became disillusioned with Koch and his "tendency to Byzantine intrigue, corruption and almost feudal airs and graces," as the historian Hans Mommsen notes.[22] Writing in July 1933, Schulenburg reminded Koch of East Prussia's sacred mission to reestablish "once and for all the Prussian lifestyle and struggle and toil." But in a thinly veiled criticism of Koch and his circle, he lamented that "there are areas where even we National Socialists have departed very far from that."[23] As Koch's power and hubris grew, Schulenburg abandoned illusions that he could do anything to stop it. He retreated from Königsberg by appointing himself as regional governmental head (*Landrat*) of a nearby seaside village. From there, he planned to institute his reforms on an even more local level, unimpeded by the politics of the capital. The other members of Koch's inner circle, even if they criticized Koch in private, remained loyal. As Koch's power grew, so too did theirs.

Although Schulenburg's plans to revolutionize the state were abandoned, Koch and Grünberg took their populist revolution to the countryside. Within weeks of the takeover, Koch proclaimed a "Battle of Labor" to tackle East Prussia's dire unemployment and mobilized 58,000 men, many of them from the poor houses of Königsberg, for public works projects across the province, including a highly publicized campaign to convert thousands of acres of marshlands in southern East Prussia into arable farmlands for German settlers.[24] The campaign proved wildly successful, and by the summer of 1933, Koch boasted that East Prussia was the first region in Germany to eradicate unemployment. East Prussia made national headlines as the frontlines of the societal transformation. As the Nazis' national party newspaper, the *Völkischer Beobachter* declared, the former "Poorhouse of Prussia" had become the vanguard of the Reich.[25]

Despite these early successes, the East Prussian revolution soon got bogged down, as transformative projects do, by economic constraints and popular opposition. The regime had to keep searching for ways to keep workers employed or else risk flagging morale, and it was forced to shuttle seasonal agricultural laborers into housing construction projects to keep them occupied between fall sowing and spring planting.[26] Plans to solve East Prussia's population crisis through settlement also stalled, as Germans continued to leave for economic opportunity in the Reich (although by 1935 outmigration came mostly from already industrialized areas and towns rather than the countryside).[27] Mass employment and subsidies became unsustainable already by the mid-1930s, and the gap grew ever wider between stagnating economic growth and publicized exponential rates of productivity. Attempts to scale back short-term relief aid prompted backlash from recipients who had come to depend on them.[28] In the drive to provide ever more tangible evidence of economic growth, Königsberg's Nazis hid problems while searching for longer-term solutions to revive the economy, still isolated from the Reich by the Polish Corridor. Nonetheless, by 1938, the party leadership could brag—at least on paper—that East Prussia's agricultural output had grown dramatically, even if much of that growth came from the global recovery from the Depression.[29]

Farmers supported Koch's campaign promises of German national renewal and gladly accepted the emergency tax breaks and debt relief; however, they opposed Koch and Grünberg's East Prussia Plan once they got wind of the details. Farmers rebelled against broader plans for economic restructuring, fixed prices, and state-led resettlement, which they denounced as quasi-socialist collectivism and the dramatic intrusion of the state into their personal affairs. Most of the opposition came from within the party itself; they did not oppose National Socialism, but rather what they saw as Koch's deviation from it. One party farm leader from the Masurian region declared, for example, that "yes, we have a Führer, but we can't support the politics of Gauleiter Koch" because Koch's plans were foolish and unrealistic, while another farm leader denounced Gauleiter Koch as "the biggest Bolshevist" amid rumors that Koch was trying to rule East Prussia in "Bolshevik style."[30] Koch's attempts to silence the opposition only made matters worse. When the *Ostpreußische Zeitung*, East Prussia's most popular rural newspaper, began openly criticizing the regime, Koch shut down the paper entirely, to the population's dismay.[31] And when another local news-paper mistakenly reported that unrest was leading to Koch's removal, international newspapers used the debacle as proof that Germans were fed up with Nazi rule.[32]

By 1935, growing resistance to the East Prussian revolution almost cost Koch his rule. Although his direct appointees remained loyal, Koch struggled to control the party's and the state's numerous organizations. He tamed the paramilitary SA by replacing its first leader, but conflicts between party and state organizations over the future of East Prussian agriculture, in particular, erupted into chaos. The Agrarian-Political apparatus, an auxiliary party organization, opposed the establishment of the *Reichsnährstand* (Reich Nutritional Estate), a government body in charge of regulating food production. The leaders of this agrarian party organization turned their ire against Koch directly, reportedly carrying out their battle in "harsh and often hateful forms" against the regional party leadership.[33] Koch simply dismantled the unruly Agrarian-Political party organization, but the rebellion soon infiltrated the ranks of the *Reichsnährstand* itself.[34] By December 1933, Robert Ley, the head of the Nazi Political Organization in Berlin, warned Hitler that East Prussia had become a "microcosm of the problems plaguing regional rule" across the Reich.

Koch's strong-arm tactics in East Prussia also provoked the ire of several high-ranking Nazis in Berlin, who attempted to curb his grow-ing power. Ley himself repeatedly discussed "the problem of Koch" with Hitler and questioned Koch's loyalty.[35] Prussian minister presi-dent Hermann Göring, *Reichsnährstand* leader Walter Darré, and the SS leader Heinrich Himmler all tried to put constraints on Koch, but were at first unable to do much to stop him.[36] In late 1935, their moment of opportunity finally came. When a disillusioned Königsberg city coun-cil member wrote Hitler a memorandum about Koch and his acolytes' rampant abuses of power and criminal activities, the scandal erupted into a so-called *Oberpräsident* Crisis. Himmler eagerly launched an SS investigation into Koch's activities, which revealed a complex web of nepotism and cronyism, with Koch presiding as a near-despotic ruler over the bureaucratic mess of his own creation. As a result of the damn-ing report, Göring forced Koch to take a temporary leave of absence as governor in November 1935.

But just one month later, Hitler intervened personally, reinstating Koch to his governor post and clearing him of all charges. Putting Ber-lin's high-ranking Nazis in their place, Hitler declared that Koch, as the embodiment of the leadership principle in East Prussia, should be subordinate only to Hitler himself. Hitler's trust in Koch was all the more extraordinary given Koch's socialist leanings. The later Nazi defector Hermann Rauschning claimed that Hitler had for a long time considered "putting Koch out of the way" as part of a purge of socialist Gauleiter.[37] (Koch's former mentor, the overtly socialist Gregor Strasser, had already been murdered the year before during Hitler's "Night of the Long Knives" purges.) Rauschning never learned why Koch survived, but Grünberg's colleague Bethke, by then serving as Königsberg district president, reportedly speculated that Koch's durability lay in networking: "Don't you suppose that Hitler would have been glad to send him to the devil long ago, if it had not been too costly a business for him? Koch, the intimate friend of Gregor Strasser! But he holds some trump cards. The man has got power in his hands. Hitler knows that if he were to take Koch by the scruff of the neck a whole bastion of the party would fly into the air, and many other honorable party members would go up with it."[38] Koch managed to survive because he cultivated important allies, including a few in Berlin. But what Bethke did not realize was that Koch's most important ally was Hitler himself. Despite his pompous airs, Koch continually demonstrated his loyalty to Hitler. Hitler, in turn, respected him as the party boss with the strength and economic vision to manage the affairs of the far-flung German East.

Koch emerged from the crisis with no viable opposition in Berlin or Königsberg. By 1937, Koch and his inner circle purged their remaining opponents to emerge even more powerful than before. But the early resistance left Koch wary of threats to his rule and cost him much of his popular legitimacy, especially among the party rank and file.[39] In June 1938, Koch organized a monumental festival, "Ten Years of Gau East Prussia," to celebrate a decade of accomplishment since his arrival to the province. It reflected his growing hubris (the event was scheduled on his forty-second birthday) and his desire to demonstrate tangible outcomes to bolster support for the regime. Robert Ley, then head of the German Labor Front and Strength Through Joy program, presented a keynote about Koch's triumph, despite having privately criticized him to Hitler five years earlier. The festival's companion volume offered a hagiography of Koch and his rule: the saint had struggled in the party's darkest hours but had never lost his faith in the Führer; his party, weak and victimized, fell prey to the "economic oppression and open terror" of its enemies, but emerged triumphant to win in 1933. Koch's battle against unemployment—still, five years later, his regime's most tangible success—became the foundation for the glorious future awaiting East Prussia. The celebration omitted the conflicts that had almost toppled Koch's reign, highlighting only the eternal present of National Socialist rule and the grateful unity of the German people.[40]

Cultivating the *Volksgemeinschaft*

The crises plaguing Königsberg's Nazi leadership stalled their plans to revolutionize the state and the economy. But over the course of the 1930s, they managed to radically transform East Prussia by reordering culture and society around new principles of inclusion and exclusion. Seeking to transcend the class, confessional, and regional divisions that had divided the German people, the Nazis sought to foster a new German national community, or *Volksgemeinschaft*. Fostering the *Volksgemeinschaft* was both about bringing Germans together through a shared sense of common past and national destiny, and about transforming and purifying the German nation, culturally and racially.

Nazi dreams of the *Volksgemeinschaft* were at once forward- and backward-looking. They called for revitalizing the countryside and creating an agrarian paradise as a counterweight to the detrimental influences of the industrialized world. They attempted to reestablish traditional gender roles in order to celebrate warrior masculinity and demure motherhood. Most of all, they tried to cleanse German cultural expression from the degenerative effects of cultural modernity and urban life. For decades, scholars rejected the Nazi notion of the *Volksgemeinschaft* as a mere propagandist myth: Marxist historians sought to show how workers became disillusioned with the dashed promises of Nazi rule, while more recent scholars have questioned the *Volksgemeinschaft* as a social reality, preferring to concentrate on widespread passive resistance (much of it from the middle-class).[41] But more recent scholarship on the *Volksgemeinschaft*, while recognizing the limits of this imagined community, shows the powerful unifying force of the myth. The Nazis fostered a sense of belonging in the German national community through rituals of inclusion. And by ostracizing those they deemed to be political, social, and racial enemies, the Nazis strengthened the bonds by involving their chosen people in the process of exclusion.[42]

Immediately following their seizure of power, the new Nazi rulers across Germany sought to sustain the image of unified support for dictatorship. This process proceeded similarly in East Prussia, where Koch and his party purged the government of their enemies and outlawed other political parties, and then assimilated all independent organizations and media into the state. Trade unions, once hotbeds of communist activity, were folded into the National Socialist Labor Front. Weimar political militant leagues, including the Stahlhelm, were first incorporated into the party structure and then eventually dissolved. The Lutheran church was coopted by the pro-Nazi wing of the leadership.[43] The few newspapers that had opposed racism and antisemitism were shut down, and the remaining newspapers came gradually under party supervision.[44] By the fall of 1933, the Nazis drove the last vestiges of the opposition underground and, despite a few communists smuggling leaflets and the occasional drunken outburst, no sizable opposition ever formed against Nazi rule in East Prussia.[45]

Even as the Nazis terrorized their opponents, most East Prussians supported Nazi rule during the 1930s because they associated it with greater prosperity and stability. Amid the enthusiasm for German national renewal, few Königsbergers protested in June 1933 when the Nazis banned alternative political parties; just as was the case across the Reich, the Nazis succeeded in framing the NSDAP's victory over pluralist squabbling as synonymous with the victory of Germany.[46] As the Königsberg propagandist Hellmut Sommer explained, eliminating alternatives meant that the party and the state could work "even more closely together in the service of the people and for their benefit."[47] Most East Prussians tied the province's economic recovery to Hitler more than to Gauleiter Koch, whose attempts to form a cult of personality mostly fell flat. But they did identify strongly with the employment campaigns that put East Prussia on the front lines of the battle for German national renewal.[48] As Koch's economist Grünberg wrote in 1934, the "belief and hope in the *Volksgemeinschaft*" in East Prussia had become so powerful that the new world was being "propelled more quickly into reality" than elsewhere in Germany.[49] Although the economic prosperity was not built on sustainable foundations, many East Prussians, comparing to what had come before, considered the years before the outbreak of war in 1939 to be, as the historian Andreas Kossert writes, "the happiest of their lives."[50]

In East Prussia, the party especially promoted unity around the region's bulwark identity. Building on borderland imagery from the 1920s, officially sanctioned nationalist and antimodern *Heimat* literature, already popular in East Prussia since the turn of the twentieth century, adopted increasingly *volkisch* language during the Nazi period, describing East Prussian Germanness through Teutonic origins,

Protestant upbringing, and generations of conflict with neighboring tribes. Genres of "beleaguered literature" emphasized East Prussians' wartime suffering during the First World War, and "borderland novels" pitted noble, pure East Prussian protagonists against corrupt outsiders—usually "the Pole," "the Lithuanian," or "the Russian." Many of these works described the hero's return from the big city to the idyllic rural life of the farm amid the lingering danger of the Corridor.[51] Spectacles of public unity promoted this East Prussian German identity through celebrations of traditional regional folk culture, music, art, and peasant attire. As the head of the *Gau* Propaganda Department, Joachim Paltzo, wrote in 1938, such festivals were designed to demonstrate the "new spirit of community and common East Prussian will" of the *Volksgemeinschaft* by performing East Prussians' shared "native values and traditions." At the grandiose festival celebrating "10 years of *Gau* East Prussia," in 1938, 1,200 German women danced in traditional costume while 2,000 SA men harmonized to "The Farmers Wanted to Be Free," and 70,000 party members marched from the Erich-Koch-Platz stadium to the Königsberg Castle, symbolically linking the bright Nazi future with the glorious Prussian past.[52]

Despite the performances of unity, determining just who belonged to East Prussian version of the German national community remained a complex affair. Eager to demonstrate the essential Germanness of East Prussia, German nationalists had long argued that speakers of Lithuanian and the Masurian dialect of Polish were indelibly German because they were loyal to the German state, were predominantly Lutheran, and had long ago adopted German cultural norms.[53] In his campaigns, Gauleiter Koch had downplayed Nazi biological racism to attract the Polish-speaking Masurian vote, directing his diatribes instead to Polish nationalists' plans to dismember East Prussia. Hitler likewise sought to capture the non-German vote: despite styling himself as the next Hindenburg who would rescue East Prussia from the Slavic hordes, Hitler declared in the Masurian town of Lyck in 1932 that "I do not believe that there is another land in Germany as loyal as Masuria"—a phrase that National Socialist propaganda swiftly stylized as the "Masurian revelation" that Masurians were German no matter what language they spoke.[54] After the seizure of power, Nazi ideologues and ethnographers continued to emphasize the inherent Germanness of Polish and Lithuanian speakers. The state's concerted economic investment in Masuria during the mass employment campaigns, especially led many Masurians, regardless of the language they spoke at home, to support the regime. As a demonstration of loyalty, many began speaking German in public or with their children, and a number of towns and villages, to conform with the new Nazi ideology, voluntarily Germanized their names.[55]

Koch and the Königsberg leadership remained less invested in race science than their national counterparts; however, by the mid-1930s "German ancestry" increasingly took priority over cultural definitions of Germanness, as numerous ethnographers and race scientists increasingly sought to define East Prussian German identity according to blood.[56] The obvious problem was that East Prussians, as Nazi researchers were forced to admit, were "racially mixed." A guide to East Prussia issued by the SS Race and Settlement Office in 1937 grappled with these apparent contradictions by asserting (dubiously) that most East Prussians belonged primarily to the "Nordic race." But even the Race and Settlement Office was forced to admit that many East Prussians, because of the great migrations of the Middle Ages, had "East Baltic" and even "Dinaric" (southern) blood. Race scientists claimed to find tall, blonde-haired, and blue-eyed Nordic types closer to the coast, but further inland, they claimed the people were of shorter stature with darker hair and eyes. Yet despite these variations, the text insisted that East Prussians remained primarily Germanic and that more dangerous racial elements (Jewish blood and eastern Slavic blood from Russian military invasions) had supposedly not contaminated East Prussia's racial stock. Although Masurian East Prussians, especially, were more "racially mixed" than Germans in the West, even they, the report claimed, were "in the German sense . . . in no way inferior." Polish-speaking Masurians, in other words, were German not only by will but also by blood.[57]

As international tensions escalated with Poland and Lithuania toward the end of the decade, Königsberg's Nazis increased their Germanization efforts. Masurians who did not sufficiently assimilate by speaking German in public risked harassment and persecution. The Gestapo began registering non-German minorities in the province, and started targeted arrests of politically oriented individuals of Masurian Polish or Lithuanian heritage. By the late 1930s, they even attempted to eliminate the Masurian Polish language entirely. Arguing that the language had been kept alive through its religious use, the Nazis shut down the long-standing Polish-language Lutheran seminary at the University of Königsberg, outlawed the publication of Polish-language prayers, and prohibited Polish from being used in church services.[58]

The state also sought to erase traces of East Prussia's polyglot history from the map entirely. Whereas Germanization of place names had been a decentralized, voluntary process in the 1920s, in late 1938, all place names with Lithuanian or Polish name origins were forcibly changed. Kurt Forstreuter, a Königsberg archivist, recalled being tasked with finding original "ancient German names" from old maps and records. He recalled that when few such names were found, the committee conjured up new names to allude to supposedly ancient German settlements, without recognition of East Prussian local naming tradition: in Masuria, Wawrochen became Deutschheide (German heath), Suchorowitz became Deutschwalde (German woods), and Sendrowen became Treudorf (loyal village); other villages adopted the names of Teutonic Knights. In 1938, 1,375 historic place names were replaced, and in some border regions, over 70 percent of all villages were renamed.[59] Forstreuter preserved his own hometown's name by arguing that "Weedern" did not sound Lithuanian (though it was). Recalling the campaign in the early 1960s, Forstreuter dismissed it as "a highly superfluous measure, since the inhabitants [of these towns] did not become any more German than before."[60] But in a way, they did; becoming German had become about the elimination of alternatives.

When it came to East Prussian Catholics, the problem of religion, language, and race were bound together from the start. Although 84 percent of the population was Protestant, including most Masurians, a significant Catholic minority lived in the southern part of the province, especially in the Warmia district along the border with Poland. Polish-speaking Catholics had been most likely to vote for Poland during the 1920 Plebiscite, and the Catholic Centre Party won absolute majorities in Catholic-dominant regions by 1929.[61] Königsberg's Nazis saw Masurian Catholics as inherently pro-Polish, and they arrested and harassed numerous Catholic political leaders in the first months after the seizure of power. Relations improved briefly after Hitler's Concordat with the Vatican in July 1933, but by April 1934, Warmia's bishop, Maximilian Kaller, lamented that East Prussia's Catholic Church found itself "in dire circumstances" after the SA shut down numerous church organizations.[62] The same dynamic played out across Germany, but in East Prussia, the conflict assumed a distinctly ethnonational tone, pitting the Nazis against Polish-speaking Catholics and sharpening the divide between Germans and Poles around religion. By November of that year, Kaller, an ethnic German who had grown up bilingual in Prussian Silesia, another polyglot border region, responded defiantly by addressing his "beloved Polish people"—his congregation—in Polish.[63] Catholic organizations maintained some autonomy till late in the decade, but a crackdown in 1937 led to the arrest of four priests and ten laypeople in the town of Heilsburg over an alleged plot to stage an uprising. When the Königsberg Special Court convicted the men to long prison sentences and eventual deportation, protests erupted, leading police to ban all remaining Catholic organizations. The revolt was quickly suppressed, and it remained the only substantial protest in the province after the first year of Nazi rule.[64]

Determining the dividing line between Germans and Poles became more complicated after 1938, when numerous former Prussian citizens migrated from Poland to East Prussia as part of Hitler's *Heim ins Reich* (Back Home to the Reich) program. The program was designed to attract racially and culturally German settlers from outside Germany as Volksdeutsche, but the authorities also feared that would-be Volksdeutsche were actually Polish saboteurs or opportunists. The Gestapo even began rounding up people with Polish connections or ancestry to determine their loyalties.[65]

The case of one Gustav Badzinski proved to be especially complex. Badzinski had been born in 1900 in Masuria in an East Prussian village near the border with Poland, which was then in the Russian Empire. He spoke German and was Protestant, but he spent all of the 1920s and 1930s living in towns across Poland and southern Ukraine. He returned to Königsberg in 1939 and tried to obtain German citizenship. Over the next five years, Badzinski attempted to establish his racial and cultural German identity, providing dozens of pages of ancestors' birth certificates, reference letters from former places of habitation, and personal biographies. Acquaintances, bureaucrats, and judges testified that "he spoke German well" and "was of German ancestry and cannot be considered a Pole."[66] But officials doubted his application because he had twice married Polish women and his children had attended Polish-language schools. In late 1942, during the Second World War, the police caught Badzinski giving food and salt to starving Russian prisoners of war and arrested him for sympathizing with the enemy. With his political and racial loyalties in question, court officials debated whether Badzinski could be deemed "worthy for inclusion."[67] Badzinski continued to assert his identity as a German even after his release, but the case was never resolved. The paper trail dropped off in the late summer of 1944, as the Red Army closed in on the borders of East Prussia. Badzinski might have been arrested as a political traitor, or he may have decided there were no longer benefits to joining the *Volksgemeinschaft*.

Masurians and Lithuanians could become German by choosing to assimilate, but assimilation was no longer available to German Jews. In East Prussia, just as was the case across Germany, the Nazis relied on antisemitism as the primary binary for defining membership in the *Volksgemeinschaft*. Königsberg's Nazis were virulent antisemites—they blamed Jewish finance for economic inequality and denounced Jewish influence on pure German culture. Initially, they focused less on biological racism and more on the idea of Jews as foreign threats to East Prussia's economic well-being and territorial integrity. But they made no special efforts, unlike many other regional parties, to develop local policies against Jews, in part because the province's Jewish population was proportionally small compared to other German regions, and because many Jewish families left after 1918, seeking greater economic opportunities elsewhere in the Reich. After 1933, Königsberg followed Berlin's lead, implementing exclusionary and increasingly violent policies against Jewish Germans. In the spring of 1933, the Nazis targeted Jewish institutions and leaders, pushed Jews out of larger financial concerns, and instituted boycotts on Jewish shops.[68] They expelled Jewish Reichstag members, government employees, journalists, and professors, and they widely publicized the burning of books by Jewish authors, along with those by other enemies of the people.[69] The Nazis escalated their antisemitic violence, burning shops and destroying provincial synagogues and cemeteries, but the exclusionary rhetoric and terror did not immediately separate Germans from Jews. The Gau Office for Municipal Politics lamented in 1935 that many Germans, despite local party leaders' "attempts to enlighten them," still socialized with Jews and frequented Jewish shops.[70] In the Masurian town of Allenstein, a Nazi district leader complained that a publicized boycott had backfired and "Jewish businesses were overflowing" with German patrons.[71]

After Germany's institution of the Nuremberg Race Laws in September 1935, Königsberg's Nazis incorporated the national rhetoric of biological racism more strongly. In the interest of protecting "the purity of German blood," the laws institutionalized Nazi race theory and created policies to legalize racial discrimination. Jews were stripped of citizenship and intermarriage or sexual relationships between Germans and Jews were outlawed.[72] The legal distinction between citizen and noncitizen underscored the divide between us and them, laying the groundwork for further discrimination over the course of the decade. Germans were called on to assert their Aryan identity by documenting Christian German ancestry with baptismal or other archival records. In so doing, they developed an increasing sense of being bound together as members of a national community that explicitly excluded Jews.[73]

After the Nuremberg Laws, the Jews, deprived of the rights of citizenship, began to feel their forced separation from Germans through institutionalized racism and increasingly cold encounters with former friends and neighbors. Few non-Jewish Germans demonstrated solidarity with their Jewish neighbors. Most Germans were not part of the murderous minority actively carrying out discriminatory policies against Jews, but the majority of Germans either remained indifferent to the plight of their neighbors or engaged in passive complicity out of fear.[74] Gestapo records reveal that in East Prussia, it was mostly simple workers and the occasional rural farmer who risked showing kindness to Jewish neighbors. Such acts were rarer in Königsberg, where anti-Jewish rhetoric was sharper and the mechanisms of social control more pervasive.[75]

The former editor of Königsberg's liberal newspaper, the *Hartungsche Zeitung*, Ludwig Goldstein, wrote poignantly in his diary about the process of exclusion. Goldstein was the atheist son of an assimilated Jewish father and a Christian mother. He wrote in the early 1940s, shortly before his death: "I have always *felt that I was German and nothing else.* It was therefore not just something repulsive, but ridiculous as well, when one day suddenly it was, 'You're not German—you're a Jew.'" "Yes, what should I say to that? Down to the innermost fibers of my being immersed in native German [*heimatliches*] thinking and feeling, I was completely unfamiliar with foreign customs because I had never learned them in any way. I loved the land and the people, my familiar surroundings with its customs and institutions, and not in the least the German language, which is sacred to me, not by any intellectual means, but emotionally, out of innate instinct, just as one loves one's mother."[76] Goldstein never came to think of himself as Jewish, even after being forced to wear the Star of David. He died of natural causes shortly before Königsberg's Jews were slated for deportation.

Rainer Radok, a teenager in the 1930s, recalled similarly how his family became Jewish in the eyes of the state. Although Rainer's grandfather had converted to Christianity in 1894, the Nuremberg Race Laws dictated that Rainer's father Fritz was a Jew, and that Rainer, like Ludwig Goldstein, was a half-Jewish *Mischling*, or mongrel. Radok's father,

Fritz, a proud First World War veteran, had worked as the commercial director for the prominent Steinfurt train car factory in Königsberg. Although the family faced increasing isolation after 1933, Radok's family remained in Königsberg even as other Jewish families began to emigrate. His father Fritz sympathized with National Socialism, at first refusing to believe that there was no place for him in Germany; only in 1938, when he was fired from his job for being Jewish, did he start making plans to emigrate. But before Fritz Radok managed to escape with his family in 1939, he was arrested twice and briefly sentenced to hard labor.[77] Likewise, the historian Hans Rothfels hoped that as a war veteran and conservative nationalist, he might be granted the status of honorary Aryan. Although Rothfels lost his professorship in 1934, he requested (unsuccessfully) an exemption from the 1935 Nuremberg Laws, believing that his identity as a German could not be officially rescinded by racialist laws of exclusion. Rothfels only emigrated in 1938, when he could no longer find any employment in Königsberg or Berlin, and when the law on Jewish given names forced him to adopt the name "Israel."[78]

For most Jews, the *Kristallnacht* pogrom shattered remaining hopes for peaceful coexistence with the Nazi state. In coordinated attacks throughout the evening of November 9, 1938, the Nazis looted Jewish businesses, arrested 450 Jewish men, destroyed Jewish cemeteries, and burned down Königsberg's main synagogue. As Goldstein later recorded in his diary, it was at that moment that he recognized that Nazi terror knew no limits. "As I crossed the Köttel Bridge, my eyes fell upon the dome of the New Synagogue. Well! It looks so peculiar, so airy! But when one looked closer, it became clear that only the iron structure remained. Were repairs being carried out? But no one mentioned anything about that! Could it be—? No, that would be unthinkable. But of course, the word 'unthinkable' [*unmöglich*] . . . no longer exists in the dictionary of National Socialism." The Israelite Orphan House next door was also set on fire—the children there were ripped from their slumber by a gang of intruders and driven outside, "frightened to death and barely dressed," before their teacher could find them and tend to them.[79]

State violence escalated quickly after *Kristallnacht*. In 1939, Gauleiter Koch forcibly resettled Jewish families in cramped communal apartments, the so-called *Judenhäuser*. From September 1941 on, Jews were forced to wear the Star of David. Königsberg's Jewish population shrank by a third between July 1933 and October 1938, when only 2,086

Jews remained out of a total city population of 339,360.[80] Emigration became increasingly difficult, and then impossible after 1939. Many of those who had succeeded in leaving Königsberg only made it as far as other German cities; even those who emigrated to neighboring European countries found themselves soon once again under Nazi rule, this time without the possibility of escape.[81]

Königsberg's Empire

Despite the rhetoric that East Prussia was a fortress and bulwark of Germandom, East Prussia's economic future still depended on establishing bridges to the East so long as the province remained severed by the Corridor. Königsberg's Nazi leaders envisioned their future in connection with Russia, even as anticommunist and anti-Bolshevist rhetoric began dominating nationwide Nazi propaganda campaigns in the second half of the 1930s.[82] When the later Nazi defector Rauschning visited Königsberg for the German *Ostmesse* exhibition in the mid-1930s, Koch reportedly announced, "Now, leave aside for once all the usual prejudices and tell me, is it not a grand, tremendous country? And the people! Magnificent raw material, eh? You can make something of them. Russia, my friend, is the world of the future. Germans and Russians, let us weld together our miserable existences. I tell you, it will bring the biggest boom in the world, the most tremendous that has ever been known."[83] Koch was the "chief advocate" among leading National Socialists for a German-Soviet alliance.[84] He even sent his economist Grünberg on a mission to the Soviet Union in 1936 or 1937 to facilitate trade relations.[85]

Unlike Hitler, Koch's inner circle initially held the view that East Prussia's and Germany's economic security lay not in the military conquest and subjugation of native populations to create a colonial space for German settler fantasies—a view they found to be naive and impractical—but in the fundamental reenvisioning of Eastern Europe as an economic sphere.[86] Rauschning recalled, when being introduced to Grünberg during a visit to Königsberg in the mid-1930s, that the planner's office was covered with specially drawn maps and schematics—not of East Prussia, but of the "whole of Eastern Europe and part of Russia in Asia." Grünberg reportedly explained that his office had charted all the power stations, natural resources, and industrial plants of Eastern Europe and the Soviet Union, "the necessary starting point for any reasonable system of planning." Königsberg's party leadership, he explained, was "not merely planning East Prussia here; we are at work on the preparations for the coming Great Order."[87] Grünberg announced with exuberance that state boundaries would be erased and all of Eastern Europe would be reorganized rationally around centers of production, raw material supplies, and transportation routes in order to facilitate a perfectly distributed German-Russian region of production and consumption.[88] The new world order would transcend politics and be run entirely by technocrats; private enterprise would coordinate with state planning to regulate the total volume of goods produced and consumed. Rauschning laughed off the idea as "complete Bolshevism," but Grünberg retorted that Bolshevism was "just an intermediate stage" on the way to the new world order.[89] Like Koch, he assumed that a close economic collaboration between Germany and the Soviet Union was both possible and mutually advantageous. Yet their vision for a pan-Eurasian economic space was as chauvinist as the racial settlement fantasies that motivated Hitler. While Koch and Grünberg expected a German-Soviet economic partnership was inevitable, they also believed that Germans would be its greatest beneficiaries. If the Soviet Union refused to cooperate, then a short, prophylactic war would be necessary to bring the arrangement about.[90]

But even as planners were scheming to bring about economic new world order, other scholars and organizations in Königsberg were plotting for East Prussia to become the base for German colonial expansion. Königsberg's nationalist scholars had long focused on demonstrating the historic expanse of the German settlement and cultural realm (*Siedlungs- und Kulturboden*) to justify Germany's historical claims to East Prussia.[91] During the 1930s, these scholars increasingly argued that not only East Prussia but much of Poland and Eastern Europe had been German settlement land. Repopulating East Prussia, the Nazi ideologue C. G. Harke declared, held critical "political-strategic" value for the future expansion of the German nation.[92] Erich Maschke, a professor of East and West Slavic history in Königsberg through 1935, likewise argued for German territorial expansion. During a 1938 party exhibition on "Europe's Fate in the East," he called for the Germans to reclaim the lands of supposed historic German settlement in order to ensure the "growth of the German national body" and to bring about the "trinity of race, nation, and space."[93] Koch and the party leadership sometimes came into friction with these institutes, but on other occasions cooperated with them. By the late 1930s, Koch, Grünberg, and the rest of the party leadership, still not completely abandoning hope for an East German economic nexus, increasingly began entertaining the *Lebensraum* fantasies Koch had once reportedly dismissed as naive. Koch worked closely with the Königsberg-based League of the German East, for example, to draft plans to revise Germany's eastern borders and destroy the state of Poland. He also collaborated with a number of Königsberg historians, including Theodor Schieder and Werner Conze (both students of the since-dismissed German-Jewish historian Hans Rothfels), to draft plans to Germanize Polish territories through mass deportations of Poles and Jews.[94]

Germany invaded Poland on September 1, 1939, unleashing the Second World War. The invasion of Poland eliminated the Corridor, reconnecting East Prussia to the body of the Reich, and the province transformed overnight from a vulnerable border region to the center of a new German empire in the East. This borderland geography, no longer a vulnerability, combined with Koch's ability to curry favor with Hitler to allow East Prussia and its party leadership to play a seminal role in the wartime occupations of Eastern Europe, more so than any other regional party in the Reich. By the fall of 1941, Koch and Königsberg's party leadership extended East Prussian informal rule into a continuous stretch of territory from the Baltic to the Black Sea. Already by the late 1930s, Königsberg's Nazis had brought their once-divergent visions for Nazi rule more closely in line with those of Berlin. Still, the German-occupied East became a colonial space where Königsberg's party leadership in many ways recreated their East Prussian ruling style; they replicated the same personal networks of rule, the same inherent bureaucratic complexities, and the same nepotistic self-enrichment. The fantasies of colonial domination and the violence of the war allowed them to radicalize their rule and its deadly effects, both at home and in their colonies.

Nazi Germany dismantled the Polish state in the fall of 1939, claiming much of the territory for their own, thus doing what they had accused the Poles of conspiring to do to East Prussia during the interwar period. Koch successfully maneuvered to claim several historically Polish territories lying along East Prussia's southern and eastern borders, including northern Mazovia, a 12,000 square kilometer territory stretching to the outskirts of Warsaw, and the Polish towns of Suwałki and Augustów.[95] East Prussia annexed these territories as integral parts of the province, complete with German administrative structure and law codes—Mazovia became the district Zichenau (Ciechanów, after the regional capital), and Suwałki and Augustów became district Sudauen.

Königsberg's leadership personally administered these territories: The Königsberg District President Dr. Hermann Bethke and Paul Dargel, Koch's deputy, each served terms as Zichenau's district president, and the police leadership also came from Königsberg or other East Prussian towns.

Although the Nazis claimed these territories were historic German settlement regions, Germans comprised only 10 percent of the pre-1939 population—80 percent were Poles and 10 percent Jews. Königsberg's Nazis saw these territories as East Prussia's personal space of territorial expansion, or *Lebensraum*. They planned to provide Polish farmsteads to the sons of East Prussian farmers, even as the SS drafted competing plans to settle ethnic Germans from Central and Eastern Europe, the so-called Volksdeutsche, who migrated to Germany as part of the *Heim ins Reich* program.[96] By November 1940, the Germans deported almost 15,000 Poles and Jews from Zichenau and Sudauen to extract wealth from their farmsteads and businesses and to make room for Volksdeutsche and settlers from the Reich.[97] By 1943, however, Germans remained only a small minority: only 57,000 living among 823,000 Poles.[98] Volksdeutsche, provided they could definitively assert their racial identity as Germans, were granted greater rights and privileges than non-Germans, although they remained subject to more stringent regulations than their counterparts from the pre-1939 territories. Non-Germans were denied citizenship, rigorously policed, and subjected to a series of oppressive regulations, forced labor, and deportations.[99] But just as in East Prussia, authorities often struggled to determine who was German and who was Polish, leading to regulations requiring Volksdeutsche to perform their racial identity by Germanizing their names, wearing swastika bands, using the Hitler salute, and eating in restaurants at different times in order to avoid socializing with Poles. Poles, meanwhile, were forced to tip their hats in deference to Germans or risk arrest; in order to underscore their separateness, newborn Polish children were forced to adopt the acquired name "Kazimiera" or "Kazimir." Yet in some cases, Poles deemed racially valuable—by physical features or character traits—were considered "capable of being re-Germanised" and treated as Germans, further underscoring the arbitrary flexibility of Nazi race science.[100]

The expansion into Poland broke down many legal restrictions and taboos previously limiting Nazi violence of exclusion. Eighty thousand Jews lived in Zichenau in 1939, compared to only 3,000 in East Prussia at the time. This first wartime encounter with a large Jewish population outside the former borders of the Reich triggered a dramatic increase in exclusionary actions against Jews and marked the transition toward genocide.[101] In the first weeks of the invasion, Wehrmacht soldiers and *Einsatzgruppen* killed dozens of Jews, expropriated their property, and set fire to synagogues. In the fall of 1939, the new civilian government attempted to rid the new East Prussian territory of Jews entirely, at first driving convoys of Jews across the border to the Soviet Union and then, beginning in January 1940, deporting them into Nazi-occupied Poland. Unable to expel them efficiently, they forcibly resettled the remaining 40,000 Jews into ghettos and work camps by January 1942.[102] The Nazis simultaneously escalated racial violence against Poles. Within months of the invasion, East Prussia became home to a constellation of labor, transit, and concentration camps to house Polish POWs, political opposition, and members of the intelligentsia, including priests, school teachers, postal employees, and eighteen-year-old secondary school graduates.[103] The largest of these, the Soldau transit and detention camp, detained an estimated 200,000 people over the course of the war. While some were released and others deported to concentration camps, "the remainder," as the camp's founder, the SS-Brigade Leader and Königsberg Security Police inspector Dr. Otto Rasch, explained, "were to be liquidated." At least 10,000 Polish prisoners were murdered, among them the eighty-three-year-old Archbishop of Płock Antoni Julian Nowowiejski.[104] The war also radicalized the Nazis' violent social engineering within the prior borders of East Prussia. Working with regional SS agencies in May and June 1940, Koch and the Königsberg leadership facilitated the liquidation of 1,558 incurable psychiatric patients in mobile gas chambers at Soldau as part of Operation Lange.[105] After the killing spree was over, the police officers who took part were treated to a night at the camp casino. To ease their remaining moral qualms, the murderers received the gift of a commemorative box designed with East Prussian amber, a vacation to Nazi-occupied Holland, and a dedication signed by Gauleiter Koch.[106] The euthanasia campaign was organized regionally and was only later folded into Berlin's notorious Operation T4. Such local murder initiatives helped set a precedent for the Holocaust.

After Hitler and Stalin divided Eastern Europe with the Molotov-Ribbentrop Pact of 1939, East Prussia found itself directly bordering Soviet-annexed Lithuania. The brief alliance between Nazi Germany and the Soviet Union meant friendlier exchanges—the Nazis toned down anti-Bolshevik propaganda, and in 1940 the Soviet Union once again took part in Königsberg's *Ostmesse* Eastern Exhibition Fair.

But the detente was short-lived. In the nearby forests of southern East Prussia, Hitler was already constructing the *Wolfsschanze*, his largest secret military headquarters, in preparation to invade the Soviet Union. Hitler personally hated East Prussia—he famously preferred the Alps to the marshy, mosquito-infested flatlands of the German East—but he spent a full thousand days in his East Prussian headquarters during the war, nearly a quarter of his total time in power. The lands around the *Wolfsschanze* became the most heavily guarded closed zone of the entire Reich. Numerous high-ranking Nazi officials, including Hans Lammers, Joachim von Ribbentrop, Himmler, and Göring, established hunting lodges and estates nearby. Hitler and his inner circle, including Koch, planned Operation Barbarossa and the Blitzkrieg campaigns from the *Wolfsschanze*.[107] On June 22, 1941, Wehrmacht Army Group North and Army Group Center launched their invasions from East Prussia. Catching Soviet defense forces completely off guard, they pushed deep into Soviet territory, capturing Kyiv and arriving at the outskirts of Leningrad and Moscow by the fall of 1941.

With the Soviet invasion, Koch and the Nazis of Königsberg further extended their domain to eastern Poland, Belorussia, and Ukraine. On August 15, 1941, Koch became chief of the Civilian Administration of the newly occupied Bezirk (district) Bialystok, a 31,000-square-kilometer territory, as large as East Prussia had been before the war. Bialystok (Białystok in Polish) was not directly annexed into East Prussia but became an anomaly of the German occupations—not part of the centrally administered Reich Ministry for the Occupied Territories but an informal colony that Koch and his inner circle ruled with a great deal of autonomy. A month later, Koch became the Reichskommissar of Nazi-occupied Ukraine, the largest of all of the German-occupied Soviet territories, covering 340,000 square kilometers by September 1942. Koch and Königsberg's Nazis did not exercise the same degree of autonomy in Ukraine as they did in Zichenau and Bialystok, but their role in the occupation allowed them to become the most powerful regional party leadership in the Reich. While Koch eagerly sought control over Zichenau and Bialystok, he hesitated at the prospect of ruling Ukraine, complaining that the job would be purely negative—a recognition of the brutal occupation regime Hitler had in store. (Koch instead wanted to rule over the Baltic occupation district Reichskommissariat Ostland, which he saw as a more productive space for extending East Prussian influence.) But Hitler trusted Koch as a strongman and economic expert who could exploit the territories' resources for the war, and once Koch stepped into the role, he no longer expressed those qualms.[108] Whereas Koch and his economic planner Grünberg had once dreamed of fostering a German-Soviet cooperative partnership, Koch announced in September 1941, upon the establishment of the Reichskommissariat, that he was eager to "smash Ukrainian industry and drive the proletariat back to the country."[109]

Koch ruled Bialystok and Ukraine in the same way he did East Prussia and Zichenau, by importing his inner circle from Königsberg to serve as personal agents of his rule.[110] Many of them served in multiple roles in the three spheres of Königsberg's empire. As Jonathan Steinberg writes, occupied Ukraine in particular "became an arena in which every conceivable expert—agronomist, economist, racial and genealogical fanatic, technocrat, bureaucrat, student of Russian and Slavic cultures (the *Ostforscher*), colonizer and crank—attempted to mobilize some element of the great state apparatus to fulfill his visions."[111] A disproportionately large number of these colonizers and cranks came from Königsberg. Grünberg became the head of the Reichskommissariat Division for Population Matters and played a central role in early economic planning efforts.[112] Of the six general districts of the Reichskommissariat Ukraine, three were ruled by Königsberg party leaders. Among them, East Prussia's SA paramilitary leader, Heinrich Schöne, ruled Volhynia-Podolia and Königsberg's first Nazi party member, Waldemar Magunia, became the General Commissar of Kyiv, after having first served as Koch's representative in Bialystok. Dozens of other Königsbergers and East Prussians held positions of power: Hellmut Will, the Königsberg mayor, became Kyiv's Regional Commissar and Friedrich Rogausch, the mayor of the East Prussian town of Memel (reannexed from Lithuania in 1939), became Kyiv's City Commissar. Koch's deputy Paul Dargel, already the District President of annexed Zichenau since 1940, became Koch's permanent representative in the Reichskommissariat headquarters in Rivne, effectively running the day-to-day business of occupation while Koch spent most of his time in Königsberg.[113]

The rule in the East introduced many of the same endemic flaws of Nazi governance to the occupied territories: polycratic rule, bureaucratic infighting, and rampant opportunism among civilian officials looking to enrich themselves and enhance their careers in the Wild East. Much more so than in Zichenau and Bialystok, Koch and the civilian administration competed for power with the military and civilian agencies in Berlin, especially Alfred Rosenberg, head of the Reich Ministry for the Occupied Eastern Territories, and Himmler and the SS. Historians disagree about the extent to which these personality struggles and overlapping jurisdictions shaped rule in Ukraine. While some scholars have shown how conflicts between civilian, military, and SS rule created chaos and led to an escalation in violence, others have convincingly argued that local and regional Nazi civilian administrators nonetheless played a powerful role in determining policies on the ground, implementing an occupation regime that was brutal by design.[114]

The irony was that in Bialystok and Ukraine, many among the local population had first welcomed the Germans as liberators. Around twenty to twenty-five million people lived on the territory of the Reichskommissariat Ukraine on the eve of the invasion.[115] Most of them, especially those living in rural areas, had suffered under Soviet rule. At least 3.3 million peasants starved to death during Stalin's collectivization of agriculture, when an orchestrated famine decimated the countryside for years, and tens of thousands of families were forcibly deported from their homes as part of dekulakization and ethnic cleansing operations throughout the 1930s.[116] Many Ukrainian peasants welcomed the invading Wehrmacht soldiers with peace offerings of flowers and bread, and Ukrainian nationalist groups hoped the invasion would lead to an independent Ukrainian nation-state. The Polish region of Bialystok had fallen under Soviet occupation after the Molotov-Ribbentrop Pact; the forced nationalization of property, mass deportations, and arrests led many of the local Polish and Belorussian inhabitants also to welcome Germans as liberators.

The German occupiers viewed the Soviet territories as backward and their populations as racially and culturally inferior.[117] The fertile soils of the region were to become Germany's breadbasket, a settler paradise for German farmers, and a region to supply the natural resources needed to ensure German dominance in Europe. Ethnic Germans from across Eastern and Southeastern Europe, the so-called Volksdeutsche, would join German farmers from the West as colonists.[118] Any non-Germans living there—Jews or Slavs—were to be forced into submission or eliminated entirely. Koch never fully embraced Nazi racial theory, but he conformed to Hitler's wishes and emphasized it more strongly than he had in East Prussia. He was a committed German chauvinist and performed German cultural superiority with great bravado.[119] Koch became, as the historian Karel Berkhoff writes, a "proudly brutal Reichskommissar," who once reportedly remarked that "if I find a Ukrainian who is worthy of sitting at the same table with me, I must have him shot."[120] The civilian government, along with the Wehrmacht and SS, organized rule through racial hierarchy. Germans from the Reich served as masters and overlords, occupying luxurious apartments, shopping in special shops, and driving around in motor cars, while Ukrainians, Russians, Poles, and Jews were subject to myriad restrictions, tariffs, and curfews designed to emphasize their status as an underclass.[121] Ethnic Germans living in Ukraine were promoted to positions of authority over their former neighbors, even though the authorities remained suspicious of the ideological commitment, racial composition, and civilizational level of these Germans who had spent decades under the corrupting influence of Soviet rule.[122]

Just as in Zichenau, Nazi race science, already contradictory in theory, proved arbitrary in practice. Hitler famously preferred Ukrainians over Russians after seeing Ukrainian women and children with blonde braids and blue eyes, and postulated that useful and biologically valuable Slavs might not be Slavs at all but peoples eligible for

FIGURE 3.   Erich Koch (right), Gauleiter and *Oberpräsident* of East Prussia and Reichskommissar of Ukraine, examines the traditional folk costume of a Ukrainian woman in the occupied territories, circa 1942. The reichsminister for the occupied eastern territories, Alfred Rosenberg (center), looks on. Collection: AKG-Images.

Germanization.[123] Throughout the occupied territories, the civilian government promoted some groups within the social hierarchy—Poles over Jews, Ukrainians over Russians—as part of a divide-and-conquer politics of rule. In Ukraine, the Reichskommissariat even supported Ukrainian nationalists and permitted a parliament made up of Kyiv's "intelligentsia," many of them professors or engineers who had been imprisoned for some time by the Soviet government.[124] But by the end of 1941, Koch suppressed all Ukrainian councils and regional administration, leaving the local population with no ethnic or regional representation beyond the lowest levels.[125] Still, the Germans found many Ukrainians willing to serve in the lower levels of the Reichskommissariat, often as a means to improve their own material conditions.[126]

Ultimately, Nazi fantasies of German racial and civilizational superiority combined with economic imperatives as Koch and Königsberg's leadership pursued resource extraction at a fever pitch. They did so with no regard to the economic and social consequences for the people living there. In the later words of the East Prussian regional administrator (*Landrat*) Klaus von der Groeben, who took part in the occupations, Königsberg's Nazis saw Bialystok, especially, as East Prussia's "cow to be milked."[127] They appropriated the businesses of Poles and Jews, lining their own pockets in the process, and forced the population to produce supplies for the Wehrmacht at near starvation wages—Koch reportedly said that it would be of little importance if a few million people died in consequence.[128] In Ukraine, the Reichskommissariat cut off food supplies from major urban centers, including Kyiv, as part of a general Nazi *Hungerplan* to eliminate superfluous population and to wipe out Russian and Ukrainian urban culture. But although Koch consistently called for forced appropriations and insisted that Poles and Ukrainians were "inferior in every respect" to any German, no available records indicate that he called for, as Himmler often did, the planned mass extermination of non-Jewish peoples.[129]

By contrast, it was on the killing fields of Bialystok and Ukraine that the calculated genocide of the Jewish people began. Even before Hitler instituted the Final Solution and created a constellation of death camps and gas chambers across Eastern Europe, SS *Einsatzgruppen* and police battalions began mass executing Jews in the first weeks of the invasion in 1941 at a much larger scale than they had done during the invasion of Zichenau in 1939. An estimated 1,533,000 Jews lived on the territory of what became the Reichskommissariat, according to Soviet census records from 1939, and around 240,000 Jews lived in the Białystok region, along with another 100,000 Jewish refugees who arrived from Nazi-occupied Poland when Białystok briefly came under Soviet occupation. Some of them fled the German advance, were deported, or drafted into the Red Army; most remained on occupied territory. Between July and September 1941, *Einsatzgruppen*, a number of them organized by the East Prussian police, shot 30,000 Jews, mostly men. Poles also murdered their Jewish neighbors and looted their property in a wave of pogroms in towns such as Stawiski, Radziłów, and Jedwabne. These Poles sometimes acted of their own volition—emboldened by the German occupiers and eager to scapegoat Jews for Soviet rule—or as members of auxiliary police units (*Hilfspolizei*) under the direction of Nazi killing squads.[130] Because Soviet propaganda had understated the role of Nazi antisemitism (preferring to focus on fascist imperialism and brutality against the working class more generally), many Soviet Jews in Ukraine, especially, had assumed that Nazi rule would be no worse than communism, perhaps even preferable. But within days or weeks of the Wehrmacht's arrival, hundreds of thousands of Jews were rounded up in towns and villages and murdered in open-air mass shootings. Unlike in Western or Central Europe, where Jews were first cordoned into ghettos before being shipped to camps to be gassed, a large percentage of the 2,000,000 Jews who died in Bezirk Bialystok, Ukraine, and the Baltics died immediately, shot in the pits that would become their mass graves.[131]

Koch and the Königsberg leadership played no small role in carrying out the Holocaust after the institution of civilian rule. Early in the war, Koch and local authorities in Zichenau did not implement widespread measures to kill Jews—not out of humanitarian concern, as thousands died from poor living conditions in the ghettos, but because they prioritized economic exploitation over racial extermination. Koch and Göring visited Kolno in Bezirk Bialystok to watch local Polish inhabitants murder thirty Jews on July 5, 1941, and he personally approved of the execution of 3,000 others in the following weeks. On the eve of the establishment of the Reichskommissariat in the summer of 1941, Koch's representative, Paul Dargel, helped organize the massacre of 23,600 Hungarian Jews who had crossed the border into Ukraine at Kamenets-Podolsk, in what became at that time the largest mass murder action of the war.[132]

Upon the establishment of the civilian occupation in September 1941, the Reichskommissariat forced surviving Jews living in urban centers into ghettos, reduced their rations to starvation level, and levied high taxes on Jews and organizations employing them. But when the SS first initiated systematic executions as part of *Aktion Reinhard*, local civilian authorities in Zichenau, Białystok, and Ukraine attempted to delay the executions in territories under their control to preserve their Jewish workforce. They tried, especially, to maintain the Białystok ghetto, home by the summer of 1942 to 40,000 Jews, and twenty factories that produced clothing, uniforms, shoes, saddles, barrels, appliances, soap, chemicals, furniture, and bandages for the front. The president of the Białystok Jewish community, Ephraim Barash, strove to keep the ghetto economically profitable in hopes of sparing Jews from execution—at one point, the Białystok ghetto laundry reportedly cleaned the soiled linens of every Wehrmacht unit on the Eastern Front. Königsberg civilian authorities in Białystok even appealed successfully to maintain the ghetto until the end of the war by pointing out that it was invaluable for the war effort. But as the situation on the Eastern Front began to deteriorate in the summer of 1943, Himmler overrode objections and ordered the liquidation of the ghetto in order to transfer the industrial equipment further west. The ghetto's inhabitants staged an armed uprising in August 1943, but they were soon defeated, and the remaining 25,000 Jews were deported to Auschwitz and Treblinka.[133] Koch also at first sought to continue exploiting Jewish labor in Ukraine, but already in the summer of 1942, he changed course—abandoning economic productivity to achieve a more visible ideological goal—and allowed the SS to liquidate the ghettos and begin deportations.[134] As his deputy Paul Dargel reported in August, it was Koch's "emphatic wish" to demonstrate to Hitler that he had solved the Jewish question once and for all. By the summer of 1944, at least 1.2 million Jews had been murdered in Ukraine alone.[135]

Despite the brutality of the Reichskommissariat, some rural Ukrainians at first held hopes that conditions would improve after the war. But as the war became more desperate in August 1942, Göring and Hitler demanded greater deliveries of agricultural produce and Koch, eager to fulfill orders, squeezed the countryside to the point of starvation. Instructing his subordinates to treat Ukrainians in a "hard and uncompromising way," Koch claimed that only the constant threat of punishment would get the peasants to deliver. Around the same time, the Reichskommissariat carried out a campaign of forced labor deportations of so-called Eastern Laborers, or *Ostarbeiter*, to Germany to compensate for labor shortages in the Reich. Though *Ostarbeiter* were sent from occupied Soviet territories as early as the summer of 1941, relatively few had been sent from Ukraine. But after the summer of 1942, 2.3 million laborers were deported from Ukraine to the Reich (out of 2.8 million from the Soviet Union as a whole).[136]

The sudden heavy-handed deportations and forced requisitions triggered significant partisan resistance, and Red Army spies began mounting attacks against Koch's civilian administration in Bialystok and Ukraine. Waldemar Magunia, who was Königsberg's first Nazi party member and the commissar of Kyiv, was nearly killed in a mine attack near Brest while traveling by train between Rivne and Königsberg in December 1943. Koch and his superior Rosenberg faced several assassination attempts, and a bomb thrown by the famous Soviet spy Nikolai Kuznetsov seriously wounded Koch's second-in-command Dargel, leading to the amputation of both of his legs.[137] Similarly, while many Poles and Belorussians in Bezirk Bialystok held strong anticommunist views, Königsberg's Nazis engaged in contradictory policies that quickly undermined the regime's credibility. They attempted to cultivate relations with Polish partisan groups to fight Bolshevism but enacted increasingly harsh measures and deported at least 28,000 people, many to the Reich as *Ostarbeiter*.[138] By 1944, the occupation regime's legitimacy was so damaged that many Poles were volunteering to fight on the side of the approaching Red Army.[139]

The Second World War was arguably lost for the Germans by the fall of 1941, though it took four more years of devastation before they surrendered. The German rulers' bravado, contradictory ideologies of rule, and uncompromising economic extraction in Zichenau, Bialystok, and Ukraine played no small part in sealing Germany's fate. Though the majority of the civilian rulers in Ukraine enjoyed playing out their colonial fantasies of master-race domination, some immediately recognized the contradictions at the heart of the occupation. Detailed reports sent to Koch in the first year of the occupation called for the Reichskommissariat to improve living standards and rations in order to maintain morale.[140] The Wehrmacht leadership, although it had ruthlessly murdered partisans and Jews at the beginning of the invasion, also called for better treatment. In January 1942, for example, Field Marshall Walter von Reichenau, the commander-in-chief of Army Group South, demanded land reform, food relief, and political autonomy for Ukrainians in order to prevent rebellion. Even Koch's superior, Rosenberg, repeatedly attempted to curb Koch's brutality, asking Hitler in 1943 to remove him from office, but Hitler supported Koch, in a striking parallel to the East Prussia governor crisis of 1935.[141]

At the nearby front, Koch's old opponent Schulenburg witnessed the ruthlessness of the German occupation of the Soviet Union, which confirmed for him the deep immorality at the heart of National Socialist rule. By 1942, Schulenburg became convinced that Germany's survival depended on Hitler's defeat. He began coordinating with the Kreisau Circle, the elite group of Nazi resisters who conspired to remove Hitler from office. Among them were several East Prussians, including Carl Friedrich Goerdeler, who had served for ten years as Königsberg's deputy mayor, and his brother Fritz, Königsberg's municipal chamberlain. Heinrich Count von Lehndorff-Steinort, an East Prussian Junker who served in the Army Group Centre during Barbarossa, first joined the military resistance after witnessing Jewish children being massacred outside of Minsk. Heinrich Count zu Dohna-Schlobitten, another East Prussian Junker, left the Wehrmacht, also on ethical grounds, in 1943. Most of these men had voted for Hitler in 1933 and remained loyal through the violence and exclusionary policies of the 1930s. It was only the conduct of the war that sealed their opposition.

In early 1944, Koch and his circle had abandoned the Reichskommissariat as Soviet partisans and the Red Army recaptured Ukraine. The Germans left behind a trail of destruction after only two and a half years of Nazi rule: nearly 4.1 million civilians dead, and nearly 700 cities and towns and 28,000 villages completely or partially destroyed.[142] By July 20, 1944, the borders of Königsberg's empire had contracted almost to the prewar borders of East Prussia. As the Red Army closed in on Białystok and Zichenau/Ciechanów, the conspirators, led by Colonel Claus von Stauffenberg, attempted to assassinate Hitler at his *Wolfsschanze* lair. Had the plan succeeded, Schulenburg would have become Germany's Minister for the Interior, and Dohna-Schlobitten would have replaced Koch as East Prussia's governor. The conspirators' bomb, however, left the Führer only lightly wounded. Later that day, Hitler denounced the conspirators over Königsberg radio and sentenced them to death.[143] But the triumph was short-lived. In October 1944, the Red Army first crossed the borders of East Prussia and remained for two weeks on German soil. Hitler's inner circle abandoned their lavish East Prussian estates. As the Red Army approached Göring's *Reichsjägerhof*, Hitler ordered that his hunting estate, filled with trophies stolen from Ukraine, be burned to the ground.[144] The following month, Hitler left the *Wolfsschanze*, never to return.

Königsberg's Nazis planned for East Prussia to become the center of an eastern economic nexus and a vanguard of National Socialism for the

Reich. They developed a local variant of National Socialism based on East Prussia's Prussian heritage, its rural economy, and its borderland geography, but their National Socialist revolution became emblematic of the contradictions and nepotism characterizing Nazi rule across Germany. By the late 1930s, Königsberg's socialist economic plans for rural agriculture had fused with Berlin's *Lebensraum* fantasies of the East, and its previously ecumenical understanding of the *Volksgemeinschaft* gave way to hard-line interpretations of Germanness influenced more strongly than before by biological racism. The fallout of the *Oberpräsident* Crisis, the nationwide escalation of racial policy following Nuremberg, and the looming threat of war led Koch and his followers to adhere more closely to policies set from above. But Koch's ability to demonstrate his loyalty to Hitler allowed him to maintain significant autonomy within East Prussia. It also allowed his loyal followers to become the most influential regional party in Germany and to export their rule across Eastern Europe. Königsberg's Nazis had asserted that East Prussia, as the easternmost territory of the Reich, had a special mission to serve as a bulwark of Germandom in the East. During the war, they carried out that mission with unparalleled brutality, and Koch became infamous in the Soviet Union as Hitler's henchman and the greatest tyrant of the Nazi occupations.

Koch's inner circle long tolerated his megalomania because they personally benefited from his rule. But as the empire began to collapse, some high-ranking Nazis in Königsberg began to criticize Koch's excesses. By mid-1944, Koch's old SS rivals accused him of ruling through gangster politics and wanted to see him publicly hanged. Even the Königsberg Higher SS and Police Leader George Ebrecht claimed that Koch had completely upended any concept of legality, both in his colonial domain and at home.[145] In an attempt to spare themselves, Königsberg's Nazis began obscuring their own participation in the murderous system they had sustained.

CHAPTER 3

Downfall

During the war, Königsberg's Nazis extended their influence over Eastern Europe and transformed Königsberg and East Prussia into the de facto capital of Germany's wartime empire. As the borders of the empire contracted toward East Prussia, Königsberg's Nazis brought these harsh methods of rule to their own population at home. With the enemy at the gates, East Prussia was the first region to mobilize the home front for total war and invasion, setting the precedent that the rest of eastern Germany would follow. As the German state called every East Prussian man, woman, and child into service for the war, it combined propaganda about the unity of the German national community with increasing threats against those who failed to rally in support. The *Volksgemeinschaft* had been an aspirational myth in the 1930s, but by the spring of 1945, Germans, while scrambling to save themselves and their families, found themselves bound together into a larger community of fate, fearing the Bolshevik retribution that awaited them.

The flight of East Prussians from the Red Army in the fall of 1944 and spring of 1945 was part of one of Europe's greatest demographic upheavals and one of the most massive population transfers in human history.[1] Almost 2,000,000 East Prussians fled their homes, and hundreds of thousands of these refugees, leaving in great haste and ill-prepared for their journey, found themselves tangled in the front-lines. Briefly in the fall of 1944, and then again in the winter of 1945, East Prussia became the first German soil the Red Army entered and the site of Soviet soldiers' most brutal retributive violence against German civilians at the end of the war. Tens of thousands of German civilians were tortured, raped, or murdered by Red Army soldiers seeking revenge. Others escaped the Red Army's advance only to die from hunger and disease on their trek or in crowded refugee camps in Germany. Historians and émigrés debate about the number of people who died in East Prussia during the flight and invasion, as the population swelled and contracted with soldiers, forced laborers, camp inmates, and refugees during the German invasions of Poland and the Soviet Union and the Wehrmacht's retreat back onto German soil. According to some estimates, of the 2,490,000 residents of East Prussia in March 1944, nearly 511,000 died as a consequence of the war, of them 311,000 civilians. They died from battle, flight, from deportation, internment, hunger, disease, and cold.[2]

Hundreds of personal narratives and documentary histories tell the story of East Prussia's downfall. In popular memory, the desperate escape from the Red Army was elevated to almost mythical status; the historian Ralph Giordano, for example, declared that East Prussia belongs "to one of the darkest chapters in the history of humanity in war—orgies of violence, and probably the greatest mass rape of all times."[3] The war stories of refugees and expellees written immediately after the war, as Robert G. Moeller writes, allowed West Germans to narrate the enormity of their losses while rejecting charges of "collective guilt" briefly leveled by the victors. Instead, Germans from the East could talk about the end of the Third Reich—the loss and destruction of their homelands, their mistreatment at the hands of the Red Army, and their experiences as forced laborers in the Soviet Union—without assuming responsibility for the war's origins.[4] East Prussians emerge in these narratives as double victims—of the party's fanatical continuation of the war and lack of concern for civilian life, and of animalistic Bolshevik aggression against innocent civilians who had little to do with the crimes of Hitler and East Prussia's party boss, Erich Koch.[5] Their stories remain untethered from the murderous years of German occupation in the East, isolated from the Holocaust, and separate from the parallel tragedy of the tens of thousands of people the regime deemed other who were caught in East Prussia and became the victims of German crimes.[6] German memoirists who suffered death and destruction and the loss of their homeland begin the story of East Prussia's downfall on the eve of the first Soviet invasion in 1944. But as the historian Andreas Kossert writes, "the flight, death, and expulsions began in 1933."[7]

The Home Front at War

Numerous memoirs written in the postwar period describe East Prussia as a relative island of tranquility until the summer of 1944, when the frontlines first neared the border. German expellees tend to present peacetime and early war East Prussia through well-worn *Heimat* motifs—idyllic scenes of simple rural life, pristine landscapes of forests and dunes and a land of a thousand lakes, storks' nests and roaming elk, and large but austere estates where common farm laborers and their Junker landlords lived in peaceful coexistence.[8] These memoirs, especially those written during the Cold War, tacitly deny the province's connection to the war in the East and assert their distance from the decisions made by a fanatical National Socialist party leadership.[9] Similarly, in the hundreds of nostalgic picture and lexicon books produced in West Germany, the Nazi period receives only scant coverage. The "who's who" book *Frag mich nach Ostpreußen (Ask Me about East Prussia)* from 1976, for example, reduces the entire entry on "National Socialism" to a terse biography of Gauleiter Koch that points out that he was not a native East Prussian and that his greed and corruption led him to escape the province in 1945, leaving the rest of the population in the lurch. Countless memoirs, popular histories, and newspapers of expellees' communities completely side-skirt discussions of difficult topics about daily life in the Third Reich. For the fiftieth anniversary of *Kristallnacht* in 1988, for example, the prominent expellees' newspaper, the *Ostpreußenblatt*, focused on the international events in Paris that the Nazis had used as an excuse for launching the pogrom, while mentioning virtually nothing about *Kristallnacht* in Königsberg or the role the city's inhabitants played as perpetrators and bystanders in the crimes against the Jewish population who lived there.[10]

Contrary to the depiction of these memoirs, Königsberg and the rest of the province were dramatically transformed by the war from the start. The eastern campaigns provided Königsberg and rural East Prussia, due to their geographic proximity to the front, both great economic opportunity and disproportionate burden. The economic transformation was nearly instantaneous, as most factories, including Königsberg's most prominent industries, the Schichau shipbuilding yards and the

Steinfurt train car factory, redirected their production for the war effort, and numerous military units established headquarters across the province. New recruits drilled in East Prussian barracks, a significant proportion of the wounded from the Eastern Front convalesced in East Prussian hospitals, and Königsberg's harbor, train stations, and airport became transit hubs for men and materials heading east.[11] A steady stream of mail and supplies traveled weekly between Königsberg and the Reichskommissariat Ukraine headquarters in Rivne (which Koch and East Prussia's Nazis had established at Königsberg Street 39, renaming the street in honor of their capital).[12] Smaller local ventures also profited: Königsberg's famous bookstore and publisher Gräfe und Unzer produced bulk orders of Nazi programmatic texts for civil servants in the occupation regimes,[13] and the Head of the Reichskommissariat Press Department, the native Königsberger Kurt Nestler, coordinated special publicity trips for East Prussian journalists to document the German domination in Ukraine.[14] Yet the war also came with burdens, as East Prussian men were drafted for the Wehrmacht at a rate of twice the national average, and already by 1940, SS intelligence reports noted that Königsberg was among the cities facing critical shortages of supplies, including coal.[15] Rations for food, clothing, and fuel grew stricter after 1941, and crime rates grew alongside.[16]

East Prussia continued to project the image of an impenetrable bulwark of Germandom, but the war made borders porous by design. As a result, East Prussia's inhabitants came in constant contact with foreign peoples, diseases, and ideas. Already from 1939, troops from Romania, Slovakia, Hungary, and Italy traveled alongside Germans through Königsberg to and from the front. Epidemic diseases traveled with them, creating ongoing health risks. German troops and officials in Ukraine were supposed to be vaccinated against cholera and typhus and undergo delousing before entering East Prussia, but the government was forced to issue periodic travel bans against soldiers vacationing in popular East Prussian destinations to curb outbreaks of epidemic and sexually transmitted disease.[17] With the arrival of almost 64,000 POWs and forced laborers between 1939 and 1941, most of them from Poland, authorities warned about the risks of Germans and foreigners intermixing, fearing that East Prussian civilians would not adequately self-police the boundaries of the *Volksgemeinschaft*.[18] They warned especially about the "dangers of employing Polish POW labor in minority regions," namely in Masuria, where the Nazis' escalating attempts to Germanize the population (including banning the use of the Masurian dialect in public) had faltered. Fears surrounding fraternization were highly gendered: by early 1940 a large number of East Prussian women were sentenced to long prison sentences for encounters with Polish POWs and forced laborers, and prosecutions and death sentences grew dramatically as the war progressed.[19] In Rastenburg, for example, German women were caught visiting the quarters of prisoners, and three women in the village of Labiau were caught having sex with Polish POWs.[20] As punishment, authorities cut off the women's hair and paraded them through town in shame. In Allenburg, the mayor forced young girls to adhere to a 6 p.m. curfew to prevent them from dancing with Poles.[21] After the invasion of the Soviet Union in 1941, even stricter regulations were enacted for Soviet forced laborers, designed to stop them from being mixed with German workers at all, ostensibly to prevent disease transmission but also to prevent Germans from softening their hatred for the enemy.[22]

Living standards for most East Prussians declined after 1941 as Königsberg's factories and farms redirected their production to the war effort, and East Prussians were disproportionately called up for the Wehrmacht because farm workers were not considered indispensable labor.[23] Still, many memoirists depict the first years of the war as the calm before the storm. Although many families worried about their sons and fathers at the front, cafes stayed in business, students continued their studies at the university, and the remaining farmers adhered to the seasonal rhythms of planting and harvest. But if German civilian life remained calm, it was because forced laborers and POWs bore the brunt of the hardship. The city's remaining Jewish population, registered in 1939 at 1,586 out of a total population of 372,200, were forced to work for the war effort and were issued significantly lower rations than Germans.[24] Michael Wieck, then the thirteen-year-old child of a Jewish mother and German father, recounts wartime life in Königsberg through the increasing exclusion he faced and the indifference of his German neighbors. Once Jews were ordered to wear the Star of David in September 1941, Wieck recalls, it was no longer possible to "forget, even momentarily, that you did not belong."[25] The following month, all "German-blooded persons" were prohibited from engaging in a friendly manner with Jews, with the threat of three months punishment in a concentration camp for offenders.[26] Jews were physically assaulted and forced not to use the sidewalks alongside Germans—the visible marker of difference became, as Wieck recalls, "enough to trigger a hateful reaction, even when the person wearing the star looked no different from one's own child or parent."[27] An increasing number of Jews committed suicide after being forced to wear the Star of David, including a number of Wieck's family acquaintances. The former editor of the liberal *Hartung'sche Zeitung* newspaper, Ludwig Goldstein, wrote in his diary about his complete social and intellectual isolation, no longer having contact with former friends and being denied access to libraries, bathhouses, cafes, and bars. "One wants so badly to go 'somewhere,'" wrote Goldstein, "But where?"[28]

Königsberg began small-scale deportations of Jews in the fall of 1941, and by the summer of 1942, the city's Jewish population declined to 1,183.[29] Wieck and his mother were spared deportation because she was married to a German, and he was a half-Jewish *Mischling*. But Wieck was forced to leave school and was tasked with transporting elderly Jews to Gestapo collection points.[30] He recalls that Jews were paraded through the city as their "former fellow citizens, patients, customers, friends, or neighbors stood there doing nothing, watching or looking away. Some of them certainly with bitterness and the knowledge of the terrible injustice and their own impotence. But most of them profited without hesitation when given the opportunity to collect the goods left behind."[31] At least 1,000 of Königsberg's Jews were deported to concentration camps, including Theresienstadt, Auschwitz, and Maly Trostenets outside Minsk. Those sent to Minsk died immediately, shot and buried in mass graves. Others starved in the camps before being shot or gassed. Only a handful survived the war.[32] Forty-five Jewish families remained after the last mass transports in 1943, all of them with one German spouse and *Mischling* children. The remaining Jewish men, women, and teenagers were compelled to work in factories for ten hours a day, including Wieck, who worked at first in a furniture factory and then alongside his mother at a chemical factory. By 1943, rations for Jewish workers decreased nearly to starvation level, placing great stress on the Aryan parent to provide for the rest of the family.[33]

Wartime living conditions were also dire for forced laborers and prisoners of war. Soviet forced laborers (the so-called *Ostarbeiter*) received even worse treatment than Poles—the lowest rations, poorest accommodations, the harshest prohibitions on mobility, and near constant ridicule by German masters who treated them like slaves.[34] Soviet POWs became one of the largest groups of victims of Nazi violence, approaching the scale of the Nazi genocide of European Jews. The German Wehrmacht ignored the 1929 Geneva Convention on Prisoners of War, and instead intentionally starved them, deprived them of adequate accommodation, and treated them brutally. Intentional murder by the army or SS resulted in the deaths of between 2.6 million and 3.3 million Red Army soldiers and a total of 5.3 million to 5.7 million Soviet POWs in German captivity.[35] The racial and ideological dimension of Nazi starvation policy becomes more striking if one takes into account that more than 50 percent of Soviet POWs died, compared to 4 percent of Western POWs.[36] In East Prussia, Soviet POWs were isolated from German civilians and supervised by German soldiers at gunpoint.[37] In order not to reduce German civilians' rations in 1941, Soviet POWs were at first fed only root vegetables normally fed to cattle, and as the war progressed, camp guards systematically starved Soviet POWs to reduce their numbers.[38] By the fall of 1944, the Nazis began transferring Soviet POWs to extermination camps, but with as many as 10 to 15 percent of them collapsing or dying en route, authorities warned to leave the terminally ill in the labor camps to prevent German civilians from finding dying prisoners on the roads.[39]

In February 1943, after the Wehrmacht's catastrophic defeat at Stalingrad, Reichsminister for Propaganda Goebbels made the infamous speech declaring Germany's transition to total war. Arguing that the fate of Germany and all of non-Bolshevik Europe would be determined by the course of the war on the Eastern Front, Goebbels ordered the restructuring of the entire German economy, stricter rations and management of resources, and the broad mobilization of the civilian workforce to produce materiel for the war.[40] Public spaces were increasingly commandeered for military use—Königsberg's churches, for example, were transformed into nursery schools so that women, previously encouraged to remain housewives, could work producing munitions.[41] But in comparison to the city's remaining Jewish population and forced laborers, who had been experiencing the forced sacrifice of total war for years, German civilians continued to live significantly better, even as they faced tighter rations, the elimination of nonessential programs, and the redirection of the economy to the war effort.

By the middle of 1943, as the Wehrmacht suffered continuing defeats, police and SS reports noted that the mood among the population was growing cynical. One Königsberg barber, for example, was arrested after reportedly declaring that the people had "lost faith" in the party and that "German victory is impossible." Another of his customers had declared that the Germans would never recover from Stalingrad, and a third insisted that the German people were being "dumbed down" by increasingly falsified news reports from the front.[42] By mid-July 1944, Königsberg's occupation regime had abandoned Ukraine and the city of Białystok as the Red Army captured territories less than 60 kilometers from the East Prussian border. Mood reports noted that a "deep anxiety over the fate of East Prussia had taken hold of the population of the entire province."[43] Evacuees from Berlin, sent to East Prussia to escape Allied aerial raids, complained that they had jumped "from the frying pan into the fire" and that it would be "better to be buried by a bomb than fall into the hands of the Russians."[44]

It was in the summer of 1944 that Germans in the eastern territories of the Reich first got a sense of what complete mobilization would entail. Hitler had long denied that the war would reach German soil, but as public morale plummeted and the invasion became imminent, he announced that "the entire German *Volk*" would be summoned to defend the endangered borders of the Reich.[45] Hitler asserted that the party would take the leading role in maintaining civilian morale but should work in close cooperation with military authorities to organize the defense. But Gauleiter Koch, in his capacity as Reich defense commissar for East Prussia, commandeered the defense preparations, distrustful of the Wehrmacht and accusing its generals of "defeatism" after the army's retreat through Ukraine.[46] Co-opting a Wehrmacht plan, Koch ordered the construction of a massive *Ostwall* (Eastern Wall), an East Prussian bulwark stretching from the Baltic Sea to Warsaw. All able-bodied men in the province between ages fifteen and fifty-five were drafted to dig trenches and build rudimentary fortifications. Civil servants, shopkeepers, workers, managers, farmers, professors and students, refugees from the East, and brigades of Hitler Youth—all were ordered to report to the borders with provisions to last a few days. Lack of planning led to acute shortages and poor accommodations. Men were often forced to do heavy work by hand, sometimes even to dig without shovels. Police units, including ethnic Balts and Organization Todt units, reportedly assisted in rounding up stragglers and imposed draconian punishments on dissenters. Koch likewise issued strict travel restrictions to prevent civilians from fleeing their homes in the border regions.[47] Although the *Ostwall* brought Germans the first taste of total war, they were only mobilized for the short term and were first in line to receive scarce provisions. Forced laborers, by contrast, were mobilized for months, poorly housed, and barely fed. Tens of thousands of Jewish prisoners from satellite camps of the nearby Stutthof concentration camp were deployed to build fortifications at starvation rations, and some of the Polish workforce in the parts of Bezirk Bialystok and Zichenau still under German control were even beaten to death after collapsing from infectious bloody diarrhea.[48] Jurgis Mališaukas, then a teenage refugee from Lithuania temporarily housed in Königsberg, recalls being separated from his family in October 1944 and sent to work on the southern border. He slept in barns alongside cattle and performed hard labor for three months before being released as an invalid to find his family, who had long since evacuated further westward.[49]

The *Ostwall* was later ridiculed as Koch's hair-brained scheme; the Königsberg émigré historian Theodor Schieder, for example, derided it as "one of the most desperate and . . . useless efforts made during the last months of the war."[50] Newly dug trenches flooded because of lack of irrigation, positions lay exposed to attack, and numerous fortifications remained unoccupied because their locations were never mapped. Moreover, the mobilization of all able-bodied males damaged the East Prussian harvest, leaving the region facing food shortages for the winter, and it curtailed critical armaments manufacture. Already by the middle of August, the Red Army brushed aside fortifications in Lithuania and, unbeknownst to the public, even briefly penetrated

FIGURE 4. East Prussian civilians dig trenches to construct *Ostwall* border fortifications in East Prussia in the summer of 1944. Collection: AKG-Images.

the border before being quickly repulsed.[51] Although it failed to create an impenetrable barrier, the *Ostwall* and resulting *levée en masse* were profoundly consequential. The project set the terms for the party's continuing involvement in organizing the Reich's defense. It boosted morale in the short term by engaging worried East Prussians around the common goal. Echoing Koch's mass employment campaigns from a decade before, the party's *Preußische Zeitung* boasted that East Prussia had once again become a vanguard for the entire nation. Perhaps most important, it provided a powerful means for social control—unifying the *Volksgemeinschaft*, through both positive and coercive means, to a degree that had never before been possible.[52] Other eastern German regional party leaders soon consciously adopted the same tactics to mobilize their own populations, and in 1944–45, half a million German civilians and forced laborers were mobilized across Germany, 200,000 of them in East Prussia alone.[53]

Königsberg's inhabitants had long envisioned the city as a bulwark against foreign incursion. For most of the war, that role had remained untested—Königsberg was spared from the major aerial raids plaguing industrial cities further west. But on the nights of August 26–27 and 29–30, 1944, British bombers raided Königsberg, engulfing it in flames.[54] In those two days, over 50 percent of the city was destroyed, and over 90 percent of the city center. The Kneiphof Island, Königsberg's heart at the center of the Pregel River, with its narrow medieval streets and solemn cathedral, was almost completely razed. The nearby castle and university were also decimated, along with most of the city's treasured nineteenth-century architecture, including the opera house, state library, and stock exchange. At least 2,400 people were killed, and 130,000 to 150,000 lost their homes—almost half of Königsberg's inhabitants at that time.[55] Victims whose clothes caught fire during the raids jumped into the river to put out the flames, but as soon as they emerged from the water, the phosphorus burned them alive. Others suffocated in cellars, and their bodies shriveled from the intense heat.[56] The famous bridges of Königsberg connecting the island to the city collapsed into the Pregel River, leaving only two remaining. The city that had once imagined itself as both bulwark or as bridge found itself no longer able to serve as either.

Over the next several months, the demands on the region's inhabitants grew ever greater. Those Jews and Soviet forced laborers who survived were made to work long hours to rebuild factories, even as their rations were further reduced.[57] The party organized the recovery efforts, distributing food and supplies to the destitute and homeless, while warning that plunderers would be sentenced to death.[58] While many shops and factories reopened by the fall, city life never completely recovered. As Königsberg's émigré scribe Fritz Gause wrote two decades later, "Königsberg as a living organism was paralyzed after the two August raids. What followed was a fight to the death without hope of a favorable outcome."[59] Königsberg, once a central actor in the war, had become a victim of it.

On October 16, 1944, the Red Army brushed aside Koch's fortifications and crossed for the first time onto German soil. Over the course of two weeks, Soviet forces cut 50 kilometers deep into the province, capturing towns just 120 kilometers from Königsberg before being pushed back beyond the border.[60] Two days after the start of the invasion, Koch and Himmler stood side by side in Königsberg to announce the first mobilization of the *Volkssturm*, a nationwide network of people's militias under party control.[61] Koch promised Hitler that every man, woman, and child would defend East Prussia "with their bare hands."[62] All able-bodied men between sixteen and sixty were called to defend the province (although by that time, most men of fighting age had already been drafted). The *Volkssturm* was designed to assist the military in bringing about victory; it was also a means to further mobilize Germans through propaganda and indoctrination. Ideologically committed party members would lead the brigades, fanaticizing the civilian population to prolong the struggle on German soil. *Volkssturm* members were issued uniforms and a weapon and sent soon after to the front. A great number of them, barely trained and ill-supplied, were taken prisoner or killed in battle soon thereafter.[63]

For the remainder of 1944, East Prussians continued their lives without further attack. But the initial mobilizations intertwined the lives of German civilians more tightly with the demands of party and state than ever before. The more Germans became involved in the mechanism of war, the more many of them, at the time and in later memory, distanced their identities from the goals of the regime and constructed a different, less culpatory narrative about themselves and their homeland.

Humanity against Barbarism

The brief Soviet incursion led to fear among a growing segment of the population that defeat was inevitable. In response, the Nazis increasingly relied on anti-Bolshevik propaganda to motivate Germans to continue to fight. The Nazis had defined themselves in opposition to Marxism and communism long before 1933, but discourse on Soviet 'Judeo-Bolshevism' only emerged as part of a concerted campaign effort in September 1935. Nazi propaganda at that time introduced the idea that it was Germany's "universal mission" to save Europe from Bolshevism. The anti-Soviet campaign was part of radicalization of Nazi rule at home designed to rally support for the government by presenting global conspiracies against the German nation. It also served to discredit the Soviet alternative to Nazism and to legitimate exclusionary antisemitic legislation.[64] Publications in the latter half of the decade focused on dismal conditions in the Soviet Union to show the divide between Bolshevik promises of prosperity and the gray reality of Soviet life. In cases when the evidence did not fit the propaganda aims, they simply fabricated stories to prove the USSR was a Judeo-Bolshevik conspiracy to bring about the "tremendous oppression and impoverishment of the entire population."[65] After the invasion of the Soviet Union in 1941, the Nazis drew on this same imagery, while also asserting German racial, cultural, and (especially) technical superiority over the Bolsheviks, whom they cast as barbaric, backward, racially and culturally inferior.[66]

But as SS mood reports noted in the summer of 1942, many East Prussians struggled to reconcile propaganda depictions of the Soviet Union with their own experience. German soldiers were often surprised to find massive, modern industrial centers amid the otherwise underdeveloped conditions of Russia, and some of them reportedly began wondering whether the Soviet system had benefits to offer after all. Propaganda had presented the Soviet people, especially the enemy soldiers, as "animalistic" and "brutal"; Germans had originally responded so strongly to this depiction that they feared Soviet POWs and laborers being sent to work in the Reich. But mood reports in Königsberg and across the province noted that after encountering individual *Ostarbeiter*, many Germans were reportedly surprised to find "that these Russians were often intelligent, decent, and quick to understand how to operate complicated machinery," and that they picked up the German language fairly quickly. And while the Soviets were supposedly "racially inferior" Mongol and Turkic peoples, German soldiers were surprised to learn that "even these Mongols and Turks were good soldiers, often cleaner and more intelligent than others, and not completely falling for Bolshevism." Moreover, especially in Ukraine, soldiers were shocked to find that many peasants were "tall, blonde, and blue-eyed," leading some to question the terms for German racial superiority.[67]

After the Soviet victory at Stalingrad in early 1943, the Nazi propaganda dropped much of its former German technological chauvinism and instead presented the Bolshevik enemy as both barbaric and technologically capable. As the Soviets drew nearer and victory became more chimeric, they cast the battle as a struggle for the German spirit against the cruel inhumanity of the enemy.[68] To mark the University of Königsberg's 400th anniversary in July 1944, just weeks before the construction of the *Ostwall*, party ideologues from Berlin transformed a modest vigil planned at the philosopher Immanuel Kant's mausoleum into an elaborate three-day event, complete with keynote speakers, ceremonial processions, symphonic fanfares, and the bestowal of honorary awards. This event became a platform for this new depiction of the war as a struggle between German and European civilization, on the one hand, and barbarism, on the other. As the Reich Minister for Science, Education, and National Culture, Dr. Bernhard Rust, declared with no small sense of foreboding, "on the Eastern Front, it is not just two armies, two nations, and two states that are pitted against one another, but two worlds. It is therefore not just a battle of soldiers and people but of two spiritual worlds and therefore all spiritual strengths must be called up as never before, to be willing and ready to take up the battle of the worthy against the unworthy, the spiritual against the spiritless, the human against the inhuman and finally end this battle on the fields of spiritual conflict."[69] Other professors, including Koch's chief economist and imperial planner, Hans-Bernhard von Grünberg, who by 1944 was serving as the university's rector, and the prominent historian and proponent of ethnic cleansing, Theodor Schieder, spoke of Königsberg's historic identity as a city where humanist scholarship and military duty had long been intertwined. Another professor drew connections between Kant's concept of duty and the obligation of every German to defend the Reich. And as the enemy was swiftly approaching, Reich Minister Rust reminded his audience why such sacrifice was necessary, and why capitulation would not spare the German people from horror. In this final, decisive phase of the war, Germany was forced "not only to fight for our Reich, for freedom, and for life," but also for "our inner world," to protect it from the "deadly threat of Bolshevism," a pernicious ideology on the path to "subjugate the world itself." Disguising itself under the veil of progress by making clever promises about civil society and religious tolerance, Bolshevism had wooed European society with lies. But whereas the Soviets had made the dogma of Marxism their only basis for truth, Rust proclaimed that German civilization (and particularly Königsberg's university, that "400-year-old site of scholarship") had based its culture on not one reductive truth, but on the values of "God, Nation, and Individuality [*Persönlichkeit*]."[70] By reinserting God and individuality into the formulation of German culture, Rust and Königsberg's professors shifted away from the Nazis' previous elevation of the nation (at the expense of the individual) to emphasize the common bond between German culture and Western European civilization as a whole. In this formulation, Königsberg emerged once again as the epitome of German civilization and Europe's greatest bulwark against Bolshevism.

But with the Red Army's brief invasion in October 1944, Nazi propaganda shifted to a more visceral horror against which to rally Germans to fight—a preview of what Bolshevik rule might bring. The invasion became immortalized in wartime propaganda through the story of Nemmersdorf, a border village briefly captured by the Red Army on October 20, 1944. When the Germans reentered days later, they found the gruesome traces of a massacre. The NSDAP party organ, the *Völkischer Beobachter*, was the first to report the story on October 27.

> In a plundered apartment a woman sat on the sofa, with a blanket still covering her legs. She was clearly surprised by the murdering bandits in this position and was killed with a shot to the head. In the bedroom of another house one found a nineteen-year-old girl lying on the floor with her head leaned against the wall. The girl had been raped and then killed by a gunshot wound in the mouth. In the corner of the same room an old woman lay with her skull split open, murdered by a rifle shot at close range. By the table, the husband of the woman lay on the floor.

The report described dozens of women, children, and men murdered, all shot individually at close range, most of the women sexually violated. "After two days of bloody Bolshevik rule," the *Völkischer Beobachter* concluded, "Nemmersdorf has become a village of death, a village of silence."[71]

In hundreds of news stories and film reels released for weeks after the discovery, Goebbels used the incident to paint the Red Army soldiers as barbarian hordes seeking to destroy German and European civilization.[72] The publicized eyewitness reports of numerous Wehrmacht and *Volkssturm* soldiers, doctors from an international medical commission, and local officials coalesced around common themes: that "Nemmersdorf" stood for atrocity, outside the conventions of modern warfare;

FIGURE 5. German military personnel examine the corpses of women and children in the East Prussian village of Nemmersdorf after the Red Army's brief invasion in October 1945. Collection: AKG-Images.

that the massacre had not been the result of individual excesses but had been encouraged by the Red Army command; and that the violence had been directed against innocent civilians, particularly women. The newspapers focused especially on "crimes [that] belong to the darkest chapters of sexual pathology," as a reminder to fathers, brothers, and sons to fight to the death to keep the enemy off German soil.[73] Any Germans who failed to heed the warnings—"those criminally blind fools" who after years of war still underestimated the threat that communism posed not only to the German nation but to all of European civilization—"had only to look to Nemmersdorf in East Prussia" to see the true face of Bolshevism.[74]

This prelude to Bolshevism left a lasting mark on the German psyche, both in East Prussia and across the Reich.[75] Most East Prussians living near the border began fleeing, forcing Koch's administration to permit evacuations within thirty kilometers of the front.[76] Others were dubious, rejecting the accounts as typical Nazi propaganda. The East Prussian aristocrat and later West German journalist Marion Countess von Dönhoff was among them; as a dissenter who had been indirectly involved in the July 1944 plot against Hitler, she and her social circle "automatically assumed that everything the government printed or broadcast was a lie" and that the graphic photos had been faked.[77] Indeed, contemporary reports and early postwar testimonies reveal numerous contradictions. Newspaper reports first claimed twenty-six civilians had died but later increased the figure to sixty-one; after the war, a *Volkssturm* eyewitness, Karl Potrek, claimed to have counted seventy-two. While the news first reported that some of the women "show signs of rape," postwar testimonies asserted that every woman in the village, from children to the elderly, had been sexually abused. News reports counted multiple men among the dead, but the *Volkssturm* eyewitness Potrek insisted there had been only a single man, perhaps to underscore the violence against helpless German women. Although most of the reports insisted that not a single Soviet soldier had died in Nemmersdorf, one farmer recalled seeing the "Asiatic facial traits" of fallen Soviet soldiers on the streets.[78]

Yet the Red Army's later violence against German civilians in the spring of 1945 seemed to confirm the propaganda portrayal of Nemmersdorf. As Dönhoff writes in her memoir, she later learned that "women had indeed been stripped naked and nailed to barn doors, and twelve-year-old girls had indeed been raped; sixty-two women and children had been found murdered in their homes, and the pictures of dead women with torn clothes lying in the streets and on compost heaps were not faked."[79] Decades later, however, the evidence reveals that the scale of the massacre at Nemmersdorf had been inflated by Nazi propagandists. Witnesses later admitted that photographs had been manipulated (bodies rearranged, skirts lifted to give the impression of sexual transgression) and that some of the photos had been taken elsewhere. Although the press reported no survivors, one woman did survive, later testifying that although the Red Army soldiers did shoot everyone they found—she, too, had been shot in the head but had survived—they had not committed the sexual violence that the press and later witnesses had attributed to them. The historian Bernhard Fisch, at the time a young East Prussian *Volkssturm* member who entered Nemmersdorf immediately following the invasion, encountered no evidence of the civilian atrocity, but he concludes after piecing together the evidence that Soviet soldiers had murdered civilians in Nemmersdorf. He estimates that around two dozen civilians died, about a third of the number established by the West German government. The true scale of the violence will remain unknown.[80]

Regardless of whether the propaganda claims were inflated, the images of Nemmersdorf succeeded in fostering solidarity against the enemy. Newspapers assured the German public that what had happened in Nemmersdorf was in no way justified revenge for what Germans had done during the war in the Soviet Union. But as news of the atrocity spread, Königsbergers, and Germans at large, could not help but develop the pervasive fear that a nation that had committed unspeakable crimes could now expect the worst kind of retaliation.[81] As Michael Geyer argues, "individuals and groups felt that they were in the same boat and knew with remarkable precision who was not. They were never more German, more part of a community of fate, than in the mushrooming fantasies of the enemy's revenge which propaganda enhanced so cunningly."[82] Nemmersdorf offered Germans a vision of a future Soviet occupation, and these visions informed the way that Germans, and East Prussians especially, would later narrate their actual experiences under Soviet rule.

Flight into Death

Civilian and military memoirists and nationalist German historians in the twentieth century most often present the story of East Prussia's downfall in the mode of tragedy: the destruction of Germany, the loss of the German East, and the hardship facing Germans who lost their lives or homes in the violence of the Soviet invasion. Stories of German civilians' flight from the Red Army, in particular, have assumed the quality of myth. They are intertwined with accounts of the Wehrmacht's desperate resistance in the spring of 1945, with the argument that the continued fight was necessary to postpone the Red Army's violent orgy of revenge.[83] But these stories ignore the fact that the prolongation of the war also abetted the Nazis' work of massacring the Jews and other prisoners in Nazi camps.[84] The two national catastrophes of the spring of 1945—the flight and death of German civilians from the Red Army's revenge and the German extermination of the Jews—are inseparable. East Prussia's downfall was a tragedy both for German civilians fleeing their homes and meeting their fates at the hands of the Red Army, and for those civilians, Jewish prisoners, forced laborers, and POWs who found themselves caught in the German machinery of war.

The Christmas of 1944 assumes almost a mystical quality in postwar German memoirs, remembered for some as a final moment of the naïveté of youth and for others as the last moment of willful oblivion before the end. Felicitas Lieberoth-Leden, the daughter of an estate manager at Falkenau, remembered that the mood during the holidays was joyous and festive, with a rich spread of food for the table despite the shortages. No one, she claims, thought that the end was near, "that we were spending our last Christmas here, that we would have to leave behind our homeland."[85] Hans Count von Lehndorff, a local aristocrat and medical doctor, wrote in his diary less sympathetically how East Prussians celebrated Christmas "almost as in peacetime," complete with hunting parties.[86] Käthe Hielscher, a girl at the time, recalls how on New Year's Eve, the voices of Hitler and Goebbels addressed the nation: "It is five minutes before twelve—Germans! Believe in victory!" Hielscher and her family had already left their homes in the eastern part of the province to live with extended family in Königsberg. Upon hearing the words of Goebbels, Hieschler's mother was cynical, but her aunt still believed.[87]

Just two weeks later, on January 13, 1945, the Soviets began their invasion of Germany, the greatest offensive in military history. It was also one of the most violent wartime engagements for soldiers on both sides and civilians, as an estimated one million people died violent deaths in the first month of 1945 alone.[88] The German Army Group Center was vastly outnumbered with half a million German soldiers against the 1.6 million men and 3,800 tanks of armored vehicles of the Red Army's Second and Third Belorussian Fronts.[89] The Soviets intended to isolate East Prussia by cutting through the German Second Army to reach the Baltic Sea—in essence recreating the interwar Polish Corridor.[90] In preparation for the attack, Koch had spent months constructing fortifications of his own design, including such dilettante inventions, as they were later derided, as "frying pans" (Koch-Töpfe, a pun on Koch's name): a system of half-submerged concrete turrets for German machine gunners. But like the Ostwall, the fortifications proved no match for the Soviet tanks, which simply rolled over them, crushing the soldiers inside. By January 20, only a week into the offensive, the Red Army had stormed halfway across East Prussia.[91]

Although Koch had allowed some strategic evacuations in the fall of 1944, reducing East Prussia's population from an estimated 2.4 million in March 1944 to about 1.75 million at the end of the year, he continued to prevent mass evacuations until after the winter invasion began.[92] Germans in the 1939-annexed Zichenau district, for example, were only given permission to leave on January 15, 1945, two days after the Soviets had crossed the nearby border. Refugees fled from the southern and southeastern parts of the province toward Königsberg and other ports on the Baltic Sea.[93] By January 20, the roads were completely jammed with fleeing Wehrmacht columns and refugees—the road to the town of Thorn was backed up with wagons for over twenty kilometers.[94] The villagers from Marion Countess von Dönhoff's estate, Dönhoff recalls, were en route for a few days, poorly prepared for the weather and already running out of food, when they began to consider their options. "If we're to end up in Russian hands," explained one of the estate employees, Mr. Klatt, "then let it be at home." They all agreed that the Russians would surely execute Dönhoff as the aristocratic owner of an estate, whereas they themselves would "simply go on milking cows and threshing grain, [but] for the Russians." Rationalizing their desperation, many refugees interpreted Nazi propaganda's depiction of Bolshevism as the vulgar elevation of class over race as a cause for hope that simple workers and peasants would be spared the wrath of Soviet vengeance.[95] As Dönhoff later lamented, "neither they nor I had any inkling how mistaken we were to think that nothing would happen to the workers."[96] One of Dönhoff's secretaries, Miss Markowski, "a passionate believer in the Führer who had greeted every victory bulletin with undisguised joy," managed to reach Danzig to secure passage on a refugee ship.[97] She joined tens of thousands of other refugees who boarded the *Wilhelm Gustloff*, a cruise ship converted for mass civilian transport.[98] The ship departed on January 30, but less than a day later, it was torpedoed by a Soviet S-13 submarine and sank into the Baltic Sea. Of the estimated 9,000 people on the ship, only nine survived. Half of those who died were children.[99] The sinking of the *Gustloff* stands as one of the largest maritime disasters in world history (1,513 died in the sinking of the *Titanic*).[100] The disaster drew international media attention and was offered as more evidence of the Soviet disregard for human life, even though later it turned out that the *Gustloff* had also been armed, and among the passengers there were thousands of German soldiers.[101] The *Gustloff* disaster nonetheless became inscribed in the German postwar memory as one of the greatest civilian tragedies of the war.

Within two weeks, the Red Army reached the outskirts of Königsberg. Until the eleventh hour, the party prohibited evacuation, but on January 27, they commanded that the population leave immediately. The city's administrators and elite party members managed to organize safe passage on a few boats available in the harbor, but over 100,000 Königsbergers and refugees scrambled to escape by train, boat, and foot. One refugee waiting at Königsberg's main train station reportedly told Lehndorff that she did not know where she was going, but added, to his surprise, that "our Führer will never permit the Russians to get us; he'd rather gas us first."[102] Koch himself had packed up his possessions and evacuated days earlier to join the military command at the front further to the west.[103]

One refugee described the scene at the westernmost port of Pillau at the end of January, when 28,000 people arrived from Königsberg to board one of the few civilian transport ships. Throngs of people pushed toward the ships, and "human beings became animals" in the crowd.

> Women threw their children into the water just in order to keep up or in order that they not be crushed to death in the crowd. The general confusion was now made even greater when completely disorganized military units streamed into the city and into houses, looted, intermingled with the refugees and also pushed to get themselves onto the ships. In order to get through the cordons to the harbour, soldiers took children from their mothers and claimed they wanted to bring their families on board! Others put on women's clothing and thus attempted to get away on the ships.[104]

The majority of the city's inhabitants, unable to escape by train or boat, got caught in the frontlines while fleeing by wagon or on foot. Annaliese Kreutz and her family, who lived ten kilometers south of Königsberg, were among those who failed to escape. She and other refugees caught on the road could hear the "grumbling of the front" behind them; "automobiles, people, and horses stretched out westward in an unbroken column like a black snake in the white snow."[105] Trapped, they turned back to Königsberg, not knowing that another road to the West was still open. By the time they discovered it, that road too was cut off, and there were no means to escape.[106] By the end of 1944, just before the spring evacuations, East Prussia's population had already declined to about 1.75 million. From the start of the mass evacuations until the end of fighting on the Samland Peninsula in late April 1945, an estimated 451,000 inhabitants managed to escape by ship, and another 180,000 to 200,000 on land or frozen ice over the narrow Vistula Spit. The remaining inhabitants, as many as half a million people, were overwhelmed by the invading army.[107]

The German tragedy was intimately bound to the fate of the Jewish population in the last months of the war, as the Nazis escalated the Final Solution on the heels of the Red Army's advance. In the spring of

1944, the Stutthof concentration camp, located on the Baltic seacoast just east of Danzig, had established satellite camps throughout East Prussia to house surviving Jewish forced laborers evacuated from ghettos in Kaunas, Riga, and other Baltic cities. In the chaos of the invasion, the camps were evacuated and 13,000 Jewish prisoners, the majority of them women, were marched to Königsberg, where they were slated to work in a camp set up at the Steinfurt train car factory.[108] But as the Red Army closed in on the city, the SS shot as many as 3,000 of the prisoners and piled their corpses in the street.[109] On January 26, they marched another 5,000 to 10,000 to the Baltic Sea coast.[110] Up to 2,000 of the prisoners died on the fifty-kilometer march, many of them from weakness and starvation. Others were beaten or shot by SS guards for moving too slowly or trying to escape.

German civilians who witnessed the march could no longer deny the long-standing rumors of German atrocities in the East. In the first decades after the war, memoirists recounting their wartime experiences tended to separate their suffering from the state's machinery of death. Indeed, neither eyewitnesses nor the editors of the high-profile multivolume testimony collection appearing first in 1953, *Die Vertreibung der deutschen Bevölkerung aus den Gebieten östlich der Oder-Neisse* (published in English as *The Expulsion of the German Population from the Regions East of the Oder-Neisse*), commented on German exploitation of non-German nationalities as forced laborers.[111] Memoirists writing in more recent decades, many of whom had been children or young adults in 1945, more frequently grapple with their experiences as witnesses, however. Many of them had been young boys drafted into the *Volkssturm*. Then fourteen-year-old Hans-Dieter Willuweit later remembers his horror upon witnessing the column of "gray-brown clothed" people marching without shoes, with their feet bound in rags.[112] The air force helper Gert Herberg recalls the shock of seeing his commanding officer follow the path of the prisoners to shoot stragglers lying on the road. Then ten-year-old Klaus Lemke remembers seeing traces of the march in his village of Kumehnen; the morning after the prisoners passed through, the SS forced Polish and Russian POWs to "pile up the stiff, frozen bodies on the edge of the village," creating a "mountain of corpses" while the women who had been shot "struggled around and begged for mercy."[113]

German eyewitnesses also became perpetrators as they were swept up by the rapidly escalating violence of the war. On January 27, 1945, the same day the Red Army liberated Auschwitz, the SS marched the

3,000 surviving Jewish prisoners into Palmnicken.[114] The seaside town was the center of amber manufacturing in East Prussia, and at the suggestion of Gerhard Rasch, the director of State Amber Manufacturing in Königsberg, an unused amber mining pit was designated as a mass grave. A few of the mine's local administrators, however, resisted taking part in the murder, insisting that German morality defined itself in opposition to what they saw as Bolshevik-style atrocities. According to one postwar war crimes testimony, the amber factory manager and local *Volkssturm* commander Hans Feyerabend declared to the SS squad leader Fritz Weber that he could not allow any more Jews to be killed, because he could not "allow this to become another Katyn!"[115] The SS leader Weber explained that the front lines were rapidly approaching, calling for desperate measures, and that he had been given his orders and had to fulfill them. According to a witness testifying after the war, Weber seemed shaken by Feyerabend's condemnation and admitted that he had not been told originally that the prisoners were to be executed.[116] The factory manager Feyerabend attempted to feed the prisoners potatoes from the *Volkssturm* reserves and recruited nearby village women to prepare soup. But once the news reached SS authorities in Königsberg, Feyerabend was punished for attempting to protect the Jews. He and one hundred of his *Volkssturm* men were ordered to depart for the most dangerous part of the front, an assignment tantamount to a death sentence. Soon thereafter, Feyerabend's *Volkssturm* members found him dead with his own gun in his mouth. No investigation was conducted to determine whether it had been murder or suicide.[117] The official cause of death was listed as "fallen in battle with the enemy."[118]

At the amber pit, SS guards assembled Hitler Youth and young *Volkssturm* members to supervise the prisoners, and these younger witnesses also became perpetrators, sometimes reluctantly, sometimes eagerly. Martin Bergau, the teenager who had witnessed the march of the prisoners days before, recalls how an SS leader named Friedrichs handed him and his classmates some schnapps and led them to the pit. "Now I understood for the first time," writes Bergau, that "I had found myself in an execution squad."[119] Bergau was told to stand guard at the end of the long columns of prisoners. One woman asked Bergau in good German if she could move forward a few places in line and offered him a piece of jewelry she had preserved on the journey as payment. "I would like to be shot together with my daughter," she explained. Bergau refused her gift but allowed her to go. As she stepped out of line, one of Bergau's fellow classmates, Lothar, beat her with the butt of his rifle.

"You dirty punk," Bergau growled, "I gave the woman permission!" Bergau helped her up and escorted her to her daughter. Bergau claims to have shot no one that day, but a few of his classmates joined in the massacre, including a boy named Alfred, who shot the surviving stragglers. "Was it showing mercy," he asked, "or an inflamed lust to kill? . . . We had been forced into becoming accomplices of mass murder."[120]

Running out of time and ammunition, the SS squad marched the surviving prisoners to the sea coast on January 31. They forced them to wade into the freezing water and shot anyone who tried to swim back to shore. Celina Malinewicz, who was then twenty-three years old, was stationed toward the end of the kilometers-long column of prisoners being forced into the sea.[121] As she later testified, they were so starved, weak, and demoralized that "death seemed to us to be a merciful deliverance, but still we did not have the courage to collapse on the path because a glimmer of hope still slept within us that at the last moment, as if by miracle, we would come away with our lives."[122] When they reached the water, Malinewicz and her friends tried to back up. The commanding SS officer yelled at them, "Why do you not want to go forward? You'll be shot like dogs anyway!" Because the officer had run out of ammunition, he beat her unconscious with the butt of his gun. When she woke, she found herself floating atop a heap of bodies. Once the guards retreated, she and two other young women waded to the shore and assembled clothing for themselves from the bodies of the victims.

Victims' testimonies and memoirs juxtapose the general indifference or outright cruelty of many Germans they encountered with rare acts of bravery and kindness. Malinewicz testified that as the women made their way to the closest village, they convinced a reluctant farmer named Voß to hide them. But a week later, he decided to turn them in—believing that the Germans would still win, he would no longer risk his life to protect them. "Just shoot us, then!" cried Malinewicz's friend Genia. "That is for others to do!" he answered.[123] While the farmer fetched the police, another neighbor, Loni Harder, hid them in her coal shed.[124] Harder and her family protected the girls for the next two and a half months, giving them German names and instructing them to pose as German-Lithuanian refugees who had lost their documents. Because of the women's emaciation and shaved heads, Herder told the villagers that her 'relatives' had been typhus patients. The Harders were not the only civilians to shelter survivors: doctors and nurses at the Palmnicken hospital took in a severely wounded girl, and one doctor by the name of Schöder operated on an escapee, Maria Blitz, to remove her tattooed prisoner number. Two Polish forced laborers, Stanisława and Romualdo Zbierkowski, also protected some surviving Jews.[125] But most bystanders simply looked away, feeling powerless. As the Palmnicken resident Helene Zimmer returned from her unsuccessful attempt to flee, she came upon the site of the massacre. "As far as I could see," she later testified, "those lying on the shore were all dead, and every now and then we could hear desperate cries coming from the water. . . . I was so shaken at the sight that I covered my eyes with my hands. . . . We then quickly went on walking because we could not stand the sight."[126]

Malinewicz and her friends managed to escape detection, although they attracted the attention of German soldiers who wished to ask them on dates. Harder, afraid to say no, gave permission for Malinewicz to go on a date with one interested officer, as long as she did not stay out long. They strolled along the shore and ended up at the same spot on the sea "where I spent the most terrible night of my life." Testifying in 1961, Malinewicz recalled what the officer told her about the fate that awaited them both as Germans. "On this spot, our people murdered ten thousand Jews. It is abhorrent what Germans became capable of. I can only tell you that when the Russians march in, which is only now a matter of days or weeks, they do the same to us as we did to the Jews. A German will hang from every tree. The woods will be full of German corpses." As Malinewicz and the officer walked back to the village, he told her that 200 Jews had survived the massacre, but the local population had turned them over to the police to be shot. Malinewicz was one of just over a dozen who survived the war.[127]

In early February, the teenager Bergau, who had become forced to supervise the columns of prisoners at the amber pit, rode his horse along the coast and discovered the lifeless forms piled in the sand: "the ice had given up the bodies and new victims washed ashore for weeks." Bergau escaped the Samland Peninsula by boat on February 28, but as a Hitler Youth soldier, he was later captured by the Soviets and sent to a labor camp in Siberia. He worked for years building the Murmansk rail line, where he almost died from exhaustion, "in order to experience," he wrote in his memoirs, how "we Germans had exterminated six million people of Jewish faith." (As the Soviets saw it, he was atoning not for the suffering of the Jews, in particular, but for that of all those who had perished because of Germany's inhuman war.) Years later, Bergau found out that his Hitler Youth classmates, Lothar and Albert, had also been sent to Siberia, where they died from typhus and starvation. Unlike the Germans, the Soviets did not shoot their prisoners: "their punishment for the crimes of an unscrupulous Hitler Youth leader was of a different sort."[128] But the man who had induced the boys to murder, *Ortsgruppenleiter* Friedrichs, escaped to the West on April 15. He was imprisoned by the British at the end of the war, released in 1947, and was issued a comfortable West German pension. He later denied involvement in the Palmnicken massacre, only confessing under interrogation in 1961.[129]

The massacre survivor Malinewicz recalled that the evening before the Soviets captured the village in the spring of 1945, the same officer who walked with her along the shore brought her a suitcase full of canned food and begged her to evacuate with him. Otherwise, he said, "you will suffer so much if the barbaric Russians get ahold of you here!" Malinewicz could not tell him she was waiting for those "barbaric Russians" and claimed that she could not desert the Harder family. She begged him instead to throw away his uniform and pretend to be a civilian farmer. "I cannot do that," he reportedly said in tears, "I have to play my part in this evil play until its evil end."[130]

Fortress Königsberg

The Red Army's Third Belorussian Front surrounded Königsberg by the end of January 1945. The city was cut off from the outside world for the next two months, except for occasions when the German counteroffensive punched a narrow passage through the Soviet blockade or when ice cover connected Königsberg with pockets of German resistance along the western coast of the Samland Peninsula.[131] Hitler declared Königsberg to be one of several "Fortress Cities" on the Eastern Front to be held at all costs, and he demanded the total mobilization of its inhabitants and the final realization of Königsberg as bulwark against the East. He promoted General-Lieutenant Otto Lasch, the commander of the Königsberg Military District since October 1944, to the rank of general and put him in charge of the defense.[132] Lasch was a former *Freikorps* fighter, long-time East Prussian resident, and career Wehrmacht officer since the mid-1930s. During the war, he commanded regiments and divisions comprised mostly of East Prussian soldiers. He first rose to prominence as the conqueror of Riga for his role as a regimental commander for an East Prussian division that stormed the city in 1941, and he led a mostly East Prussian division in the siege of Leningrad.[133] In 1944, he fought in the retreat from northern Ukraine, where his unit, consisting of a core of East Prussians, was defeated within four months. In November 1944, as the second invasion of East Prussia loomed large, he was appointed to the administrative role of *Wehrkreis* I (military district) commander for East Prussia, only to be called back into combat duty to defend Königsberg. Gauleiter Koch, having evacuated before the Soviets arrived, appointed the party *Kreisleiter* (district leader) of Königsberg, Ernst Wagner, as the "Commissar for Party, State, and Economy" of the fortress. Wagner issued orders from the party headquarters inside the ruins of the Königsberg Castle and worked on cooperation with General Lasch.[134] Koch occasionally returned to Königsberg when a narrow opening permitted, but he never appeared during the day, as General Lasch later wrote derisively, "afraid of showing himself to the Königsberg population, whom he had cowardly left in the lurch."[135]

Trapped inside Königsberg were as many as 150,000 German civilians, a large number of them refugees, 15,000 foreign laborers, 30,000 to 35,000 Wehrmacht members, and 6,500 to 8,000 men drafted into the *Volkssturm*.[136] Lehndorff had decided to stay in the city as it was being encircled, volunteering to take over a military hospital that had been abandoned without medical supervision when many of the doctors had fled. Lehndorff wrote incredulously that the fact that Königsberg had become a "small remote island" surrounded by the Soviets seemed to be—at least in Lehndorff's estimation—a distant reality to most of the town's German inhabitants. Indeed, the party attempted to fabricate a sense of normalcy to maintain morale.[137] Although much of the population was living in makeshift housing, the city maintained its electricity and water supply, and shops remained open, mostly staffed by women and invalids who escaped mobilization into the *Volkssturm*.[138] Lehndorff wrote in amazement that "streetcars are running as usual, and people are having their hair cut and going to the movies" as if the end were not near.[139] Official reports to Berlin painted equally rosy pictures: an SS report from February 15 assured that the civilian population felt "confident," and a civilian government report noted that food supplies remained good and that "the mood among the population, despite the special circumstances, is not bad, even hopeful."[140] By contrast, Soviet spies and escaped POWs reported later in that month, with some overstatement (but not entirely without evidence), that conditions were dire, that civilians were being given only subsistence rations, and that there was a "high rate of fatality in the city" from military casualties and infectious disease.[141] Lehndorff, despite his glib presentation of civilian oblivion, had himself noted that civilians were taking their own lives out of desperation; archival documents confirm at least 120 suicides during the first week of the siege.[142]

Nazi rhetoric guaranteed the inevitable triumph of the Reich and attributed the seemingly hopeless situation to Hitler's cunning military plan—as one Nazi Public Relations Officer told the employees at Lehndorff's hospital—"to let the Russians in, the more surely to destroy them."[143] Propaganda posters began appearing throughout the city to convince the Königsbergers to maintain the defense. A placard from February 9, 1945 called for all men, women, and children to stand "shoulder to shoulder" with the soldiers of the Wehrmacht and the *Volkssturm* to build an "indestructible fortress" to protect the city until the German army could beat back the Soviets once and for all. Propaganda films such as Veit Harlan's *Kolberg* valorized civilian sacrifice. *Kolberg* portrayed the defense of a besieged Baltic German city during the Napoleonic Wars, showing how civilian battalions banded together in the ruins to defeat the French and secure the Peace of Tilsit. Goebbels was so moved by the film's message that he had the film reels parachuted into Königsberg and Kolberg (once again under siege) for special screenings.[144] An increasing number of posters drew on anti-Bolshevik rhetoric. As Lehndorff recalled, one such poster, "Hate and Revenge," was "full of obscene expressions" about Russians and Bolshevism, and ended with a summons to destroy the enemy at all costs.[145] The message on one of the others, "Königsberg will become a Bolshevik mass grave!" led some civilians to wonder whose bodies would be buried there.[146]

As the party leadership could no longer so easily sway a war-weary people who had come to treat official propaganda with suspicion, they increasingly relied on more coercive measures to draw Germans into service for total war. Boys as young as ten were drafted into the *Volkssturm*, and the de facto head of Fortress Königsberg, *Kreisleiter* Wagner, required every resident of the city to work four hours each day clearing rubble, rebuilding damaged factories, and building fortifications. "From the ruins of our city," Wagner declared, Königsbergers will "build barricades and points of defense, from which every Bolshevik onslaught will be smothered in blood."[147] By March 5, 1945, the liquor and soap plant began producing munitions, and factories began providing makeshift housing on site to keep workers on the job.[148]

Wehrmacht soldiers and civilian defenders also found themselves under attack from within, as total war increasingly demanded total compliance. A decree by the Reich Ministry of Justice from February 15, 1945 authorized the establishment of summary courts-martial for individuals deemed guilty of cowardice, shirking their duty, or undermining the war effort. By the end of the war, the military court system in

Germany had sentenced around 4,000 soldiers to death, while another 6,000 to 7,000 were executed by summary courts-martial.[149] Any civilians displaying a white flag of surrender were to be shot immediately, and newspapers filled their pages with reports of death sentences for defeatists, shirkers, and looters.[150] Escaped Soviet POWs reported to Red Army intelligence that the German soldiers and officers had enough weapons and supplies to withstand a long siege, but the lack of food made the command fear a "hunger riot" from civilians. Soviet NKVD (People's Commissariat for Internal Affairs) reconnaissance reported in late February that hundreds of residents were being shot each day for stealing food and supplies or for refusing to fight. The number was almost certainly inflated (Soviet sources had also overestimated the remaining population by a factor of ten), but numerous sources confirm that convicted cowards and defeatists were being executed by hanging. In early February, for example, eighty German soldiers were reportedly shot at the North Train Station for refusing to defend the city.[151] On their bodies hung the sign: "They were cowards and died anyway."[152]

Conditions deteriorated significantly by March. Munitions shortages damaged morale, and frontline soldiers reportedly began declaring that the German Fourth Army was being martyred. On March 17, SS reports warned that the city only had enough energy supply to last to the end of the month, after which time Königsberg would no longer be able to produce munitions to defend itself. Severe food shortages meant no food or milk for children, who were forced to survive on their parents' already lower rations.[153] From late February to mid-March, the party and military attempted to evacuate women and children—ostensibly for their safety, but actually to lower the drain on scarce food supplies, gas, and electricity.[154] Rumors about even worse conditions in the Reich led many to resist leaving Königsberg, but still tens of thousands were evacuated while one exit road remained open. Due to evacuation and casualties, the city's population sank to a reported 55,000 to 70,000 civilians (down from the highest reported number of 135,000) by late March.[155] *Kreisleiter* Wagner ordered lower-level party officials to execute at least 1,700 starving Soviet POWs and forced laborers to prevent them from undermining the defense.[156]

By early April, the frontlines had moved well beyond East Prussia to Pomerania, Brandenburg, and the outskirts of Berlin.[157] Königsberg and the Samland Peninsula were isolated pockets of resistance cut off from the main front, but the Soviet command decided to end the siege of the city with a full-scale assault to demonstrate to Germans everywhere the futility of maintaining resistance. As the gunfire became heavier in early April in preparation for the offensive, Soviet loudspeakers blared appeals to the population to surrender. Understanding that the end was near, the police and SS relocated residents from their apartment buildings, refugee camps, and makeshift dwellings into bomb shelters in the center of town.[158] Lehndorff, as a medical doctor, was permitted to walk freely in the city, by then so altered by barriers and barricades that it seemed to him possible for the first time to imagine it was an actual fortress. Knowing the end was near, Lehndorff's medical colleagues at the Samaritan Hospital began learning Russian words of welcome and propped up a photograph of Churchill on the dining room table.[159] A frequent joke at the time was that LSR [*Luftschutzraum*], the name for designated bunkers, actually meant *Lern schnell Russisch* (learn Russian quickly).[160] Käthe Hielscher, then a teenager, recalls how, as they waited in their bunker, her aunt ripped the NSDAP badge from her blouse and threw it away. Hielscher, who belonged to the League of German Girls, did not think to do the same.[161]

When the final siege began on April 6, 1945, the Soviet forces outnumbered the Germans by more than five to one—a quarter of a million Red Army soldiers to only 35,000 to 55,000 Wehrmacht soldiers and upwards of 8,000 *Volkssturm* men. One-third of the Soviet air force launched the attack with not a single German fighter plane to defend.[162] Soviet fronts from the north and south attacked the concentric rings of German fortifications, breaking through two lines of defense within a day.[163] German counterattacks on April 7 caused heavy losses on both sides but did not slow down the advance, and the Red Army's two fronts soon met up at the Pregel River running through the center of town. Koch's Deputy Gauleiter Ferdinand Großherr and the Fortress Königsberg leader Wagner died in the first days of the siege. Another eighty party leaders reportedly committed suicide by detonating a *Panzerfaust* rocket inside their bunker.[164] Others remained behind, instructed by Wagner to undermine the Soviet occupation from the inside.[165]

General Lasch radioed Hitler to ask permission to surrender, but Hitler refused. Lasch and General Friedrich-Wilhelm Müller, the commander of the Fourth Army on the Samland Front, at first ordered soldiers to continue the fight. But by the morning of April 9, as General Lasch conceded, "the tactical situation in Königsberg . . . was hopeless" and he "understood that it was now necessary to surrender the fortress to a brutal enemy who knew no mercy."[166] Although he later claimed he surrendered to save the lives of the civilians and soldiers and to bring an end to the meaningless war, he waited until he had little choice. Only seven tiny isolated pockets of resistance remained, one of them around Lasch's bunker, which by that point had begun to flood.[167] More German soldiers were killed between July 1944 and May 1945 than in the entire previous five years of the war.[168] January and February 1945 were the bloodiest months, with over 450,000 soldiers killed in January alone, the majority of them in East Prussia. Civilian deaths were just as high, and tens of thousands of East Prussians were sent to forced labor in Siberia.[169]

Lasch surrendered on the night of April 9, 1945, and Hitler sentenced him to death for cowardice. On the morning of April 10, Red Army commanders escorted Lasch and his cohort from their bunker and cataloged the prisoners for transport. Soviet courts sentenced Lasch to twenty-five years of labor for the atrocities committed by soldiers of his East Prussian division. Lasch later claimed it was a "sheer political act of revenge," as neither he nor his soldiers had committed any atrocities, nor had they ever been in the villages where the atrocities supposedly took place. Thus Lasch preserved the myth of the "good Wehrmacht," the heroic fighters, outnumbered and doomed, who prolonged the city's defense in order to spare civilians from the Red Army's vengeance.[170] By doing so, he exonerated himself for the deaths of thousands of German soldiers and civilians and Soviet soldiers who died in those two months of futile defense before he surrendered and ignored his own participation in the long course of the war. Lasch spent the next eleven years in various prisons and work camps near Moscow, Leningrad, Karabas in Central Asia, Vorkuta on the Arctic Sea, Asbest in the Urals, and in Stalingrad before being released as part of a mass amnesty of German POWs in 1955.[171]

Gauleiter Koch survived the war unscathed. He departed Königsberg for the last time in March 1945 and remained in the western Baltic port of Pillau until late April 1945, escaping by plane just before the city fell. He hid for four years under the pseudonym "Rolf Berger" until being apprehended by the British in Hamburg. He was turned over to Poland for his wartime crimes against the Polish people in the occupied territories Ciechanów (Zichenau) and Białystok and spent the rest of his life, unrepentant, in a prison in Barczewo, Poland (formerly Wartenburg, East Prussia), until his death at the age of ninety in 1986.[172] After the war, generals, émigrés, and scholars almost invariably placed the blame on Koch for the civilian tragedy that unfolded in the last months of the war. Baron Bernd Freytag von Loringhoven, the final adjutant to Colonel-General Guderian, later testified that the officers found it "unbearable" that the population had not been given the possibility to evacuate.[173] Dr. Paul Hoffmann, the Königsberg district president (*Regierungspräsident*) between 1936 and 1941 and himself a party member since 1932, denounced Koch as "doubtlessly . . . responsible" for the unfolding of the flight tragedy, even as he recognized that Koch was also following orders from above.[174]

First Contact

In the spring of 1945, Soviet soldiers looted and pillaged towns across the province and raped and murdered tens of thousands of German civilians. The German doctor Hans Deichelmann estimated in his diary that about 80 percent of the surviving women in Königsberg were raped or violently mishandled in the first weeks of the occupation.[175] Lehndorff, who served as a doctor in a German internment camp set up outside Königsberg immediately after the fall of the city, wrote in his diary that one woman there reported with "unmistakable pride" that she held the record for rape; "she counted up to a hundred and twenty-eight times."[176] Few were immune to the violence: Soviet soldiers reportedly raped the sick and injured women inside Königsberg's hospitals and even Soviet forced laborers, either because they were suspected to be traitors or simply because the orgy of violence knew no limits.[177] German diarists and memoirists emphasize the barbarity of Soviet soldiers raping their own; Deichelmann wrote in April 1945 how "our Russians" at the hospital "were also dragged about (*hineingezerrt*)."[178] Lehndorff wrote that "our plucky little Russian nurse" was found at his hospital "with blood streaming over her face, not stirring" after trying to intercept the soldiers before they raped the hospital patients.[179] Women tried to make themselves less desirable to these soldiers, as Wieck recalls in his memoir, by altering their appearance, covering their heads in scarves and smearing dirt on their faces, in order to look "like old, hunchbacked grandmothers."[180] The young woman Lucy Falk wrote in her diary that women had learned to claim they were sick with tuberculosis or a venereal disease because the soldiers' fear of infection proved to be one of the few reliable deterrents. But if a woman who tried to disguise herself was exposed, she risked the chance that the soldiers' violence against her would be more brutal than if she had acquiesced when the soldier first singled her out.[181]

Nazi propaganda gave Germans a language to narrate their experiences of violence during the invasion and occupation, and these images likewise shaped Cold War anticommunism. Postwar accounts of the violence tend to share the sense that German women were, in the historian Atina Grossmann's words, victims of "a surging Asian flood and marauding Red Beast tearing through what was supposedly still a pacific, ordinary German land."[182] The West German scholarly commission set up to document the fate of civilians expelled from the German East—a commission supervised by the former Königsberg historian Theodor Schieder and numerous other Königsberg émigrés—explained in the early 1950s that "it is clear that these rapings [sic] were the result of a manner of conduct and mentality [that is] inconceivable and repulsive to the European mind."[183] That behavior, the commission argued, was the natural inheritance of Mongol primitiveness; in the "traditions and notions of the Asiatic parts of Russia . . . women are just as much the booty of the victors" as cash, jewelry, furniture, and booze from shops and homes.[184]

The doctor and East Prussian aristocrat Lehndorff, although emphasizing his long-time opposition to National Socialism, employs the same imagery in his diary (edited and first published in 1947). Powerless and subject to the whims of the Soviet soldiers, he "felt like someone who'd gone bear-hunting, and forgotten [his] gun."

> They made short, growling noises and carried on methodically with the work. Other Russians, meanwhile, came out of the main block, hung round like sleigh-horses with the most fantastic objects. They too ran their hands over us; my fountain pen vanished, money and papers flew all over the place. My shoes were too bad for them. They hurried away with a short-legged gait over the ruins and through bomb craters to the other block and disappeared in the doorways. Their mode of locomotion left us gaping: when the situation suggested it they dropped on their hands and ran on all fours.[185]

Elsewhere in his published accounts, Lehndorff compares the Red Army's approach to a "flood of rats that exceeded all of the Egyptian plagues." As Robert G. Moeller writes, "such images of animalistic hordes carrying disease, deployed in Nazi propaganda to describe Jews," served a new function to describe the Soviet invasion. "Goebbels's prediction had come true, and his rhetoric remained apposite."[186]

Other memoirists, especially those who were young adults in 1945, reflect on the Soviet malice and refusal to accept ordinary German civilians' lack of individual complicity with the crimes of the regime. Käthe Hielscher (née Urban), the then-fifteen-year-old girl hiding with her aunt in the bunker, was among the first in Königsberg to be interrogated as the Soviet troops entered the building where her family was hiding. In her memoir, written in the 1970s but first published in 1998, she describes how a Soviet officer saw the swastika sewn to her League of German Girls shirt and pushed her angrily into the commandant's room for interrogation. " 'Name—screamed a Russian officer at me. 'Urban,' I answered, 'Käthe Urban.' 'You fascist!' The Russian opened his mouth wide, his eyes gleamed with hatred and a derisive smile dodged around the corners of his mouth. I didn't understand anything. What is a fascist. My personal details were registered, and I was pushed through a door into another room, where other young people were already waiting."[187] Hielscher adopts the narrative voice and perspective of her naive teenage self ("What is a fascist.") to underscore her innocence and the brutality of the occupiers. Even decades after the war, some memoirists describe Russian and other Soviet soldiers as less human than Germans, and therefore indifferent to their suffering. As Wolfgang Lehnert recalled in 2001, "The street ditches always offered the same image: . . . dead horses, dead men, injured German soldiers in mortal agony moan with pain, but the Russian soldiers showed no compassion and pointed at us: 'You are all criminals!' "[188] Few German civilians had the knowledge or capacity in 1945 to acknowledge the scope of the murderous war the German state had waged in the East—the calculated enslavement, starvation, and murder of millions of people. Fewer still were willing to accept as individuals the burden of collective guilt for the suffering inflicted in their name. Those who were did not think it was the punishment they deserved.

The Soviet Union lost more people than any other combatant nation: an estimated 26 to 27 million people, about 13.5 percent of its prewar population. More than 8.6 million soldiers died, including almost 3.4 million lost from the ranks or imprisoned and deliberately starved to death in German camps. Between 700,000 and 1,000,000 Soviet civilians died in besieged Leningrad alone. In other words, the violence, hunger, and deprivation that East Prussians experienced in the final months of the war had defined the lives of Soviet citizens on the battlefield and the home front for the previous four years.[189] On their march toward East Prussia, Soviet soldiers liberated millions of forced labor slaves, rescued concentration camp prisoners, witnessed the horrors of the Nazi death camps, and uncovered countless mass graves. To the Red Army soldiers entering East Prussia, it was the Germans who were the true barbarians.

One of the mass graves the Red Army discovered was in the East Prussian village of Palmnicken, where the Nazis' death march to the Baltic coast had ended. Rudolf Folger, a German civilian who became that village's Soviet-appointed liaison between the Germans and occupiers, later testified about what happened when the Soviets first arrived and discovered the full extent of the massacre of Jews. "The Russians," he testified, ordered him to "collect a large number of women to dig up the mass grave for Jews behind the mine building" and round up German men to dig a new mass grave for the victims. The women were forced to line up alongside the dead bodies they had exhumed, and then "the Russians set up two machine guns and pointed them" at the grave diggers. Folger recalled that a Red Army officer, "a Jew," made a speech in German: "He made it clear that the Russians could do to the people of Palmnicken the same thing that had been done earlier to the Jews, but that they would not, because they would not stoop to the level of Hitler's criminals."[190]

Folger emphasized the reversal of fates—the image of a now powerful Soviet Jewish soldier, wielding a gun over powerless German civilians in retribution. What Folger could not see was that this officer wanted to portray the Red Army's mission as one of humanist liberation, not of barbaric vengeance. But amid the violence of the occupation, few Germans could take such assertions of moral superiority seriously. As Palmnicken's last pastor, Johannes Jänicke, later testified, "much worse was to come. That [they did not kill us then] is close to a miracle."[191]

Chapter 4

Liberation and Revenge

"My previous happy mood is gone," wrote Iurii Uspenskii, a Soviet officer in the 39th Guard Army, on the eve of the East Prussian invasion in January 1945. "Sarina is near death, and my friends aren't writing. The war has been raging for more than three years, millions of people have died, and millions must suffer agonizing torment. Mother is dead, I was not with her, haven't seen her and wrote her very little, but she wrote me more often. Father, whom I've hardly seen, has fallen. My sister doesn't write what's going on with her. My grandmother and aunt are living terribly, and I am not doing anything to help them."[1] While German civilians in East Prussia saw the Soviet invaders as unrivaled in their cruelty, Soviet soldiers invading East Prussia in 1945 insisted that the Germans were the true barbarians. Their understanding—and their anger—was shaped not by technological chauvinism or illusions of racial superiority, as had been the case for the Germans fighting on the Eastern Front, but, as Uspenskii wrote in his diary, by their own experiences of the German war.

As Red Army soldiers invaded Germany in 1945, they saw themselves as defenders of their motherland, liberators of humanity from the crimes of fascism, and avengers called upon to punish the German beasts in their own lair. East Prussia, as the first German territory the Soviet Union invaded, was the place where Red Army soldiers first took

out their long-awaited revenge. As the soldiers raped and executed German civilians and pillaged East Prussian towns and villages, Soviet perpetrators and bystanders sought to justify, rationalize, or condemn the
violence. In diaries, memoirs, and military correspondence from the rear
of the Red Army, Soviet soldiers, officers, and propagandists grappled
with the question of how to punish the fascists for their crimes—how
to pay back the Germans for their barbarism without becoming barbarians themselves. In debating these questions during the invasion and in
the decades that followed, Soviet soldiers and veterans wondered what
their encounter with the German enemy meant for their self-identity
as an army of liberators and for the professed humanist mission at the
heart of the Soviet project.

German Fascists and Russian Humanists

Soviet soldiers brought to East Prussia an understanding of the German enemy shaped both by their wartime experiences and by two decades of evolving Soviet discourse about fascism—what it was, where
it came from, and what role the German state and the German people
played in perpetuating it.

Soviet theorists had defined communism in opposition to fascism
almost from the start. As the Nazi movement grew in the late 1920s,
they diagnosed "German fascism" as merely an extreme version of the
general European variety. In these early formulations, Soviet ideolo-
gists avoided blaming specific features of German history and culture
for fascism, in large part because the Bolsheviks saw German historical
development as a template for their own. While Lenin had conceded
that there were unfortunate characteristics of German national behavior ("brutal imperialism," for one), he insisted that Germans also
"personify . . . the principle of discipline, organization, harmonious
co-operation on the basis of modern machine industry" that the Soviet people should adopt on their own path to prosperity.[2] The two
countries, moreover, seemed to share revolutionary prospects: the destruction of the First World War and the collapse of the German and
Russian empires had given birth to the world's two greatest communist
movements, two unconnected halves of socialism, Lenin explained, developing "like two future chickens in the single shell of international
imperialism."[3] Even when German communists failed to usher in the
world revolution in 1918, Germany remained the country with the most
conscious working class and strongest Communist Party in Europe,

and it continued to serve as the model for the Bolsheviks' plans for state-led modernization. Soviet officials recruited numerous German "bourgeois specialists" to develop their industry and agriculture, and leading Bolshevik intellectuals spoke German, hired German tutors for their children, and included the classics of German literature in their cultural canon.[4]

After 1933, Soviet propagandists portrayed Nazism not as a deeply, quintessentially German disease but, in Marxist-Leninist terms, as a combination of late-stage capitalism, imperialism, and the diabolical aims of a small minority of fascist thugs—the so-called Hitler clique. Soviet propaganda at first insisted that German workers who voted for Hitler had been only temporarily misled by Nazi lies. In most of the Soviet press in the 1930s, Nazi Germany was not a major preoccupation; many news items minimized Nazism's significance and reported widespread German worker dissatisfaction with conditions in the Reich.[5] But as Hitler's power grew and the German communist opposition was destroyed, the Soviet press shifted to more essentialized portrayals of Germans as imperialists and eternally war-mongering Teutonic raiders. By the late 1930s, these images began to predominate, but they abruptly disappeared after Stalin and Hitler forged a nonaggression pact in August 1939 to divide Eastern Europe between themselves.[6]

Soviet Marxist critiques of fascism had understated the role of violence, biological racism, murderous antisemitism, and genocidal fantasies of *Lebensraum* in Nazi ideology and practice. For that reason, few Soviet citizens had a real sense of what the German invaders had in store. Many Soviet soldiers in the summer of 1941, drawing on their internationalist Soviet educations, assumed that it was only capitalists and landlords who had waged war, and that ordinary soldiers had only been driven to fight because they were afraid of getting shot.[7] Daniil Granin, then a twenty-two-year-old member of a hastily constructed militia, remembers that he "didn't associate the Germans with the fascists and the soldiers who had invaded our country." He and his fellow soldiers even tried to awaken the class consciousness of a German prisoner by reciting the names of history's great Germans: "Marx, Engels, Thälmann, Clara Zetkin, Liebknecht, even Beethoven." Recalling the popular 1931 film *Sniper* (in which a tsarist soldier in the First World War is moved by the discovery that the German soldier he had killed was a fellow steelworker), Granin offered an enthusiastic "Workers of the world, unite!" to a German prisoner of war, who simply sneered back at him, "'You will all be destroyed.'"[8]

For the first year of the war, Stalin spoke in ruthless terms about German occupiers but remained generous to the German people, careful to distinguish "fascist thugs" and "Hitlerites" from Germans at large. Yet, as Karel Berkhoff shows, Soviet war correspondents and other writers, with toleration and even tacit encouragement from above, often flattened the distinction between Germans and fascists in order to bolster flagging soldier morale against a seemingly invincible foe.[9] Several of these Soviet wartime writers and correspondents, including Konstantin Simonov and Vasilii Grossman, became famous voices of the era. Undoubtedly the most influential was Ilya Ehrenburg, a regular columnist for the Red Army's main newspaper, *Krasnaia zvezda* (Red Star). During the war, Ehrenburg wrote over two thousand articles, and his words helped give shape to Soviet soldiers' understanding of themselves and the German enemy.[10] Ehrenburg had little in common with most Soviet workers and peasants fighting at the front. He came from a distinctly intellectual milieu, had spent much of his life since the Russian Revolution living abroad in Paris, and had even been an erstwhile anticommunist. But Ehrenburg managed to find words that went straight to the Soviet soldier's heart. According to a popular anecdote, soldiers often ripped up old newspapers to roll their cigarettes, but they preserved Ehrenburg's articles to read and share.[11] Abandoning early economistic explanations for German fascism, Ehrenburg his fellow war correspondents focused instead on the deep corruption of the German people and German culture at large.[12]

Ehrenburg blamed the soldiers' early underestimation of their German enemy on Soviet education of the 1920s and 1930s, according to which "every Soviet schoolboy" had been taught that cultural achievement was measured "in mileage of railway lines, numbers of cars, or the existence of a technically advanced industry, the spread of education and of social hygiene." Publishing excerpts from German soldiers' captured diaries and letters, Ehrenburg revealed the typical German to be cruel, shallow, and obsessed with earthly possessions.[13] Germans soldiers, Ehrenburg wrote, thought of the entire Soviet campaign as a shopping spree for their wives back home; while Red Army soldiers were fighting for honor and the defense of their homeland, the Germans, he decried, were scrambling for "a pair of stolen boots."[14] This German greed went hand in hand with sexual depravity; in the article "Gretchen," Ehrenburg pointed out the contradictions between Fritz's theories of exclusive racial supremacy and his impure sexual practices. Looking through captured German soldiers' wallets, he found that "in one half there'll be naked girls and the addresses of bordellos, in the other (Fritz is accurate, he doesn't mix them up) a photograph of a blond-haired German woman with round porcelain eyes." German women were just as corrupt: although this "Gretchen" appeared to be a "harmless, fair-haired damsel," in fact, Ehrenburg explained, "she's a real shark"—one of the many "cowardly and selfish bitches" who would "lie down with the first comer," but, once the tables had turned, became "animals [samki] who scream because the hour of retribution is approaching."[15] The true measure for the Soviets' superiority over the Germans in this formulation was not material wealth but ethical behavior and socialist humanism.[16]

The Soviet-German war, in these terms, was a battle for the progressive legacies of Soviet (and European) culture against the superficiality and cultural corruption of the fascists. Yet it was simultaneously, as the Soviet worldview understood it, an ethnonational struggle between the archetypical Russian Ivan, the simple, peace-loving Slavic peasant defending his village, and the technologically savvy but morally depraved German Fritz. This association of socialist virtue with the Russian people, in particular, had been a recent development in the Soviet Union, stemming from the official promotion of ethnic Russian national identity—a kind of Russocentric national Bolshevism beginning in the mid-1930s.[17] Although the Bolsheviks were decidedly internationalist, they were also committed ethnophiles. Understanding the allure that nationalism held for ethnic groups in the prerevolutionary Russian Empire who had been oppressed by forced Russification, Soviet leaders actively promoted national consciousness among non-Russians. They created over a dozen national republics and autonomous regions within the Soviet Union in order to rectify legacies of imperial injustice, at the same time they hoped that doing so would minimize the allure of separatist movements. Performance of national identity was designed to be, in Stalin's words, "national in form, socialist in content"; that is, national groups were encouraged to express their individual Ukrainian, Tajik, or Uzbek identities through native language education, press, and literature, national costume and traditions, and national communist parties, so long as they remained politically committed to the Soviet Union, socialism, and the dictatorship of the proletariat.[18] Within this constellation, the Soviet leadership initially did not encourage the expression of Russian national identity, although Russia remained the implicit developmental template that the Bolsheviks expected 'backward' nations to follow on their path toward modernization. Amid the broader shifts in Soviet policy in the 1930s, however, cultural producers and political propagandists, with Stalin's guidance, reintroduced the official celebration of Russian culture, ostensibly to bolster support for the regime after the hardships of Stalin's massive industrialization campaigns and in response to the Soviet Union's increasing global isolation. When Soviet discourse began propagating essentialist depictions of Germans as imperialists and Teutonic raiders in the late 1930s, Soviet official culture simultaneously rehabilitated once-taboo political and military figures from Russian history and reinstated the great figures of Russian literature, art, and music into the cultural canon.[19]

After the Nazi invasion, Soviet propagandists such as Ehrenburg and Grossman (both of whom were not ethnic Russians, but Russian-speaking Soviet Jews), channeled this Russian national patriotism into more cosmopolitan articulations of socialist humanism. As Katerina Clark argues, they formulated a moral vision of Soviet (and, especially, Russian) culture in contrast to the German enemy.[20] Soviet soldiers who drew on the words of Ehrenburg, Grossman, and other war correspondents to give voice to their experiences thus drew on two overlapping tendencies inherent in Soviet socialism. The internationalist tendency, prominent in the Soviet project from the start, understood socialism to be a liberating force that would bring the legacies of world revolution to all peoples, including the Germans. The nationalist tendency, growing from the reintroduction of Russian nationalism in the 1930s, by contrast, perceived fascism as an intrinsic quality with deep roots in German culture and perceived the Germans to be irreparably corrupted.

As the war progressed, the nationalist tendency became predominant. Soviet propagandists increasingly encouraged hatred of the enemy, and despite the Soviet Union's continuing rejection of racism, they sometimes adopted racialized language to describe the German foe. Soviet propaganda never became fully dehumanizing as Nazi propaganda, however. While the Nazis depicted entire races as poison, rats, or maggots, Soviet propaganda focused on "poison" as a metaphor for fascist ideology rather than humans themselves. Still, Soviet propaganda referred to fascists—and sometimes simply Germans—as "beasts" and "cannibals" who had turned away from humanity.[21] By 1945, such propaganda increasingly merged class and nationality to treat all Germans as inherently criminal bourgeois philistines.[22]

Although this essentializing tendency—which Ehrenburg fully embraced—provided a powerful rallying cry for Red Army soldiers, the internationalist tendency remained vital to how many soldiers, officers, and propagandists understood their role in the war. Soviet propagandists and war correspondents, and Ehrenburg, in particular, projected these values onto ordinary Soviet soldiers, whatever their nationality. Unlike the Germans who bombed and pillaged and burned entire cities to the ground, Ehrenburg explained, Red Army soldiers "will never kill German children," and would never "burn down Goethe's house in Weimar of the library of Marburg." In March 1944, Ehrenburg explained the origins of this Soviet—and Russian—virtue in "Our Humanism": "The Russian people more sharply and fully than others have recognized the value of man . . . Foreigners call Russian literature the most humane literature . . . In songs, folk tales, and legends the nation repeated what is expressed in the slogan 'The soul is not a neighbor—you can't avoid it.' Our nation was soulful and conscientious."[23] This virtue, Ehrenburg revealed, did not originate in the dedicated study of Marxism-Leninism, loyalty to the leadership of the communist party, or the international solidarity of the working class, but in the innate goodness of the ordinary Russian.

Precisely because of this great humanity of the Soviet people, Ehrenburg told the soldiers to hate the Germans. In the article "Kill," written in the fall of 1942, Ehrenburg warned the Germans that the Soviets "remember everything. Now we understand the Germans are not human. Now the word 'German' has become the most terrible curse. Let us not speak. Let us not be indignant. Let us kill. . . . If you do not kill a German, a German will kill you. He will carry away your family, and torture them in his damned Germany. . . . If you have killed one German, kill another. There is nothing more joyful for us than German corpses."[24] The Red Army's mission was not only defense but also retribution—for the sake of the Soviet people and for all of Europe. As Ehrenburg wrote in May 1944, on the eve of the invasion, "our magnanimity demands punishment suited to the crime."[25]

During the war, Goebbels seized the opportunity to depict Ehrenburg as a smarmy cosmopolitan Jewish Bolshevik who called for the destruction of the German people. After the war, many German civilians, refugees, politicians, and historians likewise looked to Ehrenburg's words to explain the Soviet troops' wartime violence against German civilians.[26] Yet even as Ehrenburg told the Soviet soldiers to "kill the German" and to avenge the suffering of the Soviet people, he attributed to them a sense of heroic justice that demanded no violent retribution. The Soviets were supposed to kill the Germans, but "it is not of vengeance that our soldiers dream," because "vengeance is repayment in the same coin, a retort in the same language."[27] But Red Army soldiers, he explained, had "no common language" with the fascists. They hated the fascists "because we love people, children, land, the trees, horses, smiles, books, the warmth of a friendly hand, because we love life."[28] The Soviets, in this socialist humanist worldview, were "protecting Man from the fascists, his past and future, his dignity, his right to be unique, complicated, and great."[29] Red Army soldiers would be hailed by all the mothers of the world and celebrated by thinkers and artists as "the protectors of true humanism." If anywhere a seed were to sprout, "from which in a hundred years a mighty tree" would grow, if ever a schoolboy were to become the next Shakespeare or Tolstoy, it was only because "the Red Army is defeating death, trampling fascism, killing the German sociopaths. The blood on the soldier's bayonet is the dawn of happiness, the salvation of man."[30] The Red Army came to Germany on a sacred mission to liberate, to punish, and to be the representatives of European civilization. As Ehrenburg concluded in May 1944, "Our love is too abundant to forgive this. We are the conscience of the world."[31]

In the Lair of the Beast

"What great responsibility must the fomenters of this war, Hitler and his consorts, bear?" wrote Uspenskii in January 1945, just as the Soviets first invaded East Prussia. Frontline newspapers covered the liberation of the first Nazi concentration camps, especially Majdanek, and shared stories of the horrors of German slavery from forced laborers who had fled in the Wehrmacht's retreat.[32] Uspenskii, upon watching the newsreels of liberated civilians in Belgrade, was moved by the images of gaunt faces smiling at Red Army tanks and the emaciated bodies of people grateful to be alive but still feeling the grip of death around them. Filled with righteous anger, he asked himself how Soviet soldiers could possibly respond to the cruelty the Nazis had brought into the world. "What kind of terrible punishment must they receive! It is a crime to love war and to exalt it in song. No, it is already a crime even to say a good word about war. No utterance of a word, no note of music, not a single brushstroke of color should be allowed for the glorification of war!"[33] Uspenskii prepared to avenge the suffering the Nazis caused to his family, his homeland, and all of the victims scattered across the continent. He joined thousands of soldiers who came, in the words of the frontline newspaper *Krasnoarmeiskaia pravda* from the eve of the first invasion in October 1944, with the "sacred duty . . . for the sake of virtue and in the name of the memory of those murdered" to go "into the lair of the beast" to punish the fascist criminals: "The blood of our comrades fallen in battle, the agony of the murdered, the groans of those buried alive, the unquenchable tears of mothers call you to unsparing revenge."[34] The time had come for Red Army soldiers to destroy in the name of peace all those who glorified the war.

East Prussia played an outsized role in the soldiers' imaginary as the site of the first Red Army entrance onto German soil. Propagandists and historians writing in the pages of frontline newspapers combined long-standing European stereotypes about Prussian militarism with Nazi propagandists' insistence on Prussia's ancient mission in the East. The resulting imagery looked remarkably similar to Königsberg's Nazis' self-image, only with the moral values reversed. Beginning on the eve of the first invasion in October 1944, news articles in *Krasnaia zvezda*, for example, denounced the province as the most fascist place in Germany, the "homestead of the German military clique," and the "most important foothold of Hitler's fascism."[35] Building on increasingly prominent wartime depictions of German history and culture as perennially corrupt, propagandists and historians cast Königsberg, as East Prussia's capital, as the geographic origin of fascism—the place where the Teutonic Knights first launched their raids against the peaceful Slavic and Baltic peoples and built an empire of conquest. This *longue durée*, primordialist explanation of fascism assumed an ancient material base of German conquest upon which fascism had formed. The germ-seeds of fascism, the propagandists argued, were rooted into the East Prussian soil as part of the feudal agrarian system, sprouted in the Prussian monarchy, and were ultimately transplanted directly from Königsberg to Hitler in Berlin.[36] The invasion of East Prussia assumed a heightened symbolic significance, therefore, as part of both the international socialist humanist mission to fight fascism and as the ethnonational battle against the wellspring of fascism at its historical source.

The act of crossing the East Prussian border into Germany, so often remarked on by imperial Russian and Soviet travelers, assumed an almost spiritual quality in contemporary soldiers' accounts and later reminiscences. Ehrenburg himself recalled how, when he first entered East Prussia following the Red Army's advance in February 1945, the long-awaited arrival was almost too much to contemplate. He had written so much about that day when the Nazis were marching on the Volga, but now, driving along "a good smooth road bordered by lime-trees[,] I saw an old castle, a town hall, shops with German signboards, and could hardly believe it: was it possible that we were in Germany?"[37] For others, penetrating the border brought a more visceral elation. Lev Kopelev, later a Soviet dissident who served as a propagandist and German interpreter during the war, decided to celebrate the occasion "in an appropriate fashion" by urinating to mark the territory. "It seemed humorous to us," he remembered, "standing in a row by a ditch, solemnizing our entry onto enemy soil."[38] Anatolii Genatulin's novelized wartime memoir captures the simultaneous sadness and anticipation many soldiers felt. The hero of Genatulin's story, the soldier Talgat Gainullin, recalled how, fighting their way westward, through the "streams of people's blood," they had witnessed the destruction of their homeland and passed through "ashes of villages, the smoky ruins of cities . . . soldiers' graves and unburied human bones." Believing that the victory was finally near, soldiers wrote letters to their mothers, wives, and girlfriends with "words of life, words of hope: 'the war is over.'" They could not have imagined then, as Genatulin explained, that seven more months of battle still lay before them.[39]

As had been the case for generations of imperial Russian and Soviet travelogues, the East Prussian landscape seemed to reflect the soldiers'

FIGURE 6.   Soviet soldiers direct traffic at the East Prussian border. The sign reads, "There she is, accursed Germany!" Collection: Russian State Archive of Film and Documentary Photography (RGAKFD) Krasnogorsk.

preconceptions of Germany. Soviet propagandists had created an exotic picture of East Prussia, casting the territory as visibly fascist because of the unfamiliar, distinctly German, landscape. As the veteran P. A. Pirogov recalls, when "the front drew closer to the borders of Germany, the propaganda of hate not only of the German army, not only of the German people, but even of the German land itself took on a more and more monstrous character."[40] Veterans' memoirs echo the dual nature of East Prussia in the wartime Soviet imaginary: a landscape at once modern, geometrical, and rational, yet oppressively dense, dark, and medieval. Passing through the southern East Prussian town of Allenstein for the first time, Genatulin's hero Gainullin noted that "it was the first European, or rather, first German city in my life," but he emphasized how towns such as provincial Allenstein appeared sinister, like a "dark, high-rise city with solid walls of grim grey buildings" and narrow cobblestone streets, with dwellings that seemed to have been "carved out of dark, massive cliffs not so much for housing, but for adorning the city (turrets, cornices, balconies, columns, sculptures, gargoyles)."[41] East Prussia, in particular, seemed to display the linkages between ancient Teutonic and contemporary fascist oppression. In late April 1945, the officer Nikolai Inozemtsev wrote to his father that Stettin, further westward into Germany, was much more picturesque and joyful than East Prussia had been: "there everything is too grey, stern, and unwelcoming."[42]

At the time of the invasion, however, many commenters focused primarily on the visible wealth of East Prussia, sharing the diarist Uspenskii's remarks that "finally we've come to a wealthy land!"[43] As the historian Brandon Schechter writes, Soviet soldiers responded to foreign goods with an alternating sense of superiority and inferiority, and with both covetousness and rage.[44] Inozemtsev recalls in his memoir how, within a few kilometers of the border, he and his scouts indulged in German luxuries. Finding a large store of food hidden in the woods ("canned food of all kinds, cheese, biscuits, sausage, beer—in general, anything you could ask for"), the men laughed about Prussian hospitality as they enjoyed their fill of French champagne, Danish cheese, Bulgarian preserves, and Dutch chocolate.[45] For many of the soldiers, discovering such abundance only compounded their frustration. The common question, as one soldier explained to the US journalist Alexander Werth in Berlin, was why the Germans had gone to war at all. "They lived well, the parasites. Great big farms in East Prussia, and pretty posh houses in the towns that hadn't been burned out or bombed to hell.

And look at these datchas here! Why did these people who were living so well have to invade us?"[46]

Much of the German civilian population had evacuated on the eve of the invasion, so Soviet soldiers first took out their revenge on already abandoned towns and villages. Uspenskii crossed the border at Eydtkuhnen to find only a "half-destroyed little town" full of soldiers and cargo trucks, and the neighboring town also lay in ruins. Just over a week into the invasion, however, Uspenskii wrote that he heard that much of the damage had not come from battles, but that "it was our soldiers who set the fires."[47] As Grigorii Pomerants, then an infantryman and later a well-known Soviet philosopher and cultural theorist, recalls that Red Army soldiers started pillaging and were "shooting with their machine guns at the crystal china that wasn't possible to stuff into their bags" before setting whole towns ablaze. "And so the soldiers' hatred turned against those who were profiting from the war. Destroy everything. The fires were spreading so fast that the rear units were forced to move from one place to another several times. The flames bursting out of control, senselessly and ruthlessly. If you think about it, it said a great deal, but I did not want to think about it."[48] What Pomerants had not wanted to contemplate was the fact that his fellow soldiers, who had begun affectionately to refer to themselves as Slavs (in opposition to the Teutonic Fritzes), had found moral authority for their actions in the war, not in the ideals of international humanist socialism, but in ethnic nationalism. Pomerants, who was not a Slav but Jewish, recognized, perhaps more than those around him, the exclusionary power of imagined tribal bonds.

The violence of "sacred revenge" was self-perpetuating. Kopelev first ventured into East Prussia with a band of German POW graduates from his antifascist reeducation school to act as "Commissars of Panic," posing as German soldiers and spreading rumors about the Soviet advance. When houses were burning in some of the first villages they encountered, Kopelev asked whether it had been due to fighting or exploded German mines, but the soldiers answered that they had just done it themselves as a matter of course.[49] Evgenii Plimak, then a young sergeant major and translator, also recalls that the soldiers set the towns on fire, not fulfilling any direct orders, but out of the shared conviction that German cities should burn in retribution.[50] The diarist Uspenskii wrote with delight about "destroyed German trucks and the corpses of German soldiers" as his troops passed by. He explained that while the unending columns of German POWs and captured machinery created an "ominous" picture for the Germans, the "magnificent" scene was "the payback for everything that the Germans have done to us. Now its cities will be destroyed, and its people are experiencing what that means: war!"[51]   .

Many of the soldiers also took the opportunity to collect as many goods as they could to send back to their families at home. By 1944, Soviet civilians on the home front were suffering from hunger and extreme shortages as the entire economy had been directed toward supplying the troops to win the war.[52] In late December 1944, just two weeks before the East Prussian invasion, official policy dictated that soldiers could ship packages home—up to five kilograms of goods per month for soldiers, ten for officers, and sixteen for generals.[53] The shift in policy served, in effect, as unofficial encouragement to loot. Although many soldiers collected canned foods, clothing, and valuables to send to their families, other soldiers collected trophies as an end in itself (an ironic parallel to Ehrenburg's description of the German occupiers being obsessed with material goods). The historian Norman Naimark argues that Soviet soldiers ignored the warnings of the newspapers and political commissars not to be diverted by the riches of the West, as they were eager to explore "the strange and delicious world of bourgeois decadence."[54] But collecting such trophies of this world elicited, as Schechter writes, a combination of attraction and revulsion, one that embodied the "dynamics of inferiority and superiority that have been a leitmotif of Russian—'Western' interactions for centuries."[55] In post-Soviet oral histories, former soldiers recall that such collection of "trophies" was widespread, although interviewees tend to downplay their own participation. Rostislav Zhidkov remembers that food was more valuable than material goods, but he did manage to collect some impractical and decidedly philistine trophies, including a few paintings, a black wooden table, an armchair, and some champagne. But his efforts mostly went to waste: in the battles around Königsberg, the pictures caught fire, leaving only the frames, and the furniture ended up destroyed.[56] The veteran Lev Polonskii, who describes looting as a widespread obsession, recalls only taking a few watches and a couple of cameras for himself. At one train station, he was even offered free transport of a whole wagon's worth of goods by a sympathetic officer, but he turned it down, not out of modesty or morality, he explains, but because he had nowhere to send anything: the Germans had destroyed his home, and his father, mother, and brother were all engaged elsewhere in the war.[57]

For some soldiers, the dynamics of destruction created cause for concern. One mustached soldier reportedly approached Kopelev, remarking bitterly, "'The word is: "This is Germany. So smash, burn, and have your revenge." But where do we spend the night afterward? Where do we put the wounded?'" Another reportedly lamented, "All that stuff going to waste. Back home, where I come from, everyone's naked and barefoot these days. And here we are, burning without rhyme or reason."[58] Pomerants was especially unsympathetic to the soldiers' desires to collect trophies. He recalls a junior-lieutenant Tovmasian, an old communist "who preserved some of the rigor of the first years of the revolution." Tovmasian was, Pomerants claims, the only righteous one among his command, leaving Germany the same way he came: in a motor car, with only the possessions he had brought with him. The rest of the officers, corrupted by the promise of material gain, "dragged wagons of booty" behind them. The commander of Pomerants's division reportedly took five or six truckloads of cameras and various trifles and a few wagons of furniture.[59] The righteousness of the old communist Tovmasian, Pomerants explained, stood in distinction to the self-serving greed of the Slavs. (The fact that Pomerants was Jewish and the surname Tovmasian is typically Armenian adds another dimension to the critique.)

Blood for Blood

When Red Army soldiers finally came in contact with German civilians during their advance, they raped and murdered countless people in an ongoing act of fury and revenge. It is impossible to determine the total number of German women raped by Soviet soldiers in 1944–45. The figures cited by different scholars vary from twenty thousand to one million, with a conservative estimate of around one hundred thousand different women having been raped in Berlin (many of them more than once), and up to 1.9 million German women in all of Germany.[60] East Prussia, as the first German territory the soldiers entered and a place where so many refugees were intercepted during their flight, suffered the worst violence of any German conquered territory, including even Berlin. The historian Mark Edele estimates a rate of .6 rapes per Red Army soldier in East Prussia, amounting to over one million cases of rape.[61] Soviet troops sometimes raped every female between the ages of twelve and eighty before looting and burning villages to the ground; a village captured on February 26, 1945, for example, was systematically plundered and virtually all the women were raped, and the screams of help from the tortured could be heard day and night. Twenty-five to thirty women were left pregnant, and around one hundred contracted a venereal disease.[62]

Soviet official histories and post-Soviet Russian official narratives of the war deny charges that Red Army soldiers raped and murdered civilians. Numerous Soviet archival reports, however, testify to the scope and scale of mass violence, confirming the accounts of German victims and bystanders. An NKVD report from March 1945 noted cases of mass rape in the Baltic seaside town of Cranz; one resident, Wilhelm Schedereiter (Russ. Shedereiter) explained during filtration that on the night of February 12, "several soldiers raided his apartment and began to rape all of the women, little girls, and old women." According to the report, Schedereiter's daughter, Gertrude, who was raped multiple times, said that the Germans who had fallen behind Red Army lines "expect famine, epidemics, and NKVD repression soon to come."[63] In the village of Schpaleiten (Russ. Shpaleiten), NKVD soldiers collected reports from several German women who had been raped repeatedly by soldiers. One of them, Emma Korn, reported the following:

> Before their retreat, the German Army command recommended that we evacuate to Königsberg, explaining that the "Red Asiatics" would carry out unimaginable atrocities against the German population. According to the advice of German soldiers, [however], we did not evacuate and stayed in the village of Schpaleiten. On February 3rd of this year, the advance units of the Red Army came into our village, the soldiers broke into our basement and, pointing their weapons at us, ordered me and two other women to go into the courtyard. In the yard, twelve soldiers took turns raping me, and the other soldiers did the same with my roommates. That same night, six drunken soldiers broke into the basement and raped us in front of the children. On February 5th, three soldiers came, and on February 6th, 8 drunken soldiers, who also raped and beat us. Influenced by the German propaganda that the Red Army would humiliate the Germans and seeing it actually come true, we decided to end our lives by committing suicide, and so on February 8th we slashed the veins on ours and our children's right hands.[64]

Korn, who gave this testimony, survived the suicide attempt, but hundreds of others across East Prussia managed to kill themselves and their children.[65] Germans apprehended by the Red Army reported rumors and fears that the Soviets were planning to sterilize German women— a mirror of Nazi Germany's own policies reflected onto the invading enemy.[66]

One of the most chilling portrayals of revenge comes from Alexander Solzhenitsyn, who immortalized the orgy of violence in his poem *Prussian Nights*.

> Zweiundzwanzig, Höringstrasse
> It's not been burned, just looted, rifled.
> A moaning, by the walls half muffled:
> The mother's wounded, still alive.
> The little daughter's on the mattress,
> Dead. How many have been on it
> A platoon, a company perhaps?
> Reduced to the simple words:
> DO NOT FORGET! DO NOT FORGIVE!
> BLOOD FOR BLOOD and tooth for tooth!
> A girl's been turned into a woman.
> A woman turned into a corpse.[67]

Solzhenitsyn's poem captures the contradictions of violence against civilians. Soviet soldiers were superior to the Germans—they had not started the war, but had suffered at the Germans' hands. That suffering called for retribution, and the soldiers allowed themselves every means to carry it out. The destruction of fascism and the Hitler clique remained unsatisfying and abstract, but inscribing the punishment onto the physical body of the enemy felt undoubtedly real.

During the Cold War, many Western scholars, particularly in West Germany, focused on the ideological functions of Ehrenburg's propaganda to explain Red Army violence. Most of the German discussion revolved around a couple of texts: Ehrenburg's article "Kill" and an untitled leaflet with the key phrase "racial pride." (The discovery that the "racial pride" text had not been penned by Ehrenburg and was written by an anonymous author after the war did little to change the discussion.)[68] Scholars built a monolithic explanation that combined the totalizing features of Bolshevik ideology with Ehrenburg's propaganda. They argued that the violence was incited from above, thus pinning responsibility on Red Army commanders, on Stalin, and ultimately on the corruption of the entire Soviet project. By arguing that the excesses were central to military policy, they sought to discredit the Soviet Union's purported mission of liberation.

Contrary to the West German Cold War consensus, the violence was not part of a calculated central policy. Within the Red Army, reactions to the troops' behavior varied according to division, but there seems to have been no high-level directive instructing the troops to terrorize civilians. There is also little evidence that Soviet commanders purposely condoned violence in East Prussia as an example for the rest of Germany to surrender.[69] Explanations for the violence go deeper than Ehrenburg's propaganda or any Soviet ideological failing. Although Red Army rape was the largest in scale, actors on all sides—the United States, Britain, France, Germany, Japan, and the Soviet Union—perpetrated sexual violence against both enemy and allied women.[70] Recent histories of the German occupation of Soviet territory show how sexual violence, sexualized violence, and drunkenness were also endemic in the Wehrmacht, even amid Nazi ideological taboos against racial defilement. Both German soldiers and Soviet troops frequently gang-raped women on the Eastern Front as an act of male bonding and performance of misogynic masculinity.[71]

The scale of Red Army rape and other forms of sexualized violence has been explained as the result of wartime brutalization on the front and lack of consistent discipline, especially during the first weeks of the invasion.[72] But it might also have much to do, more generally, with the soldiers' understanding of their mission. As Susan Brownmiller argues, armies of liberation often have a different attitude toward local women than armies of conquest (and subsequently show them more respect), which helps explain, in part, why Soviet soldiers only engaged in sporadic rape against Polish or Bulgarian women but widespread rape against Germans.[73] Greater cultural differences between perpetrator and victim also correlate with more violent encounters: rape was generally a less common feature in friendly countries and Slavic-speaking regions (owing perhaps to the rhetoric of liberation, pan-Slavic brotherhood, or merely the morality of mutual intelligibility).[74] There were also occasional reports of mass rape in Serbian Yugoslavia and Poland, countries allied with the Soviet Union. A number of accounts note how Red Army members did not hold back against their own fellow citizens—Soviet women and girls coming out of German forced labor in Silesia, for example, were rerouted into work camps there and raped by entire companies of soldiers.[75] When the Yugoslav communist Milovan Djilas complained that Soviet soldiers were raping Serbian women,

Stalin reportedly replied, "Can't he understand it if a soldier who has crossed thousands of kilometers through blood and fire and death has fun with a woman or takes some trifle?"[76] Stalin's quote shows the contradictory nature of sacred revenge: even if the violence was not directed from above and sparked concern among frontline commanders, it was also seen as an understandable and increasingly self-justifying act. The soldiers felt they deserved to be compensated for having made the ultimate sacrifice to win the war and rewarded themselves through any means of their choosing.

In East Prussia, although soldiers were expressly prohibited, even early on, from mistreating civilians, the military turned a mostly blind eye to the first wave of violence and thus effectively permitted it to continue.[77] But from the beginning, military reports also complained that many soldiers were using their weapons against civilians, including women and invalids, pointing out that "in most cases, the perpetrators were drunk." Already in late October 1944, for example, NKVD border guards reported with concern that two men "dressed in Red Army uniforms" returned from East Prussia to Lithuania to sell pilfered goods to the local population and threatened them with violence. Shortly thereafter, on November 3, 1944, NKVD border guards were alerted to search for an officer and soldier who had reportedly abandoned their ranks, got drunk, "raped a woman, killed two local residents and wounded a third, and disappeared in an unknown direction."[78] At least one order commanded that "these disgraceful incidents" be stopped immediately, and that those involved be held responsible with "iron discipline." Similar military sanctions were published in *Krasnaia zvezda* as early as December 1944.[79] At the beginning of the January offensive, Stalin supposedly issued an order demanding "that no violent acts against the German civilian population be permitted."[80] On January 22, 1945, the head of the Second Belorussian Front, Marshal Konstantin Rokossovskii, issued an order concerning the discipline of his troops in East Prussia;[81] other documents suggest that organs of political education and military justice continued to condemn looting, plundering, arson, and mass drinking.[82] Above all, frequent complaints appeared about the soldiers' "refusal to fulfill orders."[83] Much of this concern from the official Soviet military perspective was pragmatic: the spoils of war were prolonging the very war whose end the soldiers were prematurely celebrating. Soldiers raped German women, became drunk on captured liquor, and escalated the cycle of violence. The spoils of war themselves were toxic; just as sexual violence against German women created an epidemic of venereal disease, captured Wehrmacht alcohol stores, often poisoned by the retreating Germans, led to scores of poisoning deaths among the soldiers.[84]

The threat of sexually transmitted diseases increased dramatically once the mass rape of German women began, and such rapid spread of disease threatened the mobility of the troops. In the late summer of 1944, Marshal Aleksandr Vasilevskii noted the "significant rise" of cases of venereal disease, particularly in the liberated territory of Romania, which he blamed on widespread prostitution, both individual and in brothels. From that point, all soldiers and officers in the army were required to undergo monthly medical inspections to stop the spread of chlamydia, gonorrhea, and syphilis.[85] For the soldiers who marched into East Prussia from Belorussia and the Baltic countries, rape and violence had not been considered an endemic problem before their entrance into Germany. Monthly medical reports for the rear of the Third Belorussian Front, for example, noted only isolated cases of venereal disease throughout the summer of 1944, but the reported rate increased dramatically after the troops crossed into Germany.[86] The soldier Vasilii Krysov recalls how one of his commanders had picked out "the most beautiful" women in the village of Groß Ottenhagen (Russ. *Grosottenkhagen*), and "he did his thing there, but three days later it started to drip [*u nego zakapalo*]." The regimental doctor, Krysov recalls, covered for the commander by claiming that an old infection had reappeared. Otherwise, "you'd be sent to the penal battalion. That made touching German women dangerous."[87] (Krysov claimed that he could not rape "for moral reasons.")[88]

The Soviet leadership recognized that the continued mishandling of the German civilian population was damaging the Red Army's reputation and ultimately prolonging the war. The Wehrmacht continued its futile defense of Fortress Königsberg for over two months, even as the frontlines reached the vicinity of Berlin; Soviet intelligence reports noted that Germans continued to fight or chose to take their lives because they feared that "the Red Army will exterminate everyone." One report described an epidemic of suicide across the province, including thirty-five cases of suicide in the town of Soldin, which the report attributed, perhaps in partial rationalization, to "mostly members of fascist organizations." Interrogated civilians explained that Nazi party members were especially prone to committing suicide because they figured that "the Red Army would shoot them anyway."[89] In the village of Wohlitz (*Volits*), one survivor reportedly told interrogators that "the

Germans understand that they must bear responsibility for all of the destruction and murder that the German Army carried out on Russian territory" and decided to kill themselves rather than face retribution. "Better a horrible end," these Germans pointed to the familiar proverb in the last months of the war, "than horrors without end."[90] Although such reports primarily blamed German fanaticism, they also implied that the soldiers' revenge was in part to blame.

Even as Red Army officers began to recognize that the violence was damaging the war effort, few had the power to stop it. Formally documenting widespread violence meant damaging the Red Army's reputation, and accusers themselves risked retaliation or counteraccusations of going soft on the enemy. When Solzhenitsyn and Kopelev questioned their fellow soldiers' behavior in East Prussia, they were each arrested for their misplaced sympathy and shipped off to the Gulag. Pomerants recalls how one political officer tried to bring charges on a lieutenant who had taken part in mass rape, but his supervisor then sealed the case, destroying all of the paperwork before anything could be done.[91] Krysov recalls being sent on a days-long mission as an interpreter to question a German girl about her attacker and compile a case, but when he filed the report, the man was given five days of house arrest and released without further action.[92]

Reports tended to describe atrocities against civilians only in veiled terms, refraining from assigning direct blame to Red Army soldiers. Reports frequently noted "men dressed in Red Army uniform," implying that the perpetrators were more likely spies or partisans, and in other cases, they focused on incidents by auxiliary armies—not true Red Army soldiers. An NKVD report from March 1945 pointed out that soldiers in the First Polish Army of the First Belorussian Front were known for "particular cruelty toward the Germans": instead of sending captured German soldiers and officers to designated collection points, they simply shot them en route. Troops of one infantry division reportedly captured eighty German soldiers, but only two arrived alive at the collection point. In another case, soldiers shot nine prisoners who had surrendered voluntarily.[93] Such summary executions were nothing new on the Eastern Front—the Germans had frequently shot POWs and civilians as part of sanctioned mass killing operations, and Soviet NKVD officers often executed military and political prisoners, including almost 22,000 Polish officers and intelligentsia as part of the infamous Katyn massacre. But with the rise in such executions on German soil, some Red Army officials expressed concern. Veiled denunciations continued until the end of the war, though few risked questioning the collective behavior of Red Army soldiers directly.

In the spring of 1945, military authorities first pursued a soft approach to address the violence, attempting to direct vengeance into service of the greater cause. Political officers lectured soldiers about their conduct on foreign soil, encouraging them to balance their right to vengeance with the need to maintain discipline. Just over a week into the invasion, one such political leaflet issued to the troops, titled "How I Understand Soldier's Revenge," attempted to contain the soldiers' excesses.[94] The author, Sergeant S. Krasnov, describes how the "Russian heart" was overflowing with anger at the Germans and how he and his fellow soldiers came to East Prussia to "destroy, burn, and exterminate." But once he crossed the border, he realized that Red Army soldiers should destroy the enemy army mercilessly, but not loot or pillage. Towns and factories needed to be preserved "down to the last screw" for the occupying forces to use; only then could the Soviet Union be repaid.[95] The leaflet refers continually to "the German" in the homogenizing singular as the target for revenge and calls for soldiers to punish "enemy soldiers and officers" mercilessly. But it remains silent on the topic of German civilians—should they, too, bear the brunt of "sacred soldier's revenge"? Were they, too, "the German" who would be punished? The author's stern warning not to waste time, resources, and blood on retreating Germans sits in uneasy juxtaposition with the final call to "turn anger against the German beast, beat him, the reptile, with bullet and bayonet [and to let] their black blood pay for our burned-out cities, for the tears and suffering, for our mothers, wives, and children!"[96] Soldiers were supposed to punish the Germans and to take their "sacred soldier's revenge" but limit their rage to the battlefield. But revenge, in that formulation, would remain abstract, no different from the previous three and a half years of the war.

Many Red Army memoirists, eager to uphold the reputation of the units in which they served, maintain that violence tapered off after the first weeks, while others say that it continued unabated until mid-April 1945, when the head of the Soviet Communist Party Central Committee Propaganda and Agitation Department, Georgii Aleksandrov, penned a now famous *Pravda* article, "Comrade Ehrenburg Oversimplifies."[97] The article, approved and perhaps even written by Stalin himself, blamed Ehrenburg for the violence. Aleksandrov denounced Ehrenburg, in particular, for an article in which Ehrenburg had called the Germans "one colossal gang" of fascists. Citing Stalin's offhand remark from 1942 that "the Hitlers come and go, but the German state and the German people remain," Aleksandrov criticized Ehrenburg for the monolithic portrayal of the Germans as evil. On the contrary, he insisted, many Germans had resisted Hitler, and even among the German leadership there had been dissent in the ranks. Alexandrov's *Pravda* article marked a dramatic turning point in Soviet rhetoric and policy: the Red Army would no longer see itself as the army of avengers but only as the army of liberators. Ehrenburg, who had given voice to the Soviet mission—both to liberation and to revenge—was sacrificed for the cause. His articles disappeared from the frontline newspapers, and he was prohibited from reporting on the Soviet victory in Berlin. Although Ehrenburg was publicly criticized for his incendiary rhetoric, he, too, was horrified by the soldiers' violence against German civilians in East Prussia. Ironically, one of the reasons for his calculated fall from grace was that he had dared to criticize the Red Army's behavior and the officers' inability to control their men.[98]

Aleksandrov's corrective marked a public turning point. With an eye toward the postwar occupation, official Soviet rhetoric began re-emphasizing the redemptive, liberating mission of antifascism. Soviet newspapers resurrected earlier Soviet depictions of Germans not as perennially evil, but as temporarily misled by the lies of Nazi propaganda and therefore potentially redeemable after the war. Königsberg fell in early April 1945, and with the front lines extending already to the outskirts of Berlin, the myth of Königsberg as the wellspring of fascism disappeared from the headlines. On a more pragmatic level, the Red Army found itself, particularly in the decimated German lands, responsible for sustaining the lives of the very people they had conquered. But some memoirists recall that mass violence only really tapered off in the weeks after Stalin issued another directive, which denounced the ongoing violence, although still blamed it not on Red Army soldiers directly, but on penal battalions, enemy agents, and malcontents.[99] After that, as Pomerants recalls, the risk of punishment became too great. The soldiers, Pomerants explained, could no longer use the pistol as "the instrument of love."[100] (The German civilians who remained in Königsberg at the end of the war, however, remembered differently—namely that the pistol served as an instrument long thereafter.)[101]

During the Soviet period, discussions of Red Army violence did not appear directly in the press, official sources, or published memoirs. Memoirs and military histories during the Soviet period note how the desire for revenge melted into magnanimity when faced with the real human suffering of German civilians—even those who had opportunistically benefited from the fascist system. Marshal Rokossovskii, the commander of the Second Belorussian Front, writes in his 1970 memoir primarily about grand strategy, tactical considerations, and the heroic deeds of his men. The troops' interactions with German soldiers and civilians are mentioned only in a passage toward the end that appears different in style from the remainder of the text and seems to serve as a political declaration. In it, Rokossovskii emphasizes how the military council had created a cohesive policy on "the question of our people's behaviour on German soil." As Rokossovskii explains, it was their duty to prevent Red Army soldiers' legitimate hatred "from degenerating into blind revenge against the whole German nation." Party and Komsomol activists continually reminded the men of the essence of the army's mission of liberation, and Rokossovskii concluded that "on German soil our people displayed genuine human kindness and magnanimity."[102] Even today, the Russian collective remembrance of the war does not include the public recognition of atrocities. In Russian historiography, especially in light of recent laws in the Russian Federation against historical revisionism of the Soviet Union's role in the war, the theme of atrocities of the Red Army in Germany remains taboo.[103] Most former soldiers interviewed after 1991 do not acknowledge widespread violence; while some admit there were occasional excesses, others maintain they saw no violence at all. Valentin Aver'ianov, a pilot during the battle for Königsberg, remembers that relations with the Germans were peaceful, and that no one touched them.[104] The soldier Mikhail Zharovskii explains that because his division rarely came in contact with civilians, he could not comment on any alleged "barbarism of Soviet soldiers."[105] Dmitrii Kiriachek also remembers that relations with German civilians were good, with a few notable exceptions; he arrived once at an estate and saw that the German family there had been shot, but he insists it was "hard to say who did it."[106] But even those who admit that soldiers often indulged in violent acts insisted that not every sexual encounter was forced. Isaak Kobylianskii heard a story about how a few scouts found three good-looking German women, and the soldiers enjoyed themselves greatly, "without even resorting to pressure." That was back when those sorts of things were still not punished, as Kobylianskii recalls.[107] In cases when interviewees recall witnessing violence, it was always the work of other soldiers. None of them admit to having taken their own revenge.

The small number who talk openly about what happened are generally highly educated veterans, many of them also Jewish, who later

actively opposed the Soviet regime. Solzhenitsyn, Kopelev, and Pomerants all became dissidents, and they trace their first disillusionment
with the Soviet project to their experiences in East Prussia. Many dissident memoirs recount scenes of encountering a German woman by her
bedside after she had been attacked and left for dead. Solzhenitsyn's
Prussian Nights is filled with such encounters; Pomerants recalls entering an apartment where he found an elderly woman lying injured. "Are
you sick?' 'Yes,' she says, 'your soldiers, seven of them, raped me and
then shoved a bottle up there, so now it hurts to walk.'" As Pomerants
explains, the women reported "matter-of-factly," more surprised than
offended, as she was "around sixty years old."[108] Kopelev recalls finding
a woman with a fur hat, covered with blankets and quilts. Her eyes were
closed and she moaned hoarsely. He raised the covers and found blood
on the sheets—she had been stabbed in the breast and the stomach with
a makeshift dagger, "the kind our men make from the Plexiglas off of
downed aircraft." Kopelev recalls with contained horror how his partner Beliaev entered the room in search of loot, took one look, and said,
"Let's go. Nothing worthwhile here."[109]

More often, veterans' narratives of the war engage with the problem of rape less directly, but grapple more generally with the question
of whether retaliation demanded repayment in the same coin. Some
memoirists and interviewees recall their great desire for revenge before
entering East Prussia, but their reluctance after encountering German
civilians for the first time. One soldier testified not long after the war
that witnessing the German bombing of a railway station full of civilians had led him to decide "that as a soldier, I must some day try to
get back to Germany to get even for such things." But when finally got
there, "all of a sudden I started feeling some sympathy for them." He
remembered seeing the "horrible things were done there, especially by
drunken tankists. They shot whole columns of refugees, burned villages in East Prussia. And I was almost sick in reacting to it. It was not
that I felt sorry for them after all they had done, but because it was
unworthy, it was no way of treating people; it was bound to confirm
the view that we were Asiatics."[110] Just before crossing the border from
Poland, the Soviet Jewish poet David Samoilov spent the evening with
two elderly German men and their wives. They spoke about music, not
with words, but with the melodies of Brahms and Tchaikovsky, and he
pitied them for having been too weak to flee. He wrote then in his diary
(although perhaps in a passage added later, before publication) that
"the German tragedy, the well-deserved tragedy, passed before my eyes,

and I vowed never to hurt the wives and children of my enemy."[111] But in wartime, such sympathy had its limits. Kiriachek, although remembering having no real contact with German civilians during his stay in East Prussia, did recall seeing the body of a young German boy who had been killed. He felt pity for the boy, but at the same time, he reminded himself that if the Soviets did not kill the Germans, the Germans would kill them.[112]

Genatulin's protagonist Gainullin first felt a twinge of sympathy toward German civilians when coming across the body of an elderly woman. "Small, dressed all in black, wearing a hat, her face was buried in the cobblestones and she grew stiff in a pool of her own blood. Why did she not leave the city? Didn't have time? Didn't want to? How did she get shot? What surprised me was not that an old woman had been killed but that such ordinary old ladies could live in a town like that."[113] Perhaps Gainullin could feel real compassion for the old woman because it was not he who had killed her but the circumstances of the war. Later, Gainullin met her living analog—an elderly estate worker with a grandson. Gainullin showed her true human compassion even though she mistrusted him and expected revenge. He took pleasure in the thought of confusing the prejudices of this woman: the "Asiatic" (Gainullin was ethnic Teptiar and spoke Bashkir) had demonstrated himself as the true humanist, and the German woman was forced to question her assumptions about the barbarians.

The more time that self-proclaimed humanists spent in East Prussia, the harder it became for them to rationalize eye-for-an-eye payback. Although some expressed misgivings out of compassion for the suffering of individual German civilians, just as often, soldiers reacted with practical and moral concern for the behavior of their fellow soldiers. The officer Inozemtsev wrote a letter to his father in November 1944, declaring each Soviet soldier had compiled a personal account for all the friends and loved ones who had died, and he demanded a "terrible reckoning" from the Germans for their suffering.[114] But when witnessed the violence in East Prussia, Inozemtsev recalls, he and a friend wondered whether the cost was worth it. "You know," said the friend, "I don't feel sorry for the Germans at all, let [the soldiers] shoot them and do whatever they want with them." Whatever the Soviets were doing in East Prussia could never compare with what the Germans had done, "either in terms of it being state-sponsored or in scale." But it was a shame, he continued, that "all of these rapes are debasing the army in general and every individual Russian in particular." The "unleashed animal instincts" had lowered army discipline and were becoming difficult to rein back in. Inozemtsev recalls that every time the troops received another order against arson, pillage, or rape, he was reminded of "the now-discarded Ehrenburg formula" to leave the punishment up to the soldier's conscience. "It took a lot of effort and energy on the part of the officer corps to undo the damage."[115]

For some, the greatest concern was that the Red Army soldiers, as representatives of Soviet socialism, were stooping to the level of the fascist criminals they had fought to defeat. After at first feeling jubilation at the destruction of East Prussia, Uspenskii wrote in early February 1945 that the revenge had spun out of control. The Red Army, he argued, needed to destroy the German war machine and the fascist state, but "we don't want to become 'Majdaniki' who murder women, children, and the elderly."[116] In his memoir, Pomerants grapples with the question of whether doling out punishment came necessarily with consequences for the victors. During the march westward, he recalls, the soldiers repeated a favorite anecdote. The first soldier would ask, "Where's my wife now? Probably sleeping with a German." Another would answer, "Oh well, let's get to Berlin—we'll show the German women!" Pomerants describes how he became increasingly frustrated with this logic of payback: "Why do humanists need to repeat the fascists?" Even the party had supported this line, Pomerants complained. "Where did real humanism go, the logical foundations for communism? I didn't ask myself this question at the time, but I remembered it in 1945."[117]

The soldiers marched to the words of Ehrenburg, who had encouraged them to avenge their suffering, but they had forgotten the humanist message behind Ehrenburg's vitriol. "The war," Pomerants explained, "freed the soldiers of all fear. They had gotten used not to pity anyone, their own skins or the enemy. They had gotten so accustomed to it that anything was permitted to us heroes. I remember that feeling very well in October 1944 right before we invaded East Prussia.... Cross that border (they put up a black sign right there: Germany), and take revenge to your heart's content."[118] When Red Army soldiers and officers such as Kopelev, Pomerants, and Uspenskii witnessed the behavior of their fellow soldiers—the mindless vengeance, the animal aggression, the looting, and rape—they feared that the soldiers' behavior was a symptom of the corruption of the communist project and a cause for it: the communist revolution had not been fully secured at home, and now it was being exported by men and women who had only undergone half of the transformation. Pomerants deliberately calls on the formula from Fyodor Dostoevsky's *The Brothers Karamazov*, the consequences of moral relativism: "If there is no God, then everything is permitted." But in East Prussia, the question came in reverse: if everything was permitted, did it mean that there was no God? In other words, did it mean that Soviet socialism's claims of moral authority over fascism had no basis? Did it mean that the protectors of European civilization were themselves not civilized, the heirs of socialist humanism not truly humane?

At the end of the siege, the memoirist Boris Gorbachevskii recalls, there was only one place in the center of Königsberg that remained undamaged: "an old church, which held the remains of the great German, the scholar and philosopher Immanuel Kant." Rumor had it that Stalin ordered for the mausoleum to be saved, Gorbachevskii writes, because "somewhere in Karl Marx the great leader had read that he thought highly of the philosopher."[119] Most of the Kneiphof Island, including the cathedral in the center of the old town, had been destroyed during the siege, but Kant's mausoleum remained mostly undamaged. Gorbachevskii must not have seen it himself, or else he would have noticed that the actual sarcophagus had cracked apart in the bombing,

FIGURE 7.   Soviet soldiers fight street battles during the siege of Königsberg in April 1945. Collection: AKG-Images.

exposing the philosopher's bones. Soldiers scrawled their names and the date on the walls to mark their victory. Among the inscriptions, one proclaimed, "Now you understand that the world is material." Next to it, another asked, "Did you think that the Russian Ivan would be standing on your grave?" Marxist internationalism and nationalism could go hand in hand.

Inozemtsev returned to the city a week after the siege and took a tour of the remains of Königsberg. After photographing his fellow officers in front of monuments to Bismarck and Friedrich the Great, he wrote that "the bronze Bismarck looks out of one lonely eye (half of his head has been blown off by a shell) at the Soviet signal woman, at the cars passing by, at the horse patrols, as if asking: 'Why are there Russians here? Who let this happen?'"

> Yes, the Russians are here. And the Germans, mostly elderly men and women or women with children, with knapsacks on their shoulders, drag themselves wherever the Russian escort guard orders them to go. Their faces are blank, a deathly silence, the feeling of shame and defeat imprinted on all of them without exception. One, two, three, four years ago they lost their sons and fathers in far-away Russia, then lost faith in Germany, and now they are losing everything: their homes, their family, their homeland. It's hard to tell what they are thinking as they pass by Bismarck: thinking about how much stupider and smaller the current rulers of Germany are than their great predecessors, or thinking about a crust of bread for tomorrow. The heart of Prussiandom and militarism, the hotbed of the Teutonic Order and its deluded ideas, the true bulwark of fascism—has fallen to pieces.[120]

The army that entered the remains of Königsberg claimed to represent both European civilization and merciless retribution. They considered themselves to be humanists by virtue of being Russians and socialists, but they were also an army of avengers. The people they found in Königsberg seemed to represent both betrayed humanism and pathetic humanity. They were also, by most accounts, the beast in its lair. On the eve of the invasion, Königsberg's Nazis had claimed—in the name of a different humanism—to be defending the legacy of Kant against the barbarians. Now it was the Soviets' turn. The city lay in ruins, but the Kant Mausoleum survived mostly undamaged.

CHAPTER 5

City of Death

The invasion of East Prussia and siege of Fortress Königsberg marked the collapse of the Nazi party, the German state, and, as it seemed to the Germans who remained, the very foundations of German and European civilization. More tangibly, it brought about the destruction of an entire ecosystem—the urban and rural environments designed to sustain life. Five days after the Red Army captured Königsberg, Red Army reconnaissance reported that the city had been reduced to a "heap of rubble." Allied bombing in August 1944, Wehrmacht sabotage, heavy street fighting, and Red Army soldiers' pillaging destroyed more than 60 percent of the city and 90 percent of the historic center.[1] The entire Kneiphof Island and areas surrounding the Königsberg Castle were left in complete ruins. Fires burned across the city for over a week from soldiers' arson and exploded mines, and the bodies of fallen soldiers and horse carcasses littered the streets. As the Red Army officer Nikolai Inozemtsev wrote in his diary after touring Königsberg in late April 1945, "there was a smell of death in the air (quite literally, for hundreds and thousands of corpses were decaying underneath the ruins)."[2]

The air of death also lingered among the living. Between 150,000 and 200,000 German civilians remained in northern East Prussia, and the majority of them were hungry, weakened, and ill.[3] Some had chosen to remain in place, while others had been thwarted during their flight by the Red Army advance. Most of them were uprooted from their former homes, living in makeshift refugee camps or bomb shelters. Between 55,000 and 70,000 civilians, along with 35,000 captured German POWs and several thousand forced laborers from the Soviet Union and elsewhere in Europe, had survived the onslaught of Fortress Königsberg by living in air raid shelters and surviving off dwindling supplies of military provisions.[4] The prolonged siege and heavy fighting completely destroyed the foundations required to support urban life. Bridges, roads, and railway tracks had been destroyed or were buried in rubble, impeding movement through the ruins. Electricity generators had been sabotaged, leaving most neighborhoods without power. Water supplies were contaminated when sewer lines back-flowed into the Pregel River. The squalid conditions became ripe breeding grounds for epidemic disease.

Environmental collapse coincided with dramatic political and economic transformation. Königsberg and the northern third of East Prussia fell under direct Soviet control immediately at the war's end, not in cooperation with any Allied occupation government. The territory was slated to be made Soviet—to become, in some form, part of the Soviet Union. Violence and exclusion were inherent in the Soviet project. Just as the Nazis imagined the world as a perennial struggle between nations, the Soviets imagined the world as one of class struggle and, more generally, as one divided sharply between those supporting the revolution and those opposed to it. The Soviet revolution, wherever it was exported, led, in the name of eliminating opponents of that revolution, to the violent exclusion of political rivals and intellectual alternatives and to the installation of one-party rule. In one way or another, it also led to the complete nationalization of commerce and property into a centralized state-led economy and the reconfiguration of public and private space. Recent works have shown, however, that the processes of postwar Sovietization were not handed down, prepackaged, from above, but were more decentralized than formerly assumed. The course of Sovietization, and to some extent, even the outcomes, were shaped significantly by local circumstances.[5] As E. A. Rees shows, Sovietization, in general, involved an all-embracing, transforming conception of politics with a "visionary aspiration to reshape geographic space."[6] In Königsberg, extreme privation meant that the first stage of Sovietization was initially guided less by any ideologically driven, planned transformation of people and space, and more by the exigencies of time—by the urgent race to rescue the rural and urban environment and the people living there from death.

The entire region became a zone of death in the wake of wartime devastation. In this sense, it was the continuation of a longer cycle: the closed spaces created by Nazi Königsberg's empire—the camps and ghettos across Poland, Belorussia, and Ukraine, where millions had perished from hunger and disease—folded back into Fortress Königsberg in the last months of the war, spurred on by the Germans' unyielding defense. In the last days of the siege, the hunger and disease of these closed environments spread finally to German civilians themselves.[7] Wartime devastation, compounded by geographic and administrative isolation in 1945, served to prolong and widen an already unfolding demographic catastrophe, arguably the worst in postwar Europe. To the Germans remaining in Soviet Königsberg, the squalid living conditions, hunger, and epidemic disease seemed to be an intentional extension of the Red Army's violent wartime retribution. But whereas the Nazis had combined economic resource extraction with racial hatred to weaponize hunger and disease, postwar Königsberg became deadly not by design, but in large part as a long-term byproduct of the destruction of the war. After the war, Moscow's administrative and financial neglect of the region—due more to budget constraints and administrative confusion than ideological calculation—served to perpetuate the destructive cycle of privation.

As was the case elsewhere in the Soviet sphere of occupation, the Red Army soldiers who had come to liberate the world from fascism and seek their revenge against the German fascists found themselves called on to become caretakers—to assume the role of the state they had destroyed or risk demographic catastrophe that would threaten even their own lives. Their task was to rebuild, and in doing so, to demonstrate that their revolution and way of life were superior. In order to succeed, they needed to engage with the German population, whom many Soviet soldiers had understood to be a perhaps irredeemable enemy. These Germans, likewise, had seen the Soviet soldiers, by virtue of Nazi propaganda, their own cultural and racial prejudices, and by their horrific experiences at the end of the war, as savages and demons who had brought about Hell's dominion on Earth.[8] As the German population teetered on the verge of death, the new Soviet rulers of Königsberg struggled to demonstrate that their revolution was more just and more humane and that they would never stoop to the level of Hitler's criminals.

Königsberg and East Prussia, cut off from the mainland of the Reich in the 1920s and 1930s, had become, through isolation and hardship, a petri dish for a local variant of National Socialism. In 1945, Königsberg, once again isolated, became the contained site of another revolution—this time, the Soviet project to build communism on the ruins of fascism, rescue the German people from death, and, perhaps, redeem them from their sins.

Sovietization in Isolation

For all the grand ideological transformations associated with Sovietization, Königsberg became Soviet virtually without a plan. Stalin had taken great interest in claiming Königsberg during wartime negotiations with Churchill and Roosevelt, but he paid little attention to it after he had secured it. The northern third of East Prussia was a mere ink blot on the redrawn map of Europe, accounting for less than 1 percent of new land falling into the Soviet sphere of influence. Königsberg, no longer part of a postwar German state, was not deemed geopolitically important for establishing a new postwar order. And as a former fascist city in a region uninhabited by Soviet citizens, it fell low on the Kremlin's priority list for rebuilding.[9] As the historian Per Brodersen points out, widespread confusion among Moscow leaders about where and what this new Soviet territory was, let alone who lived there, reigned for years.[10] The territory remained under a placeholder Red Army occupation for a full year. On May 10, 1945, one day after the victory in Berlin, a Special Military District was established under the command of 11th Guards Army general Kuz'ma Galitskii of the Red Army's Third Belorussian Front. Königsberg's Special Military District was separate from the civilian government of the USSR and from other occupations in Eastern Europe and outside the jurisdiction of the Soviet occupation government in Berlin.

Architects and planners had begun planning the reconstruction of Soviet regions while they were still under German occupation, drawing up blueprints and appointing funds to begin rebuilding following liberation.[11] But Königsberg, only captured in April 1945, had no Soviet-led planning committee to direct the rebuilding and no established budget to carry it out. Unlike other territories entering the Soviet sphere of occupation, no hopeful antifascist government-in-exile had been waiting in the wings with ambitious plans to reconstruct the city and refashion its society. While the Soviet occupation forces in Berlin relied on German émigré communists and local German antifascists to run low-level occupation administrations, in Königsberg, the Red Army organized the administration entirely on its own.[12] They received little guidance from Moscow about how to make Königsberg Soviet—only a few general orders to rebuild the region's industry and agriculture and to filter the population, both Germans and Soviet repatriates (former POWs or forced labors who ended up on German soil at the end of the war), to identify opposition figures, spies, and other dangerous elements.[13]

Yet Königsberg was becoming Soviet even without a plan from above. The first wave of transformation began as a violent and immediate consequence of the Red Army invasion. Because East Prussia was the first land where the Soviet invaders saw the bulk of the civilian population not as victims to be liberated but as the fascists themselves, occupation forces established their rule more violently than they had when liberating German-occupied territories. But even as the soldiers destroyed farms and villages and raped and executed tens of thousands of German civilians, they started to transform the ruins of the old civilization in their own image as a natural consequence of their scramble to organize an occupation.[14] By commandeering large aristocratic estates and small farms houses to quarter the soldiers, they ended up nationalizing private property; by dismantling the remains of factories and sending tractors and other farm equipment to the Soviet Union as reparations, they began to reorganize Königsberg's industry, even as they dismantled it, and to collectivize formerly private farms.

On the surface, the Königsberg region provided an auspicious stage for rapid Sovietization. Because the majority of the Nazi party and government elite had fled or had died in the invasion, there were virtually no groups left to oppose Soviet rule besides a few straggling bands of *Werwolf* guerilla fighters, quickly apprehended by the late summer of 1945.[15] Wartime devastation likewise eliminated the traces of virtually all German government institutions and most private commerce. By contrast, underground nationalist groups and guerilla fighters mounted harsh resistance to Sovietization in the Baltics and western Ukraine well into the late 1940s. And in the reannexed Baltic republics of Lithuania, Latvia, and Estonia, unlike in Soviet East Prussia, private farms and businesses continued to operate in the first postwar years, despite initial Sovietization in 1940–41.[16]

Yet Königsberg's great demographic and political upheaval proved not to be a clean slate, but ultimately the greatest challenge to establishing

Soviet rule. East Prussia was one of the most heavily damaged regions in Eastern Europe. The Wehrmacht's scorched-earth retreat combined with Red Army pillage to decimate the countryside, and the extended wartime occupation and mass flight of the rural population destroyed East Prussia's farmlands, most of which remained barren during the critical spring planting season. Dwindling food supplies and contaminated water left the remaining civilian population and POW population weak and vulnerable to disease. The region's administrative and geographical isolation further compounded these problems: the Kremlin and Soviet military command in Berlin ordered the Special Military District to rebuild with virtually no outside funding or supplies and offered little specific guidance about how to go about it.[17]

Königsberg's Sovietization thus was guided especially by the Red Army's local administration. Although the leadership of the Special Military District's provisional government were well-established military leaders—forty-seven-year-old Galitskii had been named a Hero of the Soviet Union for his role in storming Königsberg—the majority of officers and soldiers were on average young and inexperienced outside their service in the war. Most of them had not completed higher education, and many had not made it far past elementary school; others had their studies cut short when the war broke out in 1941. Many of the local military leaders were Communist Party members. Whereas in Nazi Germany, party membership had been easy to obtain, in the Soviet Union, membership in the Communist Party was supposed to be endowed only after rigorous training, earnest study of communism's sacred texts, and a prolonged period of candidacy. But in 1945, a large percentage of Communist Party members were new recruits who had been fast-tracked into party membership as a reward for bravery in battle. Their wartime political training had been superficial, meaning that their understanding of socialism came less from the dedicated study of Marx, Lenin, or Stalin, and more from shared assumptions about the values of the Soviet project, based on their own life experiences and shaped especially by the war.[18] Furthermore, while the party's political officers operated within the Special Military District, Soviet Königsberg had no central hierarchy of Communist Party organs in operation. That meant, in practice, that although communist ideology was an implicit force steering Königsberg's Sovietization, there was little actual institutional oversight to ensure ideological purity. Whereas Königsberg's Nazi leadership had been well-educated economists, politicians, and ideologues who planned to hatch their version of the revolution in Königsberg as preparation for a greater national rebirth, Soviet Königsberg's revolutionaries were children of a revolution that was already in the middle of its life cycle. Soviet Königsberg's leaders were not individual schemers imagining what communism should be, but military administrators trying to import and implement state control according to an already-established Soviet model.

The Special Military District was compelled to act with significant autonomy. But it was not completely independent. It had to contend with large-scale directives from above, many of them out of touch with conditions on the ground. Such monumental yet unrealistic orders for construction and economic output were part of a common center/periphery conflict in the highly centralized command economy of the Soviet Union. Moscow often announced grand targets that failed to take into account local infrastructure, supply, and labor constraints, leaving regional authorities scrambling to fulfill the plan or risk harsh punishment. This dynamic was not unique to Königsberg, especially given that devastation and shortages were endemic across the Soviet Union in 1945, but it was especially pronounced because officials in Moscow had little understanding of what was happening in the faraway, newly acquired borderland.

Königsberg's German Problem

Although Moscow often issued unrealistic, big picture directives, it remarkably gave little indication about the long-term future of the territory or the role the remaining German population would play in it. The available archival record obscures the reason, but it seems to be the consequence not of intentional policy but of administrative neglect. From the summer of 1945 onward, the directors of newly established Soviet organizations and industries in Soviet East Prussia sent numerous requests to the Special Military District in the attempt to figure out how to deal with the Germans—how to register them, how to employ them, how to pay and feed them.[19] But the Special Military District had no answers, as it did not have the autonomy to determine the status of the German population on its own. Moscow agencies also issued no clear guidelines, leaving Königsberg administrators remained trapped in what the historian Ruth Kibelka calls "a general decision-making vacuum."[20]

One thing that was clear, however, was that Moscow made no plans to expel the Germans from Soviet East Prussia.[21] In the summer of

1945, millions of Germans were being driven out of Eastern and South-eastern Europe by their Polish, Czechoslovak, or Hungarian neighbors. The Allies' Potsdam Conference of July–August 1945 sought to regulate these wild expulsions by organizing them into "organized and humane" transits to the Allied Zones of Occupation.[22] But none of this applied to Königsberg's Germans. Königsberg and the surrounding lands, as Soviet territory, were outside the jurisdiction of the Potsdam agreements, the fate of the remaining Germans there was left entirely to the Soviet Union to decide.[23] Until the Potsdam Conference, German refugees who had fled westward during the invasion were even encouraged to return to their homes east of the Oder-Neiße Line, including to northern East Prussia; in some towns, the number of returnees was as great as 30 percent, and about 10 percent of the total population returned at the end of the war. Once the borders between Polish and Soviet East Prussia became fixed in mid-July 1945, however, no more Germans were permitted to return to Soviet East Prussia, and those already there were forbidden to leave.[24]

The lack of a plan to expel the Germans from Soviet East Prussia is especially remarkable given that the Soviet Union deported more people

FIGURE 8. German civilian refugees, unable to escape westward before the Red Army's arrival, return to their homes in East Prussia in the winter of 1945. Collection: Russian State Archive of Film and Documentary Photography (RGAKFD) Krasnogorsk.

than any other European state—about eight million between 1929 and 1952—and ethnic-based deportations and expulsions by the late 1930s had become a standard tool of Soviet population management. The Soviet Union deported or expelled over a dozen ethnic groups and forty class-based or political groups, including population exchanges and repatriations of ethnic Germans from the western borderlands after the Molotov-Ribbentrop Pact. After the war, Soviet authorities in the newly annexed western borderlands frequently used deportations as a preemptive security measure against potential resistance, to target the civilian base of guerrilla support, or for geopolitical reasons. Yet while deportations in the old territories of the Soviet Union became highly ethnic-based and indiscriminate by 1943, in the new western borderlands, Soviet policy did not take the form of indiscriminate mass ethnic cleansing. Instead, deportations remained selective and served to enforce traditional Soviet security and social policies—to weed out internal enemies (real or imagined), to destroy perceived fifth column support for foreign powers, to eliminate secessionist menaces, and to enforce collectivization.[25] In this context, the Germans of Soviet East Prussia, utterly defeated and posing little active security threat in 1945, did not become primary targets for mass deportation.

Yet while the Germans were set to remain on Soviet territory, it was also clear in the summer of 1945 that Soviet East Prussia was not slated to become a German Soviet socialist republic. Indeed, at Truman and Churchill's suggestion at the Potsdam Conference that East Prussia be set up with a temporary German administration and oversight by the four Allied powers, Stalin sharply retorted that if a German administration were established in Königsberg, even provisionally, "we'll throw it out, we'll definitely throw it out."[26] Thus, Stalin's wartime slogan that the "Hitlers come and go but the German people and the German state remain" proved only partially true in Königsberg, where only the German people were left.[27] The civilian population became a stateless people, no longer citizens of the defunct Third Reich, but not automatically citizens of the Soviet Union by virtue of living on Soviet territory.

Just as was the case with the region's reconstruction, Soviet administrators were left to improvise their handling of the Germans. In doing so, they were guided by their wartime experiences and by competing wartime discourses about fascism and the German enemy. During the first months of the occupation, the Red Army rhetoric regarding the German population remained one of conquest, following the wartime depiction of the Germans as perennially evil fascist beasts. Official discourse shifted in mid-April 1945, as the soldiers' uncontrolled violence threatened to prolong the war and damage the Red Army's reputation. With an eye to the postwar occupation, official Soviet discourse, while continuing to celebrate Great Russian virtue and heroism over the depraved German fascists, once again emphasized the universalist ideals of liberation, antifascism, and world socialism. Along with it, they revived the idea that not all Germans were irreparably fascist, and that some Germans were capable of being redeemed.

These rhetorical distinctions meant little in the first weeks of the occupation, however. Just as in the Allied occupations of Germany further to the west, the Soviets arrived in Königsberg as a victorious army rather than as liberators.[28] They treated the entire population as potentially complicit, and in order to secure the territory and weed out opposition, NKVD border guards began the process of filtration, rounding up all German civilians, POWs, former Soviet *Ostarbeiter*, and other forced laborers. Interrogators focused on determining who among the German civilian population, POWs, and Soviet repatriates had been active fascists or willing collaborators—ideologically committed Nazis, high-level officials, and members of party organizations. The filtration process was more extensive and longer-lasting in Soviet East Prussia than in the Soviet Zone of Occupation (future East Germany), where some low-level former Nazi party members even maintained prominent positions in government.[29] In Soviet East Prussia, violent interrogations lasted weeks, as the entire population of the province was quartered in makeshift internment camps, abandoned German barracks, and former Gestapo prisons. Tens of thousands of Germans and former forced laborers were revealed to be party activists, *Werwolf* guerrillas, or double agents.[30] Those deemed guilty were sent to detention camps, forced labor in Siberia, or were executed.[31] Thousands more died or succumbed to disease from the squalid conditions of detainment.[32] These filtrations also lasted longer than in the Soviet Zone of Occupation in Germany, well into the spring of 1946.[33]

Yet the ostensible purpose of these filtrations was not only to excise the irredeemably corrupted, but also to leave behind those who might still be saved. Elsewhere in the Soviet sphere of occupation, once unreliable elements were eliminated, new antifascist governments were permitted, with close oversight by Moscow, to build a socialist state. Remarkably, in the Allied Zones of Occupation in Germany and in German-majority areas in Poland and Czechoslovak territories (at least until the German expulsions), the Soviets were the first and most

willing of the Allies to encourage antifascist German political participation.[34] Local participation was the norm even within Soviet borders. In
the newly reannexed Baltic Republics, after the sweeping filtration of
populations, reinstated communist governments, with strong Moscow
guidance, were declared to be run by Lithuanian, Latvian, or Estonian
communists. These linked processes—purging unreliable elements and
setting up communist-led local governments—allowed for the titular
nationality of the territory to be declared collectively liberated from fascism, granted citizenship, and dissociated en masse from the crimes of
complicity and collaboration.[35] In Königsberg, by contrast, the Special
Military District established its own Provisional Administration for Civilian Affairs in the first weeks after the war to tend to the local German
population and the rebuilding process.[36] The crucial difference between
this government and others within the Soviet sphere was that, although
it was ostensibly set up for the Germans, it was not organized by them.
In Soviet East Prussia, the Königsberg Special Military District did not
permit the establishment of German-led antifascist institutions and
merely appointed local mayors (Russian: *burgomistry*, German: *Bürgermeister*) to serve as conduits between the Soviet officials and the German
population.[37] This absence of even a nominal German-led government is
striking, especially in contrast to Königsberg's Nazis' own imperial occupation: even Gauleiter Koch's Reichskommissariat Ukraine established
a Ukrainian National Rada to provide the illusion of national liberation
and sovereignty amid an inhumane, colonial occupation.

This divergence had profound consequences. The absence of a
German-led government meant that there was no ready mechanism
for mass redemption. That is, there was no means by which morally
uncompromised German antifascist leaders could, with Moscow's
blessing, declare the mass of the civilian population liberated from the
fascist regime and morally disentangled from its crimes. The German
civilians released from the first violent waves of filtration were allowed
to return to Königsberg and other towns and villages in Soviet East
Prussia. Just as was the case in the occupied zones in Germany, they
were tasked with rebuilding the devastated urban and rural environments.[38] These German civilians, however, fell somewhere on the spectrum between guilt and innocence—they had not been revealed during
interrogation to be 'active' fascists, nor had they been charged with
any specific crimes. But they were understood to be still in some way
complicit, corrupted by fascism. Although they comprised virtually
the entirety of the population of Soviet East Prussia, they remained

stateless, not deemed collectively liberated by virtue of being citizens of a postwar antifascist state. They were, as a result, not explicitly designated as the beneficiaries of the new, more humane society they were tasked with building. The Germans' redemption from fascism was partial and unfinished. In 1945, the terms by which they could be declared definitively rehabilitated, either collectively or as individuals, remained unclear.

This ongoing legal and moral ambiguity had profound consequences. Budget problems related to the Germans' indeterminate status further deepened conditions of privation. The Special Military District's provisional administration frequently made requests to the Military Command in Berlin and to civilian institutions in Moscow for food and money to feed the Germans and pay them for their labor, but no external organizations felt obligated to include provisions for Soviet East Prussia's German population in their already over-stretched budgets.[39] Uncertainty about what role the Germans would play served to prolong the violent wartime relations between the Soviet occupiers and German civilians. Relations between Germans and Soviets improved rapidly in the first weeks of the occupation of Berlin and Breslau/Wrocław; however, sexual violence, looting, and theft remained widespread in Königsberg for several months.[40] A less tangible but long-term profound consequence was that the Germans' unclear pathway to integration into Soviet society left a sense among Soviet local leaders that Germans still needed to be converted in some way in order to be redeemed.

Laboratory of Death

Amid this ambiguity surrounding the Germans' fate, postwar Königsberg became a laboratory of death—an experiment in what happens to human beings in extreme hardship. Wartime devastation, isolation and endemic shortages, and the violence of early Sovietization combined to destroy the natural and built environment's ability to sustain life. Germans inside Fortress Königsberg had begun to suffer from food shortages already in the last weeks of the siege, and heavy fighting between Soviet and German soldiers destroyed water and sewer systems, demolished food production plants, and created prime conditions for the spread of disease. But the Red Army's acts to secure the territory, necessary from a military standpoint, perpetuated the unfolding catastrophe and made it all the more deadly. As a result, food shortages remained more dire and longer-lasting than elsewhere in the Soviet-occupied territories. All of the former German East became an epidemic zone in the immediate postwar period, but Soviet East Prussia, because of the wartime occupation and the peculiarities of its occupation, had the worst conditions of all. In Soviet East Prussia, continual epidemic outbreaks of typhus, typhoid fever, and dysentery led to the greatest infection rates and mortality in all of postwar Europe.[41]

The Red Army filtrations in East Prussia were more violent, wide-sweeping, and prolonged than further west because they were the first filtrations to take place on German soil.[42] The initial filtrations took place over the course of the spring and summer of 1945, but the single largest action took place in Königsberg after the siege. In order to scour the city for hidden mines and to root out opposition, the Red Army marched every inhabitant outside the city—primarily German civilians, but also POWs and forced laborers—on extended "propaganda marches," as Germans disparagingly referred to them, in an uneasy analog to the Nazis' death marches just two months before.[43] Because the marches were swiftly organized and civilians were marched at gunpoint, civilians had little opportunity to prepare for the journey, and Red Army soldiers, eager to collect trophies to send home, confiscated food and valuables and forcibly exchanged clothing on the spot— a soldier upgrading his ragged shirt and worn boots by identifying a better-dressed German of similar size. Because there were few places to house tens of thousands of captives, the marches sometimes lasted weeks, traveling in circles, as the prisoners became dehydrated, hungry, and increasingly suffering from intestinal ailments. By the time they reached their internment camps—often an old church, an abandoned estate, or former military barracks—many of them were barefoot with only the shirts on their backs.

Uprooted from the means to produce or procure their own food, the German civilians became completely dependent on their captors. The conditions of containment, however, only worsened the spread of disease. Michael Wieck, the German, half-Jewish teenager who had survived the war in Königsberg, recalls that when his group of civilians reached Rothenstein, a former barracks a few kilometers northeast of the city, they were crammed into windowless cellars with twenty to forty men sleeping on top of one another.[44] They were fed once a day a thin watery soup and stale bread covered in mold, but because there were no bowls, only those who could fashion some makeshift container had any way to eat.[45] Most German women and girls were raped by Red Army soldiers during the internment, often repeatedly, leading to the rapid spread of sexually transmitted diseases.[46] As Wieck remembers, the sounds of women being raped were "unbearable" to the imprisoned German men who could do nothing to stop it: "screams, cries for help, shots, whimpering, and more cries for help. . . . The backdrop to all of it was Königsberg newly engulfed in flames."[47] Doctor Hans Count von Lehndorff, the East Prussian surgeon and aristocrat who assumed control of a military hospital at the end of the siege, was recruited by the Soviet administrators of the camp to care for the sick. The contaminated water supply and squalid living conditions led to a mass epidemic outbreak, and by the end of April, Lehndorff wrote that he and his fellow doctors had to spend a part of each day collecting the dead. "In time there were about thirty-six corpses," he wrote one day in his diary, "all men, piled up in a heap three feet high in the wash-room. (The women hold out longer.) Many were almost naked, their clothes having been appropriated by others against the cold."[48] Internees in all of the Allied Zones of Occupation were housed in makeshift camps, where they frequently lacked adequate food, clothing, and medical care. But whereas relatively few prisoners starved in these other internment camps, including in the Soviet Zone of Occupation, in the harsh conditions of Soviet East Prussia, a great number of them died.[49] The surviving civilians were released, weeks later, to Königsberg and other towns and villages, but they found conditions even worse than those they had left. Much of the city's housing had already been destroyed in the August 1944 bombing, and even less remained after the protracted siege and the soldiers' jubilant arson in the wild first weeks of occupation. When Wieck and his family returned to the city after weeks of internment, they found that their apartment building, still habitable in the days after the surrender, had been burned down to the cellar. "Ruins, nothing but ruins. Only seldom here and there was there a half-burned and—shockingly—a fully undamaged house."[50]

As the remaining civilians sought shelter in the ruins, the Special Military District instituted a forced labor regime to begin rebuilding. Just as in other spheres of Soviet and Allied occupation, authorities required Germans civilians and POWs to clear the rubble from the streets and bury the dead.[51] In the occupied zones in Germany, US, British, French, and Soviet administrations tended to assign unpleasant tasks (agricultural work, grave digging, manual labor) to former Nazi party members and reserved lighter tasks, such as peeling potatoes, for women. But forced labor lasted far longer in Soviet East Prussia, and the terms were more severe. All able-bodied Germans, from teenagers to the elderly, were forced to work ten or more hours per day, seven days per week. By contrast, in some other Allied occupation zones, mandatory labor was only required for party members; the US administration in Mannheim required all Germans to work, but only for one day a week.[52] In Soviet East Prussia, women were tasked with hard manual labor because so few able-bodied men remained among the civilian population. Käthe Hielscher, a teenager at the time, recalls in her memoirs the dread she and her mother felt when the work commandos came for them in the mornings, shouting in a mixture of German and Russian, "*Raustreten, dawei, dawei!*" ("Come out! Come on, come on!"). In 1945 alone, Hielscher worked at several construction sites, cleaned furniture for storage, hauled rail ties to change German tracks to Soviet gauges, and sorted German soldiers' uniforms for recycling. Hielscher and her mother were dispatched on short notice to a farm for the summer, where the workers, most of them women, the majority of them barefoot. The work was arduous, and they were only allowed to return to Königsberg after falling ill with typhoid fever.[53]

Forced labor was necessary to separate the living from the dead and to create the conditions for the city once again to sustain life. But not enough food was available to feed the workers, and not enough workers were available to produce food. Although the military command immediately established rations for workers, in the wild and destructive free-for-all of victory, weeks passed before dwindling Wehrmacht food stores could be organized and distributed. German civilians and former foreign laborers were left to scour bomb shelters for canned foods and to carve meat from the corpses of dead horses in the streets.[54] Wieck recalled how he and his family rummaged through cellars for "Dr. Oetker's pudding mix, vanilla sugar, a can of vegetables, or, when someone had great luck, meat and sausage conserves. You ate whatever you could find."[55] Over the summer of 1945, as food ran out, more Germans became weakened from malnutrition and disease, and the number of able-bodied workers declined, further delaying the urgent tasks to restore city life. Only about half of the German civilians registered in Königsberg in October 1945 were adults of working age (36,270 out of a total registered population of 65,137). But only around 17,000 of them—one-quarter of the registered German population—were deemed by Soviet authorities as being able-bodied enough to work.[56]

Caught in this cycle, Königsberg became a site of mass death. Disease outbreaks, especially typhoid fever, reached epidemic proportions across Eastern Europe in the wake of the German defeat, but Soviet

East Prussia had the worst disease and mortality rates.[57] The incomplete archival record make it impossible to determine exactly how many Germans died from hunger or disease in the first year. After the borders stabilized, a territory-wide count on September 1, 1945 registered 129,614 German civilians remaining Soviet East Prussia (down from a broad estimate of 150,000 to 200,000 in April 1945), just over half of them in Königsberg. Using Soviet population counts, the Kaliningrad historian Iurii Kostiashov estimates that about 30 percent of the German population died between the end of the war and November 1946, when the reported German population sank to 90,991.[58] The German doctor Hans Deichelmann estimated in the summer of 1945 that nine out of ten infants in the hospital where he worked did not survive, and that 40 percent of all of the patients were buried in the yard behind the building.[59] Incomplete reporting and seasonal labor migration makes it impossible to determine comprehensive mortality rates, but even Soviet archival records indicate approximately 20 percent mortality for the city of Königsberg's German population between June 1945 and January 1946. The entire German population of Soviet East Prussia decreased an additional 8 percent in the following four months between February and May 1946. Population counts had stabilized and borders were mostly closed by that time, meaning that almost all of the decline came from death.[60] By comparison, one-third of the 122,671 people interned in the Soviet Zone of Occupation's prison camps—where prisoners faced the harshest, most inhumane living conditions in all of postwar Germany—died between 1945 and 1949.[61] But in Soviet East Prussia, at least a quarter of the free German population, by even modest estimates, died from malnutrition or disease in the first year alone.[62]

In the city caught between death and life, all of the green spaces that did not become kitchen gardens to feed the population became cemeteries to bury the dead. Wieck, then a young teenager, recalls how he was tasked with searching the rubble for corpses to bury; among the bodies he found on his first day was that of a partially naked young woman who had dried blood crusted on her mouth and vagina. She had "a fine, soft face," he wrote, and he and his teammate carried her by the arms and legs out onto the street and "threw her into the nearest crater."[63] Iurii Ivanov, a Russian teenager who survived near-starvation in the Leningrad Blockade and made his way to Königsberg by traveling with the Red Army, also recalls these ever-present encounters with death. In his novelized memoir, the young narrator likewise finds himself on a funeral team, working together with Russian and German hospital patients to bury the stacks of bodies lined up outside.[64] The symbolism of death was not lost on the people who survived. Wieck named a chapter of his memoir "Cemetery Königsberg." Ivanov named his memoir *Tantsii v krematorii* (*Dances in the Crematorium*). Deichelmann, who worked at a hospital for infectious disease, published his diary under the title *Ich sah Königsberg sterben* (*I Saw Königsberg Die*).

The most prominent diarists and memoirists to chronicle the German experience in postwar Soviet Königsberg were medical doctors such as Deichelmann—they were among the most well-educated witnesses to remain in the city as other civilians fled the Red Army's advance. These German doctors focused especially on the high incidence of epidemic disease in their diaries and later memoirs. The infectious disease doctor Wilhelm Starlinger blamed the "hermetically sealed space" of Königsberg for the outbreak, noting that "it seemed . . . as if fate and nature wanted to test what human beings could endure and how they would handle themselves during rampant epidemics."[65] Lehndorff pointed out that the epidemic diseases plaguing Soviet East Prussia, namely typhoid fever, typhus, diphtheria, dysentery, and malaria, were all diseases civilized Central Europe had pushed outside its borders at least eighty years prior.[66] For Lehndorff, the epidemic outbreak was evidence of the barbarity of the Russians, the flood of primitive conditions into a civilized land.

But these conditions, while exacerbated by the forceful implementation of Soviet rule, had been, in a larger sense, already created by the war itself. Soviet POWs, Jews, and other Soviet citizens had suffered similar fates at the hands of the Nazis during the war. The destitute conditions in Nazi camps and ghettos had been created by design and were perpetuated intentionally to bring about the mass extermination of people they deemed unworthy of life. To the German civilians living and dying in postwar Königsberg, the Soviets appeared to be equally anti-humanist. Numerous German witnesses and generations of later historians argued that the Soviets merely exploited the Germans for their labor and allowed them to starve thereafter—an analog to Nazi policies in Ukraine. The memoirist Hildegard Rosin recalled decades later, for example, that "the Russian authorities did not seem to be concerned" about the Germans' mass death, while the popular historians Eberhard Beckherrn and Alexej Dubatow argue that "it seemed that the Soviets wanted to get rid of the Germans simply by leaving them to their fate."[67] But in the case of Königsberg, no evidence exists that the Soviet authorities condoned the conditions that created mass death or celebrated the outcome. By contrast, the record suggests that, after the initial violent establishment of the occupation, local Soviet authorities tried everything in their limited power to reverse the unfolding catastrophe. By then, however, it had spiraled out of control.

The Struggle over Space and Time

The Red Army had arrived as an army of conquest, but in establishing an occupation, it found itself called on to assume the role of the state. After the first weeks of interrogations, the Red Army's pressing task was to rebuild the devastated city and countryside. They sought to do so in large part to contain the epidemic contagion, which threatened the lives of the German population and increasingly the lives of the Red Army soldiers and officers themselves. Because Germans constituted virtually the entirety of the population and the primary workforce, the tasks of rebuilding the city and rescuing the Germans from death proved to be inseparable. Success depended on the Soviet occupiers' ability to assert control as quickly as possible over the collection, production, and distribution of the city's remaining resources. This process of Sovietization became a battle for the mastery over time and a struggle to assert control over space. Yet the military's efforts to rebuild and improve living conditions were constrained by the region's ongoing privation and its geographic and administrative isolation. Practices of Sovietization utterly transformed Königsberg in the first year after the war. But Königsberg started to become Soviet less so in response to the military occupation's plans, and more so in organic and pragmatic response to constant crisis.

The military government's greatest struggle was to nationalize the city's remaining resources. The most valuable and urgently needed of these, by far, was food. Hunger had already plagued the Soviet home front for years: the Soviet Union was the only major combatant to face mass starvation mortality during the war, in large part due both to the loss of agricultural lands to the German occupation and the extreme, long-term mobilization of the home front to produce supplies for the defense.[68] When Fortress Königsberg fell on April 9, 1945, the Red Army issued orders immediately to collect the city's remaining stockpiles and Wehrmacht supplies. By mid-April, it established the first rations for the German and Soviet population of the conquered territory. The Soviet state had developed a complex wartime ration system designed to feed Soviet soldiers and civilians, structured around

FIGURE 9. Soviet soldiers and cargo trucks transit through the ruins of Königsberg on April 10, 1945 after the end of a three-day siege. Collection: Russian State Archive of Film and Documentary Photography (RGAKFD) Krasnogorsk.

basic hierarchies of allocation: soldiers at the front were fed better than civilians in the rear, and provisions were based roughly on a labor principle of caloric expenditure.[69] The Special Military District adopted a similar practice at the end of the war. The number of calories and types of food varied by group—German POWs, injured soldiers in hospitals, German civilians, and Soviet citizens all had different rations—but the main determinant for the number of calories was based not on being German or Soviet, but according to the difficulty of labor. Construction workers, no matter their nationality, were slated to receive more food than those working less strenuous labor, and certain groups of Soviet citizens and former forced labor repatriates, along with German POWs and civilians working under direct Red Army command, were slated to be fed according to the Third Norm, the military's standard rations for noncombat troops.[70] Still, because supplies were so scarce, the rations for all workers, even Soviets, were insufficient. Early proposed rations were as low as 200 grams of bread per day (about 500 calories) for nonarduous labor, although they doubled on average by mid-May 1945. And in practice, these rations existed mostly on paper. Funds and food were invariably not available to feed the workers according to the stated norms. In August 1945, for example, the Military Council of the Third Belorussian Front, instead of delivering a month's worth of rations for the civilian population and Soviet administrators of the Special Military District, provided just five to six days' worth of rations for administrators only, refusing to send any food to feed the Germans at all. General-Major Mikhail Pronin, the first head of the district's Provisional Administration for Civilian Affairs, begged the Military Soviet of the Front to reconsider, explaining that if Königsberg did not receive the funds from somewhere, "the personnel I bear responsibility for will be left with nothing to eat."[71] As numerous diaries and memoirs note, Germans, especially, were often left to fend for themselves. "We lived almost entirely from Russian kitchen scraps," recalls Marga Pollmann, who scrounged to feed herself and her small children with "potato peels, bones, and fish carcasses."[72]

In a rush to produce more food, the new government utterly reshaped both the rural and urban environments. Within a year, all private farms in Soviet East Prussia were collectivized—that is, conglomerated into large central farms under direct state or military control. This rapid transformation of agriculture was, in many ways, a telescoping of the Soviet revolution: collectivization in the old territories of the Soviet Union had begun in the late 1920s but had taken a few years to complete. That first collectivization in the Soviet Union had also been especially violent. In the early 1930s, around the same time that Koch and Königsberg's Nazis were forced to postpone their "Bolshevik-style" plans for agriculture amid resistance in the countryside, Soviet leaders pushed through the collectivization at all costs. Stalinist zealousness, forced grain requisitions, and the suppression of peasant resistance led to a famine that killed six to eight million people in Soviet Ukraine, Kazakhstan, and Russia.[73] After the war, Soviet East Prussia was collectivized more rapidly than any other European region undergoing Sovietization because the population was completely uprooted and many farms abandoned. The Red Army established numerous military state farms already in the spring of 1945, and amid dire demographic conditions and the German defeat, no organized resistance emerged to slow the process. That summer, the Special Military District transformed green spaces within Königsberg, including parks, city squares, and front lawns, into garden plots for potatoes and root vegetables.[74] These kitchen gardens blurred the distinction between city and countryside, just as the forced deployment of over 10,000 German city dwellers from Königsberg to work in the fields in some sense 'urbanized' the rural environment. By the start of the 1946 planting season, the entirety of East Prussian agriculture had been folded into state farms. East Prussia's collectivization was the most rapid in the Soviet sphere of influence. The neighboring Baltic republics only slowly began collectivization in 1948, by contrast. In East Germany further west, collectivization only took place over the course of the 1950s, and even then it was a process marked by opposition and reversals.[75]

Rapid collectivization failed miserably. A disastrous harvest the first year left much of the population facing even greater hunger by winter. Wartime devastation played a role here, too, as the Wehrmacht and Red Army's destruction of the fields and the flight of the rural population during the invasion delayed planting and damaged the soil. But as the historian Arūnė Arbušauskaitė points out, much of the destruction of agriculture took place in the summer of 1945.[76] In East Prussia, the tragedy stemmed not explicitly from some inherent unsuitability of state-led mass agriculture (although forceful collectivization had also led to poor grain yields and a terrible harvest in the Soviet Union in the 1930s). After all, Königsberg's Nazis had dreamed of such a model for East Prussia in their technocratic fantasies to address the region's harsh climate and poor soil. Instead, the disaster stemmed in part from the early violence of the occupation, in which soldiers continued to treat the region as foreign soil, pilfering rural estates for trophies to send back home, despite the administration's attempts to curtail the practice. Even worse, while the Special Military District scrambled to produce food, Soviet reparations teams, under national orders, were collecting the mass of East Prussia's agricultural equipment and raw materials—tractors, plows, hand tools, and even livestock—to send back to the Soviet mainland as reparations. The stripping of the land caused lasting damage to agriculture and hindered its recovery for several years.[77]

The mass flight of the population and delayed spring planting left the Red Army occupiers little choice but to establish collective farms. But, without necessary local knowledge about the landscape, they imported Soviet mass farming practices ill-suited to East Prussian soil.[78] As a large expanse of East Prussia lay on converted marshlands, the soils required complex drainage networks, many of which Gauleiter Koch had rallied Germans to build in his early depression-era employment campaigns. But Red Army state farms employed Soviet soldiers and German civilians and POWs who had little agricultural experience. The field workers dug too deep, bursting irrigation pipes and flooding the fields. By February 1945, the head of the Provisional Administration for Civilian Affairs Viktor Gerasimovich Guzii lamented that "the quality of the land is getting progressively worse" because the fields had been left unfertilized for spring and the drainage networks had fallen apart. Over 20,000 hectares of arable land had flooded, turning much of East Prussia into a swamp.[79]

Meanwhile, the Special Military District also struggled to gain control over the region's existing resources.[80] In the jubilation of the victory celebrations, Red Army soldiers had become accustomed to treating food and material objects as personal trophy, and they resisted turning these goods over to the state.[81] Because food remained scarce, pilfering, petty theft, and 'skimming off the top' were often the only ways to guarantee a meal, especially because the state did not always provide the rations it promised. On August 27, 1945, for example, the military tribunal reported the case of three Red Army soldiers caught stealing potatoes. They had served with the 50th Army but had been hospitalized with typhus infections. They were sent to work at a city warehouse upon recovery, but because their status in the military budget then became unclear, they were not issued rations cards. As the tribunal reported, "They did not receive food as Red Army soldiers, so they went to a garden plot in the Fifth Military District and dug up twenty potatoes to eat. Along with that, they said that German women were also there with baskets. It was known to them that the German women frequently came to the garden for potatoes. It needs to be said that the majority of potato theft is by German women because of the absence of security."[82] The military tribunal, while admitting that the soldiers had not been paid or fed, still charged them with theft. When the city's population—Germans and Soviets alike—became victims of the broken distribution system, they had to break the law in order to eat. At first, the administration treated petty theft as a problem of organization and discipline. It frequently issued orders reminding soldiers that German consumer goods, warehouse stores, and food supplies were no longer their personal trophies. But by November 1945, as the first winter set in, the military command denounced the ongoing pilfering as an intentional act committed against state power.[83] But as long as there was not enough food to go around, pilfering remained as endemic as hunger itself.

Even as the Special Military District was struggling to feed the population, organizations in Moscow began issuing their own targets for reconstruction and export. Their demands came with little understanding of the endemic shortages plaguing the city. Soviet expansion into Eastern Europe was driven more by motives of geopolitical security rather than colonial-style economic resource extraction (in contrast to Nazi plans for the East). But Stalin and other Soviet leaders did view Königsberg as a major economic prize. In the spring of 1945, still during the siege, Soviet reconnaissance teams reported on the city's economic potential for the Soviet state. In May 1945, a Moscow special commission ordered that a number of the city's large-capacity wartime industries be revived, including the Schichau shipbuilding plant, two paper milling factories, and the Steinfurt train car factory, as well as smaller industries connected to Königsberg's harbor.[84] German and Soviet labor teams were tasked with reconstructing these factories alongside smaller plants that tended to Königsberg's local food supply and construction economy: flour mills, bakeries, brick factories, lumber yards, repair garages, metal-working factories, spirits factories, a meat production plant, the radio station, telephone and telegraph stations, a laundry service, and the natural gas works. A few of these plants came into operation by the winter of 1946, employing an estimated 11,000 German POWs as the primary workforce.[85] Continuing delays and shortages, however, led to production bottlenecks.[86] Shortages of raw materials thwarted efforts to produce building supplies and construction equipment, meaning that other factories remained in ruins for years.[87] Vehicle and fuel shortages likewise created roadblocks to reconstruction. Most of the captured German cars and trucks fell into disrepair by the winter of 1946, and without parts to repair them or gasoline to fuel them, city work crews could not transport materials to construction sites. The provisional government petitioned central authorities numerous times for more vehicles, but as late as May 1947, local officials complained that the repeated requests "still remain unmet."[88] In one particularly absurd example of the mismatch between Moscow's growing expectations and conditions on the ground, USSR Council of People's Commissars minister Aleksei Kosygin ordered in February 1946 that three coastal villages be transformed into official workers' vacation resorts and supplied with 200 horses.[89] A week later, however, a representative from the Military Soviet explained that the district only owned 588 horses, making it impossible to transfer one-third of them to a seaside resort.[90] Pressure to rebuild for industrial export only worsened living conditions, especially when combined with the poor harvest and the military administration's ongoing struggle to gain control over the region's resources.

Still, Königsberg was slowly becoming Soviet. The change did not always come from the new regime's plans for the intentional transformation of space and place—many of which were plagued by setbacks and inefficiency—but from the organic rebirth of city life between the cracks of those efforts. As a new Königsberg was emerging from the rubble, the city's previous German foundations guided its development. Surviving walls and foundations dictated the placement of reconstructed buildings, and the old town's cobblestone streets, once cleared from debris, guided traffic through the ruins along familiar prewar routes. Wartime factories, once revived, began producing the many of the same goods as before, and even the physical structures of the Nazi state apparatus found new life with strikingly similar uses. Nazi barracks housed the soldiers of the victorious army, former prisons run by Germans became internment camps to house them, and the Gestapo headquarters became the base of operations for the Soviet NKVD.

But bric-a-brac, pragmatic reconstruction in the first year also began to reshape Königsberg into a dramatically altered city. Because the historic city center was over 90 percent destroyed, a new locus of urban life developed in the once-stately northwest suburbs of Hufen and Amalienau just outside the old city ring, where the damage from bombing and siege was still significant but estimated at only 60 percent. The Hufen district had once showcased the city's most prominent Weimar-era projects to encourage trade with the East, including Königsberg's once-famous *Ostmesse* (Eastern Exhibition Center) and the House of Technology—the ruins of these buildings became ad hoc open-air market places. Nearby remained the grand turn-of-the-century villas that just months before had housed the Nazi elite, including Gauleiter Koch.[91] As the provisional military administration established its headquarters there, it repurposed old buildings in new ways, transforming commercial spaces into housing for soldiers and refitting stately residential homes into military command offices or makeshift store fronts.[92]

Despite Soviet attempts to nationalize supply and distribution, a market economy popped up in this new center of urban life, as entrepreneurial Germans opened private shops in old store fronts, apartment buildings, and cellars to sell household goods gathered from the rubble. The reemergence of the barter economy shows the flexibility of Sovietization: the military administration mostly tolerated this spontaneous growth of private trade because it was unable otherwise to produce and distribute household goods. By the fall of 1945, Soviet authorities even levied taxes on the stores' proprietors, initially in German marks and later in Soviet rubles.[93] Once official Soviet-run state shops began to open in the winter of 1945–46, these private stores gradually disappeared. But because the official stores still could not supply the population with sufficient rations and food, informal local markets popped up once again in the ruins. Improvised trade turned into an established network of buyers and sellers, a genuine second economy in a region that still struggled to establish an official one.[94]

The rest of the city developed in small pockets on the far outskirts of the old city center, where damage from bombing and fires was less significant. But these neighborhoods were separated from the new de facto city center by as much as ten kilometers of wasteland with no public transportation to connect them. Utility plants and major municipal organizations were rebuilt in their original locations, making the separation of these neighborhoods more pronounced, as critical city services were scattered in several inaccessible places. For example, Königsberg's surviving hospitals, mostly located in the old city center, were surrounded almost completely by ruins. The single office set up to register births, marriages, and deaths was located over a dozen kilometers from other neighborhoods in town. With the population scattered over great distances, the newly established post office sometimes took weeks to deliver telegrams and months to deliver letters. As Königsberg's surviving roads radiated from an empty city center, traveling between neighborhoods remained arduous even after rudimentary public transit was reestablished in late 1946. The new city center lay on the northwest side of the Pregel River, but many of the reestablished factories were located on the southwest, meaning that the old "seven bridges of Königsberg" problem became a conundrum of a different sort: with only two surviving bridges crossing the river, workers had to travel several kilometers out of the way to reach the industries on the other side.[95]

Victors and Vanquished

The ongoing privation in this rubble city served to further broaden the divide between Soviets and Germans. With not enough resources to go around, the Red Army took care of its own first, and then other Soviet civilians. The Germans, as a stateless population still complicit with fascism, got what little supplies remained. Unequal access to goods created an economy of shortages—an emergent hierarchy along the lines of citizenship but corresponding with ethnicity. In Nazi Germany, ethnic and biological racism had served as an explicit organizing principle for government and was used, especially in the occupied East, to justify the inhumane treatment of populations under German rule. The multiethnic Soviet Union publicly denounced such racism and exclusionary ethnic nationalism. Despite rising wartime Russian patriotism, it positioned itself in direct opposition to fascism's vulgar, anti-humanist elevation of race over class.[96] Postwar German historians denounced the Soviet treatment of the remaining German civilians, especially the emerging ethnic hierarchy, pointing to it as evidence of the Soviet occupiers' ongoing malicious revenge and the hypocrisy of Bolshevism.[97] But the worsening conditions of the Germans in Soviet Königsberg did not stem primarily from Red Army's continuing desire to punish them. Instead, they arose first and foremost as a consequence of the structural funding problems. These problems were further compounded by the Germans' ambiguous legal and moral status in the eyes of the new Soviet government.

By all accounts, the military occupation remained violent in the early days. Mass rape was endemic for weeks after the siege, as soldiers continued exacting their revenge in drunken victory jubilations. Soviet authorities did not condone the violence, however. Military command offices began stationing guards around German settlements in Königsberg, restricting soldiers' access to alcohol during celebrations, and threatening any soldiers who visited German quarters at night with arrest for disorderly conduct.[98] The administration even attempted to prevent cohabitation or other informal contact between Soviets and Germans entirely. At first they cited security concerns. But the real danger, as reports admitted, was that large numbers of soldiers were "having contact with the German population" (a euphemism for sexual violence), leading to a dramatic "increase in the percentage of venereal disease."[99] Separation measures proved impossible to enforce, and Germans and Soviets settled spontaneously throughout the city, on the same streets, in the same buildings, and sometimes even in the same apartments. By the early summer of 1945, Soviet authorities managed to crack down on mass sexual violence. But because the Germans had no local government representation designed to advocate for their interests and no formalized procedure for reporting crimes committed against them, individual Soviet soldiers and civilians continued pursuing German women as targets for their lust and rage. The German memoirist Hielscher recalls that the threat of rape remained constant for years, particularly when bosses turned a blind eye to their Soviet employees' escapades. The rapists, no longer able to conduct their business in the open, instead picked off women one by one during the day and took them to private quarters out of sight. Hielscher was first raped in the summer of 1945—it was the first sexual encounter she had ever had in her life.[100]

Although overt violence against Germans decreased in the summer of 1945, Germans remained an underclass in the economy of shortages. When food was scarce, Germans were the first to have their rations reduced. Red Army soldiers, Soviet civilians, and even former Soviet forced laborers (who were deemed suspect for having spent time abroad) were gradually incorporated into the military's standard rations system and were fed through a combination of outside funding and local resources. By contrast, rations for virtually all German workers had to come from local supplies. That meant that they varied significantly each month. In a draft budget from late October 1945, for example, administrators set modest rations for Germans that included various types of produce and even supplemental rations for highly qualified workers. But after new inventories revealed that pilfering and a poor harvest had significantly curtailed food stockpiles, the final budget removed all supplemental rations and downgraded total rations by 25 percent or more.[101] Whereas Germans employed in certain construction projects were slated to receive a cooked meal each day, by November 1945, meals for these German workers were eliminated because, as a report explained, "at the current moment, the People's Commissariat of Defense has completely stopped delivering food," and remaining supplies had to be used to feed Soviet citizens. The administration ambitiously set guidelines for supplying rations to German children and nonworking invalids as early as May 1945; in practice, however, the administration's ongoing struggles with supply and distribution meant that even able-bodied German workers were not consistently fed.[102] Children sometimes received dependent rations, but invalids and the elderly only rarely. The economy of shortages left German workers to divide their already meager bread rations with family members. Hielscher, a teenager at the time, recalled working extra shifts to earn food to share with her family, but her grandmother still starved to death within months.[103]

Likewise, because housing in the smoldering city ruins was scarce in April 1945, the administration occupied the best spaces and pushed out German inhabitants. Postwar expropriation of private property was common in all occupied German territories, but the housing shortage in Königsberg was especially acute, and the Special Military District required significant space per capita. Germans returning from weeks-long internment in May 1945 often found their former homes transformed into barracks or Red Army command offices. Housing shortages became even worse after the first weeks: Red Army officers and Soviet civilians arriving in Königsberg to work were guaranteed housing on arrival, so they were instructed to seek out an apartment not already inhabited by Soviet citizens. Germans living in those apartments were sometimes given as little as a few hours to vacate, and the furniture they had assembled from the ruins had to be left behind as the communal property for use by Soviet citizens. Wieck recalls that he and his parents were forced to move six times to successively more cramped and dirty accommodations.[104] Hielscher recall that in the spring of 1946, all of the Germans on her street were given a week to resettle to the neighboring street to make room for arriving Soviet citizens.[105] The Soviet new settler Manefa Shevchenko remembers this process of finding her own apartment when she arrived the following year:

> As I began to work in the school in 1947, it was hard for me to reach it because there were no trams. So my husband and I were given a permission slip to take possession of any house in the district of the school. We looked for a very long time and finally found a house that we liked. Four Germans lived there. The representatives of the housing administration told them to move out within twenty-four hours. Part of that, can you imagine, was that they were not allowed to take their things with them. That meant that they were allowed to take a bundle with them, but not more than two kilograms, and only in certain cases.[106]

By the summer of 1946, Germans for the most part no longer lived on the main floors of apartment buildings but in the cellars and attics of buildings inhabited by Soviet citizens or in semi-segregated neighborhoods in the ruins on the outskirts of town.[107]

Still, even with priority over the Germans for accommodation, the military administration and new Soviet settlers also suffered from housing shortages. After three months of reconstruction, many officers were still being housed in barracks together with soldiers, while others lived in apartments with absent or leaking roofs, missing windows, broken doors, and no water supply.[108] Despite ongoing reconstruction efforts, useable space in the city a year after the war remained at only a tenth of the prewar total. The Special Military District's offices and housing alone occupied 40 percent of it.[109]

Shortages and unequal distribution combined to make the winter of 1945–46 deadly. Food stores for the district were mostly depleted by November, and firewood collected for the German population ran out soon thereafter.[110] By early 1946, an average of eighty Germans in Königsberg were dying from starvation or cold each day.[111] During this hard winter, the Special Military District was able to petition successfully for supplemental resources for Soviet citizens: Soviet officers and their families received emergency supplements from the Military Trade Department while various organizations of the USSR Council of People's Commissars began providing funds for Soviet civilian workers. But although the Special Military District made repeated requests to fund the German population's rations, no organization agreed to take on responsibility. The USSR Council of People's Commissars finally incorporated the German population into a unified civilian trade and distribution system in January 1946. The measure was purely symbolic, however, as funding was still supposed to come entirely from local resources. As the commander of the Special Military District, General-Major Galitskii, warned in a report to Moscow in February 1946, "in so far as there are no resources in the District at all," the conditions for the Germans would only get worse. Galitskii blamed "insufficient food provided to the German population" for the "widespread dystrophy/starvation [*distrofiia/istoshchenie*]" and mass death that winter.[112] He fully understood the origins of the problem. He explained that the German population had been completely uprooted, "deprived of property and tools for production, [and] does not have its own farms, land, or apartments." The situation had been created "during the period of military action, when the population fled from our soldiers and upon returning found their apartments destroyed or occupied by other tenants," and was further aggravated by the frequent forced resettlements, "dictated by the military situation and by the necessity of quartering the troops."[113] Galitskii's report to Moscow shows that the Special Military District did not seek to perpetuate this ethnic hierarchy, nor did it rationalize it as a fitting punishment for the Germans' wartime crimes. Instead, the Soviet leadership saw it as an unfolding demographic tragedy that it had no power to stop. To solve the problem, he requested more funding and more food—for rations for German workers and invalids to be incorporated into the USSR Trade Department's budget.[114] The longer the delay in providing funding, he warned, the more

Germans would become sick and unable to work, thus continuing the deadly cycle into the next spring planting season.[115] Yet Galitskii's requests, at least for the duration of that winter, remained unmet.

Soviet leaders in Königsberg remained unable to resolve the ambiguity surrounding the Germans' legal status. They had no apparent means to redeem the Germans collectively—no ability to declare the Germans liberated en masse and eligible for Soviet citizenship. Yet, remarkably, amid the extreme hardship and emergent ethnic hierarchy, local Soviet officials did make efforts to resolve the ambiguity surrounding the Germans' moral status. Recognizing that the Germans had been contaminated by fascism, they tried in varying ways to rehabilitate the Germans individually and, in doing so, incorporate them into the socialist system. The suspicion that Germans were deeply, perhaps irreparably, corrupted with fascism still served as a deep story for many Soviet soldiers and officers. But at the same time, the Soviet military administration operated from the conviction that the world-historical victory over fascism had definitively proven the superiority of the socialist system and Soviet civilization over Nazi barbarism.[116] And, in line with the deeper internationalist tendency within Soviet ideology, they operated from the assumption that the Soviet mission was to spread the good news of socialism, even to former fascists.

The Soviet Union was a party-state conglomeration—like Nazi Germany, the Communist Party was supposed to provide ideological rigor and oversight to the activities of the government. But while numerous Red Army officers and administrators were party members, and while numerous party cells operated within the Special Military District, there was no full hierarchy of Communist Party organs in Königsberg's provisional government, and political education remained unsystematic well into 1947. Poor ideological training was also the case in Berlin and the rest of the Soviet Zone of Occupation, but in Königsberg, extreme isolation meant that no centralized authority was guiding local efforts to rehabilitate the Germans.[117] Antifascist political education had been set up to recruit German POWs during the war, but those methods were designed to encourage wartime resistance against Hitler. Meanwhile, postwar methods for political work developed in Berlin had no direct institutional means of spreading to Königsberg.[118]

Left to improvise, local Soviet administrators developed their own crude antifascism efforts. Early on, these grew out of the urgent need to resurrect the city from death and thus focused primarily on the redemptive power of hard work. Labor played a central role in Soviet ideology. Honest, socialist labor (labor for the good of society) was portrayed as a pathway to conversion and redemption. This rhetoric was in place in the Soviet Gulag camps—the idea that all human beings, no matter their prior conflagrations, could reform themselves through work to earn a place in the socialist collective. Despite the promise of redemption, living conditions in the closed-off world of the Gulag were as deadly and inhumane as in immediate postwar Königsberg. But the Gulag camps, unlike Nazi concentration camps, were also sites of mass release, where, in theory and at least some times in practice, redemption was possible.[119] Following this implicit template, local officials in Königsberg adopted the rhetoric that the German population could become the designated beneficiaries of socialism by aiding in its construction. To incentivize productivity, they attempted, even amid the forced labor regime, to incorporate rudimentary socialist labor incentives in the form of food bonuses for those who surpassed their work quotas. Because most of the population were women, children, and elderly who suffered from malnourishment, however, few could ever attain these bonuses. Perennial budget shortages, moreover, often prevented them from being paid.[120]

Still, the language of rehabilitation increasingly informed Soviet administrators' conversations over the course of 1945–46. Rhetoric gradually blurred the line between getting the Germans to work harder simply to raise their productivity and seeing their labor as a tool for converting them to socialism. This implicit connection appears in numerous party meetings in the summer and winter of 1945, during which Soviet officials emphasized the need for Germans to be educated about the value of collective labor. At the Closed Party Meeting of the Civilian Affairs Administration in Königsberg on June 20, 1945, for example, in discussions about improving German workers' productivity, one speaker, Shedov, called on communists to act as role models in order to "demonstrate culture to the German population," while another speaker, Livshits, pointed out that they should first focus on themselves. Livshits argued that "the outward appearance of officers, including communists" was poor, in part because communists did not "subject themselves to discipline." He called on communists to fight to fulfill daily orders and to increase their own productivity. Then, he explained, "we communists need to take the struggle to the German population to strengthen labor discipline."[121]

In the wake of mass rape and violence against the German civilians, many party speakers used these familiar tools of Bolshevik self-criticism to smooth relations between victors and vanquished. Likewise, a number of party members' speeches in the spring of 1946 echoed the need to set a good example in order to reform not only Germans (so they would work harder and recognize the superiority of the socialist system), but also the high number of Soviet repatriates who remained on the territory (an estimated 8,839 in May 1946).[122] In March 1946, for example, one communist, Major Gran, called on fellow party members to live according to high principles because they "come in contact not only with Russians, but also with the German population and should not forget about that, and should work so as not to discredit themselves." These speakers, by mentioning both German civilians and Soviet repatriates, considered the groups to be in a similar situation: morally compromised by exposure to fascism and therefore in need of individual rehabilitation.[123] These early speeches have in common an emphasis on the transformative power of labor (Germans and repatriates could be redeemed through education and labor discipline) and an inward direction of focus (communists needed first to improve themselves).

From the start, the tendency to focus on rehabilitating the Germans through socialist labor contained the possibility for failures in reconstruction to be directed outward—onto the Germans themselves. A case from the winter of 1946 illustrates this tendency. In February, the head of the Special Military District, Galitskii, and his assistant, Guards General Major Kulikov, issued a resolution addressed directly to the German population in response to the mass hardship. They rationalized the ongoing food shortages by pointing to harsh wartime battles, mass evacuations, and labor shortages in 1945. The administration's job, Galitskii and Kulikov explained, was to reconstruct the economy as quickly as possible. German civilians, they pointed out, were being given ample opportunities to improve their material situation through "honest and conscientious labor," and tens of thousands of Germans, "working honestly in industry and on farms," they insisted, were "receiving pay and a good supply of food." Speaking the language of rehabilitative labor, Galitskii and Kulikov reiterated to the German population that those Germans who worked toward socialist reconstruction would become its direct beneficiaries. But while blaming earlier food shortages on wartime destruction, the report explained that some "individual Germans" were "still not freed from the influence of lying Nazi propaganda, setting the German population against the Soviet government and the Red Army. By sabotaging the implementation of economic activities of military and civilian authorities, this part of the population harms itself and hinders the implementation of measures to improve the economic status of the entire German population." Galitskii and Kulikov's assignment of agency to the German population was a subtle shift of responsibility away from the administration. This resolution to the German population in Soviet Königsberg came the very same month that Galitskii wrote to Moscow to blame the Germans' mass death objectively on the endemic shortages and the failure to include the Germans in the Soviet budget. But when addressing the Germans directly, the Special Military District tied the Germans' physical well-being and their pathway to redemption directly to their labor. In this formulation, the failure of living conditions to improve was connected not to shortages, but to German intransigence and "the influence of lying Nazi propaganda."[124] Through this reversal, Germans' living conditions came to serve as a gauge of the Germans' successful rehabilitation, or the reverse—of their lingering fascist sympathies.

Almost one year after the war, Soviet Königsberg remained a city trapped between death and life. The ambiguity surrounding the German population's fate, combined with Königsberg's geographic isolation and dire material conditions, had led to a demographic tragedy in the wake of complete environmental collapse. As was the case elsewhere in Soviet-occupied Europe, Königsberg's Germans had been forced to work to rebuild. However, they received lower food rations and succumbed to malnourishment and epidemic disease at significantly higher rates. They also suffered treatment from their Soviet overseers that resembled, far longer than for German civilians elsewhere, the violent wartime dynamic between victors and vanquished.[125] Yet even as a de facto ethnic hierarchy emerged between Germans and Soviets in the postwar economy of shortages, Soviet officials raced to stop the unfolding catastrophe, rebuild the city, and keep its population alive.

In a report to the USSR Council of People's Commissars on the economy of Soviet East Prussia in February 1946, at the height of the Germans' mass death that winter, the head of the Special Military District Galitskii and the head of the Provisional Administration for Civilian Affairs Guzii presented a sobering account of the state of affairs. They argued that the Special Military District was supposed to be a temporary administration, not designed to manage Königsberg's reconstruction for so long. Insisting that the underfunded military occupation could survive no longer, they requested that the USSR "expedite the process of establishing organs of Soviet power" in Königsberg—that is, to fully incorporate the territory into the civilian government of the Soviet Union.[126] The transformation began less than two months later, on April 9, 1946—one year to the day since the Red Army conquered Fortress Königsberg. Soviet East Prussia was reconfigured as Königsberg Oblast and became merely one of nearly four dozen such districts within the Russian Soviet Federative Socialist Republic (RSFSR). On July 4, 1946, both city and oblast were renamed in honor of the recently deceased nominal head of state Mikhail Kalinin. They became Kaliningrad—the city of Kalinin.[127]

Although Kaliningrad was born, the transformation remained incomplete. It took almost two years for the full array of Soviet government and party institutions to be established in the new oblast. In the meantime, Kaliningrad's development was guided by a new Civilian Affairs Administration, which itself only gradually wrestled control from the military over the course of 1946 and 1947. Although the transition to civilian rule was supposed to rectify the problems created by the underfunded and disorganized military administration, the new Soviet city of Kaliningrad continued to suffer from many of the same problems as before. The oblast was not incorporated in time to be included in the Soviet Union's grand postwar five-year plan for economic development, meaning that it continued to fall through the cracks of the Soviet budget.[128] Kaliningrad remained desperately underfunded, and its leaders struggled to garner the attention of state and party institutions in Moscow in their appeals for money, labor, and supplies. The territory remained, as it had for much of the twentieth century, a borderland isolated from its empire's center of power but still dependent on it for survival.

CHAPTER 6

Living Together

Königsberg's Germans and new Soviet settlers to Kaliningrad lived together for over three years. Nowhere else did such a concentrated population of German and Soviet civilians come together after the war, and nowhere in East Central Europe did Germans remain for so long before their eventual expulsion.[1] Although the two groups met as representatives of mutually antagonistic ideologies, they slowly built a shared life together. For over a year, this process unfolded organically, in the absence of state oversight or through the cracks of state control. Germans and Soviets struggled side by side to survive in Kaliningrad's economy of shortages and, in doing so, developed new practices of everyday life in dialogue. The de facto ethnic hierarchy established at the end of the invasion shaped this encounter. With wartime roles reversed, Soviet citizens, many of them former *Ostarbeiter* in East Prussia, became the new dominant group, while Germans, the former 'master race' of Königsberg, lived on as Kaliningrad's underclass.

When the transitional civilian government took shape in the summer of 1946, its leaders sought to contain the development of this organic rubble civilization and reshape it in a Soviet form. The new civilian government's visions for socialist Kaliningrad were the same as those at the heart of the Soviet revolution. Soviet socialism, like Nazism, rejected western individualism in favor of a new form of collective. But in contradistinction to Königsberg's Nazis, who sought cultural renewal in rural pastoralism, the torch-bearers of Kaliningrad's revolution embraced industrial modernity and large-scale urbanity. They imagined the noncapitalist USSR to be the embodiment of the future. They planned to rebuild Kaliningrad as a beacon of socialism in the West, a showcase of Soviet cultural and technical superiority.[2] The new society, they imagined, would be modern, rational, and clean, designed to improve the quality of life of the workers who lived in it. Their visions were shaped both by Soviet ideology and by deeper Russian cultural values and assumptions. When the first Soviet revolutionaries sought to create a new, modern worker's paradise, they also set out to overcome the perceived cultural and economic backwardness of the former Russian Empire vis-à-vis Western Europe. When the Soviets exported their revolution from abroad to the lands of Eastern Europe after 1939, they brought along the idea of Sovietization as state-led, anticapitalist modernization and antidote to backwardness. They applied this template even to societies that were already more economically developed than many parts of the Soviet Union.[3] As Tarik Cyril Amar writes of the Soviet western borderlands, "the Sovietizers made fundamental distinctions between . . . those who bring progress and those who must catch up" in the same way in which Western empires viewed their colonies, the Russian Empire viewed its periphery, and Cold War development projects viewed the Global South.[4]

The new civilian government took a similar approach to dealing with the people of Kaliningrad. The Bolshevik revolutionaries understood that their chosen people—the working classes, the peasantry, and formerly oppressed non-Russian nationalities—would need to be transformed into modern, socialist subjects. The Sovietizers of the 1920s and 1930s brought modern practices of public health, literacy, and 'cultured' behavior with them wherever they exported their revolution.[5] After the war, the Soviet state brought this template to Kaliningrad.

Most remarkably, it applied this civilizing template to Kaliningrad's Germans. Although Kaliningrad's leaders still operated with significant autonomy and little guidance from above, they sought to integrate the Germans and make them beneficiaries of the new socialist society they were forging. They attempted to rectify the inequality wrought by the postwar economy of shortages. Most important, they set out to convince the Germans, by example and by reeducation, of the superiority of the socialist system. They approached the treatment of former East

Prussians in the same manner as they did Soviet citizens, but in the case of Kaliningrad's Germans, the Soviet civilizing mission required not only modernization, but also an antifascist conversion.

Living with the Enemy

Until the summer of 1946, Kaliningrad was, by most accounts, an ethnically German city in an ethnically German countryside. The leadership was entirely Soviet, but German civilians and POWs in local camps comprised the vast majority of the population. In October 1945, in addition to the soldiers of the Special Military District, there were only 4,838 Soviet civilians in Königsberg, growing by April 1946 to an estimated 12,000.[6] Some were family members of military officers, but the majority were former forced laborers, including some who arrived from further west. Zoia Ivanovna Godiaeva, for example, arrived in Soviet East Prussia in the summer of 1945 after three years in German captivity. She had been traveling on an Allied transport train back to her native Smolensk, but after failing to locate any surviving family members, she decided during a train transfer in East Prussia simply to remain.[7] Soviet authorities issued numerous orders to filter these repatriates and return them to the center of the Soviet Union, but a large number of them stayed put. As of June 1946, when the Soviet population had grown to 43,743 across the oblast, nearly one in five of them were former *Ostarbeiter* and POWs. Over the first year of the oblast's existence, the Soviet population grew at a trickle as technical workers and officials were transferred to Kaliningrad on assignment. Germans remained the majority with 116,737 registered inhabitants, constituting over two-thirds of the total oblast population.[8]

In the fall of 1946, the trickle became a flood. The USSR Council of Ministers initiated a centralized settlement program to populate Kaliningrad with collective farmers to revive the region's decimated agriculture and with industrial workers to rebuild its factories. The first mass transports of Soviet settlers began in late August 1946, and by November of that year, 11,675 families were settled onto 295 newly established collective farms (kolkhozy) throughout the oblast.[9] By late August 1946, the Soviet population of Kaliningrad grew to 90,000, with 37,000 Germans constituting the city's new minority, while still remaining the majority population in the oblast until early 1947.[10] The new Soviet settlers were mostly young: 40 percent of them were under thirty years old and 60 percent under forty.[11] Settlers arrived primarily from the western regions of the Soviet Union most devastated by the German wartime occupation, including the western Black Earth lands and Volga River region of Russia, along with Belorussia and Ukraine. Over 90 percent of the settlers came from eastern Slavic nationalities: a census from 1950 registered 77 percent Russians, 9.4 percent Belorussians, and 5.8 percent Ukrainians.[12] Even though Soviet recruiters sought primarily to populate new collective farms, urban civil servants, laborers, and technical specialists arrived at a faster rate.[13] Still, 84 percent of those arriving between 1945 and 1950 were of peasant origin, even if they no longer worked on farms. For many, traveling to Kaliningrad offered the chance to escape the poverty of the Soviet countryside to find greater social mobility in the city.[14]

Soviet historians later presented this campaign as a crusade of young communists eager to build socialism on the ruins of fascism. But the majority of settlers came for more personal reasons. Sixteen percent of applicants, for example, listed as their main motivation the loss of their homes during the war. Raissa Kusminichna Eshkova recalls being drawn to Kaliningrad because "one couldn't get enough to eat with a ration card" in the town where she was living after the war. Her family decided to make the trip after they had sold all their prewar possessions in exchange for food.[15] Collective farmers, in particular, were promised special incentives to resettle. Advertised amenities included free train fare, the transfer of cattle and household possessions, financial support in the amount of 1,000 rubles for the head of household and 300 rubles for each additional member of the family, a loan of cereal grains, a credit of up to 10,000 rubles to build or repair a house, and release from paying taxes for three years.[16]

As a western border region of the USSR, Kaliningrad Oblast was a Closed Zone, meaning that applicants were supposed to be extensively filtered before receiving permission to travel. Between 3 and 12 percent of applicants were rejected, most of them because they had spent time outside the Soviet Union. Still, many settlers slipped through without filtration, especially because recruiters were desperate to attract settlers.[17] Mikhail Ivanovich Ivanov arrived in 1947 to work at Factory 820, the former Schichau shipbuilding plant. He recalls how the factory recruiter "painted life in Kaliningrad in the most beautiful colors." Ivanov was dubious—he had fought in East Prussia in 1945 and had witnessed the destruction—but he decided to go nonetheless.[18] In order to meet quotas, collective farm leaders often nominated their most unskilled workers, drunks, or troublemakers. Other settlers came of their own accord but lied to meet the necessary criteria. Families applying to move to Kaliningrad were required to have two working adults, for example, so many single mothers organized fictitious marriages to qualify for the incentives. Others, especially civil servants and young Komsomol youth league members, were sent on mandatory assignment but traveled only reluctantly. Many of them were not eager to give up more comfortable life circumstances, especially so soon after the war.[19]

To these Soviet newcomers, the word Kaliningrad meant little. Because the city and oblast had only just been renamed, most settlers imagined they were traveling to Germany or to Prussia.[20] As had been the case with generations of Russian and Soviet travelers, many of them thought of East Prussia as a gateway to the West. Anna Andreevna Kopylova recalls that "from the ruins you saw outside the train window, you could already tell that you weren't in Russia anymore." Everything around her seemed "interesting, unfamiliar and a little frightening."[21] Many of the first Soviet settlers remember, however, that their most powerful first impression was horror. When Alexandr Avgustovich Melngalv arrived in Kaliningrad in January 1947, he was shocked to find "a wasteland." As he recalls, "my heart felt so sad. I turned and said to Mama, 'Let's go back before it's too late.' She answered, 'But they gave us money,' and calmed me down with great effort."[22]

New Soviet settlers were also surprised to find so many Germans living among them. Like their soldier counterparts, most of them had ample personal experience to confirm the wartime propaganda depicting Germans as fascist beasts, and they carried their grief with them to Kaliningrad. When Nina Moiseevna Vavilova first arrived, she searched the city's wartime cemeteries in vain hope of finding traces of relatives and acquaintances who had been deported from occupied Belorussia during the war. Under a bridge near the former Steinfurt train car factory, she found an inscription that read, "one day, you will come and will read about our suffering and forced labor." The POWs stationed there had scrawled messages about their travails: the German guards had beaten them with whips and fed them like cattle. Fifteen of them had died in a single night.[23]

Decades later, most Soviet settlers recall not ongoing animosity toward German civilians but a range of feelings between indifference and compassion.[24] According to an oft-repeated recollection, new settlers arriving for the first time at the train station would be greeted by the sight of German children waiting, clean and orderly, but weak and emaciated. When these German children begged in a mixture of German and Russian for bread, the new settlers recall feeling deep pity for them and collecting food to share.[25] Direct contact with these pathetic Germans thus served to extinguish Soviet civilians' long-simmering desire for revenge. These memories, from a series of interviews with Soviet settlers in the 1990s, are filtered through decades, once old hatreds had softened with age. They also reflect the antifascist 'friendship of the peoples' trope common in official postwar Soviet narratives of Red Army liberators. At the time, however, even though many Soviet civilians surely forgave old grievances after living amid the vanquished, the wounds of the past would probably have been too fresh to heal entirely.

Making Do

Amid the constant threat of death, Kaliningrad's Germans and Soviets built a new life together. During the first year, the provisional military administration had created a quasi-socialist society by nationalizing private property and attempting to control supply and distribution, but it had been unable to offer social welfare to the population in exchange. The German population and early Soviet settlers learned to survive by making do with what little this system provided and by finding novel ways to procure what it could not.

For Germans, especially, daily life was shaped by the all-consuming struggle to find food, maintain shelter from the elements, and secure sustainable employment. As Michael Wieck recalls, "to discover food leftovers in the ruins, to carry out the commanded work, to not constantly freeze, to find water, to protect oneself against arbitrariness demanded all of one's strength, intelligence, and concentration." Whereas early German testimonies about life in Kaliningrad focus primarily on suffering and hardship, memoirs written decades later, such as Wieck's, focus also on the determination and ingenuity that some Germans channeled in order to survive. As Wieck noted, "one first had to come around to the idea that, even in fully burned-out ruins without staircases to connect the floors, some charred tin cans could have some still edible content under rusted crusts. With help of a ladder and at the risk of collapse of the ruins, you could climb up there. From semi-decomposed horses you could cut off meat, roast it and eat it, although I could not bring myself to do it."[26] Wieck presents himself as someone particularly skilled in the art of adaptation. In part, these skills were shaped by his life in wartime Königsberg, when he had been forced as a Jewish *Mischling* to work long hours in a chemical plant. Along with his mother, he was one of only a handful of Jews to survive the war.[27] Wieck received no special treatment in Kaliningrad for his wartime suffering—interrogating Soviet officers refused to believe that any Jews had survived. Wieck lived in Kaliningrad as other Germans did, gathering not only food from the ruins, but all sort of goods: clothing, furniture, linens, cookware, fine china and artwork, scrap metal and tools.[28] Everything held potential value, if only because it might someday be fashioned into something to be used or sold.

Securing this wealth proved to be a harder task than collecting it. Already in late April 1945, the German doctor Hans Deichelmann noted in his diary how some Germans attempted to disguise their appearance and to hide their valuables from Red Army soldiers. These cunning "members of the bourgeoisie," he writes, smudged dirt and leaves on their clothing to make them appear less valuable. "The many stains and patches are often just purposeful artificial productions," he notes. "A tattered coat won't get ripped off, so you'll sew a few patches on it. Then you're not so easily a 'capitalist.'"[29] After the open violence of the first months tapered off, Soviet civilians were less likely to accost Germans and take their goods. But theft remained rampant: without locks on the doors to basements, attics, and cellars where they lived, German and Soviet inhabitants alike could return from work to find that their goods had been carted off by opportunistic thieves of either nationality.

Work was mandatory in the first year. During that time, the bulk of the workforce was German, while supervisors were almost exclusively Soviet. Germans worked throughout the city as factory workers, farmers, construction workers, bakers, cabinet makers, electricians, janitors, and gardeners. Some, such as doctors and nurses, worked in specialized trades in which they had been trained, but most worked in jobs for which they had no prior experience. Nearly all postal delivery workers were German, as they knew the city streets. So, too, were the first streetcar drivers when service was reinstated in the fall of 1946.[30] Many workplaces remained predominantly German even after new Soviet settlers arrived. As of January 1947, 93 percent of Kaliningrad city construction workers were German, along with 65 percent of communal service employees and 69 percent of tram workers.[31] Hospitals employed almost entirely German doctors, nurses, and staff well into 1947; Mariia Timofeevna Surygina recalls being the only Soviet civilian working together with six German master stylists at Kaliningrad's first hair salon.[32]

The postwar world altered the hierarchy of haves and have-nots. Germans soon learned that those who secured a job in food production fared better than those who relied solely on a ration card. Farm workers had direct access to vegetables, grains, and occasionally eggs and dairy, although they were also strictly supervised to prevent pilfering. Fishing brigades off the Baltic coast could feast on their catch and sometimes hide away extra to sell. Those with some kind of technical skills—particularly medical doctors and engineers, but also those in skilled construction trades—could earn the coveted title of specialist. Technical expertise was highly valued in Soviet society, and German specialists earned better treatment and even admiration from their Soviet colleagues. They also received substantially higher wages than unskilled workers, either German or Soviet.[33] These Germans sometimes also taught their Soviet coworkers new methods—cleaner techniques for surgical incisions, new procedures in shipbuilding, sturdier construction methods. German skilled labor was in such demand that Soviet civilian and military officials often poached carpenters and other craftsmen working in lower priority sectors, such as German hospitals, to work in city reconstruction projects.

Many Soviet employers preferred to hire German men and women over Soviet citizens because they believed that Germans were more meticulous than Soviets. Isaak Mendeleevich Fishbein remembers that at the shipbuilding plant where he supervised five German POWs and five Soviet workers to repair a coast guard ship, "our guys worked quickly, in a great whirlwind," while the Germans "worked very slowly, without hurrying." But when the Soviet team tried to assemble their pieces, the holes were misaligned, and the pieces could not be assembled. But the Germans, he recalled, "laid the iron together piece by piece and began to drill, and everything worked great for them."[34] Such scenes were common not only in Kaliningrad: German POWs, especially the skilled engineers and construction specialists, were admired for their fastidious work building apartment buildings in Moscow and throughout the Soviet Union.

Most German specialists were men, but around 80 percent of able-bodied Germans were women. Many of them found themselves working in heavy construction for the first time in their lives. Whereas many Soviet employees commended German specialists, they criticized unskilled laborers—usually women—for their lack of resilience. When the teenage girl Käthe Hielscher nearly fainted from carrying heavy rail tracks in 1945, she and her fellow workers complained to their boss.

He laughed that "in Russia, women always do this kind of work," but called in more women to lighten their load. Hielscher appreciated this boss, whom she called Kostian, as a gentle, sophisticated student from Moscow. In contrast to the brutish soldiers who had previously supervised her, Hielscher recalls, "he doesn't scream and doesn't beat the broken-down skeletal women."[35] Erna Ewert, a woman working in nearby Cranz, felt no such positive feelings. She complains in her diary that her Soviet boss loved "commanding German women only too well, criticizing them and saying; 'Puh, German *Kultur* bad, Russian woman work better. So, so, tak, tak. Hmm, hmm'—for a half hour, okay. But not for ten hours a day." The boss only left the women alone once they agreed that Russian women worked harder than Germans.[36]

Over time, the divide grew between those whose skills allowed them to adapt to the new system and those who became victims of it. As Ewert struggled to maintain a steady job, she complained bitterly about the inequity of the postwar society. Even more than she resented the Soviets, she resented the Germans who had found a way to succeed. "Yes, fishers in [the village of] Sarkau live good, wonderful days. The women get fatter and fatter and have forgotten in their dumb pride how they used to haul the fish to our house with all that praise and fuss. Now they bend over (*buckeln*) for the Russians and can't do enough of 'Herr Brigadeur here and there.' But one day this grandeur will also come to an end, even if I won't live to see it."[37] By the time Ewert wrote this passage in her diary in 1947, her mother and her young son had died from hunger. Because both her Russian and German neighbors refused to loan her a shovel for fear that she would steal it, she had been forced to dig her son's grave with her bare hands.

As more Soviet civilians arrived, Germans and Soviets increasingly encountered each other outside the workplace. Some of the more damaged streets became unofficial German-only neighborhoods, similar in effect (if not by design) to Gauleiter Koch's formal creation of "Jewish buildings" just half a decade before. But in most cases, despite security bans on cohabitation from the spring of 1945, Germans and Soviets lived on the same streets, in the same buildings, and sometimes even in the same apartments. German families were increasingly pushed to the attics or basements of their former dwellings; the Soviet new settler Mariia Dmitrievna Mashkina recalls her shock when she first went to the cellar of her new apartment building to fetch water and discovered "that a family lived there and they spoke German." The Germans, she remembers, were friendly, and the older man even helped her carry her bucket upstairs.[38] Many Soviet settlers remember such encounters with meek and helpful German neighbors. As Germans had no guaranteed housing, one adaptation strategy was to ingratiate themselves with their Soviet neighbors by offering their services cleaning, cooking, or doing handiwork.

From the German perspective at the time, Soviet civilians appeared to have all of the advantages. But Soviet archival records and personal narratives reveal that Soviet civilians, too, experienced great hardship. Many settlers remember facing great hunger on their journey, only to arrive to find no housing awaiting them.[39] Many of them came to Kaliningrad with only their clothes on their backs. The new settler Daniel'-Bek, who was fourteen at the time, had no shoes and was forced to survive an entire season barefoot.[40] Life in Kaliningrad felt apocalyptic even for those who arrived from villages devastated by the Nazi occupation. Soviet civilians, like their German counterparts, recall being forced to clear away rubble with their bare hands and excavating decomposing corpses from the ruins of factories.[41] Others recall the ever-present danger of hidden munitions, which took the lives of several Soviet children.[42] Long after they arrived, settlers complained about the absence of municipal services, including water, electricity, transport, medical services, and entertainment (a particular complaint among collective farm workers who had been promised films and dance evenings, but found themselves with nothing to do after sundown). Disgruntled Soviet settlers complained that military personnel had occupied all the undamaged apartments. Collective farmers bemoaned a lack of adequate equipment or grain, and the fact that they were forced to live in half-destroyed ruins, sometimes without windows or doors. Others complained that they were "hungry, barefoot, poorly dressed" and felt "doomed to die" in Kaliningrad. "We live like primitive people," complained new settlers from Yaroslavl Oblast to the USSR Council of Ministers in 1947, upon discovering that their new villages lacked even the most basic supplies of matches, soap, or kerosene.[43]

Conditions were especially bad for Soviet factory workers, who were sent to Kaliningrad in large numbers on short notice. These workers, who were often young, recent graduates of trade schools, were already destitute, having faced extreme shortages on the home front during the war. The 227 young graduates arriving from a trade school in Omsk in July 1946, for example, each had only one pair of underwear, a threadbare suit, and no shoes because they had been forced to trade all their possessions for food during their long train journey. In Kaliningrad, local government and factory managers were ill-prepared to receive them. Their assigned living quarters were covered in layers of soot, with no place for them to sit and no pots to boil drinking water. The workers were forced to wash their clothes in the contaminated water of the Pregel River, furthering the spread of disease.[44] Workers arriving in October 1946 to work at the Electrical Coil Factory were housed in apartments with broken windows, no heating, and no hot water; eleven people were crammed into a single twenty-two square-meter room. The workers slept on the bare floor. With no way to bathe, they all became infested with lice.[45]

After the forced labor regime ended in the summer of 1946, employment remained the primary means to earn a ration card. But as rations remained insufficient, both Germans and Soviets sought other ways to make ends meet. Entrepreneurial Germans, eschewing formal employment, had already developed a second economy in the summer of 1945. The provisional military administration tolerated such private commerce in tacit recognition that the state was not yet able to provide for residents. At a time when official employment required long work days and no days off, market trade offered flexibility and a potentially lucrative means to make a living. As one German market trader explained to the diarist Lucy Falk, the benefits of illegal trade outweighed the risks because she was "free, not bound to any hours, and can live and spend my time how I want."[46] The markets became so dominated by German traders that they were nicknamed "German bazaars," but Soviet citizens also bought and sold goods there. Early on, Germans primarily sold household goods, and when those items ran out, they sold handicrafts or specialty baked goods made from pilfered flour. Vendors of agricultural produce, however, were primarily Soviet citizens (Russians or farmers crossing the border from Lithuania).[47] German women, as a rule, succeeded in market trading because they appeared less devious to Soviet consumers than German men, and German children became especially savvy merchants because they could appeal to Soviet citizens' soft spots—a character trait Germans sometimes attributed to Russian underdevelopment.[48] Cigarettes were the most lucrative wares, which entrepreneurial German children sold individually, along with matches.[49]

At the market, Germans and Soviets gained insight into another way of life. "The quality of life in East Prussia had been noticeably higher than ours," remembers Irina Iosifovna Lukashevich. "In front of the school in [the town of] Cranz, there was a market, and I used to go there as if going to a museum: silver, dishes, rugs. . . . I saw crystal for the first time there. Often the Germans sold these things for a pittance. For example, a crystal vase went for a total of three rubles."[50] Soviet citizens especially sought out items that symbolized the end of wartime sacrifice and a return to domesticity. As one German dressmaker reported to Falk, most Soviet settlers arrived in Königsberg in rags. Their "greatest wish," she explained, was "to get pretty clothing." Soviet women, especially, bought tailored dresses made by skilled German seamstresses from salvaged prewar fabrics.[51] After Falk lost her official job, she decided to try her hand at market trade. Hearing that "the Russians like to buy pictures," Falk resigned to selling a historic oil painting she had rescued from her brother's home. While Soviet customers snatched up the paintings sold by her fellow merchants, they dismissed hers as *"Plokho!"* (bad) and *"Nicht gutt [sic], alt!"* An experienced German merchant explained to her that Soviets preferred cheerful paintings and that she needed to "paint more sunshine in it." Falk stenciled in yellow sunbeams, a red hull for the ship, and bright highlights on the dark water. Although her German roommates mocked her efforts, she managed to sell the painting the next day. The buyer, she wrote in her diary, seemed stunned that she asked for only a loaf of bread as payment.[52]

Because market trading remained illegal and unregulated, it held dangers for buyers and sellers of both nationalities. Deichelmann wrote in his diary how Soviet officials—or at least uniformed men waving documents in Cyrillic—could appear at any moment and confiscate a seller's goods or impose a large fine. Other German sellers got duped by Soviet customers who took the products with the promise of payment "saftra." As Deichelmann explained in late May 1945, "they tell us this word is supposed to mean 'tomorrow,' but the seller usually has every reason to translate this word as 'never.' "[53] But German sellers also learned to swindle: a particularly cunning German market trader supposedly sold a piece of furniture to two Russians at once—while the first one left to fetch his truck, she collected payment from the second and then disappeared while the two men argued about who was entitled to the goods.[54] Buying meat at the market posed an especially high risk—authorities documented numerous cases of human flesh for sale, as it remained in ample supply when the other types became scarce.[55] While enforcement remained inconsistent, Germans and Soviets alike could face harsh punishment; an unfortunate Frau Pflaumbaum, for example, was reportedly sentenced to seven years of hard labor for dealing in hand-knit stockings.[56]

Like those in the workplace and at the market, encounters in Soviet homes were specialized according to nationality and were highly gendered. In a reversal of prewar roles, German women served as housekeepers for the families of high-ranking Soviet military personnel or even simple Soviet working families, tidying their apartments, washing laundry, and preparing meals. Iurii Nikolaevich Tregub remembers how his father brought one 'Frau Reinhard' to live with the family. She had been on the street one day, "about to die from hunger," when Tregub's father offered her a room in exchange for helping around the house. "My parents worked, and we young children, what could we cook?" Tregub explains. "She made soup, cleaned the rooms, and went to buy bread."[57] Ewert likewise developed good relations with a few Soviet families who arranged for her to do odd jobs. Some families recruited her to sell goods on the black market so they could preserve their public reputations as upstanding communists. Ewert writes in her diary about a Soviet general who treated her well; even though a clear power imbalance remained between them, they made each other laugh on occasion, sometimes on purpose and other times by accident. As Ewert wrote in 1946, "I often had to tell him about our films and theaters. Then he told me about a Russian film. It was a tragedy piece. But in his German it sounded so funny that I was often on the edge of laughter. But for God's sakes I couldn't laugh because it was something sad. He said among other things: 'There sits the woman on the bench and it cries and cries' [*Da sitzt das Frau auf das Bank und weint und weint*]. I was glad when the sad film was over."[58] Ewert documents the anger and despair she felt over the hunger and perpetual hardships she faced, but moments such as these reveal how, amid the suffering, human encounters allowed both Soviets and Germans the opportunity to relate as individuals.

While Germans, bitter about their hardship, often judged their Soviet neighbors to be backward or unsophisticated, Soviets were more likely to appreciate Germans as cultured. *Kultura* (translated loosely as cultural sophistication or civilization) was a central focus of the Soviet modernizing revolution. In the 1920s, public health and education campaigns emphasized the value of proper hygiene, literacy, and educational attainment. Even as Soviets denounced bourgeois capitalist culture, by the 1930s, Soviet ideology embraced the western cultural canon as evidence of socialist refinement.[59] Soviet observers noted, in confirmation of centuries-old stereotypes, that Germans displayed many of the outward signs of culture that Soviet propaganda campaigns had

instructed their own citizens to aspire to. For instance, new settlers recall how Germans maintained meticulous standards of hygiene even
amid great hardship. Irina Vasil'evna Poborzeva remembers how the
Germans "put value in cleanliness, maintained order and beauty." She
and her daughter were greatly impressed by the fact that the German
women cleaned the streets every morning, washed their linens daily, and
every evening rolled their hair in curlers.[60] Anna Ryzhova remembers
her astonishment at how her German neighbor fastidiously washed the
clothes of her children every three days. Because each of them had only
one outfit, she made them put the wet clothes back on to dry.[61]

Soviet civilians saw Germans as a valuable resource for attaining culture, and German women, especially, marketed their services as culture
bearers by teaching Soviet children foreign languages, music, and art.
Falk, the German diarist who sold her family's oil painting at the market, marvels at the emphasis Soviet citizens put on education, which
she identifies as a "striving for 'Kultura.'"[62] She writes about how her
brilliant young Soviet piano student Pole Goldmann, having already
mastered the waltzes of Strauss, approached her, tears falling into her
handkerchief and sobbing in a mix of Russian and German, "Pole nix
kultura?" ("Pole is not cultured?"). Falk, astounded, assured her that
she was. Falk writes in her diary about how she relayed the story to
her Soviet supervisor, "Frau Spiwak," at the German school where she
also taught. "Is it not strange that an eight-year-old girl asks such a
question?" Falk asked. "No German child would ask whether or not
she was cultured." Spiwak reportedly replied that each group was most
concerned with what it lacked: "the Russians with culture, the Germans with food." Falk agreed that she was certainly right about the
Germans.[63] In the Soviet Union, the surnames Spivak (Spiwak) and
Goldman (Goldmann) were almost invariably Jewish, adding another
dimension to the supervisor's commentary.

Because Kaliningrad was a city populated disproportionately by Soviet men and German women, the potentially most advantageous—but
fraught—means for a German woman to survive in Kaliningrad was
to ally herself with a Soviet man. Even after the violent encounters of
the first months became less frequent, coercive encounters remained
commonplace. Gradually, Soviet men pursued German women not at
gunpoint but with romantic overtures, whether or not the resulting sex
act was consensual. Some women, in an attempt to better their chances
of survival, found Soviet boyfriends, and despite periodic bans issued
against cohabitation, many Soviet soldiers and civilians found live-in

German girlfriends.[64] Sometimes the arrangement was purely business, the exchange of sex for food and protection. Wieck recalled how the mother of one girl had "wisely allied herself with a Russian officer" to secure enough food for both her and her daughter to survive. The memory of her mother's "prostitution" haunted the girl for the rest of her life.[65] Other sexual encounters blurred the lines between coercion, opportunism, and romance, and in some cases, real love blossomed between German women and Soviet men. Such was the case for Gerda Preuß, a young Königsberg woman who had learned Russian during the war for her secretarial job at a Nazi economic institute working on expanding the German East. After the war, her knowledge of Russian allowed her more quickly to see past the stereotypes, find gainful employment, and fall in love with a Soviet soldier.[66] Most German personal narratives, however, omit mention of sexual encounters. While men's diaries and memoirs describe mass rape and sexualized violence in order to assert German national victimhood at the hands of the barbarians, German women's narratives from the former East Prussia tend to allude to sexual violence only in passing, often referring to other women's experiences rather than their own.

Hielscher's memoirs, written in the 1970s and published in 1998, provide an insightful exception. Hielscher talks openly about rape, sexual coercion, and the conflicting feelings she felt coming of age in a world of vulnerable German women surrounded by powerful Soviet men. Hielscher, who was fifteen in 1945, had been a member of the Hitler Youth; her parents were Hitler supporters, and her father had even sported the characteristic "little *Schnauzer* under his nose" (the Hitler mustache). Like many other East Prussian memoirists writing during the Cold War, Hielscher does not dwell on the crimes of National Socialism. Instead, she presents the story of a young girl's innocence, naïveté, and undeserved punishment in postwar Kaliningrad. Hielscher had numerous encounters with Soviet men between 1945 and 1948, almost always while at work. She was raped at least twice, the first time in the summer of 1945, when a Russian man surprised her on the street from behind, drew her aside, and whispered "I love you" in pidgin German. In Hielscher's depiction, Russian men appear either as aggressors or protectors: the aggressors declare their love forcefully and expect sex in exchange for gifts of food; the protectors act as father figures, deflecting the advances of the aggressors. In the internment camp in the spring of 1945, Hielscher survived because of the kindness of a civilian Russian who got her a job in the kitchen. He attempted to woo her until she convinced him that she was too young. Recognizing that he had a daughter the same age, he agreed instead to friendship, giving her food and protecting her against sexual advances.[67]

In 1947, by contrast, a young Polish translator took a fancy to Hielscher, surreptitiously filling her backpack with bread, preserves, and Wehrmacht chocolates. After she rejected him, he became cruel, forcing her to perform backbreaking labor while Russian soldiers laughed, then dragged her away to rape her. She was spared at the last minute (presumably—Hielscher obscures the outcome) by another Russian boss who chastised both the translator and the soldiers. But Hielscher's German coworkers criticized her harshly for denying him: if she continued to anger her suitor, they argued, he might find a way to ship the entire work crew to Siberia. "Why are you being like this?" they asked. "When it comes down to it, you're just young and so is he. He is actually a good looking guy. Just go through with it. It would be much better than to put us all in danger!" Hielscher writes with anger about the terrible pressure she faced from these women who forced her "to submit to the Pole."[68] When Hielscher consented to a date, 'the Pole' again declared his love; when he offered her a glass of vodka, she claims to have passed out immediately. Hielscher implies that he raped her while she was unconscious; she woke up to find herself lying horizontally, her dress smudged with dirt. Thanks only to the intervention by her Russian boss that the Pole was transferred away, saving her from his proposal of marriage.[69]

Hielscher claims never to have consented to sex; she declares that she refused out of "national pride" (*Nationalstolz*) as a German. Other women, however, seemed not to feel the same loyalty to the nation, and Hielscher describes their consensual affairs with Russian lovers with disdain.[70] At the same time, she records numerous positive interactions with Soviet men and even describes on multiple occasions her first adolescent feelings of lust for her protectors. One Soviet civilian who supervised her concrete-mixing brigade had been a student in Moscow; she felt "an unfamiliar warm feeling" through her body when their eyes met. With another protector, she writes, there was "an unspoken taboo agreement" about their attraction, but Hielscher was spared from her own desire when the man fell in love with a Russian woman.[71] Hielscher presents these encounters as school girl joys—she desires these men precisely because they did not pursue her.

Even as many relations between Soviets and Germans remained shaped by dynamics of power, both in the workplace and in everyday life, an increasing number of positive interactions by the summer of 1946 seemed to point the way toward tolerance and gradual integration. The Kaliningrad historian Iurii Kostiashov even argues that the deep animosity most Soviet settlers had felt toward Germans during the war dissipated more quickly in Kaliningrad than elsewhere, aided by this extended civilian encounter.[72] Old animosities slowly gave way to friendships, while others turned into marriages of convenience or even of love.[73] German and Soviet soccer teams played pick-up games at the former Erich Koch stadium and even formed an intramural league. The German-Jewish teenager Wieck played the violin for a dance orchestra at an officer's club, where Soviet soldiers and civilians danced with German and Soviet women alike.[74] The most popular dance hall in town, however, was the German Club. Iurii Tregub, the young man whose father employed a German woman as a houseworker, recalls how well Germans and Soviets got along there, and how he "can't remember any fights ever breaking out." When the Germans danced to their own folk songs, the Soviet youth asked them to play "more popular music" that everyone could enjoy, like the foxtrot or the tango. "There were lots of boys and girls at these dances," Tregub recalls. "We liked the German girls a lot."[75]

Building Socialism

When the region transitioned to Soviet civilian government in the spring and summer of 1946, Kaliningrad's new leaders faced many of the same challenges as before. Administrative confusion about the territory continued, and the new oblast government still struggled to garner Moscow's attention.[76] The city lay in ruins and faced an acute housing crisis, especially as the military remained a strong presence and maintained control over the best facilities, housing, and land. Dire shortages of labor and supplies thwarted the civilian government's efforts to rebuild, and the population—both German and Soviet—continued to face significant hunger. The transition to civilian government, however, marked an important turning point. Whereas the military had raced to rescue Königsberg from near-certain death, the new civilian government sought to bring a new Soviet Kaliningrad to life.

Once again left to operate with significant autonomy but limited funding, the new Civilian Affairs Administration set out to bring the wild city in line with standard Soviet practices. Between April 1946 and March 1948, that job fell to Vasilii Andreevich Borisov, the newly appointed head of the Civilian Affairs Administration of Kaliningrad Oblast, the transitional government established in 1946 in anticipation of elections for representative state institutions established in 1948. Borisov was thirty-seven years old when he arrived in Kaliningrad, a child of the Russian Revolution and one of its beneficiaries. Originally a skilled weaver from a small town in the Smolensk region west of Moscow, Borisov became a Communist Party member in 1930 and rose through the ranks to become first a factory supervisor and then a member of the Moscow Oblast Soviet (representative council) from 1939 to 1946 before being sent on assignment to make Kaliningrad Soviet.[77]

Borisov and his administration attempted to put an end to Kaliningrad's chaotic development. While corresponding with Moscow to draft a master plan for long-term construction, the Civilian Affairs Administration at first focused on smaller-scale projects to repair infrastructure, housing, and industry.[78] Even these municipal repair projects demanded significant resources to complete because the devastation was so widespread. Over 30 percent of Königsberg's road surfaces had been destroyed; of its twenty-three bridges, only two were still standing.[79] Only three of the city's eight electrical stations survived, and only one of nine sewage pumping stations, meaning that sewage continually flowed backward into the Pregel River, contaminating the source of much of the city's water supply.[80] The new administration dedicated significant resources to these construction projects, and over the course of the year, the pace of reconstruction grew significantly. The renovation doubled Kaliningrad's available living space (although the military still controlled half of it), and work crews succeeded in restoring some of the city's electrical supply, two bus lines, and rudimentary streetcar service by the end of 1946.[81] Other projects took far longer, however, and it took years to establish the full range of city services.

Much of the civilian government's efforts focused on standardizing institutions, reconstructing the ruins, and providing housing and services for the quickly growing Soviet population. But Sovietization was also about transforming people. Although the civilian government was established to tend to the entire population's needs, its main ideological challenge was to Sovietize the German population, the majority of the region's inhabitants in 1946. Across the Soviet western borderlands, Soviet authorities assumed that, while being liberated from fascist occupation, new populations also had to be educated to understand the superiority of the socialist system and prepared to take part in it fully.[82] Kaliningrad's Germans, as only provisionally redeemed from fascism

FIGURE 10. A Soviet surveyor, a Soviet foreman, and a Soviet construction worker discuss plans to renovate a typical steep-roofed Königsberg residential building in the late 1940s. Collection: Russian State Archive of Film and Documentary Photography (RGAKFD) Krasnogorsk.

and not granted automatic Soviet citizenship, were deemed even more suspect. But just as was the case across the Soviet western borderlands, Kaliningrad's Soviet leaders assumed that the Germans, with the right intervention, could be incorporated, converted, and redeemed.

The provisional military administration's efforts to engage Kaliningrad's Germans in socialist labor alone had not resulted in their successful rehabilitation. The decision-making vacuum surrounding the Germans' fate continued through the transition to civilian rule. For example, in July 1946, when new identification papers were issued to everyone in the oblast, Soviet citizens were given new passports or updated registration details on their old ones. Germans, however, were issued only local identification papers valid for three years, printed both in German and Russian. The original draft of the order had called for the Germans to be issued "passports," but the word was later crossed out and replaced with the phrase "temporary identification" (*vremennoe udostoverenie*), reflecting the ongoing local confusion about the Germans' status.[83]

Still, the establishment of the civilian government in mid-1946 seemed to be the beginning of a golden age of integration. It marked a significant increase in government efforts to integrate the Germans into the system—to make them the beneficiaries of their labor, to provide them with social welfare, and to convert them to socialism through education and example. The administration's efforts started small and were relatively decentralized, but they increased dramatically as organs of the civilian government began operations over the course of the year.

The first step was to fully incorporate the Germans into the Soviet economy. The Civilian Affairs Administration worked especially to end the chaotic practices surrounding Germans' employment, rations, and wages. Although orders had already been issued in the summer of 1945 to employ only Germans who were properly registered, many factory managers and military units, facing labor shortages, were still hiring unregistered Germans to avoid the complex paperwork.[84] Borisov's Civilian Affairs Administration required that all residents be properly registered in order to work or receive a ration card. The goal was not to penalize the Germans, but to incorporate German workers into standard budgets and ensure that employers were documenting their workers and paying them fairly. The civilian government also ended the forced labor regime and standardized wages and rations for workers by type of work, regardless of citizenship or nationality.[85] As was the case across the Soviet Union, compensation varied widely: within the Oblast Civilian Affairs Administration, for example, janitors earned as low as 200 rubles per month, barely a living wage; heads of divisions, workshop leaders, and translators earned between 600 and 800; and the highest-level managers earned up to 1,300. Factory managers and highly specialized engineers working in construction or technical fields could earn as high as 3,000—a wage that unskilled workers would have seen as wealthy.[86]

The ongoing threat of contagion led the civilian administration, especially, to prioritize public health. Kaliningrad continued to have the highest rate of infectious diseases in the Soviet Union. In addition to water and food-borne illnesses, the problem of venereal disease was so significant that the USSR Ministry of Health organized a thirty-person fact-finding mission to the newly formed oblast in July 1946 and at least two other expeditions by 1948.[87] The civilian administration established an Oblast Health Department and dozens of treatment centers and pharmacies across the oblast. Notably, it incorporated Kaliningrad's remaining German hospitals, still in operation but facing significant shortages and in varying states of disrepair, into the Health Department budget. Because German doctors and nurses had not been paid rations or wages in months and had begun leaving the hospital to seek other employment, the new Oblast Health Department stream-lined and modernized hospital operations and provided the medical personnel with months of back pay in order to retain them.[88]

The administration also attempted to improve living conditions by establishing full state control over supply and distribution. It launched a campaign against what Borisov denounced as "serious shortcomings in the development of trade and communal nutrition," including ongo-ing food shortages, long lines for groceries, and widespread violations of Soviet hygiene codes. New facilities for food production, storage, and sale were established, along with a quality control system to minimize the transmission of food-borne illnesses. The new government also cracked down on private market trade by threatening fines and arrests for any civilians who produced or sold goods, including food, without a permit.[89]

The administration focused especially on demonstrating the superi-ority of Soviet socialism by providing programs for social welfare. Early on, the primary focus was on improving the Germans' dire living condi-tions. By the fall of 1946, the Oblast Health Department incorporated the remaining German hospitals, which previously had been operating with virtually no food or supplies, and made significant efforts to im-prove patient treatment.[90] The government also established a small net-work of nursing homes to care for 700 elderly Germans by May 1947. The available beds could not accommodate the large number of inva-lids, and budget constraints limited their further expansion. But the establishment of eldercare for the German population nevertheless showed the government's intention to provide for their well-being.[91] Likewise, high mortality in 1945–46 left thousands of German children orphaned and homeless. The new government responded by establish-ing eighteen orphanages across the oblast to care for 3,300 children by May 1947. These orphanages were remarkably well-supplied, given oblast-wide funding constraints, with dedicated funds to pay staff, em-ploy medical personnel, feed children, and outfit each building with furniture and equipment.[92] Some of the orphan children reportedly remained "emaciated and ill" in late 1946; by April 1947, however, Bor-isov reported to Moscow that all children were receiving excellent care.[93] German civilians had a similar impression at the time; Falk wrote in Au-gust 1946 about watching the neatly groomed orphans walk through town, arranged into orderly single-file lines by their caretakers. The boys wore uniforms and had their hair cropped close in Russian style, no longer with the long, wavy locks common for young boys in Königs-berg.[94] In some cases, German parents willingly surrendered their children to these orphanages. When Marga Pollmann lost her arm in a train accident and could not work, she chose reluctantly to deposit her children in the orphanage to ensure they would still be fed.[95]

The Civilian Affairs Administration also expanded efforts to incorporate and rehabilitate Germans through education—an urgent priority, since German children were becoming feral, living without adult supervision while their parents were at work. Children got into fights, worked as pickpockets, stumbled drunk through the streets, and engaged in prostitution in exchange for food. Although some German witnesses later denounced this corruption of the German youth as evidence of the depravity of Soviet socialism, the local Soviet government saw the problem as the result of an absence of Soviet control. The military administration had already set up schools for the few Soviet children living in Königsberg in the summer of 1945, but had made no efforts to do so for German children, admitting in February 1946 that with few resources available, "control over their education and schooling [had been] practically impossible." Meanwhile, Lutheran churches, which had continued to operate (at first because of the absence of control, but then ostensibly in demonstration of the Soviet constitution's progressive policies regarding the freedom of religion), had begun to offer day care and schools of their own to curb the unruliness of German children, heightening the new civilian government's sense of urgency in providing official Soviet education.[96]

By the end of 1946, the civilian government created twenty-six schools for German children, expanding by April 1947 to forty-four schools across the oblast, with 142 teachers and almost 5,000 registered pupils.[97] Soviet nationalities policy, in order to demonstrate the Soviet Union's dedication to anti-imperialism, afforded all national minority groups the progressive benefit of native language education. The Oblast Education Department established these schools in accordance with the standard protocol for non-Russian Soviet nationalities living within the RSFSR, providing instruction and textbooks in the German language. These schools operated alongside numerous Russian-language schools opened for Soviet children.[98] Resources remained scarce, but the Education Department's efforts showed their dedication to educating German children, not just for antifascist reeducation, but also to provide training in literacy, science, and mathematics. German parents were initially reluctant to enroll their children in the new schools, fearing either exposure to propaganda or the loss of a member of the household economy, but most eventually relented because school students received their own ration cards.[99]

German teachers were recruited from the local population. Whereas around 85 percent of teachers in the postwar Soviet Zone of Occupation had been party members during the Third Reich, in Kaliningrad, more intense filtration and the absence of local German administration meant that virtually no former party members were permitted to teach. Because many recruited teachers had never taught before, Soviet school administrators met with them weekly to discuss pedagogy and coordinate lesson plans. Soviet supervisors also worked with them to have them practice Russian and learn about the history of the Soviet state and the cultures and peoples of the USSR.[100] Falk became one of these teachers, after working a variety of odd jobs. She wrote in her diary about the pride she felt working as a teacher and about studying Russian in order to communicate with her Soviet supervisors.[101] In late 1946, school administrators sought greater pedagogical training for both Soviet and German teachers and requested funds to establish a dual-language pedagogical institute. The curriculum for Russian and German schools was similar, although the German children received less instruction in history and geography, subjects considered too politically sensitive to be trusted to the German teachers without proper training.[102] Because Nazi-era textbooks were deemed politically dangerous, the Education Department in the fall of 1946 requested that Soviet textbooks designed for the Soviet Union's own German minority, the Volga Germans, be sent to Kaliningrad to determine their suitability for use in German schools. (Later that year, however, the RSFSR Council of Ministers called for Kaliningrad to develop specialized textbooks, perhaps in belated recognition that Kaliningrad's Germans, as noncitizens and recent enemies, required special pedagogy.)[103]

Whereas children were intuitively understood to be less complicit in the crimes of fascism and more easily redeemed, Soviet authorities understood that German adults required more explicit antifascist education. The provisional military administration had made few efforts at direct reeducation, but in February 1946, on the eve of the transition to the civilian administration, it set up an official Antifascist Club. Recruitment posters for the club were printed and displayed throughout the city, calling particularly on Königsberg's intellectual elite (teachers, doctors, engineers) to join, and branches were established in several larger workplaces. The club was designed to be, as Deichelmann noted in his diary in February 1946, an "asset for the defeat of fascism in all its forms, for the establishment of a true democracy and for the creation of peace among nations."[104] The teacher Falk and the doctors Lehndorff and Deichelmann were all invited to join the club's special intelligentsia section, geared toward Kaliningrad's educated German population. The club hosted lectures, along with a lending library of socialist-friendly German literature and translations of Lenin. Under the civilian administration, the club expanded its repertoire to offer concerts, dance nights, and sporting competitions, including an intramural soccer league with German and Russian teams. Members of the club heard lectures about their responsibility and guilt for the war and the importance of their collective effort in building a bastion of democracy on the Baltic Sea.[105] By April 1947, the club had also presented numerous entertainment programs (approved by censors), including 171 concerts throughout the oblast, with a total German audience of 50,000.[106]

Königsberg's few surviving German communists worked for the club as propagandists. By April 1947, five German lecturers hired by the Oblast Department of Culture and Enlightenment presented 983 talks throughout Kaliningrad and the oblast, to a reported total of 120,650 attendees, on topics including "The Stalin Constitution: The Constitution of Victorious Socialism," "Fascism, the Worst Enemy of Humanity," "The Five-Year Plan for the Establishment and Development of the Economy from 1946 to 1950," "On the Democratic Restructuring of Germany," "Lenin: Leader and Teacher of Workers across the World," and "The Soviet Electoral System: The Most Democratic in the World."[107] A German radio hour provided news and lectures in German, and the *Neue Zeit* newspaper, which came into circulation in August 1947 at the same time as the Russian-language newspaper *Kaliningradskaia pravda*, offered translations of Russian news articles and local special-interest stories written by or for the German residents of Kaliningrad.

Although they remained small in scale, the numerous programs to rehabilitate the German population reveal the civilian government's assumption that the Germans would remain long-term in Kaliningrad and be incorporated, in some way or another, into Soviet life. Despite cynicism in later German testimonies and memoirs, there is also some evidence that these programs, even in their rudimentary forms, were starting to be effective. Hospitals improved their standards of care by the late fall of 1946. Orphan children were on average better fed and clothed than children who remained with their parents. German-language schools, despite shortages of textbooks and supplies, succeeded in facilitating improved relations between Soviets and Germans of all ages. Falk, as a teacher in one of these schools, wrote in her diary about her positive experiences in the classroom. Although she also criticized the Soviet government in private, archival Soviet Education Department reports reveal that Falk had learned in public to "speak Bolshevik"—to act as if she truly believed in the Soviet system and its values—and perhaps had begun to experience a conversion herself. For example, at a teachers' meeting, she gave a spontaneous speech about the progressiveness of the Soviet system, which allowed women to serve as school directors, something, she explained, that would never have been possible in Nazi Germany. Falk also became an active member of the Antifascist Club, read Russian literature classics in translation for the German radio hour, and contributed short stories and op-eds *Neue Zeit*.[108]

Whither Rehabilitation?

Problems remained amid these integration efforts. Although conditions improved in 1946, both formally and informally, the Germans' indeterminate status and the economy of shortages prolonged the two-tier system based officially on citizenship but in effect on ethnicity.

By May 1946, for example, the new civilian government consolidated German-operated stores into state control. The remaining state shops catered to different segments of the population: eight were designated explicitly for "Russian citizens" (*russkikh grazhdan*) and seven for "the German population" (*dlia nemets. naseleniia*). These stores instituted a separate-and-unequal regime: stores for Soviet citizens offered greater supplies and varieties of goods, particularly in times of shortage.[109] As housing remained in short supply, new Soviet settlers to Kaliningrad continued to push Germans out of the best apartments to occupy them for themselves.

Despite calls to standardize pay so that Germans and Soviets received equal pay for equal work, in practice, even when Germans and Soviets were paid from the same state funds, ongoing shortages meant that Soviets received their pay first, and German wages were garnished. The records of the Train Car Factory (the former Steinfurt factory) reveal the conflicting tendencies guiding Soviet treatment of German employees and the range of experiences these workers had in the socialist system. Among the list of employees for the main floor of the factory in early 1946 were numerous young workers recently sent on assignment from Russia, and one German among them, Karl Günther, who was hired as a construction engineer at the respectable salary of 600 rubles per month, well in line with his Soviet colleagues. The Train Car Factory also had a farm to grow crops and livestock to supply food to the factory, and many workers in this "Agricultural Division" were German. In the summer of 1946, a draft list was created to award bonuses for outstanding work; of the nine workers slated to be rewarded, four were German and five were Russian. Three Russian veterinary workers each earned 100 rubles as a bonus; a Russian milkmaid and a herder each earned 100; the four Germans, including three milkmaids and a herder, were also promised 100 rubles each. But when the factory director, Vasilii Petrovich Gorbunov, signed the order, he crossed off the names of the Germans from the list. Gorbunov may have faced funding shortages, or perhaps an agricultural team leader had nominated the Germans, but Gorbunov decided that the German workers were undeserving. Even in the case of labor, the supposed great equalizer of the socialist system, ethnicity (which in this case overlapped with citizenship), played a stronger role in determining outcomes.[110]

Equal opportunity also remained a mirage. Apart from a limited number of German technical specialists, team leaders, supervisors, and department heads were invariably Soviet citizens. Even learning Russian could not open doors to management roles, which meant that the majority of Germans remained in low-paying, unskilled jobs. Able-bodied Germans, unlike Soviet citizens, were in practice only guaranteed benefits if they worked, but they were not guaranteed employment. Ewert wrote about her constant struggle to find a steady job to feed her two children. After two months of searching, she found work as a night guard but was fired soon thereafter because she could not learn to pronounce Russian commands. After she lost her means to earn a ration card, one of her sons died of starvation.[111]

Kaliningrad's Soviet leaders understood that the Germans' poor living conditions were a problem and made efforts to incorporate the Germans in ways that went beyond just lip service.[112] They expected that more resources and better state control would eventually raise the standard of living for all. Deichelmann's Soviet acquaintances told him repeatedly that life in the rest of Russia was much better than in Kaliningrad, just as Falk's supervisor promised her that "next summer" would bring well-furnished classrooms, vacations on the beach, and plenty to eat for everyone, including the Germans.[113]

Still, the existence of programs to integrate and rehabilitate the Germans raises questions about their objective. What was the end goal of educating the Germans about the superiority of socialism? When—and how—might the Germans be considered effectively redeemed from fascism to become full participants in the society they were building? Kaliningrad officials touted the benefits of socialism, but Germans were allowed to play only a subsidiary role. They were not allowed to create their own antifascist organizations (in dramatic counterexample to Berlin) and were prohibited, as noncitizens, from participating in Soviet government institutions. The Antifascist Club (renamed the German Club not long after its founding in tacit recognition that national character was easier to demonstrate than true belief) encouraged participation, but the desired participation amounted to listening to German communists' lectures, scripted by Soviet superiors, about German guilt and Soviet superiority. Because Germans were not Soviet citizens, they had no rights or possibilities to advocate for themselves. In an all-too-common case from the fall of 1946, Soviet civilians broke into an apartment where a few German women lived and stole all of the clothing, including the shirts off the women's backs. Left naked, the women were unable to go to work the next day, and so their supervisor fired them. The victims were left with no jobs, no clothes, and no means to procure sustenance.[114] "The German here has absolutely no rights," wrote Ewert angrily in 1946. "He has to work without exception, and if he can't do that, then he'll die."[115] Allowed no independent initiative, Germans were expected to rely on a government that advertised benefits, the majority of which, as non-Soviet citizens, they were not entitled to receive.

Aside from these inherent contradictions, the government's social welfare and reeducation efforts continued to grow over the course of 1946 and 1947. In that short time, they failed to reach most Germans. Although the more educated diarists inside Königsberg, such as Falk, Lehndorff, and Deichelmann, wrote about their experiences with orphanages, schools, political lectures, and the German Club, other German witnesses deny that the Soviet government made any effort to help or educate them. Olga Golobova (formerly Klein), one of the few German women who managed to stay in Kaliningrad after the majority of the German population left, recalled that "No kind of social or political work was carried out with the Germans. Who would have

needed it? I never heard anything about the newspaper *Neue Zeit*. There
were no artistic performances or dances for the Germans. We were not
thinking about dances but about oats and saltbush, about how to survive."[116] The government's antifascist efforts primarily reached children
or workers employed by major institutions. As a cashier in a small hair
salon, Golobova simply might never have been exposed to the state's
rudimentary antifascist efforts.

For other Germans, the problem was not that they had not been sufficiently exposed but that the message seemed suspiciously familiar.
As Deichelmann pointed out, the German communists hired to offer
workplace lectures shared some uncanny similarities with Königsberg's
previous political zealots. "The hospital has got a 'Political Boss' (Paul).
Naturally a communist, formerly a Pillau waterman, very simple, primitive man, about fifty. With a formal, pompous voice he delivers a personal speech for everyone, which sparkles with talk about work for the
community, preservation of our German national culture (*Volkstums*)
and similar phrases. With some difficulty I suppress a 'Heil Hitler,' so
much did it remind me of the wholly identical speeches of my former
Blockleiter."[117] In trying to convert the Germans to socialism, neither
the German communists nor the Soviet administrators talked much
about true internationalism. Defaulting instead to the nation as the
meaningful value of a people, German communists proposed preserving German national culture through communism. At the same time,
their Soviet supervisors instructed them to emphasize the superior ac-
complishments of the Soviet Union, itself a product of Russian culture.

Increasingly, the German communists were caught between advocat-
ing for the German population and acting as the German face of Soviet
rule. For example, in August 1946, Paul, the German communist at
Deichelmann's hospital, announced that much of the hospital's furniture had been illegally "procured" (*organisiert*) from private possessions,
and as the rightful property of the state was subject to redistribution.
Whenever a new Soviet citizen arrived, Deichelmann complained, "he
appeals to this protocol and pulls furniture, carpets, lamps, etc. out of
the rooms accordingly," despite the fact that the hospital, while primarily serving Germans, had supposedly been incorporated into the Soviet
budget.[118] But even Kaliningrad's few remaining German true believ-
ers struggled with these contradictions of socialist redistribution. The
same month, a group of three German communists wrote a scathing
letter to the head of the Civilian Affairs Administration, Borisov, ostensibly filing a complaint about the capricious behavior of a particular

District Commandant, Pirov, but pointing to larger problems that Germans faced while building socialism in Kaliningrad. Pirov had instructed his *Blockleiter* (the German communists had adopted the same Nazi term for party cell leaders) to collect all the upholstered furniture in the district, with the threat of arrest for noncompliance. But ultimately, all furniture was collected, not just the upholstered items, with no regard to whether the Germans would be left with anywhere to sleep or sit. Even worse, Pirov granted arbitrary exemptions (usually to beautiful young women, they claimed), and even allowed some Germans (including the wife of a former Nazi party leader) to pick out the best furniture for themselves to take home. Meanwhile, because the confiscated furniture had been so haphazardly stored, up to half of it was destroyed by rain.[119]

The German communists explained that such episodes "discredit the Soviet Union and its political presence among the population" and "hinder the desire to work and damage the political image of the Soviet Union." But even these German communists, who ended their letter with their solid antifascist credentials (all three had served jail time under the Nazis), understood that demanding intercession meant accepting the tacit ethnic hierarchy justified by Germany's war guilt. They asserted that they were ready to help provide for the needs of new "Russian settlers" to Kaliningrad and insisted that if the socialist distribution of property were better explained, Germans would be more amenable to "downsizing voluntarily, and giving over what each could afford to spare."[120] But the question remained: how could German communists spread the message of antifascism if German civilians were expected to give up everything, receive nothing in return, and listen to lectures about how it was all for their own benefit?

German workers increasingly were under the impression that they were no longer even nominally the beneficiaries of their own labor, and that they lived in a racial state with the hierarchies reversed. Farmers sowed German seeds to grow crops for Russian workers; construction workers built roads for Russians to drive (German) trucks and used German bricks to construct apartments for Russian families; electricians rewired German churches to become Russian dance halls and sports centers; and artists painted oversized posters of Stalin's head for state holidays now that the two most important days in the year were not Christmas and Easter, or Hitler's birthday and the anniversary of the Seizure of Power, but Victory Day and the anniversary of the October Revolution. For each holiday it was necessary to start making preparations weeks in advance, and, as Deichelmann wrote in his diary, German workers did more of the "voluntary work" of clearing the streets of rubble for the parade route than the Russians did. At the hospital, the German employees helped decorate the grounds: the central decoration was a giant wood-framed portrait of the Soviet leader. As the craftsmen hoisted it above the entrance portal, they gleefully warned passers-by, "Watch out, we're hanging Stalin here!"[121]

Even the government programs designed to incorporate the Germans into the Soviet system ended up exacerbating the ethnic divide. By creating separate programs organized by nationality, such as non-Russian schools and the German Club, the Soviet government institutionalized a separate-and-unequal regime, at first unwittingly, but then increasingly as standard protocol. As newly established departments had to squeeze German programs into their budgets while failing to meet targets for programs designed for Soviet citizens, the distinction became starker between the appointed beneficiaries of the regime and the Germans. Non-Russian schools, designed to provide progressive native-language education according to common Soviet standards, ended up with fewer resources when Russian-language schools competed for funding; German orphanages and German nursing homes found their budgets capped when programs for newly arriving Soviet settlers began stretching already tight budgets.

In perhaps the most insidious example, the new First Oblast Hospital (until mid-1946, the German Central Hospital) adopted a policy of separating German and Soviet patients, at first for the ostensible reason that Germans were more likely to be suffering from epidemic disease. Subsequently, it became a matter of standard practice to divide treatment centers by ethnicity, even though, because of a shortage of Soviet medical staff, German doctors and nurses initially treated both groups of patients. As more Soviet settlers arrived in Kaliningrad, a quota was placed on the number of German patients to guarantee beds for Soviet citizens, despite the significantly higher illness rates of the Germans.[122] By 1947, the hospital's average death rate was among the highest in the Soviet Union. The hospital directors justified the high mortality rate in the 1947 annual report to Moscow by noting that while 14.5 percent of Germans died, "the majority of them were *distrofiks*" (from *distrofiia*, the Soviet medical euphemism for starvation). The death rate for Soviet patients, the report assured, was only 4.1 percent, close in line with the Soviet average. To address the problem, the hospital further reduced the number of German patients admitted, gave the new beds to Soviet patients, and discharged chronic German patients in order to avoid having to document their deaths. Even so, 78 percent of those who died in the hospital in the year 1947 were German.[123]

The civilian administration was plagued with similar funding problems as before; yet it tried not just to resuscitate the ruins but to build socialism. Extending the language of antifascism to the promise of inclusion in a just and humane socialist society, the new government sought to incorporate Germans and Soviets as equals: they standardized wages according to job rather than nationality, established schools to provide native-language instruction, incorporated dilapidated German hospitals into Soviet budgets, and set up a large network of orphanages to provide social welfare. They also recruited prewar Königsberg's few surviving German communists as lecturers, hosted educational and cultural programming in an official Antifascist Club, and established the *Neue Zeit* German-language newspaper to document the crimes of German fascism and tout the progressiveness of Soviet socialism.[124]

The Soviet government was formed ostensibly to tend to the affairs of the German population but never involved formal German representation. The unintended consequence of this fateful decision was that no "good" German communists could serve as representatives for any emergent state narrative of German heroic resistance against the Nazis or collective victimhood at the hands of the "Hitler clique." Language barriers meant that the Soviet government's antifascist rhetoric geared toward the German population appeared in only limited forums promoted by the state. Few Germans felt motivated to adopt this language themselves because, despite promises of equal pay for equal work, they remained noncitizens with no formal rights or recourse. Antifascism could only take root as legitimating rhetoric when it could also be mobilized by individuals as a language of entitlement; that is, to benefit their material circumstances and to bolster their own position in the new postwar society. As the historian Felix Ackermann shows, successful Sovietization entailed "autosovietization," a bottom-up process of integration carried out by the Sovietized peoples themselves. But Kaliningrad's Germans, as a stateless people, were supposed to receive the message but had no incentive or means to mobilize it.[125]

As more Soviet citizens arrived in the summer of 1946, the message of antifascism increasingly operated for two audiences, one German-speaking and one Russian-speaking. Whereas antifascism for the Germans had been a unidirectional language generated by the state, antifascism among Soviet new settlers, government employees, and party members worked as a language of multidirectional negotiation. New settlers voiced their frustrations about their terrible living conditions and joined local government officials to begin calling, over the course of 1947, for better housing, food, and services for the growing population of Soviet citizens. It was time, they demanded, for Kaliningrad to become a truly Soviet city, to establish a real Soviet government in the spirit of socialism. They articulated these expectations by celebrating the Soviet Union's moral victory over fascism and, just as Soviet citizens did across the Soviet Union, by insisting that the Soviet people's wartime sacrifice to defeat the Nazis should now be repaid through a better life.[126] But these calls to make the city Soviet were made against the backdrop of the German landscape and architecture of the city and in the mirror of the German civilians who remained. The ruins of a more materially abundant Königsberg reflected poorly on the new city still struggling to be built on its foundations. The bodies of starving German civilians, likewise, seemed to be an implicit judgment against the supposed superiority of the Soviet way of life. In the face of ongoing shortages and reconstruction delays, socialism—understood either as order, rationality, government control, or as improved standards of living—still seemed a long way off.

CHAPTER 7

Slavic Soil

The expulsion of Kaliningrad's Germans in 1947–48 was one small episode in the largest population transfer and unmixing of peoples in human history, as between twelve and fourteen million Germans left Eastern Europe and the Soviet Union in voluntary or forced migrations between 1945 and 1950.[1] Across Eastern Europe, these expulsions coincided with the shifting of borders and the reconfiguration of legitimating myths to assert the remaining population's rightful ownership of the land.

The lands expelling their German populations were also those falling, to varying degrees, into the Soviet sphere of influence. Some regions, such as northern East Prussia and the Baltics, were incorporated into the Soviet Union directly; others, such as Poland, Czechoslovakia, and the German Democratic Republic, underwent indirect but forceful Moscow-led Sovietization and the elimination of noncommunist parties. The new governments of these lands, operating with some measure of local autonomy, appealed in particular to the legitimating myth of antifascism, arguing that socialist one-party rule was the only true protection against fascism's return.[2] In the case of the future German Democratic Republic, the antifascist myth was used to legitimize the Socialist Unity Party regime as a necessary prophylactic against Nazism, while functioning to both omit Germans' broad support for the Nazi regime before 1945 and sustain the fiction that the majority of Germans had been victims of Hitler's ruling clique.[3] In the case of the Soviet Union, antifascism gradually became integral to the postwar Soviet state's self-conception, forming a "cult of the Second World War" that presented the Soviet Union as the morally righteous victor in the battle against fascism and safeguard against its postwar resurgence.[4]

Kaliningrad, as a newly annexed former German territory, became one of the first places in the Soviet Union in which the postwar ideology of antifascism was articulated and reconfigured. Soviet leaders used antifascist rhetoric to justify the military occupation and subsequent Soviet civilian rule to both the defeated German civilian population who remained and the new Soviet settlers who arrived. Multiple and competing ideals underpinned this myth as it developed over time—and for different audiences—to legitimate the Soviet annexation.

While Kaliningrad's new civilian government first used antifascism to mobilize the German population to build socialism, by the spring of 1947, Soviet leaders began turning antifascist rhetoric against the Germans, demonizing them as irredeemable "fascist" obstacles to socialist construction. Given the xenophobic political climate of the early Cold War and the larger pattern of forced migrations and expulsions of Germans from East Central Europe, it seems at first glance inevitable that Kaliningrad's Soviet inhabitants would sooner or later turn on their German neighbors. Yet this mobilization of antifascism against the Germans only began in the spring of 1947, as the civilian government was escalating its efforts to incorporate the Germans and convert them to socialism. It arose locally rather than at Moscow's direction, in response to the tensions inherent in the Germans' provisional redemption and to the increasing need on the part of Kaliningrad's leaders to rationalize dire living conditions and ongoing delays in reconstruction.

The new Soviet government used antifascism to unify Soviet citizens around Soviet rule in Kaliningrad, while simultaneously delegitimating the German population's right to live there. But while the rhetoric of antifascism became a powerful legitimating myth in Soviet Kaliningrad, it did not fully suffice to explain why the Soviet Union had annexed land that had no previous historical connection to the Soviet Union or Russian Empire. In the context of the rising Cold War, Soviet local leaders and new settlers turned to other resonant myths of state legitimacy, including, ultimately, nationalism and ethnic primordialism. By the end of 1947, these legitimating myths came together in new ways in order for Soviet citizens fully to stake claim to a once German land.

Accountability

In 1945, the Red Army had entered East Prussia triumphant. Victory on the battlefield also signified the victory in the contest over the future of civilization. The Soviet way of life had proved itself superior in technical and industrial capacity, in the unbroken spirit of its people, and in socialist humanism against fascist inhumanity. Kaliningrad's new leaders set out to build a Soviet city that reflected this triumph, to demonstrate socialism's superiority, and to make a better postwar life to honor the sacrifices made by the Soviet heroes and victims of the war.

Given the wartime devastation and the limited resources available, the civilian government made remarkable progress. It resurrected numerous factories and municipal services and doubled the available amount of living space within a year. The economy grew in nearly every sector. Depending on the industry, output increased by the end of 1947 from 1.5 to 4.5 times the production of the previous year.[5] But compared to other Soviet and Central European cities, Kaliningrad was a wild frontier. Food shortages remained endemic. Most of the city had no consistent water and electricity supply well into 1948.[6] Abandoned buildings lay crumbling while new settlers faced housing shortages. The total useable living and office space remained still at only one-sixth of the prewar stock, and most of it lay in disrepair. Bric-a-brac construction continued unabated, in some cases further damaging reconstruction efforts. Individual industries and even the city's own municipal services department, working to fulfill orders, would often dismantle the ruins of two buildings to construct a single one, diminishing the total available living space. New settlers frequently chopped away the upper floors and ceilings of their apartment buildings for firewood to keep warm.[7]

By late 1946, the region also faced new pressures from above. After Kaliningrad became an oblast of the RSFSR in the spring of 1946, Moscow state and economic institutions began issuing quarterly and annual production targets for Kaliningrad's institutions and industries. Without the resources to carry them out, Kaliningrad's leaders had to report widespread failures. As the State Planning Committee (*Gosplan*) representative for Kaliningrad Oblast, V. Vakhrov, conceded, production in 1947 suffered from "significant plan under-fulfillment" in almost every area of industry. Trams worked at only 40 percent of target efficiency; the city had constructed only one-third of the required communal bathhouses; workers succeeded in rebuilding only four of the ten bridges in Kaliningrad's city center.[8] The two cellulose paper plants met only an average of 42 percent of the targeted output, while the shipbuilding plant fulfilled only 57.6 percent.[9] The head of Civilian Affairs, Vasilii Andreevich Borisov, likewise reported to the RS-FSR Council of Ministers that Kaliningrad's food industry remained in shambles: without the necessary raw materials, little besides bread, beer, and vodka was being produced.[10]

Such reports of plan under-fulfillment were common features of the Soviet economy, but Kaliningrad's state of affairs was especially dire. By 1947, Soviet leaders could no longer point to wartime destruction to rationalize failure, and it was politically dangerous to blame Moscow for raising expectations without supplying the necessary support. Borisov and other city and oblast officials began pinning the blame on individuals. In quarterly and annual reports, they pointed to workers' and administrators' shortcomings, especially poor training, shoddy work, and bureaucratic ineptitude. They often emphasized the inexperience and poor suitability of newly arriving settlers. For example, reports noted how one-third of Kaliningrad's collective farmers had never before worked in agriculture. Of the 3,000 workers arriving at the Shipbuilding Plant 820, only five had any experience building ships. Among the 5,000 workers sent to work in the Pulp and Paper Mills were a large number of "ill, invalids, . . . and those who needed to be sent back home." A group of newly arriving lumberjacks included forty-one women, fourteen men, and seventy-three children—among them many invalids, women with nursing infants, and women in the final stages of pregnancy.[11]

Kaliningrad's leaders also faced pressure from these new settlers themselves. Moscow's mass settlement campaign had brought 20,000 to 30,000 new settlers each month starting in the fall of 1946.[12] These settlers had been lured with promises of abundance: they had been told that the formerly German land was wealthy, that the soil was fertile and the climate mild, and that the streets were lined with fruit trees. New settlers were dismayed to discover conditions much worse than those they had left behind, and the government struggled to assure them that their lives would soon improve. Newspaper and radio editorials presented visions of a future Kaliningrad with modern amenities and social services and encouraged the new settlers to work to bring the new socialist city into being. These same forums, however, also allowed Soviet citizens to voice their frustrations. Frequent letters to the editor in *Kaliningradskaia pravda* criticized the poor functioning of city services. Like civilian government leaders, they also frequently blamed individuals, particularly low-level administrators.[13] A letter to the editor on February 4, 1947, for example, complained that telegrams sent in January were not received until February, and customers were simply given a shrug of "better late than never."[14] During the Second Session of the Kaliningrad City Soviet in February 1948, one speaker noted that letters had been flooding in daily about electricity shortages, asking, "When will the employees of Kaliningradenergo stop abusing us? When will we have electricity?" Kaliningradenergo employees, when asked when the situation would improve, reportedly "gave no clear answer, claiming that the Ministry had not sent staff, there were no funds, not enough workers, no materials, and dozens of other objective reasons supposedly justifying the terrible state of the electrical supply."[15]

Dissatisfied by poor living conditions, many new settlers simply packed up and left.[16] Workers on the Cherniakhovsk (Insterburg) railway junction complained in early 1948 how their relatives back home had "plenty of goods in the shops, but you can't always even buy black bread here without a line, so we request you to please fire us from our jobs [so we can go home]." Other workers began selling off the furniture from their workshop and from a nearby state farm to save money for train tickets.[17] The local administration found itself powerless to stop this exodus. Although most Soviet citizens remained tied to their place of residence, Kaliningrad's new settlers had been granted internal USSR passports in order to travel, and they used these same passports to return home or to other regions of the Soviet Union. For the first ten years of the history of the oblast, the Soviet population remained unstable, as people arrived, stayed a few months, and then left. During many years, the same number of people left Kaliningrad Oblast as those who arrived.[18]

The mass settlement campaign made already difficult conditions far worse. While the 1946 growing season had provided more food than the previous year, the majority of new settlers arrived after the harvest. The Civilian Affairs Administration scrambled to secure food to feed them, even requesting that the neighboring Belorussian and Lithuanian Socialist Republics send stockpiles of potatoes before the first frost. It also appealed in vain to Moscow to temporarily halt new

settlement, but these measures were of little use, and trains full of settlers continued to arrive.[19]

The winter of 1946–47 was one of the coldest on record and led to a
winter famine across the Soviet Union, in which between one and two
million people died of starvation and famine-related diseases across
Russia, Ukraine, Belorussia, and Moldavia.[20] Although temperatures
were milder than in much of the Soviet Union, many Soviet civilians
in Kaliningrad suffered great hunger.[21] Antonina Egorovna Shadrina
remembers how she and her fellow collective farmers resorted to eating grass and sorrel, while others recall that many people killed and
ate their horses, cats, and dogs to survive. Vladimir Petrovich Filatov
scoured the ruins for rotten potatoes to feed his daughter until he
could save enough money to send her back to Tula "so she wouldn't
die of hunger."[22] Antonina Semenovna Nikolaeva recalls how two of
the daughters of her neighbors' family did not survive.[23] Many new settlers, however, remember that conditions were better in Kaliningrad
than in their former homes. Ivan Ivanovich Potemkin recalls that in
Kostroma Oblast, "war veterans gave away their rations to their families
while they themselves died from hunger and cold." Aleksei Nikolaevich Solov'ev remembers that in Vologda Oblast "entire families died
of starvation" in contrast to isolated incidents in Kaliningrad. In part,
new settlers' memories depend on the time they arrived—those arriving
before the winter of 1946 tend to describe devastating conditions, while
those who arrived at the end of the famine remember Kaliningrad, by
comparison to their former homes, as a land of abundance.[24] The juxtaposition between wartime deprivation and the beginning of a new life
in Kaliningrad also colored the memories of the new settlers. Archival
records reveal that food shortages remained endemic through the end
of the decade. Aleksandra Aleksandrovna Rusakova remembers that it
only became possible to live more or less normally starting in 1953.[25]

Mortality rates for Soviet citizens in Kaliningrad were lower than
those in other Soviet regions hit by famine, but German mortality rates
were among the worst.[26] Soviet settlers likewise recall that Germans
starved disproportionately, German children in particular. Galina Pav-
lovna Roman recalls seeing frozen German bodies piled on the streets
each morning during her walk to school.[27] Other Soviet inhabitants,
especially those living in the countryside, claimed to have tried to help
when they could, offering milk from their cows or a slice of bread when
they could afford to spare it. Antonina Semenovna Nikolaeva remembers finding a German girl with her mother in a neighboring farmhouse.

The little girl pointed to her mother and explained with sign language that she had died. Then the girl showed Nikolaeva the grave of her little sister, who was already buried in the garden. They buried the mother alongside her, gave the little girl something to eat, and took her from the house. But because Soviet settlers were also going hungry, many of them turned against their German neighbors, plundering their homes and stealing their possessions. Anna Ivanovna Trubchanina remembers how her fellow collective farm members had no hay to feed their hungry cattle and no money to buy any, so they took hay from neighboring German farmers at gunpoint.[28]

By March 1947, conditions had become so bad that the Civilian Affairs Administration characterized German starvation in Kaliningrad as "mass death." Germans were dying of hunger in hospitals and clinics, in their apartments, and even on the streets. Corpses had to be exhumed daily from the basements and rubble of abandoned buildings. The Civilian Affairs Administration's report explained that the Germans' poor living conditions resulted from a lack of housing and food ("as could be seen by the frequent occurrence of Germans scrounging for scraps from the trash") and mentioned how these poor conditions accounted, in part, for the "noticeable growth" of crime, including child prostitution. But while the report called for several measures to improve the German population's "complicated situation," most of them sought only to establish administrative clarity on various topics. None of the measures called for more food—the only solution to starvation, but the one least possible to implement.[29]

The Enemy Within

For two years, Soviet leaders had mobilized the language of antifascism to appeal to the German population. With no power to change their collective status locally, they instead focused on rehabilitating them as individuals. The military administration had appealed to the rehabilitative power of socialist labor, while the Civilian Administration attempted to reeducate the Germans, convert them to socialism, and integrate them into the socialist system. These efforts remained decentralized, haphazardly implemented, and internally contradictory, but they also demonstrated the inclusionary impulse in Soviet ideology. The problem, however, was that there remained no gauge for success.

With no means for Kaliningrad's leaders to declare the German population collectively redeemed and no formal measure for individual rehabilitation, the Germans' redemption became tied implicitly to the pace of reconstruction. This tendency emerged early on: records show how in February 1946, the head of the Special Military District, Kuz'ma Galitskii, had blamed food shortages on the continuing obstinacy of some "individual Germans."[30] This language of German intransigence also appears sporadically in the summer of 1946. At a party meeting in the Civilian Affairs Administration about improving labor productivity, for example, one speaker, Comrade Chirkin, denounced his fellow Soviet Communist Party members for getting accustomed to a "people who are hostile to us." As Chirkin explained, "the Germans are working for us, but we are not actually controlling them. They take advantage of that and have a mercenary attitude toward work, do not fulfill their quotas. Our revolutionary vigilance has slackened. Control over hiring of the members of the German population must be thorough. We need to oversee their labor on a daily basis."[31] Whereas Galitskii had denounced "individual Germans" for failing to engage in socialist labor, Chirkin called for vigilance against the German population at large. "Revolutionary vigilance," in other words, was not about converting the Germans to socialism but defending socialist construction against them.

The discourse of a "threatening outside" infused everyday life in prewar Stalinism, and as Tarik Amar argues, it was this illiberal Stalinist civilization that was exported to the new western borderlands of the Soviet Union after 1939. But in practice, postwar Soviet ideology still, despite the hypocrisy and oppression, continued to adhere to "the axiom of the perfectibility of categorically all." In Kaliningrad, that meant ongoing contradictory tendencies of integration and marginalization.[32] Only toward the end of 1946 did material and demographic pressures in Kaliningrad converge, tipping the scales toward exclusion. First, although the civilian government introduced programs geared toward German reeducation and integration, the region's designated status as an oblast within the RSFSR necessitated that the new civilian government understand its mission—and its budgetary priorities— to be to tend primarily to the needs of Soviet citizens. Such was the case especially by early 1947, at the height of the Winter Famine, when the Soviet population of the oblast grew to 278,000, almost triple the remaining German population.[33] Second, although individual Communist Party cells had previously operated in a decentralized fashion within military units and in workplaces, the full array of district, city, and oblast party organs was introduced in the spring of 1947, creating a chain of ideological accountability from Kaliningrad to the Kremlin. Because few qualified candidates could be recruited to relocate, most of these new positions were staffed by military and civilian party members already living in Kaliningrad. They were especially young and inexperienced; over 70 percent had been granted party membership during the war, mostly for bravery in battle, and only one in seven had attended university.[34] Few of them had spent much time studying the sacred texts of Marxism-Leninism; their understanding of Soviet socialism was based on intuition and experience.

These material and ideological factors triggered a splitting of the language of antifascism. At least formally, German audiences continued to receive inclusionary language and even an increase in government programs designed to rehabilitate them. But more and more often, Soviet officials, in search of a scapegoat for the poor state of affairs, began describing the German population as an enemy within.

The dramatic change first appears in the records of the first Kaliningrad Oblast Party Activists' meeting in December 1946—the first main gathering of local party leaders in anticipation of the establishment of the full range of party organs in the spring of 1947. During a discussion about Kaliningrad's first staging of USSR-wide elections, in which many speakers complained about ongoing reconstruction delays, Evgenii Rudakov, the head of the Oblast Ministry for State Security (MGB, the successor organization of the NKVD), demanded increased vigilance to defend the integrity of the elections. He reminded his listeners that Kaliningrad "differs a little from other cities" that had staged elections before because "a pretty significant number of Germans live here—our open enemies." Rudakov identified, along with a few other industrial sites, the milling plant where many German worked as a potential target for arson and "all kinds of sabotage . . . of interest to the enemy." Rudakov pointed out that security at the plant was weak, and every day thieves were stealing food and supplies. One guard there (presumably a Soviet citizen, although Rudakov did not specify) had even conspired with "German crooks" to smuggle out ten sacks of flour. Rudakov insisted that food production sites in Kaliningrad were targets of terrorism, and that the enemy stood to benefit from sabotaging the Soviet elections. He did not mention that Germans were starving, a fact well known to anyone living in Kaliningrad. Petty theft and pilfering were common among Soviets and Germans alike, but Rudakov cast this tactic for survival during the winter famine as a German crime of sabotage against the Soviet state.[35]

This overt condemnation of the Germans by the Soviet leadership was new, but Rudakov was responding to widespread anxieties about the territory's fate. Rumors were spreading across Russia that Kaliningrad was a dangerous frontier outside Soviet control. In the fall of 1946, for example, the Ministry of the Interior reported that potential new settlers from Yaroslavl Oblast had heard that Russians were being killed by the dozens by German bandits who stole all of their property; other rumors circulated that Germans were preventing new settlers from staying.[36] A particularly extravagant rumor claimed that Germans had hanged a Russian soldier on the outstretched arm of the Kaiser Wilhelm monument on the anniversary of the October Revolution; on his chest, Germans had reportedly hung the defiant sign "Königsberg was and shall remain!"[37] Fears spread in Kaliningrad and among potential settlers elsewhere that the territory would not remain Soviet; the police chief of the Mordovian Autonomous Republic reported that several potential new settlers refused to be resettled in Kaliningrad because they feared they would find themselves in a battle zone.[38] One of the engineers for the city's printing press claimed that even Aleksei Kosygin, the Soviet minister overseeing Kaliningrad's development, had admitted he was openly hesitant about dedicating resources to Kaliningrad because the city might eventually end up back under German control.[39]

Despite these rumors, there is little available evidence that the Germans posed any true conspiratorial threat. Although many of them resented Soviet rule, Germans in Kaliningrad were generally marked by their lack of resistance, either organized or individual.[40] Even German children adapted to their status as an underclass, learning not to react or defend themselves when Soviet children became angry with them, threw rocks, or cursed at them as fascists.[41] Some new Soviet settlers do recall occasional acts of German defiance—one old German man, bitter about being forced from his home, reportedly burned himself alive along with a few neighboring houses rather than leave them to the Soviets.[42] But most Soviet interviewees recall that their German neighbors were passive.

Although some early inhabitants recall rumors that German women living in Soviet homes were SS agents sent to kill Soviet children, available police reports from 1946 and 1947 also document relatively few actual violent crimes. In the spring of 1947, a few Germans were arrested for distributing anti-Soviet song lyrics, but by far the most common documented crime was theft.[43] While in neighboring Lithuania, underground nationalist groups posed a significant challenge to Soviet rule, only fifty-four Germans were convicted of political crimes in sabotage in the second half of 1947. The Germans' primary "counter-revolutionary" crime in Kaliningrad was stealing potatoes.[44]

Nevertheless, the language of "German enemies" spread quickly in the spring of 1947. Local party and government leaders drew on familiar scripts to denounce the Germans as a fifth column of fascist wreckers. German petty theft, black market trading, prostitution, and even hunger-driven cannibalism were cast as organized anti-Soviet opposition. The Germans' emaciated bodies, as the carriers of epidemic and venereal disease, served as outward proof not of the failure of Soviet social welfare but of the Germans' contamination with fascism. By attacking the Germans as fascists, local Soviet leaders could justify Soviet rule: despite the ongoing material hardship, Soviet rule became the necessary safeguard against fascism's resurgence. Remarkably, this rhetoric was not initially shared by visitors from Moscow. For example, during a visit in February 1947, the Council of Ministers' Representative for Religious Cults G. Ia. Vrachev noted that while Kaliningrad's few German Catholics held a "strong anti-Soviet position," German Lutherans (the majority in Kaliningrad) had significant potential to ally with the Soviet Union against the Catholic Church.[45]

The anti-German rhetoric was in full swing by the time Oblast First Party Secretary Petr Andreevich Ivanov finally arrived at his post in March 1947.[46] Ivanov, formerly a district party leader in Leningrad, had been awarded for his heroism in leading a partisan unit to defend the besieged city during the war. As first party secretary in Kaliningrad, Ivanov became the region's main ideological gatekeeper. Ivanov was shocked by conditions in Kaliningrad, worse than those he had experienced in Leningrad at the end of the war.[47] But when he gave his first formal speech just weeks after his arrival, Ivanov refrained from blaming the Germans. He instead referred to them in the old antifascist mode, which assumed the possibility of inclusion and rehabilitation. Ivanov criticized local party members for Kaliningrad's terrible state of affairs, prompting hecklers to taunt him from the audience. Immediately thereafter, two speakers, Rudakov, the MGB leader who had warned of German saboteurs in December 1946, and Oblast Party Secretary for Propaganda I. P. Trifonov, launched a vicious counterattack, casting the Germans as constant saboteurs and active threats to oblast security. Rudakov and Trifonov accused Ivanov of going soft on the Germans and being ill-suited to deal with Kaliningrad's problems. Ivanov, shaken by their accusations, replied that the fate of the

German population was an issue not for Kaliningrad but for Moscow to decide.[48]

Marginalization and Expulsion

Rudakov and Trifonov, representatives of Kaliningrad's most important ideological institutions, had already begun their own expulsion campaign behind the scenes. In January 1947, they wrote to Moscow, citing German criminality as a negative influence on new settlers' moral constitution and reporting rumors that the Germans were convinced that the oblast was only "temporarily occupied by the USSR."[49]

This alarmist report set off a chain reaction of discussions within the Ministry of Foreign Affairs, the Ministry of Internal Affairs, and the Politburo. The representative from the RSFSR Council of Ministers, A. Shubnikov, wrote to Deputy Minister of Foreign Affairs Andrei Smirnov in early February 1947, pointing out the "utmost necessity for immediate decisions on a number of questions concerning the legal situation of the German population of Kaliningrad Oblast and the carrying out of political work among them."[50] Smirnov, in turn, wrote to Viacheslav Molotov, then the USSR minister for foreign affairs. Smirnov expanded on the letter, casting the presence of the German population in Kaliningrad as politically dangerous, given that in some parts of the oblast, "the number of Germans significantly exceeds the number of newly settled Soviet citizens" and was "creating a mood of uncertainty" among them. Smirnov requested that Molotov appoint a special representative "to study various questions connected to the existence of a German population in Kaliningrad Oblast and the incorporation of the oblast into the USSR."[51]

Germans themselves played no small part in calling attention to their precarious situation. In early 1947, Germans in the Allied Zones of Occupation wrote requests to Moscow to permit their family members and colleagues in Kaliningrad to be reunited with their families further west. After Moscow authorities granted permission for a few hundred Germans to leave, word spread and requests began pouring in. Many Germans claim that Soviet officials seemed surprised they wanted to leave the "Soviet paradise" (the derogatory term for the Soviet Union used during the Third Reich).[52] The Lutheran minister Hugo Linck describes how a Soviet security agent expressed curiosity about why the Germans wanted to resettle, leaving Linck the delicate task of explaining that it was because of their poor living conditions. Archival records reveal how Linck, with the help of a Russian-speaking German translator, petitioned for his fellow Lutheran pastor Rosenfeld to be able to leave in July 1947. Rosenfeld had been working at a state collective farm with his family, but when he became ill from malnutrition, he was fired and hospitalized. One of Rosenfeld's sons had already died of starvation in October 1946, Linck explained, "as a result of malnutrition" (*vsledstvie nizhnii plokhogo kormlenie* [sic]) and the family had just been ordered to vacate their apartment.[53]

Although only a few hundred Germans left by mid-1947, their shocking reports about their lives in Kaliningrad risked damaging the Soviet Union's international reputation. That summer, Kaliningrad's propaganda secretary Trifonov received a translation of an article from a British Zone Berlin newspaper, *Der Sozialdemokrat*, about the situation in Königsberg, as reported by these first returnees. The stories seemed so fantastical that they could hardly be true, except that the returnees were all reporting the same conditions: dysentery in the filtration camps, food shortages, starvation of those who could not work, no public transportation or city services, no German representation in government.[54]

Officials in Kaliningrad construed these requests to leave Kaliningrad as evidence that the German population was hostile to the Soviet Union and constituted a threat.[55] The head of the Kaliningrad Oblast Ministry for Internal Affairs, General Major Trofimov, had allied with the Oblast Ministry for Internal Affairs head Rudakov and Propaganda Secretary Trifonov locally to lead the anti-German campaign, and Trofimov then escalated the case with USSR Minister of Internal Affairs, Sergei Kruglov. He described the Germans' low capacity to work, high crime rates, industrial sabotage, high incidence of venereal disease, and the potential for ideological contamination or espionage from German-Soviet cohabitation. Unlike Rudakov and Trifonov's previous hedging letters to Moscow, Trofimov declared boldly that the Germans were a negative influence and expressly requested their resettlement to the Soviet Zone.[56]

While Kaliningrad's party leaders were campaigning behind the scenes, Kaliningrad institutions began a local process of exclusion. They focused especially on marginalizing Germans from high-profile workplaces. Despite becoming the minority population in the oblast, Germans still comprised 48 percent of the total workforce, in some sectors up to 90 percent.[57] In the spring of 1947, city and oblast officials began reporting the number of workers in their institutions, separating them out by nationality: Russian and German. In doing so, they rationalized underperformance by pointing to the low number of Soviet workers.[58] Head Engineer of the City Department of Municipal Services, Konstantinova, complained, for example, that the city had less than half of the required janitors employed, and that "all the janitors are Germans." Similarly, one division of the Sewer Trust had only 449 of the required 785 workers, and "of them [only] fifty-seven are Russian."[59] This tactic allowed agencies to argue that German workers constituted both a problem of labor supply and an ideological challenge—not enough Russian workers" had been employed, while dangerous enemies continued to work for the Soviet state.[60]

Despite numerous discussions between state and party leaders in Kaliningrad and Moscow, no decision about the Germans' fate was decided by spring. As correspondence trailed off, it seemed to Kaliningrad's leaders that Moscow had sidelined the issue. After two difficult months in office, First Party Secretary Ivanov in May 1947 wrote a shrill and desperate letter to Stalin. Ivanov focused on Kaliningrad's special character to rationalize its failures in reconstruction and industrial output. Other parts of the RSFSR, he complained, sent their dregs to Kaliningrad—the youngest, least qualified workers and cadres, many of whom were invalids or drunks. Continual low output made it difficult to reestablish industry, and looting by soldiers left the new oblast with few supplies. Abandoning his earlier approach to the German population, Ivanov adopted the rhetoric of those who had attacked him in March. He described the German population as saboteurs, pointing to the arrest of 700 Germans crossing into the Lithuanian SSR in search of food during the Winter Famine as evidence of an attempt to infiltrate the Soviet Union.[61] Unlike Trofimov, who asked Kruglov to resettle the Germans, Ivanov refrained from suggesting a solution to Stalin. Instead, he requested that a commission be formed to study Kaliningrad's problems and form a plan for its development.[62]

While blaming the Germans for many of Kaliningrad's problems, Ivanov's letter made the fateful political mistake of also blaming Moscow. Stalin summoned Ivanov for a personal meeting in the Kremlin, where on June 9, 1947, the Politburo of the Central Committee met in private to discuss Ivanov's letter. Ivanov was invited into the room thereafter, along with Borisov, the head of Kaliningrad's Civilian Affairs Administration. They met with Stalin and the Politburo for an hour, and Ivanov reportedly left the meeting distraught.[63] At Stalin's direction, the head of the Council of Ministers' Bureau for Trade and

Light Industry, Aleksei Kosygin, formed a committee to study Kaliningrad's economic problems. The following week, while the commission was visiting Kaliningrad, Ivanov remained shuttered in his office.[64] On June 18, 1947, on the eve of the presentation of the commission's findings, Ivanov was found dead, shot with his own pistol. The death was reported a suicide. At the meeting the next morning, Kosygin, with no mention of the incident, named Vladimir Vasil'evich Shcherbakov, formerly the chairman of the Central Committee in Lithuania, as Kaliningrad's new first party secretary.[65]

Although it cost Ivanov his life, the anti-German rhetoric he mobilized had finally attracted Moscow's attention. In June 1947, the RSFSR announced a special "Stalin Plan" for economic development, a massive investment package designed to demonstrate to Soviet new settlers the state's commitment to building socialism in Kaliningrad.[66] The plan promised 700,000,000 rubles of support for construction and industry in 1947–48 (in some sectors, until 1950) and promised support for the development of the economy, including shipbuilding, paper production, amber mining, fishing, energy, transport, and agriculture.[67] According to reports from contemporaries, the roads to Kaliningrad were soon clogged with new combines, tractors, and farming equipment. Local newspapers and radio programs bragged about the wealth of supplies and teams of new specialist workers arriving daily.[68]

Within months, however, the familiar problems of disorganization and shortages reemerged. Once it became clear that neither Kaliningrad nor Moscow could fulfill the ambitious targets, public bravado about the Stalin Plan faded from the headlines. The fate of Oblast Party Secretary Ivanov served as an important lesson, however. Ivanov's successor, Shcherbakov, learned to handle himself delicately, suppressing the true state of affairs when reporting to Moscow. It was the last personal attention Stalin gave to Kaliningrad before his death in 1953. Although Kaliningrad was slowly being integrated into the Soviet budget, it was left again, at least for the next several years, mostly to make do on its own.[69]

Despite the hopes of those who had led the local drive for expulsion, the Stalin Plan did not address the fate of the German population. In June 1947, Kruglov proposed a limited measure, expelling orphans, invalids, and the elderly (an estimated 48,000 Germans) to reduce the burden on the oblast's scarce resources. Kosygin, meanwhile, suggested that the Council of Ministers draft a plan to deport the Germans internally to the "eastern regions of the Soviet Union."[70] Neither plan was set into motion. As many as 3,400 individual Germans were given permission to leave by the beginning of summer, many of whom were invalids in danger of starving.[71] But with no resolution from Moscow, civilian and party leaders in Kaliningrad began to assume by late summer 1947 that the Germans would remain.

Although anti-German rhetoric became a consistent feature of the oblast city and party meetings, the actual treatment of the German population still incorporated overlapping tendencies of inclusion and exclusion. While Germans were being marginalized from high-profile employment, the local government pursued policies to benefit those who remained employed. More generally, living conditions improved for both Germans and Soviets in the summer of 1947, after the hard winter famine, and both groups again began to imagine the possibility of long-term cohabitation. Germans still working in official jobs in the summer of 1947 were more likely to receive full wages and be paid on time. The government opened more grocery stores for the German population, and even though supply remained uneven, some German memoirists recall that it became easier to buy bread, butter, oil, and even fish at reasonable prices.[72] Some German workers were even recruited for specialized career training: Käthe Hielscher, who was seventeen in 1947 and had spent the previous two years working odd jobs, was selected to become a mason. The training provided her not only job stability but even good wages. For the first time, she recalls, she had plenty to eat, could afford to buy a new pair of shoes, and was even permitted to take days off.[73]

Moreover, government organizations continued to request funding to expand services for the Germans' antifascist reeducation and social welfare throughout 1947.[74] The Neue Zeit newspaper first came into publication in August 1947, at the height of anti-German rhetoric, and party officials wrote to secure more funds to expand its operation. In late September and early October 1947, Borisov and Shcherbakov sent letters to Moscow requesting more supplies and textbooks for German schools, orphanages, and daycares. Borisov and Shcherbakov even asked for funds to establish a ten-month pedagogical program to train teachers "from the trustworthy portion of the German population" and more German-speaking teachers to teach specialized subjects in German middle schools.[75] In late September, a local representative for the Education Department wrote in cooperation with Shcherbakov to request more funds and supplies for German school children and orphans, apologizing for the late request because they had been under the false impression that the Germans would be resettled.[76]

Kaliningrad's leaders were therefore caught off guard when, less than two weeks later, on October 11, 1947, the Soviet Council of Ministers issued Resolution No. 3547-1169 dictating the resettlement of the Germans to the Soviet Zone of Occupation.[77] Local Soviet officials conducted a final German census, with a total reported population of 105,558. Not all of these Germans were expelled, however: some of the names on the official expulsion lists were later annotated with "died," "taken off the list," or "given over to the MGB."[78] The first transports began on October 22, 1947. By the end of the year, 30,283 Germans had reportedly been expelled, mostly those who were sick, elderly, or invalid, but also those living near border regions.[79]

The expulsion announcement solved the long-standing problem of the Germans' provisional inclusion by deeming the entire German population collectively unredeemed and irredeemable. Deportations and expulsions had long been a tool of Soviet population management. Despite the Soviet Union's official rejection of biological racism and insistence on the primacy of class over nation, Soviet authorities sometimes conflated the two, viewing ethnic groups as class enemies—particularly the Germans, for whom being 'bourgeois' was often seen as being part of their national character.[80] Moreover, Soviet nationalities policy had already turned toward Russocentrism on the eve of the Second World War.[81] During the war, Soviet security forces, at Stalin's direction, had carried out targeted purges and deportations of ethnic groups and national minorities, especially those diaspora minorities whose geopolitical loyalties were deemed suspect. In the last year of the war, Soviet leaders also 'repatriated' Germans from the new Soviet western borderlands.[82] Moreover, the expulsion of Kaliningrad's Germans was announced in late 1947, during a time of escalating international tensions, at a time when, inside the Soviet Union, exclusionary Russian nationalism and xenophobia joined together with a shift toward hardline Sovietization policies across Eastern Europe.[83]

Yet the expulsion of the Germans, while seeming inevitable in hindsight, was not a foregone conclusion. After East Prussia was divided in 1945, its remaining population ended up in three new governments. In Masuria, the southern two-thirds of the former province that came under Polish control, the local population, some of whom spoke the Masurian dialect of Polish but many of whom had identified with Germany before the war, were allowed to remain and adopt Polish citizenship, under the assumption that these Masurians were actually Poles who had only been temporarily Germanized. The Memel/Klaipėda region became Soviet territory like Kaliningrad, but was incorporated directly into the Lithuanian SSR and governed by a Lithuanian civilian administration (at least in name if not always by ethnic composition) from 1945 on. In 1945, just as in Soviet Königsberg, the region was scoured for reparations and looted, and many of the remaining men who did not flee the Red Army's advance were deported internally to Tajikistan or Siberia.[84]

In the Klaipėda region, Russification was not a primary goal in establishing the territory as part of postwar Soviet Lithuania. The initial priorities, as in Kaliningrad, were to reestablish the economy and transform the population in the spirit of Soviet ideology so that the Lithuanian people could take part in building communism. But also as in Kaliningrad, many ethnic Russians were brought to Klaipėda to assist in rebuilding the port, fishing industry, and timber industry. In both cities, as was the case in most of the new Soviet western borderlands, Russification began not by design, but as a byproduct of this process. As Russians moved in, their language took precedent in the affairs of the state. In Klaipėda, despite the region being incorporated into the Lithuanian SSR, all of the decrees of the Executive Committee from 1945–50, with few exceptions, were issued in Russian. In 1946, five Russian and five Lithuanian schools were established, as well as two mixed schools; in the 1950s, Lithuanians made up 40 percent of the population; the others came mostly from Russia, but also from Ukraine and other parts of the Soviet Union. But the remaining inhabitants in the Klaipėda region were assumed to be assimilable, and these "Prussian Lithuanians" were permitted in December 1947 to obtain Soviet citizenship if they could demonstrate they had Lithuanian citizenship when the region was in Lithuania between 1923 and 1939.[85] In both Masuria and Klaipėda, the formerly East Prussian local population was often deemed suspect or not fully assimilated into the national culture. But even if they were unofficially treated as second-class inhabitants, they were granted formal citizenship and permitted to remain.

Only in Kaliningrad were the former inhabitants of East Prussia deemed unassimilable. But even in this case, expulsion to the Soviet Zone of Occupation was not the only possible solution. Despite the Soviet Union using expulsions and population exchanges as a population management tool during the war, wholesale expulsions were less often used after the war—instead, Soviet policy focused on selective internal deportations to punish alleged collaborators, eliminate opposition, and facilitate collectivization. In Kaliningrad, unlike in Ukraine and much of the Baltics, the Germans posed no organized political threat, and Kaliningrad's collectivization was already complete.[86] Although local leaders nevertheless turned against the Germans to scapegoat construction delays, the exchange between Kruglov and Kosygin in the summer of 1947 demonstrates that internal deportation remained an option until the very end. Either way, the Germans were understood no longer to belong in Kaliningrad. Once the territory was incorporated into not just the USSR, but the Russian SFSR, Germans became the minority in their former homes: no longer the titular nationality of Kaliningrad but outsiders.

Inside Kaliningrad, antifascist rhetoric did not end with the expulsion announcement. Even though Kaliningrad's Germans were deemed unassimilable, local Soviet officials continued to imagine socialism as humanity's most modern and advanced civilization, and they continued to try to convince the Germans of its superiority. For most of the following year, the German Club continued its work, German schools expanded their curricula, and the *Neue Zeit* newspaper continued to be printed. These efforts, however, no longer facilitated integration but merely touted Soviet superiority. In January 1948, Kaliningrad City Party Committee Secretary Bulgakov wrote to the Prisoner of War Camp Administration (GUPVI MVD SSSR), explaining the important pedagogical role Kaliningrad's German Club performed among the German population and requesting more literature to be sent from the POW camps to aid Kaliningrad's German Club lecturers, "given the importance of the club's task of providing political education in the spirit of democratic consciousness to the German population in the oblast, encouraging a friendly attitude toward the USSR."[87] Kaliningrad's Germans, despite being fascists while living Kaliningrad, might, upon arrival to the Soviet Zone of Occupation in Berlin, become good communists.

The number of registered German workers in the oblast dropped precipitously by the fall of 1947, especially in industry, healthcare, and municipal services. After the implementation of the Stalin Plan fell into familiar patterns of inefficiency, squandered funds, and undelivered supplies by the fall of 1947, the new measure for socialist reconstruction became the degree to which Germans were being eliminated from public life. Continuing a trend from the summer, speakers at government meetings and authors of quarterly reports made a ritual out of celebrating workplace purges. Reports in November 1947 celebrated the elimination of German workers from Shipbuilding Plant 820, for example, and speakers at the Kaliningrad City Soviet in December 1947 celebrated the city's greatest victory in healthcare not as the supply of new medicine or improved treatment (indeed, most of the session was spent discussing continuing poor conditions), but the replacement of German medical personnel with "Russians."[88]

The expulsion of the Germans was not designed to provide newly arriving Soviet settlers with jobs, however. Endemic labor shortages became even worse after the Germans were dismissed. Some historians of Kaliningrad thus argue that Moscow's expulsion order came against the wishes of the local administration. Bert Hoppe, for example, commenting on a complaint by the First Party Secretary Shcherbakov about declining industrial output after the first wave of expulsions in the fall of 1947, notes that "it would not be the last time that the interests of the state leadership in Moscow stood in diametrical opposition to the authorities in Kaliningrad." But such arguments fail to acknowledge the ongoing local dynamics of marginalization. Kaliningrad organizations desperately sought out Soviet Russian workers in order to lay off Germans. At first, they used the presence of German workers as a scapegoat for plan under-fulfillment; after the expulsion, they blamed failure to meet plan targets on the Germans' absence.[89]

Despite being pushed out of high-profile sectors of the economy, a large number of Kaliningrad's Germans remained for up to a year, until the final mass transport in November 1948. A few thousand more were only permitted to resettle in 1951, including some German specialists who were retained to work in industrial sectors. Other late expellees included Germans who had crossed into the Lithuanian SSR in search of food during the Winter Famine but had since been detained.[90] Most Germans had suffered terribly in Kaliningrad after the war, and many of them died. The true number of deaths will remain a mystery—inconsistent record keeping and exaggerated statistics on both sides obscure the numbers of those who survived the war in Soviet East Prussia, those who were expelled, and those who died in Kaliningrad or elsewhere during deportation. Most Western historians and Königsberg émigrés claim, based on faulty estimates of the number of Germans who remained in Fortress Königsberg at the end of the war, that 75 percent of the Germans in northern East Prussia at the end of the war did not survive and that only 24,000 Germans were expelled.[91]

Soviet expulsion records claim, by contrast, that 102,494 Germans were expelled by 1951, and that the highest registered population in the region had been 129,614 in September 1945, implying far fewer deaths.[92] But the real population at the end of the invasion had been far higher—perhaps as high as 150,000 to 200,000 before epidemics in the summer of 1945 wiped out tens of thousands, and Soviet expulsion records may also have been inflated. While the data remain inconclusive, it is possible to estimate, based on available population counts, documented deaths, and expulsion statistics, that at a minimum between 30 and 50 percent of the Germans still living in Soviet East Prussia at the end of the war died before the final expulsions.[93]

It was not uncommon for some Soviet citizens to connect the Germans' higher rates of death to their psychological defeat, believing that Kaliningrad's Germans died in part because they lost the will to survive. During the first wave of mass death in the detainment camps in April 1945, the German doctor Hans von Lehndorff's camp commander had reportedly told him that "National-Socialism must be a very emotional affair . . . to have shattered people to this extent; otherwise it wouldn't have been possible for so many people to fall ill and die."[94] New Soviet settlers echoed this sentiment even decades later. As Sergei Vladimirovich Daniel'-Bek remembers, many Germans died from hunger partly because they had lost the will to survive. "But we felt differently—it was no time to die. The war had just ended!"[95]

Germans inside Kaliningrad first got an inkling of an impending resettlement when a few hundred inhabitants were permitted in the spring of 1947 to be reunited with their families in the Allied Zones of Occupation.[96] After long hearing rumors promising the imminent arrival of Swedish ships or Red Cross missions, the memoirist Hielscher was skeptical when Soviet officials first raised the possibility. "At first we thought we hadn't understood correctly," she writes. "None of us had learned Russian. The antipathy to this harsh language is too great. And that is the little wave of national pride that has stayed with us. No, we despise this language down to the deepest abyss, and the 'nix verstehen' had gotten us out of some of the most terrible situations. But we allow ourselves to understand more and more that it is true: We will soon be allowed to leave Königsberg." That glimmer of hope, Hielscher writes in her memoir, gave the strength to the city's remaining German population to survive that summer.[97] Hielscher and her mother were passed over during the initial round of expulsions and feared that able-bodied German workers would be kept in Kaliningrad or sent to Siberia. They finally received their papers in the spring of 1948, with orders to report to the train station the following morning. With not enough time to complete the paperwork to receive her final paycheck, Hielscher and her mother had to buy food for the trip with her mother's wages alone.[98]

While most Germans were eager to leave, some desperately wanted to stay. "Tragic scenes played out before everyone's eyes," writes Hielscher mockingly about the tearful farewells she witnessed at the Kaliningrad station. "German girls said goodbye to Russian officers, to their lovers. They hang crying on their men, begging them on their knees to be allowed to stay with them. A law prohibited the marriage of a German woman to a Russian man. I can't understand any of it. Do the German women have no national pride?" Although many Soviet officials, both in the military and the civilian government, had open relationships with German women, those relationships later became political liabilities. Germans were not allowed to stay in Kaliningrad even if they so desired; in the case of mixed families, with few exceptions, the children were expelled along with their mothers, never to see their fathers again. In rare cases, Soviet men with political connections were able to keep their girlfriends in Kaliningrad arguing that their lovers were not German at all, but Lithuanians who had lost their documents.[99]

The Germans' departure from Kaliningrad is only one small story of the greater era of the unmixing of peoples in postwar Europe. But it meant the end of a decade-long violent clash of civilizations for those who lived and died through it. Interviews with new settlers after the Soviet collapse reveal conflicting memories about the expulsion. The historian Iurii Kostiashov notes that a number of settlers "supported the state's operation" at the time, while others expressed doubts. Nina Vavilova, for example, recalls asking Soviet soldiers, "why are you resettling [the Germans] when they have done nothing wrong?" Others insist that the Germans should have been allowed to stay if they wanted. But Aleksandr Furmanov, who had served as a frontline soldier, recalls that most people at the time thought it was the right thing to do: "the Soviets had won, and it was legally their land now. But then they came to understand that they had destroyed everything the Germans had left behind, and that was naturally barbarism. But understand our point of view—everything here seemed foreign to us then, German. And we had this desire to get rid of fascism and Prussiandom forever."[100]

The Prussian Spirit of the Land

Anti-German rhetoric in Kaliningrad had combined fears of fascist resurgence with Soviet language from the 1930s about internal enemies and saboteurs. Although local Soviet leaders had determined that ridding Kaliningrad of its German population was necessary to protect the territory from fascist wreckers, the measure did not prove sufficient to rid Kaliningrad of the remnants of a former way of life. Over the next several years, Kaliningrad's inhabitants continued their battle against the residual contamination of the material world and of any Soviet citizens suspected of having been swayed by it.

Whereas the original anti-German rhetoric had adopted the prewar language of wrecking, this later battle drew on the new language of the early Cold War. Over the course of 1947, rising Cold War international tensions had coincided with an increase in ideological censorship across the Soviet Union. These tensions culminated, just weeks before the expulsion announcement, in a speech delivered in Poland by the head of the Propaganda and Agitation Department of the Central Committee, Andrei Zhdanov, titled "On the International Situation." The speech, coauthored by Stalin, unveiled a new political line for the Communist Party and a dramatic shift in Soviet foreign policy. Zhdanov proclaimed that the world was divided into two camps, the anti-imperialist democratic camp, led by the Soviet Union, and the antidemocratic imperialist camp, led by the United States. Across Eastern Europe, this shift launched new hard-line policies leading to single-party communist control and greater centralized control over policies of Sovietization.[101] Inside the Soviet Union, it marked a dramatic turn toward xenophobia, anticosmopolitanism, and exclusionary Russian nationalism. In Kaliningrad, fears of internal German enemies joined together over the next several months with nationalist fears against foreign contamination at large.[102]

This language first appeared in Kaliningrad in mid-September 1947, weeks before the expulsion announcement. At a Komsomol youth activists' meeting, Trifonov once again demanded vigilance against the Germans, warning not only of the threat of fascist infiltration but now also capitalist encirclement. Using imagery similar to the interwar depictions of Königsberg as a bulwark against the East, Trifonov proclaimed that Kaliningrad, as the westernmost borderland of the USSR, was called on to stand as a Soviet stronghold against a rising capitalist tide. Whereas Königsberg's inhabitants had feared hostile forces beyond their borders, Trifonov insisted that enemies were all around—not only the Germans, but also Soviet citizens who had fallen under their influence. Trifonov denounced "the many cases of cohabitation and friendships" between "our Russian people" and German men and women. Living with Germans, even befriending them, Trifonov proclaimed, was tantamount to "the elementary betrayal of the interests of one's Russian nation, the interests of one's country." The Germans, a "people of a hostile ideology," were dangerous contaminants and so, too, were the remnants of the German material world.[103] Trifonov warned that Soviet citizens, particularly Kaliningrad's many former POWs and repatriates who had spent time outside the USSR during the war, had been lured by the false promises of bourgeois wealth and the cult of things. "And here in the oblast," Trifonov warned, "on territory which not long ago (just two years ago) was bourgeois territory, this worship of bourgeois comforts is in full force."[104]

After the expulsion announcement, the Soviets' former relations with the Germans—and with the traces of the bourgeois material world—became a litmus test for political loyalty. Any Soviet elites who had cooperated too closely with Germans, promoting them at work or befriending them, were singled out for public censure. Kaliningrad's new first party secretary, Shcherbakov, spearheaded the charge. He denounced party members for having allowed Germans into their homes, calling out three communists who, in July 1947, had organized a "Russian-German Celebration Banquet" as an excuse to dance the foxtrot with German women. Another party member, Shcherbakov decried, had hired a German nanny for his children, who reportedly spoke German better than Russian. By the end of 1947, at least nine communists had been expelled from the party expressly for cohabitating with German women. By March 1948, an oblast representative wrote to Moscow that a total of eighty-four communists had been expelled, primarily due to "amoral failures" stemming from contact with Germans and the lure of German trophy loot.[105]

In some cases, the danger of contamination was ideological, not physical; in other cases, it was difficult to distinguish between the two. At the Oblast Hospital's blood collection station, for example, blood was collected from donors of both nationalities. A hospital report noted that almost forty-eight kilograms of blood were collected between May 1947 and January 1, 1948, but in accordance with a directive from the Oblast Health Department, "Russian patients were only given transfusions of blood from Russian donors, Germans from German."

The year-end hospital report emphasized how the Russian donors out-shone their German peers; although fifty-nine Germans had donated and only thirty-nine Russians, each individual Russian had managed to donate more, as the report explained, leading to a total of 26.85 kilograms Russian blood collected compared to only 21.14 kilograms by the Germans.[106] The possibility of cross-national medical contamination combined with taboos of purity. In this case, Russian superiority was determined not only by the quality of blood but also its quantity.

Around this same time, Soviet leaders turned their antifascist crusade against the city itself. The attack drew on wartime rhetoric that had depicted Königsberg as preternaturally evil and even as the germ-seed of fascism. As the war reporter V. Velichko had written in April 1945, the city's architectural monuments—oppressive medieval fortress gates, a dominating castle, thick-walled nineteenth-century forts, and Nazi defense fortifications—contained in their façades the whole "history of the crimes of Germany."[107] Such condemnations had faded from public discourse by May 1945, however. Although historians in Moscow expounded on the East Prussian myth to justify the Soviet Union's formal annexation of the territory in October 1945, in Königsberg, neither the military administration nor the early civilian government bothered with the idea that the urban environment was in some way contaminated.[108] Fascism had been defeated, both on the battlefield and in the ideological struggle for the future of mankind. Königsberg's architecture, what little of it remained, served as a monument of a fallen civilization that no longer posed a threat. During the first year of rebuilding, the military administration's only ideological intervention was to remove the political symbols of the old regime. Swastikas were taken down, Nazi flags were trampled on, and Adolf-Hitler-Platz became Ploshchad' Pobedy (Victory Square).[109]

Until mid-1947, Soviet Kaliningrad's city planners had even lauded the city's prewar architecture, infrastructure, and municipal services, expressing no concern over supposed ideological contamination. A Kaliningrad City Soviet representative, V. Dolgushin, praised the prewar city for its "exceptionally high-level amenities," including roads, public transportation, factories, sewer networks, and parks; a city architect, Maksimov, called for Kaliningrad to use this infrastructure as the foundation for building a modern socialist city.[110] Modernization had long been a central part of the Soviet project—the Bolsheviks proclaimed their revolution would help the lands of the former Russian Empire leap over backwardness into technological modernity. Yet this framing of Sovietization as modernization met with contradictions in Kaliningrad, especially as the local government faced pressure to rationalize reconstruction delays. Prewar Königsberg's technical superiority, even in ruined form, threatened to challenge the Soviet modernization paradigm, especially as new settlers came to suspect that fascism and capitalism had provided a better quality of life.

As the expulsion and anticosmopolitan campaigns began, Königsberg's planners, architects, and government officials changed course, declaring that Königsberg had been not modern but backward. In doing so, they followed a trend in many parts of the newly incorporated Soviet western borderlands of depicting the rubble as a symbol of a dark and oppressive past.[111] The Kaliningrad Head of Municipal Services explained at a City Soviet meeting in November 1948, for example, that the city had to build communal bathhouses from scratch because prewar Königsberg had no bathing facilities. (In reality, Königsberg had a recreational bathhouse, designed for leisure because private residences before the war had indoor plumbing.) Another speaker insisted that prewar Königsberg had had "no communal services" at all, so the Soviet government was "giving out a lot of money" to establish bathhouses, hotels, and barbershops.[112]

New Soviet leaders also proclaimed that the essence of fascism was embedded in Königsberg's architecture.[113] In May 1948, Kaliningrad's head architect Dmitrii Tian, for example, declared that the entire cityscape was alien to Soviet values and therefore "unacceptable in form and content."[114] Tian found traces of "Prussian militarism" (a frequent stand-in for "fascism") in the austere facades of northern Gothic nineteenth-century architecture, while simultaneously denouncing the city's modernist architecture as an ominous "Gothic in Constructivism."[115] Tian attacked in particular the surviving buildings of Hanns Hopp, the prominent Weimar architect of several Königsberg public buildings, including the *Ostmesse* (Eastern Exhibition Fair), the House of Technology, the Devau Airport, and the Park Hotel. Whereas the Nazis had ostracized Hopp for his modernist style and sympathy for communism, Tian denounced Hopp's works as the most fascist buildings of Königsberg. (Unknown to Tian, Hopp by that time had been commissioned to design the so-called Stalin Houses, which became the most prominent showcase for communist residential architecture in East Berlin.) For Tian, the only features of Königsberg architecture that met with approval were some of the suburban housing districts built by Königsberg's Nazis in the 1930s, explaining—with no trace of irony—that the ordered principles of city planning under the Third Reich corresponded more closely to Soviet values.[116]

Because the medieval city had been designed as a Teutonic fortress, some planners even opposed rebuilding the city center in its original location, arguing that preserving the architectural form of the ring city would perpetuate the feudal base of irrationality and militarism. Yet, as discussions progressed in 1947-48, as the historian Bert Hoppe shows, planners realized that Moscow, the ideal socialist city, was also built as a ring, thereby rehabilitating Königsberg's original layout. (As Kaliningrad and Moscow architects worked together to develop a new plan for reconstruction beginning in 1948, they borrowed heavily from the 1935 plan for Moscow's reconstruction.)[117]

While the city remained in ruins, efforts to make Kaliningrad socialist focused not on reconstruction, but on making the city less fascist or Prussian—that is, less visibly German. In September 1947, Trifonov declared that the party needed to "wipe out the Prussian spirit from this land once and for all": not only the remains of Nazi monumentalist architecture and nefarious German signage ("Entrance for Jews Prohibited"), but any German signage or foreign architectural forms that might remind Soviet new settlers that Kaliningrad had once been in Germany.[118] This specter of Prussia infused public discourse for years. At a Kaliningrad City Soviet meeting in February 1948, for example, discussions about failures to establish effective sewage removal turned ideological when one member, A. Ia. Burakov, deflected criticism by insisting that the important kind of sanitation work should be "political." Kaliningrad was slated to become "one of the bright and cultured cities" of the Soviet Union, he argued, but

> wherever you go, you see reminders of fascist Prussia. How many signs, plaques, and emblems do we have with Nazi swastikas all over the city? True, some citizens are trying to learn German from these signs and street signs, but it's not really possible. I think it's time that we remove all of this junk and throw it on the garbage heap. [T]he city is Russian, and therefore the signs and street signs should be Russian. . . . And we, comrades, have the power to clear away all of it.[119]

Building socialism became synonymous with battling fascism, and the measure for declaring that Kaliningrad was truly a Soviet city was the degree to which traces of its German past were suppressed and its Soviet—and Russian—identity asserted. Yet four years later, in

May 1952, the party leaders still complained about German inscriptions and even wartime anti-Soviet propaganda scrawled on buildings throughout the oblast. Socialism—understood as either modernization or Russification—proved more difficult to achieve than Kaliningrad's Soviet leaders had imagined.[120]

The ruins of Kaliningrad became the backdrop for several postwar Soviet war films, bolstering the idea that the city was the embodiment of Prussian militarism. In one of the first films, *Vstrecha na Elbe* (*Meeting at the Elbe*, 1948), the remains of Königsberg's city center were stylized as the occupied city of Torgau (renamed "Altenburg" in the film), a scene of US and Soviet encounter. The film showed hundreds of Nazis and spies hiding in the ruins, further emphasizing the connection between the German architecture and the sinister political life of its inhabitants. As late as 1959, a full decade after Burakov's call to transform Kaliningrad into a bright and cultured Soviet city, Kaliningrad still appeared so visibly, ominously German that the film *Sud'ba cheloveka* (*The Fate of a Man*, 1959) used footage of the city's old fortifications to represent Auschwitz.[121]

Ancient Slavic Soil

Antifascism played a central role in postwar myths of state legitimacy across Eastern Europe. But new communist governments and their populations also appealed to older, still resonant legitimating myths in order to form new collective identities. The allure of national self-determination, in particular, had fueled tensions in the successor states created by the breakup of Europe's multiethnic empires. After the Second World War, the argument that the presence of large numbers of ethnolinguistic minorities in Central and East Central Europe had led to political instability and military conflict served as a rationale for the unmixing of peoples and homogenization of the nation-state.[122] The newly powerful vocabulary of antifascism came into dialogue with these nationalist discourses to justify expulsions and forced migrations, as dominant ethnic groups, with the encouragement of local communist parties, wielded charges of wartime collaboration with the Nazis against ethnic minorities, especially (but not exclusively) against ethnic Germans.[123]

These interwar national myths had also contained a deeper ethnic primordialist sentiment: the notion that nations were ancient and fixed entities and that contested territories belonged rightfully to the people whose ancestors had first settled them. These ideas about ancient inheritances had fueled interwar conflicts among Germans, Poles, and Lithuanians over the rightful ownership of the lands of East Prussia; when the territory was dismantled in 1945, Poland and Lithuania each claimed a share in the postwar settlement. Communist party leaders in these states legitimated these annexations by citing both national self-determination and ancient inheritances, while simultaneously legitimating the establishment of postwar Polish and (Soviet) Lithuanian communist governments by appealing to antifascism.[124]

The Soviet annexation of Königsberg, by contrast, could not be so easily justified through these means. Unlike the territories transferred to Poland and Lithuania, northern East Prussia had been inhabited predominately by Germans (as defined by language or by voluntary association) for over seven hundred years. Königsberg and northern East Prussia were granted to the Soviet Union not in fulfillment of some principle of national self-determination, but purely as the result of Stalin's geopolitical maneuvering. The Allies had agreed already in 1945 to dismantle East Prussia and eliminate the failed Polish Corridor. But in December 1943, when Churchill had suggested giving the bulk of the territory to Poland to compensate for the Soviet Union's 1939 expansion into eastern Poland, Stalin demanded that at least part of East Prussia for the Soviet Union in return.[125] He pointed ostensibly to the Soviet Union's need for an ice-free Baltic seaport, but he also made his own offhand appeal to historical legitimacy.[126] The Soviet Union, he explained, deserved northern East Prussia as compensation for Russia's centuries-long military sacrifices to protect Europe from German aggression. "All the more true," he added, with a nod to ethnic primordialism, "because, historically speaking, this is ancient Slavic soil."[127] Regardless of whether Stalin believed the territory had been originally inhabited by Slavs, Churchill and Roosevelt, eager to negotiate for a viable postwar Polish state, entertained his demands. They agreed to grant northern East Prussia and Königsberg provisionally to the Soviet Union, to be confirmed in the final peace settlement.[128]

Inside Soviet East Prussia in 1945, the Soviet military administration and later civilian government at first had little use for this wartime idea that the land was ancient Slavic soil. Instead, they relied on antifascism, appealing to the German population to aid in the territory's reconstruction as a means to achieve their own rehabilitation. But with the turn of antifascist rhetoric against the German population, and as the region's new inhabitants still struggled to wipe the Prussian spirit from the land, Soviet leaders, both local and in Moscow, sought more powerful ways to legitimate the annexation and tie Kaliningrad's soil indelibly to Russia.

Place names—the names of towns, streets, natural landmarks—play an important role in projecting societal values, especially in times of political transition. Just as Königsbergers had done in the 1920s and 1930s, Kaliningraders sought to reshape the vulnerable border region's identity through practices of renaming. Here, too, German-oriented antifascism had been the initial guide. In 1945, the provisional military administration simply replaced overtly Nazi names with those celebrating the Soviet victory, such as Victory Square and Avenue of Heroes (*Prospekt Geroev*). But in most cases, they adopted direct translations from existing German names so that the two could be used interchangeably by the city's inhabitants. Imagining a future for Germans in the city, street names celebrating positive German cultural figures remained, including Mozart, Bach, Goethe, Schiller, and even Clausewitz.[129] In mid-1946, the new civilian government added Russian cultural figures alongside the German, including Gorky, Gogol', Pushkin, Lermontov, Nekrasov, Tolstoy, Turgenev, and Chekhov streets, but in the spirit of antifascism, it added a street named after the German communist martyr Ernst Thälmann.[130]

The process changed significantly in mid-1946, once Kaliningrad was designated an oblast within the Russian Socialist Republic. The RSFSR Council of Ministers in Moscow initiated a project to rename towns, rivers, forests, and other landmarks across the oblast. Whereas Stalin's wartime remark that East Prussia was "ancient Slavic soil" had previously gone unnoticed in Soviet Königsberg, the RSFSR Council of Ministers sought to confirm the claim by asking scholars from the Academy of Sciences to report on East Prussia's "ancient Russian-Slavic names."[131] This process mirrored the act of renaming in the parts of divided East Prussia ceded to Poland and the Lithuanian SSR, where old Polish and Lithuanian versions of the German town names became the new official names, as an act of affirming the return of ancestral lands.

But attempts to follow the same principle of primordial inheritance soon backfired in Kaliningrad. As Moscow ethnographers explained to the Council of Ministers, the few non-German ancient place names in Kaliningrad Oblast were not Slavic but old Lithuanian; insofar as Slavic names could be found at all, they tended to be recent Polish translations from German.[132] In February 1947, members of the Institute for Ethnography in Moscow went so far as to insist that "no ancient-Slavic names exist" at all, and that (contradicting Stalin), the region "was never Slavic," but old Prussian and Lithuanian.[133] Some Soviet ethnographers therefore argued in the spring of 1947 that the region should revive the old Lithuanian names. As P. I. Pakarklis, a specialist on the Lithuanian people's struggle against the Teutonic Knights, explained, Lithuanian was the language of a Soviet republic, and some elderly inhabitants of the oblast (meaning the Germans) even still spoke Lithuanian.[134] But Soviet nationalities policy, in practice, demanded—just as in Nazi East Prussia before—that the soil be connected to a nation. If Soviet Russian farmers settled on lands with ancient Lithuanian names, the Russian SFSR risked being construed as an imperial colonizer of land rightly belonging to the Lithuanian people.

Abandoning this politically charged prospect, the Moscow renaming team chose instead to demonstrate Kaliningrad's inherent Russianness by translating the formerly German Baltic landscape into the Russian language, so that the region's flat meadows, sandy dunes, and dark pine forests, previously depicted as sinister and ominously German, became familiar spaces in Russia's symbolic geography. Half of the resulting new place names stripped the land of all historical context, whether Teutonic, Lithuanian, or ancient Slavic.

But for the other half of major oblast towns, they chose another principle for staking claim to the land, naming places in honor of the Russian and Soviet military leaders who had spilled their blood on German soil. Stallupönen became Nesterov, after a Hero of the Soviet Union martyred there in 1945; Gumbinnen became Gusev, another fallen Soviet hero. Mamonovo (Heiligenbeil), Ladushkin (Ludwigsort), Polessk (Labiau), and Gur'evsk (Neuhausen) were all named for Soviet martyrs of the Great Patriotic War. Preußisch Eylau became Bagrationovsk, after the Georgian prince who fought in East Prussia in 1807 and died for the Russian state at Borodino outside Moscow five years later.[135] Thus the soil of Kaliningrad Oblast, in fulfillment of Stalin's insistence on Russia's centuries of sacrifice against German aggressors, became rightfully Russian because it was soaked in Russian blood.

Even though the search for ancient Russian-Slavic place names was abandoned by Moscow ethnographers, Stalin's nod to ancient Slavic soil still offered a powerful language for legitimating the annexation. In Moscow, East Prussia's supposed ancient Slavic heritage continued to feature prominently in historical scholarship.[136] In Kaliningrad, the myth became a powerful means to justify Soviet rule, particularly after the expulsion announcement. In the fall of 1947, numerous local officials, from the neighborhood Komsomol youth league organizer to the oblast party leadership, began proclaiming Kaliningrad's sacred inheritance by insisting that Königsberg—the city whose architecture and people had spawned the germ-seed of fascism—had actually been built on stolen land, now reclaimed.

In this formulation, the mission to defeat fascism became inseparable from the mission to gather ancestral lands. As the head architect Tian declared in November 1947, "the territory of East Prussia—ancient Slavic soil, which found itself for centuries imprisoned—has been returned to its true owners."[137] Blending antifascism and ethnic primordialism, Oblast First Party Secretary Shcherbakov wrote that same year that the Soviet army had "liquidated the most dangerous base of war and reaction and given the Slavs back their ancient land." Such declarations soon became standard rituals in every public forum. At a neighborhood Soviet meeting in December 1947, for example, the speaker I. G. Gavrilin opened the proceedings with the incantation that Kaliningrad was "our ancient Slavic soil, which for 700 years was under the heel of the Teutonic Knights, as well as German-fascist bandits." As Gavrilin explained, these bandits had invaded the Soviet Union "to subjugate our people . . . and destroy the first socialist workers' government in the world," but "the heroic Russian people" had defended the native land and "in brutal battle with the German invaders, secured the freedom and independence of our motherland, and liberated these ancient Slavic lands from the invaders once and for all."[138] The foundational myth was thus complete: Kaliningrad proved its legitimacy not only through antifascism, but also through blood and soil: the German Teutons, themselves protofascists, had stolen the land from the ancient Prussian people, who themselves, despite being a different linguistic and ethnic tribe, became synonymous with Slavs by virtue of both their ancientness and their suffering. Just as fascism had come to mean German, so had socialism come to mean, above all, Russian.

By adopting the myth of ancient Slavic soil, Kaliningraders could present themselves similarly to the inhabitants of other Soviet and Eastern European cities occupied during the war—their land had been liberated by Soviet bravery from the fascist yoke and perennial German oppression. But Kaliningrad was different in that, even after the liberation of the soil, the cityscape itself needed to be continually reconquered, lest the city's remaining fascist elements reassert themselves and spawn an ideological contagion. The liberation myth legitimated the Soviet population's rightful ownership of the city and the land. In doing so, it helped obscure the uncomfortable reality that confronted the new settlers wherever they looked: that they were living in a city that for the past 700 years had belonged to another civilization.

Historians on both sides of the Iron Curtain during the Cold War, and even some since then, shared the basic assumption that the impetus to expel Kaliningrad's Germans came from Moscow as part of some inhumane geopolitical calculus. The West German historical commission set up in the immediate postwar period to publicize the victimhood of the Germans expelled from the territories east of the Oder-Neisse line was run by the Königsberg émigré historians Werner Conze and Theodor Schieder. They consolidated a collective understanding of the treatment of the German civilian population in Königsberg after the war that presented the three years of German-Soviet cohabitation in Königsberg as a period of intentional retribution and calculated slave labor. According to this understanding, the Soviet government deliberately used the German civilian population to rebuild the city at starvation wages and expelled them when their labor was no longer needed.[139] More recent German historians have presented the extended Soviet-German encounter in Kaliningrad it as a case of malignant neglect, in which the Germans starved as an unintentional consequence of bureaucratic ineptitude until Moscow found it expedient to expel them.[140] Soviet-era official histories, meanwhile, obscured the Germans' long postwar presence, instead focusing on the reconstruction efforts of the new Soviet settlers who arrived after 1945.[141] If they mentioned the German population at all, it was to assert, incorrectly, that their expulsion was carried out in fulfillment of the Potsdam Conference in 1945. In contrast to the dominant Soviet narrative, historians in Kaliningrad since perestroika have argued that the possibility for successful German integration in Kaliningrad was interrupted by Moscow, the result of a nefarious center/periphery dynamic in which the metropole stifled local initiatives and economic prerogatives in the name of Stalinist homogeneity.[142]

These arguments and explanations, however, overlook the coexistence of the two extraordinary features of the Soviet treatment of Germans in Kaliningrad. First, that amid the hardship, retribution, and perpetual budget shortages, the local Soviet government made concerted efforts to integrate the Germans. Second, that although the expulsion order came from Moscow, the drive to expel began locally. Kaliningrad was a place where victors and vanquished lived side by side, and the state adopted antifascist legitimating rhetoric to appeal to both but in ultimately contradictory ways. The state's use of antifascism to rehabilitate the German population failed, in part, because there was no clear means for Germans to be declared individually or collectively redeemed and therefore eligible to become Soviet citizens. Germans were supposed to rehabilitate themselves through socialist labor and loyalty to the new government, but with no other measure for success, German rehabilitation became tied implicitly to the pace of postwar reconstruction. As conditions deteriorated in the winter of 1946-47, Soviet officials, under pressure to rationalize reconstruction failures, blamed the high death rates and emaciated bodies of German workers not on the Soviet state's inability to provide but on the Germans' collective contamination with fascism.

Another factor was that the Germans themselves, unlike their Soviet civilian counterparts, could never mobilize antifascism as a language of entitlement. The Soviet administration originated ostensibly to tend to the affairs of the German population but never involved formal German representation. As a result, no good German communists could serve as representatives for any emergent narrative of German heroic resistance against the Nazis or of collective victimhood at the hands of the 'Hitler clique.' Across the Soviet sphere of occupation, including in Berlin and the Soviet Occupied Zone, antifascism most strongly took root as legitimating rhetoric for Sovietization when individuals could mobilize it to benefit their material circumstances. Kaliningrad's Germans, as a stateless people, remained perpetually complicit, with no grounds to demand rights or recourse. In the economy of shortages, Soviet citizens received priority access to scarce supplies, food, and housing, and by 1947, Soviet civilians increasingly drew on antifascism as a language of entitlement. They did so by referring to their wartime service, both in Kaliningrad and elsewhere across the Soviet Union, in what the historian Mark Edele describes as a veterans' "entitlement community."[143]

Given the resonance of antifascism, why did Kaliningrad's local officials and new settlers ultimately turn toward ethnic primordialism to justify the annexation? The case shares commonalities with other contexts in which Eastern European national majorities combined postwar antifascism with ethnic nationalism to justify expulsions and assert state legitimacy. This combination even held a strong appeal even in places such as Kaliningrad, where ethnicity-based historical claims to the territory were harder to conjure. Stalin's offhand remark that East Prussia was Slavic soil corresponded with the turn toward ethnic primordialism in Soviet nationalities policy since the late 1930s.[144] In Kaliningrad, when the ruins of a prosperous enemy civilization threatened to undermine the Soviet state's claims to technical superiority, this turn toward ethnic primordialism served to bolster the legitimacy of Soviet socialism. In denouncing the ruins of Königsberg as fascist and its former German inhabitants as occupiers of ancient Slavic soil, Kaliningrad's new residents successfully fused postwar antifascism with Russian nationalism, and in doing so, justified expelling their German neighbors and claiming a once German land.

Conclusion

Hans Count von Lehndorff was one of the many Germans who remained in Königsberg in 1945 and who later documented his experiences under Soviet rule. A landed aristocrat and native East Prussian, Lehndorff had impeccable anti-Nazi credentials— more than one member of his family had taken part in the fateful plot to assassinate Hitler in his East Prussian lair in the summer of 1944. Lehndorff had fled the Red Army's advance in the winter of 1944-45 and worked as a medical doctor for the German army in besieged Königsberg. He witnessed the city's early transformation after the war before escaping across the Polish border westward to Allied-occupied Germany. Lehndorff's evocative diary, edited for publication first in 1947 and then reissued several times over the next twenty years, helped shape public conception in both West Germany and the English-speaking world about the fate of Königsberg. His was also among the early voices to articulate how German and Russian fates in East Prussia had become so fatefully intertwined. As the historian Constantine FitzGibbon explained in the introduction to the 1961 English translation of Lehndorff's diary, *"The illness was this"*:

> the Germans, appointed by geography to convert the East while continuing to defend European civilization so long as that East

remained savage, misunderstood their role, attempted to become the masters of the Christian world, and when their bid for hegemony failed in 1914 turned increasingly to the methods of the barbarous East. The destruction of Germany began in 1933, not in 1942 or 1945. The disease that produced the first concentration camps led inevitably, one way or another, to the putrefaction, the physical putrefaction as well as the spiritual nihilism, of Auschwitz and of Russian-occupied East Prussia. And when the German smashed the Jewish shops and burned the synagogues and beat or murdered their Jewish fellow-citizens in November of 1938, it was only a matter of time—and not much time at that, six and a half years to be precise—before they, or more usually other Germans, must be treated likewise by the even more barbarous enemy to whom they had thus opened their doors.[1]

FitzGibbon's quote encapsulates the emerging postwar consensus, shared by Lehndorff and his contemporaries, that the Germans had been destined to defend Christian civilization against the East. In this view, prominent during the Cold War, the disease of National Socialism, despite the Nazis' own turn to barbarism, remained derivative of a greater barbarism, whether Asiatic Bolshevism or Slavic primitivism. The Nazis' physical putrefaction had unleashed the horrors of Auschwitz, but in the end, the greater crime was not the destruction of the Jews, but opening the doors to the barbarians who destroyed Königsberg, and with it, European civilization.

The writer Yuri Buida is one of many Russians to wonder about the meaning of this encounter, but he saw it not as destruction but as palimpsest. Buida was born in the town of Znamensk, the former German Wehlau, nine years after the war. In his short story "The Prussian Bride," written in 1998, he describes the land of his childhood not as the ruined remnant of everything that had been German, but as an "enchanted world" of "shadows and secrets" built on the German remains. Buida recounts a story—perhaps a dream—of looting an abandoned German cemetery when he was thirteen. He and his friend made their way between "crooked, rusty fences" to a "grey, lichen-spotted granite slab," where beneath lay the preserved corpse of a young girl, wearing a "white dress, made, it seemed, of gossamer or the stuff out of which butterflies' wings are cut." Upon contact with the air, the girl was reduced to dust, and a small butterfly fluttered from the socket of her skull. The boys removed a tiny heart-shaped watch, which continued to tick, a chain with a small cross, and a pale ring from the skeleton's finger. Three years later, when excavation crews plowed over the abandoned cemetery, school kids made off with German skulls and bones to frighten their teachers and classmates.

From childhood, Buida had been used to all the peculiar markers of the once German landscape—the cobbled or bricked streets, the steep, tiled roofs, the dyked marshes, the "perpetual damp and forests planted in rows." Buida learned as a child that Germans had once lived there, but by then only the fragments remained: "a Gothic echo, a quirkily shaped door-handle, part of a shop-sign." His teachers and adults offered little help in deciphering them, "not that they were not interested in the past of this land," but that they had been told that "the past of other people was no concern of theirs." The refrain was only that the land had been a stronghold of militarism and aggression, and that Kant had been born and died there. "As for the Prussians who inhabited these lands before the Germans, for some reason they were counted as Slavs." Some older people dimly remembered when Russians and Germans had lived together. When Buida asked them what life had been like, they shrugged and recounted old memories—"pavements washed with soap, fishermen who handed over their entire catch to the authorities even when they were collapsing from hunger." Once the Germans had gone, a "ten-twenty-thirty year layer of Russian life trembled on a seven-hundred-year foundation" of which Buida knew nothing. So as a child he began to invent—"gathering the fragments of that life and transforming them by the force of his imagination into some kind of a picture . . . It was the creation of a myth." Close by, a stone's throw away, "lay an enchanted world," Buida writes, "but if a Russian in Pskov or Ryazan could enter an enchanted world which he had inherited by right, what was I doing here, a man without a key, of a different race, blood, language and faith? At best a treasure-seeker, at worst a grave-digger." But Kaliningrad was also Buida's adored homeland—the place where he had been born. The shadows and secrets of that soil, "or perhaps the shadow of a shadow, the hint of a secret" became, therefore, part of the chemistry of his own soul. "My little homeland," he concludes, "has a German past, a Russian present, and a human future. Via East Prussia, German history became part of Russia's; and vice versa." Exactly as it should be, he concludes, "when we recall what a gigantic crossroads of blood the land between the Vistula and the Niemen has always been."[2]

It was in this gigantic crossroads of blood that German and Russian fates became intertwined, the place where the Third Reich and Stalin's Soviet Union each sought to claim the same soil for their chosen people. The case of Königsberg and Kaliningrad shows the powerful role of local context in shaping both ideologies and events on the ground. Such was the case across Nazi Germany, the Soviet Union, and the territories of Eastern Europe that these two states invaded and occupied, of course—the map never conformed entirely to the territory. But it was especially the case in both Königsberg and Kaliningrad. As an isolated periphery and contested borderland of both the Reich and the USSR, the place allowed for greater experimentation in adapting the revolution to local circumstances. Indeed, it demanded it. Because of geographic isolation and political and economic rupture, Königsberg's Nazis and Kaliningrad's Soviet leaders maintained a high degree of autonomy, particularly during the first years of their rule. Both operated under severe financial constraints as a result of living on a periphery, and both appealed to the city's special outpost character in order to receive support from the center of power. In both cases, the city's leaders adapted their claims and practices in response to economic constraints on the ground. But after allowing the local authority to shape Nazi and Soviet rule, the revolutions' leaders, Hitler and Stalin, chose to intervene personally in order to bring their border outposts back into the fold.

These local manifestations of Nazi and Soviet rule in Königsberg/ Kaliningrad shared more features than the national versions of these revolutions, in part due to geography. East Prussia's northern Baltic climate, low grain yields, and dearth of natural resources had hindered industrial development in the region, leading Königsberg's Nazis, more than other regional parties in the Third Reich, to deal with economic and demographic issues similar to those facing the late Russian Empire and the early Soviet Union. Just as in the Soviet Union, Königsberg's Nazis, inspired by the conservative revolutionary thought of Prussian socialism, sought to leapfrog over industrial backwardness while sidestepping the problems of capitalist industrial development. And despite their lip service to Hitler's and Goebbels's anti-Bolshevism, Königsberg's Nazi leadership, especially Gauleiter Erich Koch and his main economist Hans-Bernhard von Grünberg, openly admired the Soviet Union and proposed similar technocratic and collectivist solutions to the crisis of East Prussian agriculture. Koch and his theorists' attempts to elevate the common good of poor farmers over the property rights of estate-owning Junkers even led some East Prussian contemporaries to denounce them as Bolsheviks.

The local adaptations of Nazi and Soviet rule in Königsberg and Kaliningrad also revealed the internal contradictions at the heart of each revolution. Although each defined itself according to the contours of its community of belonging, in both cases the terms for inclusion and exclusion became ambiguous once they came in contact with human beings. Despite the Nazis' elevation of race and nation over class, it turned out when cultivating the East Prussian *Volksgemeinschaft* that belief in the German nation—the will to belong—was as important, in the case of Polish-speaking Masurians, as any objective measures of ethnicity or race, however defined. In the Soviet case, the will to belong—acceptance of the superiority of the socialist system—was already a key determinant for membership in the collective, but Soviet officials found in the case of Kaliningrad's Germans that conversion to socialism was difficult to measure. In both cases, fears of incursion and escalating threats at the borders tested the terms for belonging and fostered increasingly radical politics of exclusion and harsher tactics of unification. Ambiguity about the terms for belonging, combined with a perceived threat to the territory, led both states to assert the city's centrality to the revolution and the historic connection of the surrounding soil to the blood of the nation.

Some developments in Königsberg and Kaliningrad were shaped by isolation and geography, whereas others proved to be archetypical of greater Nazi or Soviet rule. Königsberg was shaped profoundly by personal rule, a feature of the National Socialist party-state in general but especially pronounced in East Prussia. After Koch's power got out of hand in the mid-1930s and several party leaders in Berlin conspired to oust him, Hitler intervened personally to reinstate Koch in power. He did so because he trusted Koch's personal loyalty and his commitment to "working toward the Führer" and because regional variation did little to threaten, in Hitler's eyes, the integrity of Nazi rule.[3] While Koch and Königsberg's Nazi leadership developed their own local initiatives, they also recognized that their power depended on Berlin. By the late 1930s, they shelved many of their regional plans, not because of overt political pressure but because they recognized the benefit of doing so. Abandoning their earlier visions for German-dominated trade partnerships with the East, they embraced Hitler's genocidal vision for *Lebensraum*. Königsberg's regional leaders readily assumed positions of power in occupied Poland and Ukraine. Although Koch had not previously found much appeal in biological racism, he ruled Ukraine with violent antisemitism and anti-Slavic exclusionary practices in order to impress Hitler with his strong-arm command.

The context was radically different in postwar Kaliningrad. The Soviets annexed Kaliningrad in the middle of the Soviet revolution's life cycle, when the contours of the new society had already taken shape. Still, regional variation was also a feature of Soviet rule, particularly the process of Sovietization in the western borderlands newly incorporated during the Second World War. But whereas in Königsberg, local politicians and intellectuals developed their own visions for the revolution, in Kaliningrad, Sovietization was carried out not by the revolution's fathers but by its children. The military and civilian leaders who built Kaliningrad had been raised in the Soviet Union, and they brought with them an intuitive understanding of communism based on their understanding of Soviet ideology and their experiences in the 1930s and during the war. Their plans to build Kaliningrad were shaped primarily in response to extreme privation and administrative ambiguity. Sovietization in Kaliningrad constituted a dramatic if imperfect telescoping of the Bolshevik Revolution: the violent transformation of the region's politics and economy, more rapid than any other region in Europe that was incorporated into the Soviet Union. In other ways, Soviet rule in the first years remained chaotic, as the state struggled to assert control over the economy and urban space. Kaliningrad's leaders sought Moscow's attention out of desperation and, like Königsbergers in the 1920s, mobilized fears of incursion in order to attract the attention of the center. But Stalin's intervention in the summer of 1947 proved more dramatic than Hitler's in 1935. In Kaliningrad, the Oblast First Party Secretary Petr Ivanov killed himself—or was murdered—as a result.

Both Nazi and Soviet ideologies were internally complex to begin with. Tensions within these ideologies became more apparent when the wartime encounter between Germans and Soviets forced each side to question its proclaimed moral superiority vis-à-vis the other. Early on, each side had rejected the legacies of European civilization in the name of new illiberal values. But by the time the war was unleashed, each claimed to be defending European humanism and western civilization against the barbarians.[4] Escalating violence, however, forced perpetrators, victims, and bystanders on all sides to question the foundations for these values. On the eve of the Red Army's siege of Königsberg, German civilians confronted their complicity in the regime's genocide as the Nazi leadership involved them in the murder of up to 13,000

Jews and other prisoners from the liquidated Stutthof concentration camp. Meanwhile, in seeking eye-for-an-eye punishment for the crimes of the fascist beasts, Red Army soldiers raped and murdered tens of thousands of German civilians, forcing Soviet officers, propagandists, and ordinary soldiers to debate the meaning of fitting retribution for the Germans' crimes, one that would preserve socialism's moral superiority over fascism. As German civilians and Red Army soldiers each reckoned with their complicity, they ultimately reaffirmed their civilization's superiority over the barbarians, be they Asiatic hordes or Teutonic fascists.

Soviet ideology and practice proved to be more internally complex than Nazism on both counts—in its terms for belonging and in its claims of moral superiority. These complexities became manifest in the Soviets' treatment of the Germans they inherited in Kaliningrad. Because of the extraordinariness of the circumstances—extreme administrative and geographic isolation and the prolonged ambiguity in the Germans' status—Kaliningrad's Soviet inhabitants had to grapple with the contents of Soviet ideology more explicitly than Soviet citizens elsewhere in the Soviet Union after the war. The paradoxical case of unfinished rehabilitation—in which German civilians lived in a Soviet city but were declared neither beneficiaries nor enemies of the Soviet mission—forced local Soviet officials, unable to resolve the Germans' legal and moral status on their own, to address questions at the heart of the socialist project: who gets to take part in socialism, and on what terms? Is it possible to liberate one's former oppressor, and if so, how does one measure success?

The practitioners of socialism in Kaliningrad paired the rising wartime and postwar trends of Great Russian nationalism with a persistent sense of universal human perfectibility and, along with it, the sense that fascism was a condition that could be treated and that those who suffered from it could be cured. The state mobilized the language of antifascism to rehabilitate the Germans and educate them to recognize the moral superiority of socialism. But as Kaliningrad's leaders struggled to rebuild the city, perpetual shortages led to the creation of a de facto ethnic hierarchy between Soviets and Germans. In Kaliningrad, despite a commitment to be better than the German fascists, the Soviets created a new society that reversed the hierarchies of wartime Königsberg: the city's former slaves became its new masters, while the former masters became its new underclass. In November 1948, the month of the final mass expulsion of the German population from

Kaliningrad, an op-ed in *Kaliningradskaia pravda* explained to the new Soviet settlers that Comrade Stalin's victory in the war served as "the judgment of history over Prussian militarism," one which signaled the final return of "ancestral Slavic lands back to their true homeland."[5] The Soviet Union had annexed Nazi Königsberg to replace the ethnic exclusivity of fascism with the internationalist universalism of socialism, but instead they erected Kaliningrad as a Russian national homeland, complete with a Slavic myth of origin and ethnic requirements for membership. Soviet Kaliningrad destroyed Nazi Königsberg, only to rebuild it on the same foundations.

Although it was the demographic transformation of the oblast, dire material circumstances, and new pressures for accountability that tipped the scales from integration to marginalization, the deeper explanation for local Soviet officials' inability to rehabilitate the Germans lies in the nature of the Soviet Union's nationalities policy, according to which individuals could be redeemable only as part of a nation.[6] Despite the inclusionary rhetoric, any member of a nation whose homeland lay outside the Soviet Union was considered suspect—a potential traitor based on the presumed pervasiveness of national loyalties. The inability to grant the Germans citizenship and a titular nationality status within the Soviet Union meant that local Soviet officials had no mechanism through which to offer permanent redemption. The experience of cohabitation—and unrealistic expectations from above for Kaliningraders to rebuild Königsberg—came together with cues from Moscow to lead Kaliningrad's new government to favor ethnic nationalism. In the postwar period, Germans from the former East Prussia could be liberated from Nazi oppression by becoming Lithuanians; they could be rejoined with their ancestral tribe by becoming Poles. East Prussia's Germans who were sent back to the future German Democratic Republic could embrace antifascism and become good German communists. The East Prussians' Baltic ancestors, ancient Prussians, could even become Slavs by virtue of their suffering. But the one thing that East Prussia's Germans could never become, it turned out, was Russian.

The inhabitants of both Königsberg and Kaliningrad felt that their city was both a bridge to civilization and a bulwark against the barbarians. In late 1948, after decades of engagement, opposition, and encounter, the final mass transport of Germans left Kaliningrad to become a Soviet Russian city. The German-Jewish teenager Michael Wieck, like

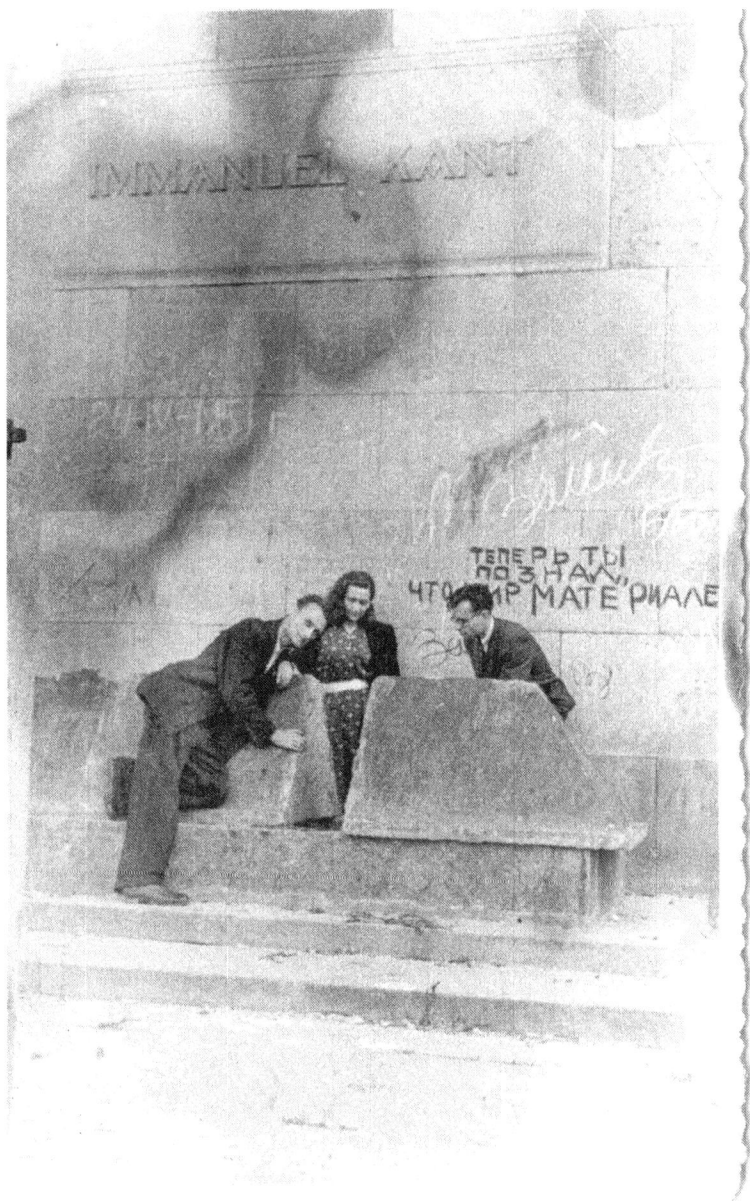

Figure 11. Soviet civilians pose for a photograph in front of Immanuel Kant's mausoleum, circa 1951. Old inscriptions on the mausoleum walls remain from 1945 and the first years after the war. The darkest inscription has been retraced and reads, "Now you understood that the world is material." A previous inscription, since faded, once read, "Did you think that the Russian Ivan would be standing on your grave?" Collection: Kaliningrad Oblast History and Art Museum (KOIKhM).

many other Königsbergers, had witnessed this transformation already beginning.

> More and more Russians were arriving in Königsberg, and we observed East Prussia becoming Russian. We hadn't really expected anything else but still, every day we were flabbergasted by what we saw. Strange clothes and uniforms, typical Russian wooden fences, the banners displaying the faces of Stalin, Lenin, Marx, Kalinin, and who knows who else. Large loudspeakers at practically every corner often emitted wonderful music as well as impressive songs of Russian soldier choruses, all of which visually and acoustically defined the character of the streets, to the extent that you could believe you were actually living in the Soviet Union.[7]

The long encounter had changed few Germans' minds. Though Wieck was one of the most self-reflective and generous memoirists, having suffered as an outsider in both regimes, most witnesses felt that their wartime stereotypes and prejudices were confirmed by their experience in 'the Soviet paradise.' In December 1947, the German doctor Hans Deichelmann asked himself, "to what degree is this murderous tyranny the work of Bolshevism or the work of the Russian national character? Put another way, what would Russia look like without Bolshevism?" Many Germans in postwar testimonies insisted that Königsberg had performed its role as a bulwark to defend European civilization, even as the city itself had succumbed to 'Asiatic Bolshevism.' If Königsberg had not martyred itself, Deichelmann speculated, "Asia would [have] overrun Europe," and the fate of Kaliningrad would have become the fate of the whole world.[8]

Kaliningrad's Soviet inhabitants understood it differently. While talk about "ancient Slavic soil" faded a few years after Stalin's death, popular memory insisted that it was the Soviets who had rescued Königsberg from the barbarians. As Polina Kaganova, who, too, was Jewish, wrote in her 1972 poem, "On the Road to Berlin,"

> Kaliningrad is not a Prussian city
> You can't get to Königsberg from there . . .
> . . . do you know, people, do you know
> how our Soviet lieutenant
> cried out to the fascists: don't shoot!
> The great Kant is buried here!
> And in that same instant as the lieutenant

[in a wave of fire . . .]
fell upon Kant's grave,
it became doubly sacred.[9]

Kaganova's reflection on the lieutenant's sacrifice at Kant's mausoleum reveals the complex understanding that Kaliningrad's Soviet inhabitants had about the land they had inherited. Thirty years after the
war, it was a Soviet soldier who spilled Russian blood to defend Kant,
the greatest legacy of Königsberg, from fascism.

Wieck was more ambivalent. Recalling his childhood in both cities,
he described the "dignified old cathedral" at the center of the Kneiphof
Island, and the words of Immanuel Kant engraved on a plaque on the
mausoleum's wall. "The words were full of admiration for the starry
heavens above, which I empathized with," Wieck wrote, "and a moral
law within, for which I later looked in vain and in which I no longer
believe."[10]

NOTES

Introduction

1. Alexander C. Diener and Joshua Hagen, "Russia's Kaliningrad Exclave," in *Borderlines and Borderlands: Political Oddities at the Edge of the Nation State*, ed. Alexander C Diener and Joshua Hagen (Lanham, MD: Rowman & Littlefield, 2010), 125. Germans used the terms "Polish Corridor" and "Danzig Corridor"; the term "Polish Corridor" entered English usage as early as 1919. Poles at the time objected to the term because of the transitory character it evoked and instead referred to the region as Pomorze (Pomerania).

2. Bohdan Koziełło-Poklewski, "Die NSDAP in Ostpreußen. Gesellschaftliche, politische und wirtschaftliche Bedingungen ihrer Entwicklung," in *Vorposten des Reichs? Ostpreußen 1933–45*, ed. Christian Pletzing (Munich: Martin Meidenbauer Verlag, 2006), 23–24; Christian Rohrer, *Nationalsozialistische Macht in Ostpreußen* (Munich: Martin Meidenbauer Verlag, 2006).

3. Wendy Lower, *Nazi Empire-Building and the Holocaust in Ukraine* (Chapel Hill: University of North Carolina Press, 2005), 107; Christian Tilitzki, *Alltag in Ostpreußen 1940–1945: die geheimen Lageberichte der Königsberger Justiz 1940–1945* (Würzburg: Flechsig, 2003), 49.

4. Andreas Kossert, *Damals in Ostpreußen: der Untergang einer deutschen Provinz* (Munich: Pantheon, 2010), 14; Norman Naimark, *The Russians in Germany: A History of the Soviet Zone of Occupation, 1945–1949* (Cambridge, MA: Belknap Press of Harvard University Press, 1995), 71–76.

5. A. V. Filatov and V. N. Patserina, *Naselenie Severo-Vostochnoi Prussii posle II Mirovoi Voiny. Pravovoi analiz. Chast' I: Pereselenie ili izgnanie? Pravovye predposylki i posledstviia* (Kaliningrad, Russia: Biznes-Kontakt, 2001), 9–25. The territory granted to Lithuania was folded into the Lithuanian Soviet Socialist Republic, also part of the Soviet Union but administered separately from Kaliningrad.

6. Bastiaan Willems, *Violence in Defeat* (New York: Cambridge University Press, 2021); Manfred Zeidler, *Kriegsende im Osten: die Rote Armee und die Besetzung Deutschlands Ostlich von Oder und Neisse 1944/45* (Oldenbourg, Germany: De Gruyter, 1996).

7. By September 1945, the documented number of Germans in Soviet East Prussia was 129,614, after executions and epidemics that summer had reduced the population by tens of thousands. Iurii Kostiashov, "Vyselenie nemtsev iz Kaliningradskoi Oblasti v poslevoennye gody," *Voprosy Istorii* 6 (1994): 186.

258   NOTES TO PAGES 3-4

8. Ruth Kibelka, *Ostpreussens Schicksaljahre, 1944–1948* (Berlin: Aufbau, 2002), 100.

9. Iu. V. Kostiashov, "Zaselenie Kaliningradskoi Oblasti posle Vtoroi Mirovoi Voiny," in *Gumanitarnaia Nauka v Rossii: Sorosovskie Lauriaty* (Moscow: Mezhdunarodnaia Nauchnyi Fond, 1996), 82.

10. J. V. Kostjašov [Iu. V. Kostiashov], "Russen und Deutschen in Ostpreußen nach 1945—Konfrontation oder Integration?" *Annaberger Annalen: Jahrbuch über Litauen und deutsch-litauische Beziehungen* 7 (1999): 161.

11. German and Anglo-American historical works present the number as higher, up to 75 percent of the population, but this higher figure is based on German expellee reports and cannot be corroborated with available archival data. See chapters 5, 6, and 7 for a discussion of German mortality in postwar Kaliningrad.

12. Hannah Arendt, *Totalitarianism* (New York: Harcourt, Brace & World, 1968).

13. The best comparative edited volumes on the two regimes are Ian Kershaw and Moshe Lewin, eds., *Stalinism and Nazism: Dictatorships in Comparison* (Cambridge: Cambridge University Press, 1997) and Michael Geyer and Sheila Fitzpatrick, eds., *Beyond Totalitarianism: Stalinism and Nazism Compared* (Cambridge: Cambridge University Press, 2009). Other prominent works have emphasized the rulers when studying the societies: Alan Bullock, *Hitler and Stalin: Parallel Lives* (London: HarperCollins, 1991); Richard J. Overy, *The Dictators: Hitler's Germany and Stalin's Russia* (New York: W. W. Norton, 2004); Robert Gellately, *Lenin, Stalin, and Hitler: The Age of Social Catastrophe* (New York: Alfred A. Knopf, 2007).

14. Christian Gerlach and Nicolas Werth, "State Violence—Violent Societies," in Geyer and Fitzpatrick, *Beyond Totalitarianism*, 133–38.

15. Overy, *The Dictators*, 54–97; Ronald Grigor Suny, "Stalin and His Stalinism: Power and Authority in the Soviet Union, 1930–53," in Kershaw and Lewin, *Stalinism and Nazism*, 26–52.

16. David L. Hoffmann and Annette F. Timm, "Utopian Biopolitics: Reproductive Policies, Gender Roles, and Sexuality in Nazi Germany and the Soviet Union," in Geyer and Fitzpatrick, eds., *Beyond Totalitarianism*, 87–132.

17. Ian Kershaw, "'Working toward the Führer': Reflections on the Nature of the Hitler Dictatorship," in Kershaw and Lewin, *Stalinism and Nazism*, 100; Yoram Gorlizki and Hans Mommsen argue that the Stalinist state contained the disorder and dynamic element of the party to subordinate it to state-building, whereas the reverse was true in the Nazi regime. "The Political (Dis) Orders of Stalinism and National Socialism," in Geyer and Fitzpatrick, *Beyond Totalitarianism*, 46.

18. Katerina Clark and Karl Schlögel, "Mutual Perceptions and Projections: Stalin's Russia in Nazi Germany—Nazi Germany in the Soviet Union," in Geyer and Fitzpatrick, *Beyond Totalitarianism*, 403

19. Sheila Fitzpatrick, *The Russian Revolution*, 3rd ed. (New York: Oxford University Press, 2008), 1–10; David L. Hoffmann, *Stalinist Values: The Cultural Norms of Soviet Modernity, 1917–1941* (Ithaca, NY: Cornell University Press, 2003).

20. George L. Mosse, *The Fascist Revolution: Toward a General Theory of Fascism* (Madison: University of Wisconsin Press, 2022).

21. Vegas Gabriel Liulevicius, *War Land on the Eastern Front: Culture, National Identity, and German Occupation in World War I* (Cambridge, England: Cambridge University Press, 2000), 8.

22. Rohrer, *Nationalsozialistische Macht*, 300–301; Hans Mommsen, *Alternatives to Hitler: German Resistance under the Third Reich*, trans. Angus Mcgeoch (London: I. B. Tauris, 2003), 154–57.

23. Clark and Schlögel, "Mutual Perceptions," 398.

24. The best edited volume exploring the entangled histories of Russia and Germany in the twentieth century is Michael David-Fox, Peter Holquist, and Alexander M. Martin, eds., *Fascination and Enmity: Russia and Germany as Entangled Histories, 1914–1945* (Pittsburgh: University of Pittsburgh Press), 2012.

25. Vejas Gabriel Liulevicius, *The German Myth of the East: 1800 to the Present* (Oxford: Oxford University Press, 2009), 4.

26. Ralf Meindl, "Vorposten und Grenzland. Ostpreussische Identitäten 1933–1945," *Acta Historica Universitatis Klaipedensis* 23 (2011): 180.

27. Liulevicius, *The German Myth*, 172; Gerhard Hirschfeld, "Nazi Germany and Eastern Europe," in *Germany and the European East in the Twentieth Century*, ed. Eduard Mühle, 69 (New York: Oxford University Press, 2003); Hans-Erich Volkmann, ed., *Das Russlandbild im Dritten Reich* (Cologne: Böhlau, 1994); James E. Casteel, *Russia in the German Global Imaginary* (Pittsburgh: University of Pittsburgh Press, 2016).

28. Ralf Meindl, *Ostpreußens Gauleiter. Erich Koch—eine politische Biographie* (Osnabrück, Germany: fibre Verlag, 2007), 249–398.

29. E. A. Rees, "The Sovietization of Eastern Europe," in *The Sovietization of Eastern Europe: New Perspectives on the Postwar Period*, ed. Balázs Apor, Péter Apor, and E. A. Rees (Washington, DC: New Academia Publishing, 2008), 1–9.

30. Felix Ackermann and Sören Urbansky, "Reframing Postwar Sovietization: Power, Conflict, and, Accommodation," *Jahrbücher für Geschichte Osteuropas* 64, no. 3 (2016): 354–57.

31. Tarik Cyril Amar, *The Paradox of Ukrainian Lviv: A Borderland City between Stalinists, Nazis, and Nationalists* (Ithaca, NY: Cornell University Press, 2015), 5; Tarik Cyril Amar, "Sovietization as a Civilizing Mission in the West," in Apor, Apor, and Rees, *The Sovietization of Eastern Europe*, 29.

32. Ackermann and Urbansky, "Reframing Postwar Sovietization," 358.

33. Three excellent studies of postwar Kaliningrad focus on urban reconstruction, memory, and the establishment of a regional identity: Bert Hoppe, *Auf den Trümmern von Königsberg, Kaliningrad 1946–1970* (Munich: R. Oldenbourg Verlag, 2000); Per Brodersen, *Die Stadt im Westen: Wie Königsberg Kaliningrad wurde* (Göttingen: Vandenhoeck & Ruprecht, 2008); Jamie Freeman, *From German Königsberg to Soviet Kaliningrad: Appropriating Place and Constructing Identity* (New York: Routledge, 2021). These works focus primarily on the 1950s and 1960s and therefore understate the role of rupture, contingency, and the encounter with the German population in shaping the nature of Soviet rule at the local level. Ruth Kibelka's evocative older study on the initial postwar years focuses on the fate of the populations in both Soviet East Prussia and the

Memel/Klaipėda Region that was transferred to the Lithuanian SSR. Kibelka, *Ostpreußens Schicksaljahre*. While Kibelka's work acknowledges the "decision-making vacuum" of local Soviet rule, it presents Sovietization as static and ideologically predetermined. Archivally rich works by historians working in Kaliningrad have explored the establishment of Soviet rule, and a comprehensive oral history project has collected the memories of Kaliningrad's first Soviet settlers. These works remain regional in focus and do not situate Kaliningrad in larger geographical or thematic frameworks. Iu. V. Kostiashov, *Sekretnaia istoriia Kaliningradskoi oblasti: Ocherki 1945–1956 gg.* (Kaliningrad, Russia: Terra Baltica, 2009); Iu. V. Kostiashov, *Vostochnaia Prussiia glazami sovetskikh pereselentsev: Pervye gody Kaliningradskoi oblasti v vospominaniiakh i dokumentakh* (Kaliningrad, Russia: "Kaliningradskaia kniga," 2018); V. Isupov, *Na etape stanovleniia: Istoriia Kaliningradskoi oblastnoi partiinoi organizatsii v period sozdaniia i ukrepleniia, 1946–1953* (Kaliningrad, Russia: Kaliningradskoe knizhnoe izdatel'stvo, 1986); V. N. Maslov, *V nachale novogo puti: Dokumenty i materialy o razvitii Kaliningradskoi oblasti v gody deiatel'nosti chrezvychainykh organov upravleniia (aprel' 1945–iiun' 1947)* (Kaliningrad, Russia: Izdatel'stvo I. P. Mishutkinoi I. V., 2004).

34. Rohrer, *Nationalsozialistische Macht*, 13.

35. Not only totalizing regimes, but also imagined national communities of all kinds undergo the process of deciding who belongs and who does not, although this dynamic has often been marginalized in discussions of the emergence of nations. John J. Kulczycki, *Belonging to the Nation: Inclusion and Exclusion in the Polish-German Borderlands, 1939–1951* (Cambridge: Harvard University Press, 2016), 1.

36. Erich Meindl, "Vorposten und Grenzland," 182; Richard Blanke, *Polish-Speaking Germans? Language and National Identity among the Masurians since 1871* (Cologne: Böhlau, 2001), 251; Andreas Kossert, *Preußen, Deutsche oder Polen? Die Masuren im Spannungsfeld des ethnischen Nationalismus, 1870–1956* (Wiesbaden, Germany: Harrassowitz, 2001); Ruth Leiserowitz, "Memel Territory," in *The Greater German Reich and the Jews: Nazi Persecution Policies in the Annexed Territories, 1935–1945*, ed. Wolf Gruner and Jörg Osterloh (New York: Berghahn Books, 2015), 145–46.

37. GARF f. 9401, op. 2, d. 95, ll. 18–9, 39–43, April 13, 1945; d. 93, l. 31, May 15, 1945; Alfred Erich Senn, "The Sovietization of the Baltic States," *The Annals of the American Academy of Political and Social Science* 317 (May 1958): 123.

38. Gregor Thum, *Uprooted: How Breslau Became Wrocław during the Century of Expulsions* (Princeton, NJ: Princeton University Press, 2011), 64–65; R. M. Douglas, *Orderly and Humane: The Expulsion of the Germans after the Second World War* (New Haven, CT: Yale University Press, 2012), 93–193; GAKO f. R330, op. 2, d. 4, ll. 8–9; d. 9, l. 1, May 15, 1945; GAKO f. R332, op. 2, d. 3, l. 47, February 28, 1946.

1. The Bridge and the Bulwark

1. Quoted in David S. Richeson, *Euler's Gem: The Polyhedron Formula and the Birth of Topology* (Princeton, NJ: Princeton University Press, 2008), 101.

2. Richeston, *Euler's Gem*, 103.

3. Michel de Certeau, *The Practice of Everyday Life* (Berkeley: University of California Press, 1984), 92.

4. Robert T. Tally, *Topophrenia: Place, Narrative, and the Spatial Imagination* (Bloomington: Indiana University Press, 2019), 2.

5. *Die Fürstliche Hauptt Statt Königsberg in Preussen*, 1503); *Königsberg* (1613); *Gru Plan der Königl. Pruss. Haupt und Residenzstadt Königsberg* (Königsberg, Germany: J. H. Bons Buch und Musikalienhandlung, 1834); *Führer-plan der Königl. Haupt- und Residenzstadt Königsberg* (Berlin: Bogdan Gisevius, 1910), 91, 93; *Gemeindelexikon für das Königreich Preußen*, vol. 1, *Verlag des Königlichen Statistischen Landesamtes* (Berlin, 1907), 118–19. The registered population in 1905 was 223,770, among them 10,320 Roman Catholics, 4,415 Jews, and 425 Poles.

6. Regiomontanus [Karl Gustav Springer], *Fremdenführer durch Königsberg in Preußen*, 3rd ed. (Königsberg, Germany: Königsberger Allgemeine Zeitung und Verlagsdruckerei, 1927), in *Reisebücher von Anno dazumal: Königsberg Pr., Reprint von 1927, 1938 und 1942* (Leer, Germany: Rautenberg, 1990), 32.

7. Alexander C. Diener and Joshua Hagen, "Russia's Kaliningrad Exclave," in *Borderlines and Borderlands: Political Oddities at the Edge of the Nation State*, ed. Alexander C. Diener and Joshua Hagen (Lanham, MD: Rowman & Littlefield, 2010), 125.

8. Henri Lefebvre, *The Production of Space*, trans. by Donald Nicholson-Smith (Cambridge, MA: Basil Blackwell, 1991); Jan Assmann, *Das Kulturelle Gedächtnis: Schrift, Erinnerung und politische Identität in frühen Hochkulturen* (Munich: C.H. Beck, 2002), 142–43.

9. Peter Fritzsche, "Historical Time and Future Experience in Postwar Germany," in *Ordnungen in der Krise. Zur politischen Kulturgeschichte Deutschlands, 1900–1933*, ed. Wolfgang Hardtwig (Munich: Oldenburg, 2007), 157. In the 1920s, the total number of tourists increased 60 percent in comparison with the prewar period. Rudy Koshar, "'What Ought to Be Seen': Guidebooks and National Identities in Modern Germany and Europe," *Journal of Contemporary History* 33, no. 3 (July 1998): 325, 334–35; Rudy Koshar, *German Travel Cultures* (New York: Berg, 2000).

10. Regiomontanus, *Fremdenführer*, 6.

11. W. Sahm, *Wegweiser durch Königsberg i. Pr. und Umgebung*, 4th ed. (Königsberg, Germany: Hartungsche Buchdruckerei, 1922); Regiomontanus, *Fremdenführer*. Cf. *Illustrierte Führer durch Königsberg i. Pr. und Umgebung*, 11th ed. (Leipzig: Woerl's Reisebücher-Verlag, 1926), a travel guide written in a more distant tone and aimed toward a German traveler arriving from afar.

12. Regiomontanus, *Fremdenführer*, 28.

13. Regiomontanus, *Fremdenführer*, 11–12.

14. Regiomontanus, *Fremdenführer*, 32, 35.

15. Regiomontanus, *Fremdenführer*, 36.

16. Regiomontanus, *Fremdenführer*, 36–38, 16, 41.

17. Fritz Gause, *Die Geschichte der Stadt Königsberg*, vol. 2 (Cologne, Germany: Böhlau, 1968), 693.

18. Gabriele Wieseman, *Hanns Hopp: 1890–1971; Königsberg, Dresden, Halle, Ost-Berlin; eine biographische Studie zu moderner Architektur* (Schwerin, Germany: Helms, 2000), 26–27.

19. Regiomontanus, *Fremdenführer*, 48–49.

20. Regiomontanus, *Fremdenführer*, 66.

21. Koshar notes that most interwar guidebooks focus on monuments, plaques, and historic architecture (especially Gothic) as the material traces of German *Kultur* and the primary objects of consumption for German tourists. Koshar, "'What Ought to Be Seen,'" 327.

22. Koshar, "'What Ought to Be Seen,'" 328.

23. Richard Bessel, "Eastern Germany as a Structural Problem in the Weimar Republic," *Social History* 3, no. 2 (May 1979): 204; Ernst Siehr, "Ostpreussische Wirtschaftsprobleme," *Zeitschrift für die gesamte Staatswissenschaft* 86, no. 3 (1929): 452–53, 461.

24. Regiomontanus, *Fremdenführer*, 46, 32.

25. Siehr, "Ostpreussische Wirtschaftsprobleme," 452; Dieter Hertz-Eichenrode, *Politik und Landwirtschaft in Ostpreußen, 1919–1930* (Cologne, Germany: Westdeutscher Verlag, 1969), 116–23.

26. Ralf Meindl, "Vorposten und Grenzland: Ostpreussische Identitäten 1933–1945," *Acta Historica Universitatis Klaipedensis* 23 (2001): 181.

27. A. I. Gerzen [Alexander Herzen], "Iz tsikla ocherkov 'Pis'ma iz Frantsii i Italii,'" in *Rossiiane v Vostochnoi Prussii: Chast' 2: Dnevniki, pis'ma, zapiski, vospominaniia*, ed. Iu. Kostiashov and G. Kretinin (Kaliningrad, Russia: Iantarnyi Skaz, 2001), 136–37.

28. Nadezhda Vladimirovna Iakovleva, "Po Prussii," in Kostiashov and Kretinin, *Rossiiane v Vostochnoi Prussii,* 177.

29. Andreas Kossert, *Ostpreußen: Geschichte und Mythos* (Munich: Siedler, 2005), 16.

30. Andreas Kossert, *Damals in Ostpreußen* (Munich: Deutsche Verlags-Anstalt, 2008), 95; Stefanie Schüler-Springorum, "Die Jüdische Gemeinde Königsbergs während des Nationalsozialismus," in *Vorposten des Reichs? Ostpreußen 1933–1945*, ed. Christian Pletzing (Munich: Martin Meidenbauer, 2006), 114.

31. Denis Ivanovich Fonvizin, "Iz 'Pisem k materi,'" in Kostiashov and Kretinin, *Rossiiane v Vostochnoi Prussii,* 71.

32. Vasilii Ivanovich Nemirovich-Danchenko, "Iz putevykh ocherkov 'Po Germanii i Gollandii'" in Kostiashov and Kretinin, *Rossiiane v Vostochnoi Prussii,* 173–76.

33. Sergei Esenin correspondence with Aleksandr Sakharov, July 1, 1922, in S. A. Esenin, *Sobranie sochinenii v shesti tomakh* (Moscow: Khudozhestvennaia literatura, 1980), 6: 123.

34. Michael David-Fox, "From Illusory 'Society' to Intellectual 'Public': VOKS, International Travel and Party-Intelligentsia Relations in the Interwar Period," *Contemporary European History* 11, no. 1 (February 2002): 10.

35. Quoted in Iu. V. Kostiashov, "Nemetsko-Russkii Klub v Dovoennom Kënigsberge," *Vestnik Kaliningradskogo gosudarstvennogo universiteta* 2 (Kaliningrad: Izdatel'stvo Kaliningradskogo gosudarstvennogo universiteta, 2003), 53.

36. Michael David-Fox, *Showcasing the Great Experiment: Cultural Diplomacy and Western Visitors to the Soviet Union, 1921–1941* (New York: Oxford University Press, 2012), 66.

37. Wiesemann, *Hanns Hopp*, 27; David-Fox, *Showcasing the Great Experiment*, 61, 66–68.

38. David-Fox, *Showcasing the Great Experiment*, 62, 70.

39. Kostiashov, "Nemetsko-Russkii Klub," 53–59.

40. Franz Fromme, "Ostpreußen und Niedersachsen," *Hamburger Nachrichten*, October 27, 1931, quoted in Kossert, *Damals in Ostpreußen*, 83.

41. *Illustrierte Führer durch Königsberg i. Pr. und Umgebung*, 5.

42. Eduard Anderson, *Führer durch Königsberg und Umbegung*, 8th ed. (Königsberg, Germany: Gräfe und Unzer, 1938), in *Reisebücher von Anno dazumal*, 114.

43. Siehr, "Ostpreussische Wirtschaftsprobleme," 467. Alsace-Lorraine was briefly invaded by the French in August 1914, but the frontlines remained near the border, and the Germans quickly forced the French to retreat.

44. Richard Blanke, *Polish-Speaking Germans: Language and National Identity among the Masurians since 1871* (Cologne, Germany: Böhlau, 2001), 183, 197.

45. T. Hunt Tooley, *National Identity and Weimar Germany: Upper Silesia and the Eastern Border, 1918–1922* (Lincoln: University of Nebraska Press, 1997), 36–37; Kossert, *Damals in Ostpreußen*, 76.

46. Fritz Gause, *Die Geschichte der Stadt Königsberg*, vol. 3 (Graz, Austria: Böhlau, 1965), 29, 18.

47. John J. Kulczycki, *Belonging to the Nation: Inclusion and Exclusion in the Polish-German Borderlands, 1939–1951* (Cambridge, MA: Harvard University Press, 2016), 16.

48. Meindl, "Vorposten," 181.

49. Blanke, *Polish-Speaking Germans*, 185.

50. Bessel, "Eastern Germany," 201; Blanke, *Polish-Speaking Germans*, 189–91. The final vote was 97.8 percent for East Prussia, or 363,209 votes, versus 2.2 percent or 7,980 votes for Poland. Seventy percent of those choosing Poland came from the predominantly Catholic area of Warmia and voted along religious lines. But even there, there only a small minority, 10 to 15 percent of the total population, voted to leave Germany.

51. Richard K. Debo, *Survival and Consolidation: The Foreign Policy of Soviet Russia, 1918–1921* (Montreal: McGill-Queen's University Press, 1992), 335.

52. Kossert, *Damals in Ostpreußen*, 72. The 1905 census listed the population as 139,738.

53. Kossert, *Damals in Ostpreußen*, 73.

54. Siehr, "Ostpreussische Wirtschaftsprobleme," 455–56.

55. *Der Große Brockhaus*, 15th edition, vol. 10 (Leipzig 1931), 382.

56. Bessel, "Eastern Germany," 209.

57. Siehr, "Ostpreussische Wirtschaftsprobleme," 450–53; Hertz-Eichenrode, *Politik*, 124–30.

58. In 1925, over half of East Prussians worked on the land, compared to less than one-third in Germany as a whole. *Statistisches Jahrbuch Deutsches Reich 1928* (Berlin, 1928), 25; *Statistisches Jahrbuch für das Deutsche Reich 1931* (Berlin,

1931), 19; Hertz-Eichenrode, *Politik und Landwirtschaft*, 101–2; Siehr, "Ostpreussische Wirtschaftsprobleme," 466.

59. Rohrer, *Nationalsozialistische Macht*, 42; Bessel, "Eastern Germany," 205, 211; Friedrich Richter, "Wirtschaftsprobleme Ostpreußens," in *Das Königsberger Gebiet im Schnittpunkt deutscher Geschichte und in seinen europäischen Bezügen*, ed. Bernhart Jähnig and Silke Spieler (Bonn: Kulturstiftung der deutschen Vertriebenen, 1993), 47–49.

60. Michael Burleigh, *Germany Turns Eastwards: A Study of Ostforschung in the Third Reich* (Cambridge: Cambridge University Press, 1988), 22–25; Meindl, "Vorposten," 181.

61. William Terry, "The Most Dangerous Spot in Europe," *North American Review* 234, no. 2 (August 1932): 161; Kulczycki, *Belonging to the Nation*, 2.

62. Quoted in Kossert, *Damals in Ostpreußen*, 84.

63. Siehr, "Ostpreussische Wirtschaftsprobleme," 454, 467.

64. Elizabeth Harvey, "Pilgrimages to the 'Bleeding Border': Gender and Rituals of Nationalist Protest in Germany, 1919–39," *Women's History Review* 9, no. 2 (2000): 218; Siehr, "Ostpreussische Wirtschaftsprobleme," 458.

65. Koshar, *German Travel Cultures*, 124; Kossert, *Damals in Ostpreußen*, 108–9; Fritzsche, "Historical Time," 157; Harvey, "Pilgrimages," 213.

66. Hanne Albrecht, "Bericht über den staatlichen Sonderkursus für Grenzkindergärtnerinnen," February 7, 1936, quoted in Harvey, "Pilgrimages," 201–2.

67. *Der Große Brockhaus*, 15th ed. (Leipzig 1931), 10:382. In 1925, only 4.6 percent of the population identified as Roman Catholic and less than 1.5 percent as Jewish.

68. Herbert Crüger, *Verschwiegene Zeiten: vom geheimen Apparat der KPD ins Gefängnis der Staatssicherheit* (Berlin: LinksDruck Verlags-GmbH, 1990), 53.

69. Kossert, *Damals in Ostpreußen*, 13.

70. Kossert, *Damals in Ostpreußen*, 13.

71. Kossert, *Damals in Ostpreußen*, 60; Kurt Forstreuter, "Vom Blickpunkt eines Archivars. Zu viele Memoiren?" in *Leben in Ostpreußen: Erinnerungen aus neun Jahrzehnten*, ed. Otto Dikreiter (Munich: Gräfe und Unzer, 1969), 74; Blanke, *Polish-Speaking Germans*, 40.

72. Herbert Gustav Marzian and Csaba János Kenéz, *Selbstbestimmung für Ostdeutschland: eine Dokumentation zum 50. Jahrestag der ost- und westpreussischen Volksabstimmung am 11. July 1920* (Göttingen, Germany: Göttinger Arbeitskreis, 1970), 63–65.

73. Hans Rothfels, "Der Vertrag von Versailles und der deutsche Osten," *Berliner Monatshefte*, 12 (1934): 18f. Rothfels, a young full professor at the university, adapted to Königsberg's nationalist political climate in the 1920s by fusing conventional histories of the state with the new politically charged field of *Volksgeschichte*. Rothfels' texts during this period adopted many "folkish" ideas, including the need for national self-assertion and emphasis on the superior cultural achievements of the Germans in East Central Europe. Jan Eckel, "Hans Rothfels: An Intellectual Biography in the Age of Extremes," *Journal of Contemporary History* 42, no. 3 (July 2007): 429–30.

74. Stefanie Schüler-Springorum, "Die Jüdische Gemeinde Königsbergs," 116.

75. Schüler-Springorum, "Die Jüdische Gemeinde," 116.

76. GStPK Rep. 2. XX. NA. Nr. 4045: Reichs- und Staatskommissar an preußischen Minister für Kunst/Wissenschaft und Volksbildung. Königsberg, June 12, 1920, cited in Kossert, *Damals in Ostpreußen*, 76.

77. Kossert, *Damals in Ostpreußen*, 94.

78. Willi Neuhöfer, "Die 'goldenen' zwanziger Jahren in Masuren," in *Neidenburger Heimatbrief* 107 (1996): 48–50, quoted in Bohdan Kozieło-Poklewski, "Die NSDAP in Ostpreußen. Gesellschaftliche, politische und wirtschaftliche Bedingungen ihrer Entwicklung," in Pletzing, *Vorposten*, 15–16.

79. Gause, *Die Geschichte*, 3:24–25; Jürgen Manthey, *Königsberg: Geschichte einer Weltbürgerrepublik* (Munich: Hanser, 2005), 542. Reichstag election results for the SPD: 1890—49.3 percent, 1893—45.22 percent, 1898—52.1 percent, 1903—49.5 percent, 1912—51.7 percent. The early strength of the Social Democrats becomes clear first when comparing to the results in the Reich as a whole. In the 1874 elections, shortly after the founding of the party, the Social Democrats received 20.2 percent of the vote in Königsberg but 6.8 percent in general; in 1877, they received 21 percent compared to 9.1 percent in the Reich as a whole.

80. Stefan Wolff, *The German Question since 1919: An Analysis with Key Documents* (Westport, CT: Praeger, 2003), 33; Rohrer, *Nationalsozialistische Macht*, 37; Manthey, *Königsberg*, 566. From 1920 to 1928, the DNVP led in East Prussia, with 31 to 39 percent of the vote. The SPD, which had 46.1 percent of the vote in 1919, remained in second place, with its strongest representation in Königsberg. Still, the city's leaders, including Mayor Hans Lohmeyer and the East Prussian *Oberpräsident* Siehr, came from left liberal parties, and the two police presidents serving during Weimar, Josef Lübbring and Hans Brandt, remained committed members of the socialist SPD.

81. GStPK Rep. 10, Tit. 36, Nr. 28, p. 124, January 24, 1927.

82. Kossert, *Damals in Ostpreußen*, 101.

83. GStPK Rep. 10, Tit. 36, Nr. 28, p. 3, May 4, 1925.

84. Kossert, *Damals in Ostpreußen*, 101.

85. GStPK Rep 10, Tit. 36, Nr. 28, p. 4. Nazi Speeches and Meetings 1925–1929, "Bericht über die am 30. April 1925 abends im großen Saale der Stadthalle abgehaltene öffentliche Versammlung der "Nationalsozialistischen Deutschen Arbeiter-Partei Ortsgruppe Königsberg," May 4, 1925.

86. GStPK Rep 10, Tit. 36, Nr. 28, p. 4.

87. Rohrer, *Nationalsozialistische Macht*, 96–97, 101–3.

88. Rohrer, *Nationalsozialistische Macht*, 75–78, 99; Kozieło-Poklewski, "Die NSDAP," 18–20. Party membership in East Prussia in 1928 remained small compared to 3,300 members in Bavaria, the first stronghold of the NSDAP, by August 1921; Peter D. Stachura, "The Political Strategy of the Nazi Party, 1919–1933," *German Studies Review* 3, no. 2 (May 1980): 264; *10 Jahre Gau Ostpreußen* (Königsberg, Germany: Ostdeutsche Verlagsanstalt und Druckerei, 1938), 14.

89. F. Bajohr, "Gauleiter in Hamburg: Zur Person und Tätigkeit Karl Kaufmanns," *Viertaljahreshefte für Zeitgeschichte* 43 (1995): 267-95, cited in Meindl, "Vorposten," 182.

90. GStPK Rep. 10, Tit. 36, Nr. 28, pp. 216-17.

91. BA-Berlin R55/1273, 234; Hans Nitram [Hans Martin], *Achtung! Hier Ostmarkenrundfunk! Polnische Truppen haben soeben die ostpreussische Grenze über-schritten* (Oldenburg in Oder, Germany: Gerhard Stalling, 1932).

92. BA-Berlin R55/1273, p. 235.

93. BA-Berlin R55/1273, pp. 236-37, 239.

94. Kozieło-Poklewski, "Die NSDAP," 23-24.

95. *Königsberger Hartungsche Zeitung*, September 15, 1930. Andreas Kossert, *Masuren. Ostpreußens vergessener Süden* (Munich: Siedler, 2001), 294, 298; Kozieło-Poklewski, "Die NSDAP," 21; Bessel, "Eastern Germany," 215-17.

96. Gause, *Geschichte*, 3:117.

97. Kozieło-Poklewski, "Die NSDAP," 23; *Statistisches Handbuch für die Provinz Ostpreußen* (Leipzig: Grenzlandverlag G. Boettcher, 1938), 64.

98. Gause, *Geschichte*, 3:113-16.

99. Thomas Mann, *Berliner Tageblatt*, August 8, 1932, quoted in *Thomas Mann. Eine Chronik Seines Lebens*, ed. Hans Bürgin and Hans Otto Meyer (Frankfurt am Main: S. Fischer, 1965), 99.

100. Kozieło-Poklewski, "Die NSDAP," 23-24.

101. Fürst Alexander zu Dohna-Schlobitten, *Erinnerungen eines alten Ostpreußen* (Berlin: Siedler, 1989), 170.

102. Wilhelm Matull, *Ostdeutschlands Arbeiterbewegung: Abriß ihrer Geschichte, Leistung und Opfer* (Würzburg: Holzner, 1973), 359.

103. Ralf Meindl, *Ostpreußens Gauleiter: Erich Koch: eine politische Biographie* (Osnabrück, Germany: Fibre, 2007), 147.

104. Anderson, *Führer durch Königsberg und Umgebung.*

105. Eduard Anderson, *Führer durch Königsberg und Umgebung*, 7th ed. (Königsberg, Germany: Gräfe und Unzer, 1934), 6.

106. Gause, *Geschichte*, 3:130.

107. Wiesemann, *Hanns Hopp*, 42; GStPK XX, Rep. 240, Nr. 93, p. 180.

108. Wiesemann, *Hanns Hopp*, 40-41.

109. Gause, *Geschichte*, 3:130.

110. Anderson, *Führer*, 8th ed. (1938), 124.

111. Anderson, *Führer*, 7th ed. (1934), 14, 16; Anderson, *Führer*, 8th ed. (1938), 120-21.

2. Empire in the East

1. "Ostpreußenpolitik ist deutsches Schicksal," *Völkischer Beobachter*, August 5, 1931, cited in Andreas Kossert, *Damals in Ostpreußen* (Munich: Deutsche Verlags-Anstalt, 2008), 104.

2. Ralf Meindl, "Vorposten und Grenzland. Ostpreussische Identitäten 1933-1945," *Acta Historica Universitatis Klaipedensis* 23 (2011): 183.

3. Erich Koch, *Aufbau im Osten* (Breslau: W. G. Korn, 1934), 65; Ralf Meindl, *Ostpreußens Gauleiter, Erich Koch—eine politische Biographie* (Osnabrück, Germany: fibre Verlag, 2007), 179-80.

4. Christian Rohrer, *Nationalsozialistische Macht Ostpreußen* (Munich: Martin Meidenbauer Verlag, 2006), 13.

5. Christian Tilitzki, *Alltag in Ostpreußen 1940–1945: die geheimen Lageberichte der Königsberger Justiz 1940–1945* (Würzburg: Flechsig, 2003), 14; Hermann Rauschning, *Men of Chaos* (New York: G. P. Putnam's Sons, 1942), 89.

6. Rohrer, *Nationalsozialistische Macht,* 300–01. The Main Franconian Gauleiter Dr. Otto Hellmuth, by contrast, focused primarily on biological racism and attempted to carry out the systematic racial examination of the entire population under his command as a means to influence his standing within the hierarchy of the Third Reich.

7. The conservative revolutionaries were inspired especially by the historian and philosopher Oswald Spengler's formulation of Prussian socialism, *Preußentum und Sozialismus* (Munich: C. H. Beck, 1919).

8. Meindl, *Ostpreußens Gauleiter,* 177–78.

9. Hans Bernhard von Grünberg, "Die Hauptgrundsätze des Ostpreußenplanes," in *Das Nationalsozialistische Ostpreußen* (Königsberg, Germany: Kaspereit, 1934), 20–21.

10. Hans Mommsen, *Alternatives to Hitler: German Resistance under the Third Reich,* trans. Angus Mcgeoch (London: I. B. Tauris, 2003), 154–57.

11. Klaus von der Groeben, *Streiflichter: persönliche Erinnerungen* (Raisdorf, Germany: Ostsee, 1997), 38.

12. Mommsen, *Alternatives,* 165, 170–71.

13. Mommsen, *Alternatives,* 154–57.

14. Hermann Bethke and Hans Bernhard v. Grünberg, *Entschuldung und Neubau der deutschen Wirtschaft* (Berlin: Reimar Hobbing, 1932), 4, 11, 23.

15. Wolfgang Schivelbusch, *Three New Deals: Reflections on Roosevelt's America, Mussolini's Italy, and Hitler's Germany, 1933–1939* (New York: Picador, 2006), 225n.

16. Schivelbusch, *Three New Deals,* 225n; Kossert, *Damals in Ostpreußen,* 115.

17. Mommsen, *Alternatives,* 154–57.

18. BA-Berlin R58/1562, p. 4, 6, January 31, 1933; BA-Berlin R58/1562, pp. 25–26, March 15, 1933; Wilhelm Matull, *Ostdeutschlands Arbeiterbewegung: Abriß ihrer Geschichte, Leistung und Opfer* (Würzburg: Holzner, 1973), 359.

19. Rohrer, *Nationalsozialistische Macht,* 250; Fritz Gause, *Die Geschichte der Stadt Königsberg* (Graz, Austria: Böhlau, 1965), 3:124. Dr. Hellmuth Will, Königsberg's newly appointed mayor, only joined the party in 1933 at Koch's request. Anton Kerschensteiner, who served as the president of the Regional Labor Office from 1934 to 1944, was never required to join, in recognition that his father-in-law, Bavarian minister president Gustav Ritter von Kahr, was murdered at Dachau in 1934 for thwarting Hitler's 1923 Beer Hall Putsch.

20. Meindl, *Ostpreußens Gauleiter,* 153. Gauleiter-*Oberpräsident* Josef Terboven in Düsseldorf, for example, was forced to cooperate with three other Gauleiter within his state district.

21. Dietrich Orlow, *History of the Nazi Party* (New York: Enigma Books, 2010), 318; Armin Fuhrer and Heinz Schön, *Erich Koch, Hitler's Brauner Zar: Gauleiter von Ostpreußen und Reichskommissar der Ukraine* (Munich: Olzog, 2010); Rohrer, *Nationalsozialistische Macht.*

22. Mommsen, *Alternatives,* 152.

23. Mommsen, *Alternatives*, 159.

24. Rohrer, *Nationalsozialistische Macht*, 266.

25. *Völkischer Beobachter* July/August 1933, cited in Ralf Meindl, "Erich Koch: Gauleiter von Ostpreussen," in *Vorposten des Reichs? Ostpreußen 1933–1945*, ed. Christian Pletzing (Munich: Martin Meidenbauer, 2006), 34.

26. BA-Berlin NS25/314, p. 156, July 16, 1935.

27. BA-Berlin NS25/314, p. 160, August 5, 1935.

28. BA-Berlin NS25/314, p. 155 July 16, 1935.

29. Erich Spickschen, "Das ostpreußische Bauerntum," in *10 Jahre Gau Ostpreußen: Festschrift zum Gautag 1938 der NSDAP* (Königsberg, Germany: Ostdeutsche Verlagsanstalt und Druckerei, 1938), 67.

30. AP-Olsztyn 389/2, 61; Rohrer, *Nationalsozialistische Macht*, 270.

31. GStPK Rep 10, Tit. 36, Nr. 40 Regierungsvizepräsident Angermann, "Politische Lage im Regierungsbezirk," December 5, 1933, 42.

32. "Zersetzung der Staatsautorität," AP-Olsztyn 389/2, 61; BA-Berlin NS22/726, 1935; BA-Berlin NS22/726, n.d. [after January 1935].

33. GStPK Rep. 10, Tit. 36, Nr. 40, p. 41f, December 5, 1933.

34. BA-Berlin NS 22/268, pp. 1–6, December 1933; GStPK Rep 10, Tit. 36, Nr. 40, p. 44, May 8, 1934.

35. BA-Berlin NS22/268, pp. 1–6, December 1933.

36. Rohrer, *Nationalsozialistische Macht*, 12.

37. Rauschning, *Men of Chaos*, 104.

38. Rauschning, *Men of Chaos*, 15.

39. Rohrer, *Nationalsozialistische Macht*, 398–99.

40. *10 Jahre Gau Ostpreußen*.

41. Omer Bartov, "From *Blitzkrieg* to Total War: Controversial Links between Image and Reality," in *Nazism, Stalinism, and Dictatorship*, ed. M. Lewin and I. Kershaw (Cambridge: Cambridge University Press, 1997), 172.

42. Peter Fritzsche, *Life and Death in the Third Reich* (Cambridge: Harvard University Press, 2008), 7–8; Thomas Kühne, *Belonging and Genocide: Hitler's Community, 1918–1945* (New Haven, CT: Yale University Press, 2010).

43. Hugo Linck, "Um Kirche und Heimat," in *Denk ich an Ostpreußen, vol. 2: Leben in Ostpreußen* (Munich: Gräfe und Unzer, 1968), 160.

44. BA-Berlin NS 22/726, NS-Zeitschriften, 1935; Jürgen Manthey, *Königsberg: Geschichte einer Weltbürgerrepublik* (Munich: Hanser, 2005), 649; Christian Rohrer, "Vom Wachstum der Erich-Koch-Stiftung. Ein nationalsozialistischer Mischkonzern und die 'Arisierung' der 'Ersten Ostpreußischen Bettfedernfabrik,'" in Pletzing, *Vorposten*, 81.

45. BA-Berlin R58/1563, pp. 66–106, February to October 1933; BA-Berlin R58/1562, p. 130, December 5, 1933; BA-Berlin, R58/1563, Geheimes Staatspolizeiamt IA, "Aus dem Lagerbericht der Staatspolizeistelle Königsberg/Pr.," August 2, 1934, pp. 62–64; Matull, *Ostdeutschlands Arbeiterbewegung*, 360–61.

46. Fritzsche, *Life and Death*, 28–36.

47. Helmut Sommer, *Wir bauen das neue Reich! Ein Tatsachenbericht* (Königsberg, Germany: J. Paltzo, 1935), 10.

48. Meindl, "Vorposten," 183.

49. Hans Bernhard von Grünberg, "Die Hauptbrundsätze des Ostpreußen-planes," in *Das Nationalsozialistische Ostpreußen* (Königsberg, Germany: Ost-deutsche Verlagsanstalt, 1934), 41.

50. Kossert, *Ostpreußen: Geschichte und Mythos*, 274.

51. Hubert Orłowski, "Das Bild Ostpreußens in der deutschen Literatur des 20. Jahrhunderts," in *Preussen in Ostmitteleuropa; Geschehengeschichte und Verstehensgeschichte*, ed. Matthias Weber (Munich: R. Oldenbourg, 2003), 265–67; Joachim Paltzo, "Nationalsozialistisches Kulturschaffen in Ostpreußen," in *10 Jahre Gau Ostpreußen*, 77–78.

52. Paltzo, "Nationalsozialistisches Kulturschaffen," 73–75.

53. Meindl, "Vorposten," 182.

54. *Völkischer Beobachter*, April 21, 1932, national edition, cited in Kossert, *Damals in Ostpreußen*, 103.

55. Andreas Kossert, "'Grenzlandpolitik' und Ostforschung an der Peripherie des Reiches. Das ostpreußische Masuren 1919–1945," *Vierteljahrshefte für Zeitgeschichte* 51, no. 2 (April 2003): 137.

56. John J. Kulczycki, *Belonging to the Nation: Inclusion and Exclusion in the Polish-German Borderlands, 1939–1951* (Cambridge, MA: Harvard University Press, 2016), 21.

57. Eduard Schwertfeger, *Ostpreußens Zukunft—eine Frage deutschen Wollens* (Königsberg, Germany: Gräfe und Unzer, 1937), 23–27; Kulczycki, *Belonging*, 21.

58. Andreas Kossert, "'Grenzlandpolitik' und Ostforschung an der Peripherie des Reiches. Das ostpreussische Masuren, 1919–1945," *Vierteljahrshefte für Zeitgeschichte* 51, no. 2 (April 2002): 142.

59. Kurt Forstreuter, "Vom Blickpunkt eines Archivars. Zu viele Memoiren?" in *Leben in Ostpreußen: Erinnerungen aus neun Jahrzehnten*, ed. Otto Dikreiter (Munich: Gräfe und Unzer, 1969), 74; Herbert Kirrinnis, "Die Ortsnamenänderungen in Ostpreußen," *Petermans Geographische Mitteilungen* 7/8 (July/August 1942): 268; Kossert, *Damals in Ostpreußen*, 119.

60. Forstreuter, "Vom Blickpunkt," 74.

61. Hertz-Eichenrode, *Politik*, 66, 102.

62. William M. Harrigan, "Nazi Germany and the Holy See, 1933–1936: The Historical Background of *Mit brennender Sorge*," *Catholic Historical Review* 47, no. 2 (July 1961): 170.

63. Quoted in Kossert, *Damals in Ostpreußen*, 122–23; Rohrer, *Nationalsozialistische Macht*, 261.

64. Rohrer, "Vom Wachstum," 83; Kossert, *Damals in Ostpreußen*, 122.

65. GAKO f.19, o.1, d.1, l. 49, July 17, 1939.

66. AP-Olsztyn 1499-1, 24, 52, Personal Akten: Badzinski, correspondence from June 27, 1941, October 14, 1942.

67. AP-Olsztyn 1499-1, 55, October 14, 1942.

68. Schüler-Springorum, "Die Jüdische Gemeinde," 115.

69. BA-Berlin R58/1563, p. 237.

70. BA-Berlin NS25/314, p. 161, August 5, 1935.

71. Quoted in Kossert, *Damals in Ostpreußen*, 124.

72. Gesetz zum Schutze des deutschen Blutes und der deutschen Ehre, September 15, 1935; Reichsbürgergesetz vom 15. September 1935.

73. Fritzsche, *Life and Death*, 76–81.

74. David Bankier, *The Germans and the Final Solution: Public Opinion under Nazism* (Oxford: Blackwell, 1993), 130–38.

75. Schüler-Springorum, "Die Jüdische Gemeinde," 117.

76. Ludwig Goldstein, *Heimatgebünden: aus dem Leben eines alten Königsbergers* (Berlin: Nora, 2015), 538.

77. Rainer Radok, *Von Königsberg nach Melbourne: Vertreibung aus Ostpreußen im Dritten Reich* (Lüneberg, Germany: Institut Nordostdeutsches Kulturwerk, 1998), 69–70.

78. Jan Eckel, "Hans Rothfels: An Intellectual Biography in the Age of Extremes," *Journal of Contemporary History* 42, no. 3 (July 2007): 442.

79. GStPK XX HA., NL Ludwig Goldstein, Nr. 1/5, pp. 137–41; Yoram K. Jacoby, *Jüdiches Leben in Königsberg/Pr. Im 20. Jahrhundert* (Würzburg, Germany: Holzner, 1983), 141.

80. Jacoby, *Jüdiches Leben*, 141. Some moved to other cities in Germany, especially Berlin, while others emigrated.

81. Stefanie Schüler-Springorum, "Die Jüdische Gemeinde Königsbergs während des Nationalsozialismus," in Pletzing, *Vorposten*, 123.

82. Anti-Bolshevism became a primary feature of Goebbels's propaganda after 1935. See Jan Claus Behrends, "Back from the USSR: The Anti-Comintern's Publications on Soviet Russia in Nazi Germany (1935–41)," *Kritika: Explorations in Russian and Eurasian History* 10, no 3 (Summer 2009): 527–32.

83. Rauschning, *Men of Chaos*, 92.

84. Tilitzki, *Alltag*, 14.

85. Rauschning, *Men of Chaos*, 248.

86. Tilitzki, *Alltag*, 18.

87. Rauschning, *Men of Chaos*, 249.

88. Rauschning, *Men of Chaos*, 254.

89. Rauschning, *Men of Chaos*, 251.

90. Rauschning, *Men of Chaos*, 256.

91. Ingo Haar, *Historiker im Nationalsozialismus: Deutsche Geschichtswissenschaft und der 'Volkstumskampf' im Osten*, 2nd ed. (Göttingen, Germany: Vandenhoeck & Ruprecht, 2002), 155.

92. C. G. Harke, "Ostpreußen—die Brücke zur Deutschen Freiheit," BA-Berlin NS22/437, p. 1, n.d. [early 1930s].

93. Robert G. Moeller, *War Stories: The Search for a Usable Past in the Federal Republic of Germany* (Berkeley: University of California Press, 2001), 177; Maschke quoted in Barbara Schneider, *Erich Maschke: Im Beziehungsgeflecht von Politik un Geschichtswissenschaft* (Göttingen, Germany: Vandenhoeck & Ruprecht, 2016), 106.

94. Ingo Haar, "German Ostforschung and Anti-Semitism," in *German Scholars and Ethnic Cleansing, 1919–1945*, ed. Ingo Haar and Michael Fahlbusch (New York: Berghahn Books, 2005), 10–14; Michael Burleigh, *Germany Turns Eastwards: A Study of Ostforschung in the Third Reich* (Cambridge: Cambridge University Press, 1988), 21.

95. Of the new annexations, only the Soldau (Działdowo) region, the small sliver of territory lost to Poland after the 1920 Plebiscite, had formerly been in East Prussia.

96. Ralf Meindl, "The Reichskommissar in the Decision-Making Process of the Ukrainian Holocaust," in *The Holocaust in Ukraine. New Sources and Perspectives* (Washington, DC: Center for Advanced Holocaust Studies, United States Holocaust Memorial Museum, 2013), 177.

97. BA-Berlin NS 19/3979, p. 3.

98. Jan Grabowski and Zbigniew R. Grabowski, "Germans in the Eyes of the Gestapo: The Ciechanów District, 1939–1945," *Contemporary European History* 13, no. 1 (February 2004): 27.

99. Grabowski and Grabowski, "Germans in the Eyes of the Gestapo," 21, 24.

100. The German National List (*Deutsche Volksliste*) provided for four degrees of Germanness based on self-identity, physical features, and even character traits such as tidiness. Grabowski and Grabowski, "Germans in the Eyes of the Gestapo," 26–27, 30; David Furber, "Near as Far in the Colonies: The Nazi Occupation of Poland," *International History Review* 26, no. 3 (September 2004): 551.

101. Most scholars point to the Soviet invasion as the start of the Final Solution, whereas others note that the first stages of genocide planning began already in 1939. See Richard Breitman, *The Architect of Genocide: Himmler and the Final Solution* (Hanover, NH: Brandeis University Press, 1991). While Breitman focuses on Himmler's plans, the local Wehrmacht and civilian actions in Zichenau highlight the local implementation of genocide.

102. Martin Dean and Mel Hecker, eds., *The United States Holocaust Memorial Museum Encyclopedia of Camps and Ghettos, 1933–1945, vol. 2: Ghettos in German-Occupied Eastern Europe* (Bloomington: Indiana University Press, 2012), 4–6.

103. East Prussia had been remarkable for having had no concentration camps before the war—after the Fort Quednau camp, the internment camp used to house political opponents, was shuttered at the end of 1933, Koch had preferred using short-term labor camps to persecute political prisoners.

104. Otto Rasch, "Report on the Operations of the Soldau Transit and Liquidation Camp," June 16, 1943, Nuremberg Trials Project, Harvard Law School Library, No. 3991, 1–4; Kossert, *Damals in Ostpreußen*, 132.

105. Rasch, "Report on the Operations," 3.

106. Kossert, *Damals in Ostpreußen*, 132.

107. Uwe Neumärker, "Spinnennetz der Macht—die 'Wolfsschanze' und andere NS-Hauptquartiere in Ostpreußen, 1941 bis 1944," in Pletzing, *Vorposten*, 176.

108. Meindl, "The Reichskommissar," 178.

109. Quoted in Karel Berkhoff, *Harvest of Despair, Harvest of Despair: Life and Death in Ukraine under Nazi Rule* (Cambridge, MA: Harvard University Press, 2004), 37–38.

110. Although much of the senior administration came from Koch's inner circle, among the rank-and-file administrators few were from East Prussia. TsDAVOU 3206, 1, 4: April–August 1942.

111. Jonathan Steinberg, "The Third Reich Reflected: German Civil Administration in the Occupied Soviet Union, 1941-4," *English Historical Review* 110, no. 437 (June 1995): 621.

112. Kazimir Kleofasovich Lavrinovich, *Albertina: Zur Geschichte der Albertus-Universität zu Königsberg in Preussen*, ed. Dietrich Rauschning (Berlin: Duncker and Humblot, 1999), 425.

113. TsDAVOU 3206, 1, 72: 7, February 15, 1942; Christian Tilitzki, *Alltag in Ostpreußen, 1940–1945: Die geheimen Lageberichte der Königsberger Justiz, 1940–1945* (Leer: Rautenberg, 1991), 48; Wendy Lower, *Nazi Empire-Building and the Holocaust in Ukraine* (Chapel Hill: University of North Carolina Press, 2005), 107.

114. Steinberg, "The Third Reich Reflected," 621; Christian Gerlach, *Kalkulierte Mord: Die deutsche Wirtschafts- und Vernichtungspolitik in Weissrussland, 1941 bis 1944* (Hamburg: Hamburger Ed., 1998), 195-96. Steinberg emphasizes the chaos of Nazi rule, while Gerlach demonstrates the methodical and often economics-driven nature of Nazi mass murder.

115. Berkhoff, *Harvest of Despair*, 36. An estimated 15 million Soviet civilians remained in early 1942.

116. Timothy Snyder, *Bloodlands: Europe Between Hitler and Stalin* (London: The Bodley Head, 2010), 53; Kate Brown, *Biography of No Place: From Ethnic Borderland to Soviet Heartland* (Cambridge, MA: Harvard University Press, 2003), 134-72.

117. Furber, "Near as Far in the Colonies," 551.

118. Berkhoff, *Harvest of Despair*, 44-45.

119. Lower, *Nazi Empire-Building*, 107; Berkhoff, *Harvest of Despair*, 47. Lower and Berkhoff refer to Koch as an extreme antisemite. Koch's foremost biographer, Ralf Meindl, points out that Koch was indeed antisemitic and actively denounced supposed financial conspiracies of international Jewry, but he generally found little appeal in race science and primarily espoused it to please Hitler. Meindl, "The Reichskommissar," 177.

120. Berkhoff, *Harvest of Despair*, 47.

121. TsDAVOU 3206, 1, 72: 44, May 15, 1942; TsDAVOU 3206, 1, 72: 8f-8b, February 23, 1942.

122. Lower, *Nazi Empire-Building*, 204.

123. John Connelly, "Nazis and Slavs: From Racial Theory to Racist Practice," *Central European History* 32, no. 1 (1999): 10-18.

124. TsDAVOU 3206.1.77.2-5, November 1941.

125. Berkhoff, *Harvest of Despair*, 52-53. In the neighboring General Government of Poland, by contrast, Ukrainians, Poles, and even Jews retained representative bodies.

126. Lower, *Nazi Empire-Building*, 205.

127. Tilitski, *Alltag*, 49.

128. BA, Ost-Dok. 8/793, 45f., cited in Tilitzki, *Alltag*, 50.

129. Quoted in Berkhoff, *Harvest of Despair*, 47.

130. Yitzhak Arad, *The Operation Reinhard Death Camps: Belzec, Sobibor, Treblinka*, revised and expanded edition (Bloomington: Indiana University Press, 2018), 168; *The United States Holocaust Memorial Museum Encyclopedia of Camps and Ghettos*, 2:858-59.

131. Berkhoff, *Harvest of Despair*, 62; Lower, *Nazi Empire-Building*, 69.

132. Andrej Angrick, "The Escalation of German-Rumanian Anti-Jewish Policy after the Attack on the Soviet Union, June 22, 1941," *Yad Vashem Studies* 26 (1998): 203–38.

133. Arad, *The Operation Reinhard Death Camps*, 169–73; *The United States Holocaust Memorial Museum Encyclopedia of Camps and Ghettos*, 2:867–69.

134. Meindl, "The Reichskommissar," 180.

135. Quoted in Berkhoff, *Harvest of Despair*, 37; Meindl, "The Reichskommissar," 179. Hitler continued to support Koch's approach, even though occupied populations in other districts met similar quotas with fewer punitive measures.

136. Lower, *Nazi Empire-Building*, 1.

137. Teodor Kirillovich Gladkov, *Kuznetsov: Legenda sovetskoi razvedki* (Moscow: Veche, 2004), 292–98.

138. Tilitski, *Alltag*, 49.

139. Tilitzki, *Alltag*, 50.

140. See, for example, TsDAVOU 3206, 1, 78: 4, January 9, 1942.

141. Berkhoff, *Harvest of Despair*, 48.

142. Lower, *Nazi Empire-Building*, 1.

143. Neumärker, "Spinnennetz," 191.

144. Neumärker, "Spinnennetz," 193.

145. Tilitski, *Alltag*, 51.

3. Downfall

1. Richard Bessel, *Germany 1945: From War to Peace* (New York: Harper, 2009), 67.

2. Andreas Kossert, *Damals in Ostpreußen* (Munich: Deutsche Verlags-Anstalt, 2008), 167; Ralf Meindl, *Ostpreußens Gauleiter: Erich Koch: eine politische Biographie* (Osnabrück, Germany: Fibre, 2007), 434–35.

3. Ralph Giordano, "Glanz und Elend der Geschichte," *Via Regia* 6/7 (1995): 7.

4. Robert G. Moeller, *War Stories: The Search for a Usable Past in the Federal Republic of Germany* (Berkeley: University of California Press, 2001), 3.

5. Bernhard Fisch, "Ostpreußen 1944/45. Mythen und Realitäten," in *Vorposten des Reichs? Ostpreußen 1933–1945*, ed. Christian Pletzing (Munich: Martin Meidenbauer, 2006), 213.

6. Moeller, *War Stories*, 12; Bessel, *Germany 1945*, 67.

7. Kossert, *Damals in Ostpreußen*, 128.

8. Christian Tilitzki, *Alltag in Ostpreußen, 1940–1945: Die geheimen Lageberichte der Königsberger Justiz, 1940–1945* (Leer: Rautenberg, 1991), 59; Marion Countess Dönhoff, *Before the Storm: Memories of My Youth in East Prussia*, trans. Jean Steinberg (New York: Knopf, 1990); Marianne Peyinghaus, *Stille Jahre in Gertlauken. Erinnerungen an Ostpreußen* (Berlin: Siedler, 1985).

9. B. Willems and J. Schuldt, "The 'European Boundaries' of the East Prussian Expellees in West Germany, 1948–1955," *Novoe Proshloe* 2 (2018): 35.

10. Klaus-Eberhard Murawski, "Die Zeit des Nationalsozialismus im Spiegel von ostpreußischen Heimatchroniken und Ortsgeschichten nach 1945,"

Preußenland: Mitteilungen der historischen Kommission für ost- und westpreussische Landesforschung und aus den Archiven der Stiftung preussischer Kulturbesitz 31, no. 2 (1993): 51–53.

11. TsDAVOU 3206, 1, 72: 2–4, February 16, 1942; TsDAVOU 3206, 1, 72: 67b, November 23, 1942.

12. TsDAVOU 3206, 1, 3: 26, May 5, 1942; TsDAVOU 3206, 1, 3: 120, November 19, 1942.

13. TsDAVOU 3206, 1, 14: 9–11, December 1–23, 1941.

14. TsDAVOU 3206, 2, 71: August 29, 1942.

15. BA-Berlin R58/148, p. 87, February 14, 1940; BA-Berlin R58/148, p. 160, February 23, 1940.

16. Tilitzki, *Alltag*, 59.

17. TsDAVOU 3206, 1, 72: 10, February 24, 1942; TsDAVOU 3205, 1, 72: 25b, March 11, 1942; TsDAVOU 3206.1, 72: 33, April 8, 1942; TsDAVOU 3206, 1, 72: 39, April 14, 1942.

18. BA-Berlin, R43 II/652, p. 25, April 1941.

19. Tilitzki, *Alltag*, 59.

20. BA-Berlin R58/175, p. 63, November 20, 1939; BA-Berlin R58/175, p. 50, November 27, 1939; BA-Berlin R58/272, p. 10, January 26, 1940.

21. BA-Berlin R58/175, p. 72, December 1, 1939.

22. BA-Berlin NS18/537, p. 8, November 8, 1941.

23. Bastiaan Willems, *Violence in Defeat* (New York: Cambridge University Press, 2021), 31.

24. Yoram K. Jacoby, *Jüdiches Leben in Königsberg/Pr. Im 20. Jahrhundert* (Würzburg, Germany: Holzner, 1983), 141.

25. Michael Wieck, *Zeugnis vom Untergang Königsbergs: Ein "Geltungsjude" Berichtet* (Heidelberg: L. Schneider, 1988), 98.

26. BA-Berlin R 58 Reichssicherheitshauptamt IV 84b–1027, p. 41, October 24, 1941.

27. Wieck, *Zeugnis*, 100.

28. Ludwig Goldstein, *Heimatgebünden: aus dem Leben eines alten Königsbergers* (Berlin: Nora, 2015), 568–69.

29. Stefanie Schüler-Springorum, "Die Jüdische Gemeinde Königsbergs während des Nationalsozialismus," in Pletzing, *Vorposten*, 124.

30. Wieck, *Zeugnis*, 112–13.

31. Wieck, *Zeugnis*, 31.

32. Alfred Gottwald, "Zur Deportation der Juden aus Ostpreußen in den Jahren 1942/1943," in *NS-Gewaltherrschaft. Beiträge zur historischen Forschung und juristischen Aufarbeitung*, ed. Alfred Gottwaldt, Norbert Kampe, and Peter Klein (Berlin: Edition Hentrich, 2005), 152–72; Schüler-Springorum, "Die Jüdische Gemeinde," 125–26.

33. Schüler-Springorum, "Die Jüdische Gemeinde," 126; Jacoby, *Jüdisches Leben*, 136.

34. BA-Berlin R58/175, p.107, October 12, 1942; Irina Scherbakova, "Oral Testimonies from Russian Victims of Forced Labour," in *Hitler's Slaves: Life*

Stories of Forced Labourers in Nazi-Occupied Europe, ed. Alexander von Plato, Almut Leh, and Christoph Thonfeld (Oxford: Berghahn Books, 2010), 270–72.

35. Reinhard Otto and Rolf Keller, "Soviet Prisoners of War in SS Concentration Camps: Current Knowledge and Research Desiderata," in *Mass Violence in Nazi-Occupied Europe*, ed. Alex J. Kay and David Stahel (Bloomington: Indiana University Press, 2018), 123; Otto and Keller point out that the primary source data to calculate death statistics is incomplete and contradictory. Reinhard Otto, Rolf Keller, and Jens Nagel, "Sowjetische Kriegsgefangene in deutschem Gewahrsam, 1941–1945. Zahlen und Dimensionen," *Vierteljahrshefte für Zeitgeschichte* 56, no. 4 (October 2008): 557–602.

36. Gesine Gerhard, *Nazi Hunger Politics: A History of Food in the Third Reich* (Lanham, MD: Rowman & Littlefield, 2015), 60, 98–99.

37. Erhard Schulz, *Childhood in East Prussia and Flight in 1944/45: Recollections*, trans. Ortrun Schulz (Norderstadt, Germany: Books on Demand, GmbH, 2003), 37, 43, 55–57; BA-Berlin NS18/537, p. 8, November 8, 1941.

38. BA-Berlin NS18/537, p. 9, November 8, 1941.

39. BA-Berlin R58/272, p. 126, September 14, 1944.

40. Omer Bartov, "From *Blitzkrieg* to Total War: Controversial Links between Image and Reality," in *Nazism, Stalinism, and Dictatorship*, ed. M. Lewin and I. Kershaw (Cambridge: Cambridge University Press, 1997), 158.

41. Gertrud Brostowski, "Vom Gutshaushalt zur Ostpreussischen Mädchengewerbeschule," in *Leben in Ostpreußen: Erinnerungen aus neun Jahrzehnten*, ed. Otto Dikreiter (Munich: Gräfe und Unzer, 1969), 36.

42. BA-Berlin DY55/V 287/162, pp. 1–2, November 10, 1943.

43. Alistair Noble, "The Phantom Barrier: *Ostwallbau* 1944–1945," *War in History* 8, no. 4 (November 2001): 443–44; BA-Berlin NS6/411, pp. 236, 239, July 14, 1944.

44. BA-Berlin NS6/411, p. 233, July 6, 1944, quoted in Alastair Noble, "The First Frontgau: East Prussia, July 1944," *War in History* 13, no. 2 (2006): 204.

45. BA-Berlin NS6/34, p. 7, August 23, 1944.

46. Noble, "The Phantom Barrier," 445; Noble, "The First Frontgau," 207.

47. Meindl, *Ostpreußens Gauleiter*, 417.

48. Kossert, *Damals in Ostpreußen*, 131; Noble, "The Phantom Barrier," 455–56.

49. Jurgis Mališauskas, "Als Schanzarbeiter in Deutschland 1944–45," *Annaberger Annalen über Litauen und Deutsch-Litauische Beziehungen* 18 (2010): 287–96.

50. Theodor Schieder, ed., *Documents on the Expulsion of the Germans from Eastern Central Europe, Volume 1: The Expulsions of the German Population from the Territories East of the Oder-Neisse Line* (Bonn: Federal Ministry for Expellees, Refugees, and War Victims, 1956), 9.

51. Noble, "The First Frontgau," 203.

52. Ian Kershaw, *The End: The Defiance and Destruction of Hitler's Germany, 1944–1945* (New York: Penguin, 2011), 105.

53. Noble, "The Phantom Barrier," 443, 447–49, 450, 452. In a study of the Wehrmacht's defense of East Prussia in 1944–45, Bastiaan Willems argues

convincingly that the Wehrmacht played a large role in the defense and was not completely controlled by Koch. I argue that Koch's powerful public role remains, however, incontrovertible; cf. Willems, *Violence in Defeat*, 63.

54. Otto Lasch, *So fiel Königsberg: Kampf und Untergang von Ostpreussens Hauptstadt* (Munich: Gräfe und Unzer Verlag, 1958), 25; Alistair Noble, "A Most Distant Target: The Bombing of Königsberg, August 1944," *War and Society* 25, no. 1 (2006): 58–59. The Red Air Force bombed Königsberg numerous times in 1941 and 1942, but the damage sustained was minor.

55. Lasch, *So fiel Königsberg*, 25–26; Noble, "A Most Distant Target," 68. Casualty estimates vary: Herta Schöning and Hans-Georg Tautorat list 4,200 dead and 200,000 homeless, while Guido Knopp and Stefan Brauberger list up to 5,000 dead but only 150,000 homeless. Herta Schöning and Hans-Georg Tautorat, *Die ostpreussische Tragodie, 1944/45: Dokumentation des Schicksals einer deutschen Provinz und ihrer Bevölkerung* (Leer, Germany: Gerhard Rautenberg, 1985), 12; Guido Knopp and Stefan Brauburger, "Die Schlacht um Ostpreußen," in Guido Knopp, *Der Sturm: Kriegsende im Osten* (Berlin: Econ, 2004), 17.

56. Schulz, *Childhood*, 93; Wieck, *Zeugnis*, 151.

57. Schüler-Springorum, "Die Jüdische Gemeinde," 127.

58. Noble, "A Most Distant Target," 64–65, 71–72.

59. Gause, *Die Geschichte*, 3:160.

60. Günter Wegmann, ed., *"Das Oberkommando der Wehrmacht gibt bekannt . . .": Der deutsche Wehrmachtbericht* (Osnabrück, Germany: Biblio Verlag, 1982), 3:302 [October 22, 1944], 304 [October 23, 1944].

61. Meindl, "Erich Koch," 37–38; Kershaw, *The End*, 107. The *Volkssturm* was the national mobilization of local militias that Koch had deployed as early as July 1944.

62. Quoted in Knopp and Brauburger, "Die Schlacht," 20.

63. David K. Yelton, "'Ein Volk Steht Auf': The German Volkssturm and Nazi Strategy, 1944–45," *Journal of Military History* 64, no. 4 (October 2000): 1064.

64. Paul Hanebrink, *A Specter Haunting Europe: The Myth of Judeo-Bolshevism* (Cambridge: Harvard University Press, 2018), 125; Jan C. Behrends, "Back from the USSR: The Anti-Comintern's Publications on Soviet Russia in Nazi Germany (1935–41)," *Kritika: Explorations in Russian and Eurasian History* 10, no. 3 (Summer 2009): 527–32.

65. BA-Berlin R58/175, p. 107, August 17, 1942.

66. Vejas Liulevicius, *The German Myth of the East: 1800 to the Present* (Oxford: Oxford University Press, 2009), 192–93.

67. BA-Berlin R58/175, pp. 107, 108, August 17, 1942.

68. Bartov, "From *Blitzkrieg*," 179.

69. [Bernhard] Rust, "Acht neue Lehrstühle für die Albertina," GStPK I Rep. 76, Nr. 882, p. 22, July 9, 1944, reprinted in Friedrich Richter, *450 Jahre Albertus-Universität zu Königsberg/Pr., 1544–1944–1994* (Stuttgart: Franz Steiner, 1994), 82.

70. Rust, "Acht neue Lehrstühle," 82.

71. *Völkischer Beobachter*, October 27, 1944, reprinted in Bernhard Fisch, *Nemmersdorf: was tatsächlich geschah* (Berlin: Edition Ost, 1997), 46.

72. Fisch, *Nemmersdorf*, 50.

73. *Völkischer Beobachter*, October 27, 1944, reprinted in Fisch, *Nemmersdorf*, 45–47.

74. *Völkischer Beobachter*, October 27, 1944, reprinted in Fisch, *Nemmersdorf*, 50.

75. Wolfgang Wünsche, "Die Rote Armee in Ostpreußen 1944/45," introduction to Fisch, *Nemmersdorf*, 9; Bessel, *Germany 1945*, 71.

76. Knopp and Brauburger, "Die Schlacht," 22.

77. Dönhoff, *Before the Storm*, 182–83.

78. Fisch, *Nemmersdorf*, 68.

79. Dönhoff, *Before the Storm*, 182–83.

80. Fisch, *Nemmersdorf*, 68; Hanebrink, *A Specter*, 157.

81. Liulevicius, *The German Myth*, 204; Bessel, *Germany 1945*, 71.

82. Michael Geyer, "Endkampf 1918 and 1945: German Nationalism, Annihilation and Self-Destruction," in *No Man's Land of Violence: Extreme Wars in the 20th Century*, ed. Alf Lüdke and Bernd Weisbrod (Göttingen, Germany: Wallstein, 2006), 57.

83. The most famous work in this genre is Andreas Hillgruber, *Zweierlei Untergang: die Zerschlagung des Deutschen Reiches und das Ende des europäischen Judentums* (Berlin: Siedler, 1996). Hillgruber's book caused a scandal during the West German Historians' Controversy (*Historikerstreit*) in the late 1980s over responsible history writing about the end of the war and the Holocaust.

84. Charles Maier, *The Unmasterable Past: History, Holocaust, and German National Identity* (Cambridge, MA: Harvard University Press, 1988), 20.

85. Quoted in Knopp and Brauburger, "Die Schlacht," 25.

86. Count Hans von Lehndorff, *Token of a Covenant: Diary of an East Prussian Surgeon, 1945–47*, trans. Elizabeth Mayer (Chicago: Henry Regnery Company, 1964), 5.

87. Käthe Hielscher, *Als Ostpreußin in russischer Kriegsgefangenschaft* (Berlin: Frieling, 1998), 60, 62.

88. Bessel, *Germany 1945*, 11–12.

89. Bessel, *Germany 1945*, 25.

90. Lasch, *So fiel Königsberg*, 32.

91. Lasch, *So fiel Königsberg*, 29–32.

92. Meindl, *Ostpreußens Gauleiter*, 435; Bessel, *Germany 1945*, 72. Primary source data lists East Prussia's spring 1944 population as 2.3 to 2.4 million.

93. Schöning and Tautorat, *Tragodie*, 40.

94. BA-Berlin R1501/1333, pp. 29–31, February 10, 1945.

95. Outside Germany, Soviet troops were more likely to spare workers and peasants. For the case of Hungary, see Alexandra Orme, *Comes the Comrade!* (New York: Morrow, 1950).

96. Dönhoff, *Before the Storm*, 190.

97. Dönhoff, *Before the Storm*, 188.

98. Guido Knopp, *Der Untergang der "Gustloff": wie es wirklich war* (Munich: Econ Ullstein, 2002), 36.

99. Knopp, *Der Untergang,* 59, 105, 138. The ship registered 7,956 passengers on January 29, 1945, not including last-minute additions and crew.

100. Bessel, *Germany 1945,* 73.

101. Knopp, *Der Untergang,* 132.

102. Lasch, *So fiel Königsberg,* 36–37; Lehndorff, *Token,* 15 [January 23, 1945].

103. Cited in Knopp and Brauburger, "Die Schlacht," 19.

104. "Erlebnisbericht des A.S. aus Pillau, Kreis Samland i. Ostpr.," in *Dokumentation der Vertreibung der Deutschen aus Ost-Mitteleuropa. Band I/1: die Vertreibung der deutschen Bevölkerung aus den Gebieten östlich der Oder-Neisse,* ed. Theodor Schieder (Bonn, 1954), 149–50, quoted in Bessel, *Germany 1945,* 74.

105. Anneliese Kreutz, *Das grosse Sterben in Königsberg, 1945–47* (Kiel, Germany: Arndt, 1988), 8–9.

106. Schöning and Tautorat, *Tragodie,* 56.

107. Meindl, *Ostpreußens Gauleiter,* 435, 447.

108. Andreas Kossert, "*Endlösung* on the Amber Shore: The Massacre on the Baltic Shore—A Repressed Chapter of East Prussian History," *Leo Baeck Institute Yearbook* 49, no. 1 (2004): 7.

109. Kossert, "*Endlösung,*" 10. Kossert puts the number of deaths at 2,000. Friedrich Ortseldorff [Russ: Ortsel'dorf], the head of the Königsberg City Jail, confessed during NKVD interrogation to personally ordering the executions of at least 3,000 prisoners, including "Germans, Poles, Estonians, Latvians, and Lithuanians." GARF f. 9401, op. 2, d. 96, l. 257, May 15, 1945.

110. Kossert, "*Endlösung,*" 10, 12; Martin Bergau, "Das Massaker in Palmnicken 1945. Ein Zeitzeugenbericht," in Pletzing, *Vorposten,* 197. Bergau cites the conservative estimate of 5,000; some survivor testimonies on the contrary mention that anywhere from 7,000 to 10,000 died in the massacre at Palmnicken, but those numbers may include other victims who joined the SS death march outside of Königsberg. Kossert cites the figure of 7,000 leaving Königsberg, from Danuta Drywa, *Zagłada Żydów w obozie koncentracyjnym Stutthof: wrzesień 1939–maj 1945* (Gdańsk, Poland: Muzeum Stutthof w Sztutowie, 2001), 235. The BA-Ludwigsburg estimate is slightly lower at 6,500. BA-Ludwigsburg AR-Z 299/1959, Bl. 944, May 27, 1964.

111. Moeller, *War Stories,* 72.

112. Bergau, "Das Massaker," 198.

113. Quoted in Bergau, "Das Massaker," 200.

114. Kossert, "*Endlösung,*" 10, 12.

115. The Katyn forest near Smolensk was the site where the Wehrmacht discovered the mass grave of nearly 22,000 Polish military officers and intelligentsia murdered by Soviet occupiers of eastern Poland in 1940. It became a propaganda centerpiece for Goebbels in 1943. Hanebrink, *A Specter,* 154.

116. Testimony of Rudolf Folger, BA-Ludwigsburg [no citation] February 6, 1961, quoted in Bergau, "Das Massaker," 198.

117. Bergau, "Das Massaker," 203; See also BA-Ludwigsburg AR-Z 299/1959, vol. I, Bl. 1–260, January 24, 1961; BA-Ludwigsburg AR-Z 299/1959, vol. II, Bl.

261–390; Testimony given in Winsen, June 23, 1961 by Kurt Friedrichs, cited in Kossert, *"Endlösung,"* 13–14.

118. Bergau, "Das Massaker," 208.

119. Bergau, "Das Massaker," 204.

120. Bergau, "Das Massaker," 204.

121. Celina Malinewicz, born July 21, 1921 in Osokow, Poland. Yad Vashem testimonies from November 30, 1958 and October 10, 1961, Jerusalem, reprinted in Martin Bergau, *Der Junge von der Bernsteinküste: erlebte Zeitgeschichte, 1938–1948* (Heidelberg: Heidelberger Verlagsanstalt, 1994), 249–59; BA-Ludwigsburg AR-Z 299/1959, Bd. III, Bl. 391–499, Testimony of Zila Manielewicz, Jerusalem, October 10, 1961, cited in Kossert, *"Endlösung,"* 16.

122. Testimony by Celina Malinewicz, November 30, 1945, Jerusalem, reprinted in Bergau, *Der Junge*, 252.

123. Testimony by Celina Malinewicz, November 30, 1945, Jerusalem, reprinted in Bergau, *Der Junge*, 253–54.

124. Testimony by Celina Malinewicz, November 30, 1945, Jerusalem, reprinted in Bergau, *Der Junge*, 255.

125. Kossert, *"Endlösung,"* 17.

126. BA-Ludwigsburg AR-Z 299/1959, vol. IV, Bl. 500–748, testimony given in Werdohl, July 3, 1962, cited in Kossert, *"Endlösung,"* 17.

127. Testimony by Celina Malinewicz, November 30, 1945, Jerusalem, reprinted in Bergau, *Der Junge*, 258. The number of survivors varies depending on the source. Malinewicz says that thirteen survived; other sources list either fifteen or sixteen survivors.

128. Bergau, "Das Massaker," 206.

129. BA-Ludwigsburg AR-Z 299/1959, vol. II, Bl. 261–390, testimony given in Winsen, 23 June 23, 1961 by Kurt Friedrichs, cited in Kossert, *"Endlösung,"* 14–15.

130. Testimony by Celina Malinewicz, November 30, 1945, Jerusalem, reprinted in Bergau, *Der Junge*, 259.

131. GARF f. 9401, op. 2, d. 93, l. 4–5, February 22, 1945.

132. Lasch, *So fiel Königsberg*, 7.

133. Willems, *Violence in Defeat*, 146.

134. BA-Berlin R1501/134, no page, n.d. [February 1945].

135. Lasch, *So fiel Königsberg*, 77–78.

136. BA-Berlin R1501/BA-Berlin RY 1/I 2/3/167, p. 1, n. d. [late 1945]; 134, no page, n.d. [February 1945]. The highest number of 135,000 is reported by the SS-Oberführer Böhme on March 3, 1945, after initial evacuations. The pre-evacuation number was 150,000 or more. Postwar testimonies estimate the numbers to be higher.

137. Willems, *Violence in Defeat*, 259.

138. BA-Berlin RY 1/I 2/3/167, p. 1 [n.d. c. late 1945]; BA-Berlin R1501/134, no page, n.d. (February 1945); Lehndorff, *Token*, 51–52 [around March 1945].

139. Lehndorff, *Token*, 16 [January 23, 1945].

140. BA-Berlin NS19/2068, p. 7, February 15, 1945.

141. GARF f. 9401, op. 2, d. 93, l. 4, February 22, 1945.

142. Willems, *Violence in Defeat*, 161.

143. Lehndorff, *Token*, 32–33 [February 1945].

144. In an ironic turn of fate, the Soviets reportedly showed the film in the Eastern Zone after the war as anti-Western propaganda. David Stewart Hull, "Forbidden Fruit: The Harvest of the German Cinema, 1939–1945," *Film Quarterly* 14, no. 4 (Summer 1961): 21–22.

145. Lehndorff, *Token*, 31 [sometime after January 30, 1945].

146. Erich Schwarz, *Abschied von Königsberg. Erinnerungen an die Jahre 1945/47* (Hameln, Germany: Niemeyer, 1997), 18.

147. Schwarz, *Abschied*, 9, 16; "Königsberger Männer und Frauen!" [Placard], February 9, 1945, reprinted in Schöning and Tautorat, *Tragödie*, 50.

148. BA-Berlin NS19/2068, p. 47, March 4–5, 1945; Geyer, "Endkampf," 62.

149. Manfred Messerschmidt and Fritz Wüllner, *Die Wehrmachtjustiz im Dienste des Nationalsozialismus. Zerstörung eine Legende* (Baden-Baden, Germany: Nomos Verlagsgesellschaft, 1987), 77–81, 305–14; Manfred Messerschmidt, "Deutsche Militärgerichtsbarkeit im Zweiten Weltkrieg," in *Die Freiheit des Andern*, ed. Hans-Jochen Vogel, Helmut Simon, Adalbert Podlech (Baden-Baden, Germany: Nomos Verlagsgesellschaft, 1981).

150. Richard Bessel, "The War to End All Wars: The Shock of Violence in 1945 and Its Aftermath in Germany," in Lüdke and Weisbrod, *No Man's Land*, 76.

151. GARF f. 9401, op. 2, d. 93, l. 4, February 22, 1945. Soviet reconnaissance reported one million civilians inside Königsberg, when there were only around 100,000.

152. Schwarz, *Abschied*, 13; BA-Berlin NS19/2068, p. 57, March 9, 1945; GARF f. 9401, op. 2, d. 93, l. 333, February 28, 1945.

153. BA-Berlin NS19/2068, pp. 69, 71, March 16–17, 1945.

154. BA-Berlin NS19/2068, p. 47, March 4–5, 1945.

155. A report from March 19, 1945 reports 55,000 civilians remaining, BA-Berlin NS19/2068, p. 74; an Army Group North report from March 24, by contrast, indicates 70,000 civilians in the Fortress, Willems, *Violence in Defeat*, 225.

156. GARF f. 9401, op. 2, d. 96, l. 259, May 15, 1945.

157. Lasch, *So fiel Königsberg*, 81.

158. Lasch, *So fiel Königsberg*, 86.

159. Lehndorff, *Token*, 57–58 [late March 1945].

160. Wieck, *Zeugnis*, 215.

161. Hielscher, *Als Ostpreußin*, 66–73.

162. BA-Berlin RY1/I2/3/167, p. 3, n.d. [late 1945] cites 35,000 Wehrmacht soldiers and approximately 8,000 *Volkssturm* soldiers, while Lasch in his memoirs cites 55,000 soldiers under his command. Lasch, *So fiel Königsberg*, 78–79.

163. V. N. Baliazin, *Shturm Kenigsberga* (Moscow: Voenizdat, 1964), 69.

164. BA-Berlin RY1/I2/3/167, p. 5 n.d. [late 1945]

165. GARF f. 9401, op. 2, d. 96, l. 259, May 15, 1945.

166. Lasch, *So fiel Königsberg*, 104, 106–7.

167. Wieck, *Zeugnis*, 218.

168. Geyer, "Endkampf," 37.

169. Knopp and Brauburger, "Die Schlacht," 16; Bessel, "The War," 73; Meindl, *Ostpreußens Gauleiter*, 438; Gerhild Luschnat, *Die Lage der Deutschen im Königsberger Gebiet, 1945–1948* (Frankfurt am Main: Peter Lang, 1996).

170. Lasch, *So fiel Königsberg*, 82.

171. Lasch, *So fiel Königsberg*, 118–19.

172. Schöning and Tautorat, *Tragodie*, 50.

173. Quoted in Knopp and Brauburger, "Die Schlacht," 19.

174. Dr. Paul Hoffmann, Aussagen vor dem Extradition Tribunal in Hamburg am 8.11.1949 und in der Spruchgerichtssache gegen Erich Koch. Schreiben vom 30.9.49 an den öffentlichen Ankläger beim Spruchgericht Bielefeld, BA-Koblenz, Ost-Dok. 10-272, quoted in Fisch, "Ostpreussen," 241.

175. Hans Deichelmann, *Ich sah Königsberg sterben: Tagebuch eines Arztes in Königsberg 1945 bis 1948* (Beltheim, Germany: Bublies, 1999), 26 [April 20, 1945].

176. Lehndorff, *Token*, 108 [April 30, 1945].

177. Deichelmann, *Ich sah*, 23–24 [April 20, 1945].

178. Deichelmann, *Ich sah*, 26 [April 20, 1945]; Michael Wieck, *A Childhood under Hitler and Stalin: Memoirs of a "Certified" Jew*, trans. Penny Milbouer (Madison, WI: University of Wisconsin Press, 2003), 66.

179. Lehndorff, *Token*, 51–52.

180. Wieck, *Zeugnis*, 228.

181. Lucy Falk, *Ich blieb in Königsberg: Tagebuchblätter aus dunklen Nachkriegsjahren*, 2nd ed. (Munich: Gräfe und Unzer, 1966), 9.

182. Atina Grossmann, "A Question of Silence: The Rape of German Women by Occupation Soldiers," *October* 72 (Spring 1995): 50.

183. The commission was led by the Königsberg history professor, former Nazi party member and *Lebensraum* advocate Theodor Schieder, and included a number of other Königsberg historians, including Hans Rothfels (excluded from the university as a Jew during the *Gleichschaltung*) and Werner Conze.

184. Schieder, ed., *Documents on the Expulsion*, 49.

185. Lehndorff, *Token*, 52 [April 9–24, 1945].

186. Quoted in Moeller, *War Stories*, 64.

187. Hielscher, *Als Ostpreußin*, 73.

188. Wolfgang Lehnert, *Die Russen kamen–und blieben: Erlebnisse eines ostpreussischen Jungen bei Königsberg in den Jahren 1944 bis 1948* (Berlin: Frieling, 2001), 21.

189. Wendy Z. Goldman and Donald Filtzer, *Fortress Dark and Stern: The Soviet Home Front during World War II* (New York: Oxford University Press, 2021), 7; Wendy Z. Goldman and Donald Filtzer, eds., *Hunger and War: Food Provisioning in the Soviet Union during World War II* (Bloomington: Indiana University Press, 2015), 1–2.

190. Testimony of Rudolf Folger, cited in Bergau, "The Massaker," 210.

191. Testimony of Johannes Jänicke, cited in Bergau, "The Massaker," 210.

4. Liberation and Revenge

1. Jurij Uspenskij, "Die Tagebuchaufzeichnungen eines russischen Artillerieoffiziers in Deutschland im Frühjahr 1945," ed. and trans. Peter Gosztony, *Wehrwissenschaftliche Rundschau: Zeitschrift für die europäische Sicherheit* 9 (September 1969): 514 [12 January 1945, near Vilnius]. This diary was the first published document to describe the violence against civilians in East Prussia from a Red Army soldier's perspective.

2. N. Lenin [V. I. Lenin], "Peace—and Our Task," March 18, 1918, printed in N. Lenin and Leon Trotsky, *The Proletarian Revolution in Russia* (New York: Communist Press, 1918), 364.

3. N. Lenin [V. I. Lenin], *The Chief Task of Our Duty* (1918), reprinted in V. I. Lenin, *Collected Works*, 4th English ed. (Moscow: Progress, 1972), 27:334.

4. On the embrace of good German culture, see Katerina Clark and Karl Schlögel, "Mutual Perceptions and Projections: Stalin's Russia in Nazi Germany—Nazi Germany in the Soviet Union," in *Beyond Totalitarianism: Stalinism and Nazism Compared*, ed. Michael Geyer and Sheila Fitzpatrick (Cambridge: Cambridge University Press, 2009), 432.

5. Clark and Schlögel, "Mutual Perceptions," 423–25.

6. Clark and Schlögel, "Mutual Perceptions," 439; Katerina Clark, "Ehrenburg and Grossman: Two Cosmopolitan Jewish Writers Reflect on Nazi Germany at War," *Kritika: Explorations in Russian and Eurasian History* 10, no. 3 (Summer 2009): 307-8.

7. Joshua Rubenstein, *Tangled Loyalties* (New York: Basic Books, 1996), 190; Ilya Ehrenburg, *The War: 1941–1945* (Cleveland: World Publishing Company, 1964), 26.

8. Daniil Granin, "Prekrasnaia Uta," in *Neozhidannoe utro* (Leningrad: Lenizdat, 1987), 195-97.

9. Karel Berkhoff, *Motherland in Danger: Soviet Propaganda during World War II* (Cambridge, MA: Harvard University Press), 168-73.

10. Rubenstein, *Tangled Loyalties*, 191; Clark, "Ehrenburg and Grossman," 608.

11. Rubenstein, *Tangled Loyalties*, 193.

12. Clark, "Ehrenburg and Grossman," 608.

13. Jochen Hellbeck, "The Diaries of Fritzes and the Letters of Gretchens," in *Fascination and Enmity: Russia and Germany as Entangled Histories, 1914–1945*, ed. Michael David-Fox, Peter Holquist, and Alexander M. Martin (Pittsburgh: University of Pittsburgh Press, 2012), 138.

14. I. G. Erenburg, "Shelk i vshi," reprinted in *Voina: iun' 1941–aprel' 1942* (Moscow: Goslitizdat, 1942), 114-15; Erenburg, "Po dva arshina," reprinted in *Voina: iun' 1941–aprel' 1942*, 53.

15. Erenburg, "Gretkhen," *Voina: iun' 1941–aprel'*, 52, 54.

16. Ehrenburg, *The War*, 26; Clark, "Ehrenburg and Grossman," 609.

17. David Brandenberger, *National Bolshevism: Stalinist Mass Culture and the Formation of Modern Russian National Identity, 1931–1956* (Cambridge, MA: Harvard University Press, 2002), 43-45.

18. Stalin quoted in Terry Martin, *The Affirmative Action Empire: Nations and Nationalism in the Soviet Union, 1923–1939* (Ithaca, NY: Cornell University Press, 2001), 12.

19. For a history of the reintroduction of great Russian nationalism in the 1930s, see David Brandenberger, *National Bolshevism*; Frederick C. Barghoorn, *Soviet Russian Nationalism* (New York: Oxford University Press, 1956); Mikhail Agursky, *The Third Rome: National Bolshevism in the USSR* (Boulder, CO: Westview Press, 1985); Erik van Ree, *The Political Thought of Joseph Stalin: A Study in Twentieth-Century Revolutionary Patriotism* (London: RoutledgeCurzon, 2002); Katerina Clark, *Moscow, the Fourth Rome: Stalinism, Cosmopolitanism, and the Evolution of Soviet Culture, 1931–1941* (Cambridge, MA: Harvard University Press, 2011).

20. Clark, "Ehrenburg and Grossman," 613.

21. Berkhoff, *Motherland*, 175.

22. Brandon Schechter, *The Stuff of Soldiers: A History of the Red Army in World War II through Objects* (Ithaca, NY: Cornell University Press, 2019), 215.

23. Il'ia Erenburg, "Nash gumanizm," reprinted in *Voina* (Moskva: Astrel', 2004), 589-91.

24. Il'ia Erenburg, "Ubei!" *Krasnaia zvezda*, October 12, 1942.

25. Ilya Ehrenburg, "Army of Life," reprinted in *We Will Not Forget* (Washington, DC: Embassy of the Union of Soviet Socialist Republics), 54.

26. Oleg Budnitskii, "The Intelligentsia Meets the Enemy: Educated Soviet Officers in Defeated Germany, 1945," trans. Susan Rupp, *Kritika: Explorations in Russian and Eurasian History* 10, no. 3 (Summer 2009): 633; Hellbeck, "The Diaries," 145.

27. Ehrenburg, "The Justification," reprinted in *We Will Not Forget*, 28.

28. Erenburg, "O nenavisti," reprinted in *Voina: iun' 1941–aprel' 1942*, 182.

29. Erenburg, "Nash gumanizm," 590.

30. Erenburg, "Nash gumanizm," 591.

31. Ehrenburg, "Army of Life," 54.

32. Konstantin Simonov, "Lager' unichtozheniia," *Krasnaia zvezda*, August 10-11, 1944; "O chëm govorit liublinskii lager' unichtozheniia," *Krasnaia zvezda*, August 12, 1944; Lieutenant-Colonel G. Ivashchenko, "Vstrecha na frontovoi doroge," *Krasnaia zvezda*, October 5, 1944.

33. Uspenskij, "Tagebuchaufzeichnungen," 514 [January 13, 1945].

34. Quoted in Manfred Zeidler, *Kriegsende im Osten: die Rote Armee und die Besetzung Deutschlands ostlich von Oder und Neisse 1944/45* (Berlin: Oldenbourg, 1996), 70–71.

35. *Krasnaia zvezda*, October 24, 1944.

36. N. P. Gratsianskii, *Kenigsberg: stenogramma publichnoi lektsii* (Moscow: All-Union Lecture Bureau of the Committee for Higher Education Affairs of the People's Commissariat of the USSR, 1945).

37. Ehrenburg, *The War*, 163.

38. Lev Kopelev, *No Jail for Thought*, ed. and trans. Anthony Austin (London: Secker and Warburg, 1977), 37.

39. Anatolii Genatulin, *Vot konchitsia voina. Povesti i rasskazy* (Moscow: Pravda, 1988), 111.

40. P. A. Pirogov, "Vospominanii o sluzhbe v armii i o begstve . . ." manuscript, Hoover Institute Archives (HIA), Nicolaevsky, box 249-9, Series 193, 9.

41. Genatulin, *Vot konchitsia voina*, 117.

42. Letter from Inozemtsev to Nikolai Inozemtsev (his father), April 27, 1945, reprinted in N. N. Inozemtsev, *Frontovoi Dnevnik* (Moscow: Nauka, 2005), 353.

43. Uspenskij, "Tagebuchaufzeichnungen," 518 [January 23, 1945].

44. Schechter, *The Stuff*, 212.

45. Inozemtsev, *Frontovoi Dnevnik*, 208 [after January 14, 1945].

46. Alexander Werth, *Russia at War* (London: Barrie and Rockliff, 1964), 983.

47. Uspenskij, "Tagebuchaufzeichnungen," 517 [January 23, 1945].

48. Pomerants, *Zapiski gadkogo utenka* (Moscow: Moskovskii Rabochii, 1998), 197.

49. Kopelev, *No Jail*, 37.

50. Evgenii Plimak, *Na voine i posle voini. Zapiski veterana* (Moscow: Ves' Mir, 2005), 35.

51. Uspenskij, "Tagebuchaufzeichnungen," 517-18 [around January 23, 1945].

52. Wendy Z. Goldman and Donald Filtzer, *Fortress Dark and Stern: The Soviet Home Front during World War II* (New York: Oxford University Press, 2021), 265.

53. Prikaz 281, no. 0409, December 26, 1944, reprinted in *Russkii arkhiv: Velikaia Otehestvennaia: Prikazy Narodnogo komissara oborony SSSR (1943–1945 gg.)*, vol. 13 (2-3) (Moscow: Terra, 1997), 344-47.

54. Lev Markovich Polonskii, interview by Grigorii Koifman, http://www.iremember.ru/index.php?option=com_content&task=view&id=430&Itemid=22, January 21, 2007; Norman Naimark, *The Russians in Germany: A History of the Soviet Zone of Occupation, 1945–1949* (Cambridge, MA: Belknap Press of Harvard University Press, 1995), 69.

55. Schechter, *The Stuff*, 214.

56. Rostislav Ivanovich Zhidkov, interview by Artem Drabkin, http://iremember.ru/gmch-katiushi/zhidkov-rostislav-ivanovich.html, July 22, 2006.

57. Polonskii interview, January 21, 2007.

58. Kopelev, *No Jail*, 37.

59. Pomerants, *Zapiski*, 95.

60. Atina Grossmann, "A Question of Silence: The Rape of German Women by Occupation Soldiers," *October* 72 (Spring 1995): 46.

61. Mark Edele, "Soviet Liberations and Occupations, 1939–1949," in *The Cambridge History of the Second World War*, vol. 2: *Politics and Ideology* (New York: Cambridge University Press, 2015), 493; Schechter, *The Stuff*, 234.

62. Naimark, *The Russians*, 74.

63. GARF f. 9401, op. 2, d. 94, l. 87, March 11(14?), 1945.

64. GARF f. 9401, op. 2, d. 94, l. 87, March 11(14?), 1945.

65. Bastiaan Willems, *Violence in Defeat* (New York: Cambridge University Press, 2021), 161.

66. GARF f. 9401, op. 2, d. 94, l. 87, March 11(14?), 1945.

67. A. Solzhenitsyn, *Prusskie Nochi* (Paris: YMCA Press, 1974), 25; translation adapted from Alexander Solzhenitsyn, *Prussian Nights*, trans. Robert Conquest (New York: Farrar, Straus and Giroux, 1977), 7.

68. See Bernhard Fisch, "Ostpreußen 1944/45. Mythen und Realitäten," in in *Vorposten des Reichs? Ostpreußen 1933–1945*, ed. Christian Pletzing (Munich: Martin Meidenbauer, 2006), 233.

69. Naimark, *The Russians*, 72.

70. Regina Mühlhäuser, *Sex and the Nazi Soldier: Violent, Commercial, and Consensual Encounters during the War in the Soviet Union, 1941–45* (Edinburgh: University of Edinburgh Press, 2021), 316–17.

71. Mühlhäuser, *Sex and the Nazi Soldier*, 316–32; Edward B. Westermann, *Drunk on Genocide: Alcohol and Mass Murder in Nazi Germany* (Ithaca, NY: Cornell University Press, 2021), 92.

72. Naimark, *The Russians*, 69–72; Catherine Merridale, *Ivan's War: Life and Death in the Red Army* (New York: Picador, 2006), 303–20; Kerstin Bischl, *Frontbeziehungen: Geschlechterverhältnisse und Gewaltendynamiken in der Roten Armee 1941–1945* (Hamburg: Hamburger Edition, 2019), 241–307; Elisabeth Jean Wood, "Variation in Sexual Violence during War," *Politics & Society* 34, no. 3 (September 2006): 307.

73. Susan Brownmiller, *Against Our Will: Men, Women, and Rape* (New York: Simon and Schuster, 1975).

74. Vojin Majstorović, "The Red Army in Yugoslavia, 1944–1945," *Slavic Review* 75, no. 2 (Summer 2016): 397.

75. Fisch, "Ostpreußen," 218; Pawel N. Knyshewski, *Moskaus Beute* (Munich: Lech 1994), 29–31.

76. Milovan Djilas, *Conversations with Stalin*, trans. Michael Petrovich (New York: Harcourt Brace, 1962), 88–89.

77. Fisch, "Ostpreußen," 220, 225.

78. RGVA f. 32941, op. 1, d. 46, l. 85, November 8, 1944.

79. *Krasnaia zvezda*, December 22, 1944, cited in Fisch, "Ostpreussen," 220.

80. A. A. Gretschko and I. V. Parot'kin, *Die Befreiungsmission der Sowjetstreitkräfte im zweiten Weltkrieg* (Berlin: Militärverlag der DDR, 1973), 437.

81. BA-Freiburg, RH 2-2470, Bl. 77, January 22, 1945, cited in Zeidler, *Kriegsende*, 155.

82. Fisch, "Ostpreußen," 224–25.

83. Fisch, "Ostpreußen," 220.

84. RGVA f. 32941, op. 1, d. 39, l. 176, January 14 –December 31, 1944; RGVA f. 32941, op. 1, d. 46, l. 75, October 29, 1944; RGVA f. 38680, op. 1, d. 3, l. 4; RGVA f. 38680, op. 1, d. 3, l. 8. Already in October 1944, the 43rd Army reported twenty-two poisonings, and military commanders issued a categorical ban against drinking captured liquids without proper testing. But despite early bans, incidences of poisoning continued to occur. According to SMERSH reports from October 21, 1944, fifteen Red Army soldiers were poisoned in Schaugsten (*Kreis* Darkehmen) from drinking poisoned liquor (twelve of them died); a report from February 21, 1945 noted that fifteen soldiers were

poisoned drinking captured alcohol in the city of Friedland. A full ban on using captured food was issued in February 1945 after a whole stockpile of poisoned food was found in Zinten (Russ. Tsinten). Frequent orders were issued to remind soldiers of the risks of drinking captured alcohol, but poisonings continued to occur throughout the spring of 1945 in and around Königsberg; RGVA f. 38680, op. 1, d. 3, l. 86, April 11, 1945.

85. TsAMORF (Tsentral'nyi Arkhiv Ministerstva Oborony Rossiiskoi Federatsii, Central Archive of the Ministry of Defense of the Russian Federation), f. 4, op. 11, d. 78, ll. 56-60, reprinted in *Russkii arkhiv*, 304.

86. RGVA f. 32941, op. 1, d. 90, l. 226, January 21-30, 1944. For example, before crossing into the Memel territory (then considered a part of East Prussia), the 31st *Pogranpolk* of the NKVD reported only three official cases of gonorrhea: one from contact with an "unknown woman," one from a maid (*domrabotnitsa*), and one chronic case that had resisted treatment. After treatment, the report promised that they would be subject to disciplinary action.

87. Vasilii Semenovich Krysov, interview by Aleksandr Brovtsin, http://iremember.ru/samokhodchiki/krisov-vasiliy-semenovich.html, July 17, 2006.

88. Krysov interview.

89. GARF f. 9401, op. 2, d. 93, l. 335, March 8, 1945.

90. GARF f. 9401, op. 2, d. 93, l. 335-36, March 8, 1945.

91. Pomerants, *Zapiski*, 95.

92. Krysov interview.

93. GARF f. 9401, op. 2, d. 93, l. 336, March 8, 1945.

94. MVS 4/46374 S. Krasnov, "Kak ia ponimaiu soldatskuiu mest'," *Frontovaia pravda*, January 23, 1945.

95. Krasnov, "Kak ia ponimaiu soldatskuiu mest'."

96. Krasnov, "Kak ia ponimaiu soldatskuiu mest'."

97. G. Aleksandrov, "Tovarishch Erenburg uproshchaet," *Pravda*, April 14, 1945.

98. Antony Beevor, *The Fall of Berlin 1945* (London: Penguin, 2002), 198.

99. B. N. Ol'shanskii, "My prikhodili s vostoka," manuscript, p. 35, HIA, Nicolaevsky, Series no. 177, 231-31.

100. Pomerants, *Zapiski*, 202.

101. Naimark, *The Russians*, 74.

102. K. Rokossovski[i], Marshal of the Soviet Union, *A Soldier's Duty*, trans. Vladimir Talmy, ed. Robert Daglish (Moscow: Progress Publishers, 1970), 288-89.

103. Budnitskii, "The Intelligentsia," 636.

104. Valentin Grigor'evich Aver'ianov, interview by Artem Drabkin, http://www.iremember.ru/index.php?option=com_content&task=view&id=159&Itemid=20, July 20, 2006.

105. Mikhail Khaimovich Zharovskii, interview by Grigorii Koifman, http://www.iremember.ru/index.php?option=com_content&task=view&id=69&Itemid=2, July 14, 2006.

106. Dmitrii Timofeevich Kiriachek, interview by Artem Drabkin, http://www.iremember.ru/index.php?option=com_content&task=view&id=95&Itemid=19, July 18, 2006.

107. Isaak Kobylianskii, *Priamoi navodkoi po vragu* (Moscow: EKSMO: Iauza, 2005), 188.

108. Pomerants, *Zapiski,* 198.

109. Kopelev, *No Jail,* 41.

110. Harvard Project on the Soviet Social System, Schedule A, Vol. 26, Case 517 (Interviewer A.D., type A4) Male, 38, Great Russian, Electrical Engineer. Frankfurt, Germany, March 1951, http://pds.lib.harvard.edu/pds/view/53711 72?n=1&imagesize=1200&jp2Res=.25.

111. D. Samoilov, *Podennye zapisi* (Moscow: Vremia, 2002), 1:210 [February 7, 1945].

112. Kiriachek interview, July 18, 2006.

113. Genatulin, *Vot konchitsia voina,* 117.

114. Letter from Inozemtsev to Nikolai Inozemtsev (his father), November 18, 1944, reprinted in *Frontovoi Dnevnik,* 343.

115. Inozemtsev, *Frontovoi Dnevnik,* 210 [end of January 1945].

116. Uspenskij, "Tagebuchaufzeichnungen," 522 [February 2, 1945]

117. Pomerants, *Zapiski,* 142-43.

118. Pomerants, *Zapiski,* 94.

119. B. Gorbachevskii, *Rzhevskaia Miasorubka: vremia otvagi, zadacha—vyzhit'* (Moscow: EKSMO: Iauza), 436.

120. Inozemtsev, *Frontovoi Dnevnik,* 222 [April 18-20, 1945].

5. City of Death

1. GAKO f. R310, op. 1, d. 7, ll. 28-29, n.d. [before October 1947].

2. N. N. Inozemtsev, *Frontovoi Dnevnik* (Moscow: Nauka, 2005), 222 [April 18-20, 1945].

3. By September 1945, the documented number of Germans in Soviet East Prussia was 129,614, after executions and epidemics that summer had reduced the population by tens of thousands. Iurii Kostiashov, "Vyselenie nemtsev iz Kaliningradskoi Oblasti v poslevoennye gody," *Voprosy Istorii* 6 (1994): 186.

4. GAKO f. R330, op. 2, d. 4, ll. 8-9, May 15, 1945; GAKO f. R330, op. 1, d. 7, l. 3, May 6, 1945; GAKO f. R330, op. 1, d. 3, l. 1, April 24, 1945. Earlier Soviet reports from April estimate much higher, around 100,000. GARF f. 9401, op. 2, d. 95, ll. 39-43, April 13, 1945.

5. Felix Ackermann, "Autosovietization. Migration, Urbanization and Social Acculturation in Western Belarus," *Jahrbücher für Geschichte Osteuropas* 64, no. 3 (2016): 411.

6. E. A. Rees, "The Sovietization of Eastern Europe," in *The Sovietization of Eastern Europe: New Perspectives on the Postwar Period,* ed. Balázs Apor, Péter Apor, and E. A. Rees (Washington, DC: New Academia Publishing, 2008), 3.

7. Bastiaan Willems, *Violence in Defeat: The Wehrmacht on German Soil, 1944-1945* (Cambridge: Cambridge University Press, 2021), 220.

8. The imagery of an other-worldly Königsberg appears numerous German diaries and memoirs. See, for example, Hans Deichelmann, *Ich sah Königsberg sterben: Tagebuch eines Arztes in Königsberg 1945 bis 1948* (Beltheim, Germany: Bublies, 1999), 27; Michael Wieck, *Zeugnis vom Untergang Königsbergs:*

Ein "Geltungsjude" Berichtet (Heidelberg: L. Schneider, 1988), 215; Count Hans von Lehndorff, *Token of a Covenant: Diary of an East Prussian Surgeon, 1945–47*, trans. Elizabeth Mayer (Chicago: Henry Regnery Company, 1964), 86 [April 24, 1945].

9. Iurii Kostiashov, "Stalin i Kaliningradskaia oblast': popytka istoricheskoi rekonstruktsii," *Acta Historica Universitatis Klaipedensis* 28 (2009): 60.

10. Per Brodersen, *Die Stadt im Westen: wie Königsberg Kaliningrad wurde* (Göttingen: Vandenhoeck & Ruprecht, 2008), 35. Brodersen points out that even in 1947, for example, a hand-drawn map of Kaliningrad Oblast for an RSFSR organization for Automobile Transport erroneously showed Kaliningrad bordering Latvia.

11. Violeta Davoliūtė, *The Making and Breaking of Soviet Lithuania: Memory and Modernity in the Wake of War* (New York: Routledge, 2013), 60–61; Karl D. Qualls, *From Ruins to Reconstruction: Urban Identity in Soviet Sevastopol After World War II* (Ithaca, NY: Cornell University Press, 2009), 11–84.

12. Richard Bessel, *Germany 1945: From War to Peace* (New York: Harper, 2009), 174–77, 184, 296; Norman Naimark, *The Russians in Germany: A History of the Soviet Zone of Occupation, 1945–1949* (Cambridge, MA: Belknap Press of Harvard University Press, 1995), 44.

13. GARF f. 9401, op. 2, d. 95, ll. 18–19, April 13, 1945; ll. 39–43, April 13, 1945.

14. Naimark, *The Russians*, 467.

15. GARF f. 9401, op. 2, d. 98, ll. 39–46, August 6, 1945.

16. Alexander Statiev, *The Soviet Counterinsurgency in the Western Borderlands* (Cambridge: Cambridge University Press, 2010), 97–99, 132, 150. For comparison with the situation in the Memel region, see Vygantis Vareikis, "Klaipėda (Memel) in der Nachkriegszeit 1945–1953," *Annaberger Annalen: Jahrbuch über Litauen und deutsch-litauische Beziehungen* 3 (1995): 61; Ruth Kibelka, *Ostpreussens Schicksaljahre, 1944–1948* (Berlin: Aufbau, 2002), 73–75.

17. Kostiashov, "Stalin," 60.

18. Naimark, *The Russians*, 16–17.

19. GAKO f. R330, op. 2, d. 4, ll. 8–9, May 15, 1945; GAKO f. R330, op. 2, l. 9, d. 1, May 15, 1945; GAKO f. R332, op. 2, d. 3, l. 47, February 28, 1946.

20. Kibelka, *Ostpreußens Schicksaljahre*, 124, 157.

21. Iurii Kostiashov, "Vyselenie nemtsev iz Kaliningradskoi Oblasti v poslevoennye gody," *Voprosy Istorii* 6 (1994): 187.

22. Norman Naimark, *Fires of Hatred: Ethnic-Cleansing in Twentieth-Century Europe* (Cambridge, MA: Harvard University Press, 2002), 108–38; Alfred de Zayas, *Fifty Theses on the Expulsion of the Germans from Central and Eastern Europe, 1944–1948* (Arlington, VA: Kearn C. Schemm and Friends, 2012); R. M. Douglas, *Orderly and Humane: The Expulsion of the Germans after the Second World War* (New Haven, CT: Yale University Press, 2012).

23. Kostiashov, "Stalin," 60.

24. Kibelka, *Ostpreussens Schicksaljahre*, 42, 91, 99.

25. Statiev, *The Soviet Counterinsurgency*, 165, 182–83.

26. *Berlinskaia (Potsdamskaia) konferentsiia rukovoditelei trekh derzhav—SSSR, SShA i Velikobritanii* (Moscow: Izdatel'stvo politicheskoi literatury, 1984), 57.

27. J. V. Stalin, Order of the Day, No. 55, February 23, 1942, Marxists Internet Archive, https://www.marxists.org/reference/archive/stalin/works/1942/02/23.htm.

28. Bessel, *Germany 1945*, 180–81.

29. Naimark, *The Russians*, 44; Bessel, *Germany 1945*, 174; Kibelka, *Ostpreußens Schicksaljahre*, 43.

30. GARF f. 9401, op. 2, d. 95, ll. 18–19, April 13, 1945; ll. 39–43, April 13, 1945.

31. Arūnė Arbušauskaitė, "Das tragische Schicksal Ostpreussens nach 1945 im Lichte neuer Dokumente," *Annaberger Annalen: Jahrbuch über Litauen und deutsch-litauische Beziehungen* 3 (1995): 13; Theodor Schieder, ed., *Documents on the Expulsion of the Germans from Eastern Central Europe, Volume 1: The Expulsions of the German Population from the Territories East of the Oder-Neisse Line* (Bonn: Federal Ministry for Expellees, Refugees, and War Victims, 1956), 64–65. Gradually, most of the German POWs were sent further east to work in reconstruction in the Soviet Union, joining an estimated 44,000 East Prussian civilians collected during the spring invasion. Few declassified archival records document the spontaneous executions or deportation of forced labor to Siberia from East Prussia. The number of civilians sent to the USSR was estimated by the postwar Schieder Commission and is difficult to corroborate with Soviet archival sources. The reported number of East Prussians sent to the Soviet Union is lower than in the other former Eastern provinces, although the commission reported that the collection of forced laborers in East Prussia involved a higher number of women and children from farms and villages and fewer workers from Königsberg because the city was still under siege.

32. GARF f. 9401, op. 2, d. 95, ll. 18–19, 39–43, April 13, 1945; GARF f. 9401, op. 2, d. 93, l. 31, May 15, 1945; Gerhild Luschnat, *Die Lage der Deutschen im Königsberger Gebiet, 1945–1948* (Frankfurt am Main: Peter Lang, 1996), 42.

33. GARF f. 9401, op. 2, d. 98, ll. 39–46, August 6, 1945; GAKO f. R332, op. 2, d. 3, l. 55, March 7, 1946.

34. Bessel, *Germany 1945*, 296; Gregor Thum, *Uprooted: How Breslau Became Wrocław in the Century of Expulsions* (Princeton, NJ: Princeton University Press, 2011), 38.

35. Bessel, *Germany 1945*, 199, 221–22, 296; Alfred Erich Senn, "The Sovietization of the Baltic States," *Annals of the American Academy of Political and Social Science* 317 (May 1958): 123.

36. V. S. Isupov, *Vostochnaia Prussiia: s drevneishikh vremen do kontsa vtoroi mirovoi voiny* (Kaliningrad, Russia: Kaliningradskoe knizhnoe izdatel'stvo, 1996), 440. The provisional civilian administration's official name changed a couple times over the course of the year, but its function remained the same.

37. Bert Hoppe, *Auf den Trümmern von Königsberg: Kaliningrad 1946–1970* (Munich: R. Oldenbourg Verlag, 2000), 25–26. These civilian representatives had no power of their own, and were only used in the first months after the war. Their presence is documented mostly from testimonies of former *Bürgermeister* after the expulsion of the Germans to the Soviet Zone of Occupation in 1947–48.

38. GAKO f. R330, op. 1, d. 3, l. 1, April 24, 1945; GAKO f. R330, op. 1, d. 7, l. 3, May 6, 1945; GAKO f. R330, op. 2. d. 4, ll. 8–9, May 15, 1945.

39. GAKO f. R330, op. 2, d. 4, ll. 4–7, May 12, 1945; GAKO f. R330, op. 2, d. 6, ll. 4–5, June 4, 1945; GAKO f. R330, op. 1, d. 7, l. 14, June 18, 1945; GAKO f. R330, op. 1, d. 7, l. 8, June 3, 1945; GAKO f. R332, op. 2, d. 3, ll. 37–38; GAKO f. R330, op. 1, d. 5, ll. 61–63, November 12, 1945.

40. Thum, *Uprooted*, 38–40.

41. Bessel, *Germany 1945*, 235.

42. Bessel, *Germany 1945*, 191–92.

43. Hugo Linck, *Königsberg, 1945–1948*, 5th. ed. (Leer, Germany: Gerhard Rautenberg, 1987), 17.

44. Wieck, *Zeugnis*, 245.

45. Wieck, *Zeugnis*, 247.

46. Luschnat, *Die Lage*, 44.

47. Wieck, *Zeugnis*, 232.

48. Hans von Lehndorff, *East Prussian Diary: A Journal of Faith, 1945–1947*, trans. Violet M. Macdonald (London: Oswald Wolff, 1963), 95 [April 30, 1945].

49. Bessel, *Germany 1945*, 189.

50. Wieck, *Zeugnis*, 238.

51. GAKO f. R330, op. 2, d. 9, l. 1, April 15, 1945; GAKO f. R330, op. 1, d. 2, l. 7, May 6, 1945; Arbušauskaitė, "Das Tragische Schicksal," 13; *Expulsion*, 64–65.

52. Bessel, *Germany 1945*, 185.

53. Käthe Hielscher, *Als Ostpreußin in russischer Kriegsgefangenschaft* (Berlin: Frieling, 1998), 96–104.

54. V. N. Maslov, "Prodovol'stvennyi vopros v deiatel'nosti sovetskoi voennoi komendatury Kënigsberga v 1945 g.," in *Vestnik Kaliningradskogo gosudarstvennogo universiteta* (Kaliningrad: Izdatel'stvo Kaliningradskogo gosudarstvennogo universiteta, 2003), 2: 47–52.

55. Wieck, *Zeugnis*, 238.

56. GAKO R332.2.7.4 n.d. [after February 1, 1946]; Bernhard Fisch und Marina Klemeševa, "Zum Schicksal der Deutschen in Königsberg 1945–1948 (im Spiegel bisher unbekannter russischer Quellen)," *Zeitschrift für Ostmitteleuropa-Forschung* 44, 3 (1995): 399.

57. Bessel, *Germany 1945*, 222.

58. Kostiashov, "Vyselenie," 187. Soviet authorities made frequent attempts to register and quantify the population, but the counts were incomplete. Many elderly and invalids, too weak to report for registration, died with their lives and deaths unaccounted for.

59. Deichelmann, *Ich sah*, 45 [July 15, 1945], 51 [August 30, 1945].

60. The borders to Soviet Lithuania remained porous, however, and some Germans fled eastward in the spring of 1946 in search of work and food. Kibelka, *Ostpreußens Schicksaljahre*, 47–49.

61. Bessel, *Germany 1945*, 187.

62. Fisch und Klemeševa, "Zum Schicksal der Deutschen in Königsberg 1945–1948," 393; RGASPI f. 17, op. 122, d. 143, ll. 78–80, June 1, 1946; GAKO f. R332, op. 2, d. 7, l. 21, n.d. [after February 1, 1946].

63. Wieck, *Zeugnis*, 239.

64. Iurii Ivanov, *Tantsy v krematorii. Desiat' epizodov kenigsbergskoi zhizni* (Kaliningrad, Russia: I. P. Mishutkina I. V., 2006), 58–59. The narrator's parallel

situation to Wieck's was by design: the two met in 1992 in Kaliningrad and shared stories of their common experiences after the war.

65. Wilhelm Starlinger, *Grenzen der Sowjetmacht im Spiegel einer West-Ostbegegnung hinter Palisaden von 1945–1954* (Würzburg, Germany: Holzner-Verlag, 1955), 23–24.

66. Lehndorff, *Token*, 32.

67. Hildegard Rosin, *Führt noch ein Weg zurück? Als der Krieg vorbei war, noch drei Jahre in Königsberg*, 2nd. ed (Leer, Germany: Gerhard Rautenberg, 1991), 64; Eberhard Beckherrn and Alexej Dubatow, *Die Königsberg-Papiere: Schicksal einer deutschen Stadt: neue Dokumente aus russischen Archiven* (Munich: Langen Müller, 1994), 131.

68. Wendy Z. Goldman and Donald Filtzer, eds., Introduction to *Hunger and War: Food Provisioning in the Soviet Union during World War II* (Bloomington: Indiana University Press, 2015), 27.

69. Filtzer and Goldman, Introduction to *Hunger and War*, 12.

70. GAKO f. R330, op. 2, d. 4, ll. 8–9, May 15, 1945.

71. GAKO f. R330, op. 2, d. 7, l. 2, August 11, 1945.

72. Marga Pollmann, "Königsberg," in Erna Ewert, Marga Pollmann, and Hannelore Müller, *Frauen in Königsberg, 1945–1948* (Bonn: Kulturstiftung der Deutschen Vertriebenen, 2006), 61.

73. Norman Naimark, *Stalin's Genocides* (Princeton, NJ: Princeton University Press, 2010), 70.

74. These kitchen gardens continued the Soviet-wide wartime practice of expanding and decentralizing food production. Goldman and Filtzer, Introduction to *Hunger and War*, 12.

75. Vareikis, "Klaipeda," 61; Karl-Eugen Wädekin, *Agrarian Policies in Communist Eastern Europe: A Critical Introduction* (Totowa, NJ: Allanheld, Osmun & Co., 1982), 63; Statiev, *The Soviet Counterinsurgency*, 178; George Last, *After the "Socialist Spring": Collectivisation and Economic Transformation in the GDR* (New York: Berghahn Books, 2009), 2–22.

76. Arbušauskaitė, "Das Tragische Schicksal," 13.

77. Arbušauskaitė, "Das Tragische Schicksal," 13.

78. Arbušauskaitė, "Das Tragische Schicksal," 11.

79. GAKO f. R332, op. 2, d. 7, ll. 5–6, 28, n.d. [after February 1, 1946].

80. See, for example, GAKO f. R330, op. 1, d. 2, l. 2, May 22, 1945; GAKO f. R332. op. 2. d. 10, l. 30–34, May 22, 1945.

81. GAKO f. R330, op. 2, d. 4, ll. 4–7, May 12, 1945.

82. GAKO f. R330, op. 1. d. 6. l. 31, August 27, 1945.

83. GAKO f. R330, op. 1, d. 2, l. 71, November 19, 1945.

84. GARF f. 9401, op. 2, d. 93, ll. 328–31, February 28, 1945; GARF f. 9401, op. 2, d. 95, ll. 40–41, April 13, 1945; GAKO f. R330, op. 2. d. 7. ll. 21–22, September 26, 1945; GANIKO f. 121, op. 1. d 4, n.d.

85. GAKO f. R330, op. 2, d. 9, l. 1, April 15, 1945; Arbušauskaitė, "Das Tragische Schicksal," 13; *Expulsion*, 64–65. POWs formed the first workforce at the Pulp and Paper Mills and shipbuilding industries, especially.

86. Isupov, *Vostochnaia Prussiia*, 454–55; GAKO f. R332, op. 2. d. 7. l. 11, n.d. [after February 1, 1946]; GAKO f. R310. op. 1. d. 7, ll. 13–14, April 18, 1947.

87. GAKO f. R310, op. 1, d. 7, ll. 13–14, April 18, 1947.

88. GAKO f. R332, op. 2, d. 7, ll. 28–29, n.d. [after February 1, 1946]; GAKO f. R297, op. 1, d. 102, l. 73, May 17, 1947.

89. GARF f. A259, op. 6, d. 3339, l. 1, February 11, 1946.

90. GARF f. A259, op. 6, d. 3339, l. 7, February 18, 1946.

91. GAKO f. R310, op. 1, d. 7, ll. 28–29, n.d. [before October 1947]; GANIKO f. 2, op. 1, d. 47, l. 9, June 1948.

92. GAKO f. R310, op. 1, d. 7, l. 31, n.d. [before October 1947].

93. GAKO f. R330, op. 1, d. 5, l. 33, November 1945; GAKO f. R332, op. 2, d. 3, l. 15.

94. S. P. Galtsova and Iu. V. Kostiashov, eds., *Vostochnaia Prussiia glazami sovetskikh pereselentsev: Pervye gody Kaliningradskoi oblasti v vospominaniiakh i dokumentakh* (Kaliningrad: Izdatel'stvo Kaliningradskogo gosudarstvennogo universiteta, 2003), 82–83.

95. GARF f. A259, op. 6, d. 3923, l. 7, n.d. [mid-1947]; GAKO R310.1.7.31, n.d. [before October 1947].

96. Rees, "The Sovietization," 18.

97. See, for example, Schieder, *The Expulsion*. This view also appears in Kibelka, *Ostpreussens Schicksaljahre*.

98. GAKO f. R330, op. 2, d. 1, l. 1, April 27, 1945.

99. GAKO f. R330, op. 1, d. 3, l. 7, June 20, 1945; GAKO f. R332, op. 2, d. 10, ll. 83–84, June 20, 1945; Fisch and Klemeševa, "Zum Schicksal," 393; Hoppe, *Auf den Trümmern*, 33.

100. Hielscher, *Eine Ostpreußin*, 92–93.

101. GAKO f. R330, op. 1, d. 5, ll. 64–70, November 12, 1945.

102. GAKO f. R330, op. 2, d. 4, ll. 8–9, May 15, 1945.

103. Hielscher, *Als Ostpreußin*, 92.

104. GAKO f. R330, op. 1, d. 5, ll. 64–70, November 12, 1945; Manefa Stepanova Shevchenko, interview by Anna Anatol'ieva L'vova, 1989, in GAKO collection, *Interv'iu s Pervymi Pereselentsami, Pribyvshimi v Kaliningradskuiu Oblast' v 1945–1950 gg.*, vol. 5, 36 [cited hereafter as *Collected Interviews*]; Wieck, *A Childhood under Hitler and Stalin: Memoirs of a "Certified Jew"* trans. Penny Milbouer (Madison, WI: University of Wisconsin Press, 2003), 173.

105. Wieck, *A Childhood*, 173; Hielscher, *Als Ostpreußin*, 118, 134.

106. Manefa Stepanovna Shevchenko, interview by Anna Anatol'ieva L'vova.

107. Lucy Falk, *Ich blieb in Königsberg: Tagebuchblätter aus dunklen Nachkriegsjahren* (Munich: Gräfe und Unzer, 1966), 86 [August 12, 1946].

108. GAKO f. R330, op. 2, d. 6, l. 16, August 4, 1945.

109. GARF f. A259, op. 6, d. 3923, l. 180, n.d. [April 1946]; GAKO f. R310, op. 1, d. 9. l. 1, 1948.

110. GAKO f. R330, op. 1, d. 5, ll. 61–63, November 12, 1945; GAKO f. R332, op. 2, d. 7, l. 18, n.d. [after February 1, 1946].

111. GAKO f. R330, op. 2. d. 3, March 20, 1946; GAKO f. R332, op. 2, d. 5, April 19, 1946.

112. GAKO f. R332, op. 2, d. 7, l. 20, n.d. [after February 1, 1946].

113. GAKO f. R332, op. 2, d. 7, l. 4, n.d. [after February 1, 1946].

114. GAKO f. R332, op. 2, d. 7, l. 18, n.d. [after February 1, 1946].

115. GAKO f. R332, op. 2, d. 7, ll. 17-19, n.d. [after February 1, 1946].
116. Rees, "The Sovietization," 18.
117. Naimark, *The Russians*, 16-17.
118. Naimark, *The Russians*, 17, 19-20.
119. Steven A. Barnes, *Death and Redemption: The Gulag and the Shaping of Soviet Society* (Princeton, NJ: Princeton University Press, 2011), 12.
120. GAKO f. R330, op. 2, d. 9, l. 1, April 15, 1945. GAKO f. R330, op. 2, d. 4, l. 8-9, May 15, 1945; GAKO f. R330, op. 2, d. 9, l. 1, May 15, 1945; GAKO f. R330, op. 2, d. 1, l. 11-14, July 2, 1945; GAKO f. R330, op. 15, d. 86; GAKO f. R330, op.1, d. 5, l. 64; GAKO f. R330, op. 1, d. 2, l. 7, May 6, 1945.
121. GANIKO f. 121, op. 1, d. 1, l. 23, June 21, 1945.
122. Kibelka, *Ostpreußens Schicksaljahren*, 100.
123. GANIKO f. 121, op 1, d. 16, ll. 64-65, March 21, 1946.
124. GAKO f. R332, op. 1 d. 1, ll. 25-26, February 15, 1946.
125. Cf. Thum, *Uprooted*, 38-40.
126. GAKO f. R332, op. 1 d. 1, ll. 28, February 15, 1946.
127. "Ukaz Prezidiuma VS SSSR ot 7 aprelia 1946 goda 'ob obrazovanii Kenigsbergskoi oblasti v sostave RSFSR,'" printed in Iu. I. Mandel'shtam, ed., *Sbornik zakonov SSSR i ukazov Prezidiuma Verkhovnogo Soveta SSSR. 1938 g.–iiul' 1956 g.* (Moscow: Gosudarstvennoe Izdatel'stvo Iuridicheskoi Literatury, 1956), 47.
128. Kostiashov, "Stalin," 60-61; GANIKO f. 1, op. 1, d. 1, l. 52, December 2-4, 1947; Hoppe, *Auf den Trümmern*, 42.

6. Living Together

1. J. V. Kostjašov [Iu. V. Kostiashov], "Russen und Deutschen in Ostpreußen nach 1945-Konfrontation oder Integration?" *Annaberger Annalen: Jahrbuch über Litauen und deutsch-litauische Beziehungen* 7 (1999): 161.
2. E. A. Rees, "The Sovietization of Eastern Europe," in *The Sovietization of Eastern Europe: New Perspectives on the Postwar Period*, ed. Balázs Apor, Péter Apor, and E. A. Rees, (Washington, DC: New Academia Publishing, 2008), 11-12.
3. Rees, "The Sovietization," 1; Tarik Cyril Amar, "Sovietization as a Civilizing Mission in the West," in Apor, Apor, and Rees, 36. On the reversal of the East-West cultural gradient, see Michael David-Fox, *Showcasing the Great Experiment: Cultural Diplomacy and Western Visitors to the Soviet Union, 1921-1941* (New York: Oxford University Press, 2012), 12, 27. On revolution from abroad, see Jan T. Gross, *Revolution from Abroad: The Soviet Conquest of Poland's Western Ukraine and Western Belorussia* (Princeton, NJ: Princeton University Press, 1988).
4. Amar, *The Paradox*, 14.
5. David Hoffmann, *Cultivating the Masses: Modern State Practices and Soviet Socialism, 1914-1939* (Ithaca, NY: Cornell University Press, 2011), 17-124.
6. GAKO f. R330, op. 2, d. 6, l. 39, October 30, 1945; GARF f. A259, op. 6, d. 3923, l. 179, n.d. [April 1946].
7. Eckhard Matthes, ed. *Als Russe in Ostpreußen: sowjetische Umsiedler über ihren Neubeginn in Königsberg/Kaliningrad nach 1945*, trans. Arne Ackermann (Ostfildern, Germany: Edition Tertium, 2002), 31, 34.

8. GARF f. A259, op. 6, d. 3923, l. 179, n.d. [April 1946]; RGASPI f. 17, op. 122, d. 143, ll. 78–80, June 1, 1946.

9. Bert Hoppe, *Auf den Trümmern von Königsberg: Kaliningrad 1946–1970* (Munich: R. Oldenbourg Verlag, 2000), 37; Arūnė Arbušauskaitė, "Das tragische Schicksal Ostpreussens nach 1945 im Lichte neuer Dokumente," *Annaberger Annalen: Jahrbuch über Litauen und deutsch-litauische Beziehungen* 3 (1995): 14–15; Iu. V. Kostiashov, "Zaselenie Kaliningradskoi oblasti posle vtoroi mirovoi voiny," *Gumanitarnaia nauka v Rossii: Sorosovskie lauriaty* (Moscow, 1996), 83.

10. GARF f. A259, op. 6, d. 3923, l. 40, August 19, 1946.

11. Svetlana Galcova, "Die Neusiedler auf dem Gebiet Ostpreußens (Kaliningrader Oblast)," *Annaberger Annalen: Jahrbuch über Litauen und deutsch-litauische Beziehungen* 7 (1999): 110.

12. Galcova, "Die Neusiedler," 110. Lithuanians comprised another 3.5 percent of the population, and the remaining were various other nationalities of the USSR, including Jews, Mordvinians, and Chuvash.

13. Kostiashov, "Zaselenie," 85; Hoppe, *Auf den Trümmern*, 38.

14. Galcova, "Die Neusiedler," 109–10.

15. Quoted in Matthes, *Als Russe*, 43.

16. Galcova, "Die Neusiedler," 111; Hoppe, *Auf den Trümmern*, 37; Kostiashov, "Zaselenie," 83; Matthes, *Als Russe*, 39–44.

17. GAKO f. R298, op. 1, d. 4, l. 10; Kostiashov, "Zaselenie," 83.

18. Quoted in Matthes, *Als Russe*, 37–38.

19. Matthes, *Als Russe*, 36.

20. Kostjašov, "Russen und Deutschen," 162.

21. Quoted in Matthes, *Als Russe*, 61.

22. Quoted in Matthes, *Als Russe*, 64.

23. Quoted in Matthess, *Als Russe*, 355.

24. Kostjašov, "Russen und Deutschen," 168.

25. Interview with Sergei Vladimirovich Daniel'-Bek, reprinted in Matthes, *Als Russe*, 75.

26. Michael Wieck, *Zeugnis vom Untergang Königsbergs: ein "Geltungsjude" Berichtet* (Heidelberg: L. Schneider, 1988), 243.

27. Yoram K. Jacoby, *Jüdiches Leben in Königsberg/Pr. Im 20. Jahrhundert* (Würzburg, Germany: Holzner, 1983), 137–38.

28. Wieck, *Zeugnis*, 228.

29. Hans Deichelmann, *Ich sah Königsberg sterben: Tagebuch eines Arztes in Königsberg 1945 bis 1948* (Beltheim, Germany: Bublies, 1999), 33 [April 20, 1945].

30. Matthes, *Als Russe*, 328.

31. GAKO f. R310, op. 1, d. 7, l. 1, n.d. [early 1947].

32. Matthes, *Als Russe*, 94.

33. Wieck, *Zeugnis*, 307; Hugo Linck, *Königsberg 1945–1948*, 5th. ed. (Leer, Germany: Gerhard Rautenberg, 1987), 75–80; Bernhard Fisch und Marina Klemeševa, "Zum Schicksal der Deutschen in Königsberg 1945–1948 (im Spiegel bisher unbekannter russischer Quellen)," *Zeitschrift für Ostmitteleuropa-Forschung* 44, 3 (1995): 399; Theodor Schieder, ed., *Dokumentation der Vertreibung der Deutschen aus*

Ost-Mitteleuropa. Band 1: Die Vertreibung der deutschen Bevölkerung aus den Gebieten östlich der Oder-Neisse (Bonn: Bundesministerium für Vertriebene, 1954), 1:144f.; Deichelmann, *Ich sah*, 209; GARF f. A259, op. 6, d. 3923, ll. 106–8 n.d. [between April and June 1946]; GAKO f. R192, op. 7, d. 2, l. 21, 150, 163 [1946].

34. Quoted in Matthes, *Als Russe*, 330–31.

35. Käthe Hielscher, *Als Ostpreußin in russischer Kriegsgefangenschaft* (Berlin: Frieling, 1998), 125–26.

36. Erna Ewert, "Tagebuch," in Erna Ewert, Marga Pollmann, and Hannelore Müller, *Frauen in Königsberg, 1945–1948* (Bonn: Kulturstiftung der Deutschen Vertriebenen, 2006), 20, 39–40 [1946].

37. Ewert, "Tagebuch," 25, 27 [1947].

38. Quoted in Matthes, *Als Russe*, 318.

39. Matthes, *Als Russe*, 48, 77–78, 107.

40. Interview with Sergei Vladimirovich Daniel'-Bek, quoted in Matthes, *Als Russe*, 99.

41. Matthes, *Als Russe*, 170, 172.

42. Matthes, *Als Russe*, 161–64.

43. Iu. V. Kostiashov, "Obratnichestvo v protsesse zaseleniia Kaliningradskoi oblasti v poslevoennye gody," in *Baltiiskii region v istorii Rossii i Evropy*, ed. V. I. Gal'tsov (Kaliningrad, Russia: Izdatel'stvo Rossiiskogo Gosudarstvennogo Universita imeni Immanuila Kanta, 2005), 217.

44. GAKO f. R298, op. 1, d. 23, l. 20, August 23, 1946; GAKO f. R298, op. 1, d. 23, l. 8, September 1946.

45. GAKO f. R298, op. 1, d. 23, ll. 30–32, October 24, 1946.

46. Lucy Falk, *Ich blieb in Königsberg: Tagebuchblätter aus dunklen Nachkriegsjahren*, 2nd ed. (Munich: Gräfe und Unzer, 1965), 83 [September 1, 1946].

47. Svetlana P. Galtsova and Iurii V. Kostiashov, eds., *Vostochnaia Prussiia glazami sovetskikh pereselentsev: pervye gody Kaliningradskoi oblasti v vospominaniiakh i dokumentakh* (Kaliningrad: Izdatel'stvo Kaliningradskogo gosudarstvennogo universiteta, 2003), 83; Hielscher, *Als Ostpreußin*, 112; Deichelmann, *Ich sah*, 74 [December 21, 1945].

48. Deichelmann, *Ich sah*, 101 [May 17, 1946]. Descriptions of the Russians' delight in children appear frequently in diaries written in Kaliningrad and in the Soviet Zone of Occupation. See Atina Grossman, "Berlin 1945: War and Rape 'Liberators Take Liberties,'" *October* 72 (Spring 1995): 60.

49. Falk, *Ich blieb*, 83 [early June to August 12, 1946].

50. Galtsova and Kostiashov, eds., *Vostochnaia Prussiia*, 83.

51. Falk, *Ich blieb*, 88 [September 1, 1946].

52. Falk, *Ich blieb*, 62–63 [March 2, 1946].

53. Deichelmann, *Ich sah*, 38 [May 30, 1945].

54. Deichelmann, *Ich sah*, 127 [November 6, 1946].

55. GARF f. 9401, op. 2, d. 136, ll. 185–86, May 6, 1946.

56. Balzer, "Eyewitness Report," in *Documents on the Expulsion of the Germans from Eastern Central Europe, Volume 1: The Expulsions of the German Population from the Territories East of the Oder-Neisse Line*, ed. Theodor Schieder (Bonn: Federal Ministry for Expellees, Refugees, and War Victims, 1956), 194.

57. Quoted in Matthes, *Als Russe*, 334.

58. Ewert, "Tagebuch," 8, 38 [1946].

59. Amar, "The Sovietization," 36.

60. Quoted in Matthes, *Als Russe*, 333.

61. Galtsova and Kostiashov, eds., *Vostochnaia Prussiia*, 83.

62. Falk, *Ich blieb*, 113 [April 20, 1947].

63. Falk, *Ich blieb*, 97 [November 17, 1946], 99 [November 20, 1946].

64. Hielscher, *Als Ostpreußin*, 118.

65. Michael Wieck, *A Childhood under Hitler and Stalin: Memoirs of a "Certified Jew*," trans. Penny Milbouer (Madison, WI: University of Wisconsin Press, 2003), 162.

66. Kostjašov, "Russen und Deutsche," 169–70; Gerfried Horst, interview with Gerda Preuß, https://www.freunde-kants.com/gerda-preuss-die-letzte-koenigsberg.

67. Hielscher, *Als Ostpreußin*, 78–82.

68. Hielscher, *Als Ostpreußin*, 152. In Hielscher's memoir, Poles appear unscrupulous, following common East Prussian cultural stereotypes.

69. Hielscher, *Als Ostpreußin*, 155–57.

70. Hielscher, *Als Ostpreußin*, 165–66.

71. Hielscher, *Als Ostpreußin*, 116, 157.

72. Kostjašov, "Russen und Deutsche," 168.

73. Kostjašov, "Russen und Deutsche," 169–70.

74. Wieck, *Zeugnis*, 398.

75. Quoted in Matthes, *Als Russe*, 345.

76. For example, the head of Civilian Affairs Borisov wrote to Moscow numerous times for permission to reorganize Königsberg's twelve military districts into civilian administrative neighborhoods (*raiony*). When the issue was finally posed to the chairman of the Council of Ministers of the RSFSR Mikhail Ivanovich Rodionov nine months later in December 1946, Rodionov's assistant dismissed the request because Rodionov did "not feel that it is worth considering this question for a [city with only a] population of 127,000 people." GARF f. A259, op. 6, d. 3923, ll. 39–40, December 19, 1946.

77. V. G. Birkovskii, *Istoriia Kraia 1945–1950: uchebnoe posobie dlia studentov-istorikov Kaliningradskogo universiteta* (Kaliningrad, Russia: Kaliningradskii gosudarstvennyi universitet, 1984), 51.

78. GARF f. A150. op. 2, d. 182, l. 1, June 24, 1946.

79. GARF f. A259, op. 6, d. 3923, l. 6, n.d. [mid-1947]; GARF f. A259, op. 6, d. 4544, l. 26, n.d. [late 1946]; GAKO f. R216, op. 1, d. 2, l. 82, February 14, 1948; GARF f. 9401, op. 2, d. 95, ll. 40–41, April 13, 1945.

80. GARF f. 9401, op. 2, d. 95, ll. 40–41, April 13, 1945; GARF f. A259, op. 6, d. 4544, ll. 22–23, n.d. [late 1946]; GARF f. A259, op. 6, d. 3923, l. 181, n.d. [April 1946].

81. GARF f. A150, op. 2, d. 182, l. 19, n.d. [1946]; GAKO f. R310, op. 1, d. 7, l. 8, April 18, 1947; GARF f. A259, op. 6, d. 3923, l. 6, n.d. [mid-1947]; GAKO f. R298, op. 1, d. 7, l. 3, September 10, 1946; GARF f. A259, op. 6, d. 4544, l. 23, n.d. [late 1946]; GAKO f. R216, op. 1, d. 2, l. 408, November 18, 1948.

82. Rüdiger Ritter, "Prescribed Identity: The Role of History for the Legitimization of Soviet Rule in Lithuania," in *The Sovietization of the Baltic States, 1940–1956*, ed. Olaf Mertelsmann (Tartu, Estonia: Kleio Ajalookirjanduse Sihtasutus, 2003), 85; Amar, *Paradox*, 14–15.

83. GAKO f. R298, op. 1, d. 4, l. 9–11, July 12, 1946.

84. GAKO f. R330, op. 2, d. 1, l. 20, July 30, 1945; Falk, *Ich blieb*, 13f.; Hoppe, *Auf den Trümmern*, 30.

85. Hoppe, *Auf den Trümmern*, 30; V. S. Isupov, *Vostochnaia Prussiia: s drevneishikh vremen do konsa vtoroi mirovoi voiny* (Kaliningrad, Russia: Kaliningradskoe Knizhnoe Izdatel'stvo, 1996), 493; GAKO f. R332, op. 2, d. 7, l. 17, n.d. [after February 1, 1946].

86. GARF f. A259, op. 6, d. 3923, ll. 106–8, n.d. [between April and June 1946]; GAKO f. R192, op. 7, d. 2, l. 21, 150, 163 [1946].

87. GStPK HA XX Rep. 99c, Nr. 37 (Dr. Martin Attz); GARF f. 8009, op. 25, d. 5, ll. 1–7, July–October 1946; GAKO f. R793, op. 1, d. 10, l. 35, August 25, 1948. Some other Soviet republics and regions also received expedition teams, but the disease rates were far lower in other places than in Kaliningrad.

88. GAKO f. R330, op. 2, d. 3, l. 61, March 20, 1946; GAKO f. R330, op. 2, d. 5, ll. 23–28, April 26, 1946.

89. GAKO f. R298, op. 1, d. 7, l. 26 September 18, 1946; GAKO f. R298, op. 1, d. 10, l. 9, November 26, 1946.

90. GAKO f. R330, op. 2, d. 3, l. 61, March 20, 1946; GAKO f. R330, op. 2, d. 5, ll. 23–28, April 26, 1946.

91. GAKO f. R332, op. 2, d. 7, l. 21, 24, n.d. [after February 1, 1946]; GAKO f. R332, op. 1, d. 2, l. 118, April 2, 1946; GARF f. A259, op. 6, d. 3923, l. 138, April 7, 1947.

92. GAKO f. R332, op. 2, d. 7, l. 24, n.d. [after February 1, 1946]; GAKO f. R332, op. 1, d. 2, l. 118, April 2, 1946; GAKO f. R297, op. 1, d. 102, l. 77, May 16, 1947.

93. GARF f. A259, op. 6, d. 4544, l. 33, n.d. [late 1946]; GARF f. A259, op. 6, d. 3923, l. 137, April 7, 1947; GAKO f. R297, op. 1, d. 102, l. 77, May 16, 1947.

94. Falk, *Ich blieb*, 86 [August 12, 1946].

95. Marga Pollmann, "Königsberg," in Ewert, Pollmann, and Müller, *Frauen in Königsberg, 1945–1948*, 60.

96. GAKO f. R332, op. 2, d. 7, ll. 23–24, n.d. [after February 1, 1946].

97. GARF f. A259, op. 6, d. 4544, l. 27, n.d. [late 1946]; GARF f. A259, op. 6, d. 3923, l. 137, April 7, 1947; GAKO f. R297, op. 1, d. 102, l. 77, May 16, 1947.

98. GAKO f. R297, op. 1, d. 110, l. 29, December 6, 1946; GARF f. A259, op. 6, d. 3923, l. 138, April 7, 1947; GANIKO R313.1.6.48, July 12, 1947; GANIKO f. 1, op. 1, d. 101, l. 58, August 12, 1947.

99. Falk, *Ich blieb*, 86 [August 12, 1946].

100. Norman Naimark, *The Russians in Germany: A History of the Soviet Zone of Occupation, 1945–1949* (Cambridge, MA: Belknap Press of Harvard University Press, 1995), 452; GAKO f. R313, op. 1, d. 5, l. 23, n.d. [late 1947 or early 1948].

101. Falk's direct supervisor, B. S. Spivak, was not impressed with Falk's Russian skills, however. In school reports in early 1948, Spivak listed Falk as

one of the few German teachers who still required a translator to take part in school meetings. GAKO f. R313, op. 1, d. 5, l. 23, n.d. [late 1947 or early 1948].

102. GAKO f. R313, op. 1, d. 5, l. 27–28, January 2, 1947.

103. GARF f. A259, op. 6, d. 4544, l. 34, n.d. [late 1946].

104. Deichelmann, *Ich sah*, 84 [February 15, 1946].

105. GAKO f. R289, op. 7, d. 4, l. 10, November 28, 1946; GAKO f. R289, op. 7, d. 7, l. 11, December 1946; GAKO f. R289, op. 7, d. 7, l. 12, December 1946; GAKO f. R289, op. 7, d. 7, l. 13, December 17, 1946; GAKO f. R289, op. 7, d. 7, l. 14, December 1946; GAKO f. R83, op. 1, d. 4, l. 10, May 1, 1947.

106. GARF f. A259, op. 6, d. 3923, l. 138, April 7, 1947.

107. GARF f. A259, op. 6, d. 3923, l. 138, April 7, 1947.

108. GAKO f. R313, op. 1, d. 5, l. 23, n.d. [late 1947 or early 1948]; Lucy Falk, "Ein schneller Entschluß," *Neue Zeit*, February 12, 1948.

109. GAKO f. R332, op. 1, d. 2, l. 163, May 1946.

110. GAKO f. R192, op. 7, d. 3, l. 26, June 8, 1946.

111. Ewert, "Tagebuch," 37–42.

112. GAKO f. R332, op. 2, d. 7, l. 20, n.d. [after February 1, 1946]; GAKO f. R237, op. 1, d. 1, l. 9, n.d. [late February to early March 1947].

113. Deichelmann, *Ich sah*, 210 [December 31, 1947]; Falk, *Ich blieb*, 122 [August 17, 1947].

114. GAKO f. R231, op. 1, d. 1, l. 13, n.d. [after August 1946].

115. Ewert, "Tagebuch," 37 [1946].

116. Interview with Ol'ga Leopoldovna Golobova (Klein), in GAKO collection, *Interv'iu s Pervimy Pereselentsev, Pribyvshimi v Kaliningradskuiu Oblast' v 1945–1950 gg*,"
11:12–13.

117. Deichelmann, *Ich sah*, 83.

118. Deichelmann, *Ich sah*, 115–16 [August 3, 1946].

119. GAKO f. R237, op. 1, d. 1, l. 22, August 27, 1946.

120. GAKO f. R237, op. 1, d. 1, l. 22, August 27, 1946.

121. Deichelmann, *Ich sah*, 67 [November 15, 1945].

122. GAKO f. R59. op. 1, d. 2, l. 4, January 1947.

123. GAKO f. R59, op 1, d. 3, ll. 1, 23–25, n.d. [early 1948].

124. GAKO f. R332, op. 2, d. 7, l. 24, n.d.; op. 1, d. 2, l. 118, April 2, 1946; GARF f. A259, op. 6, d. 3923, l. 138, April 7, 1947; d. 4544, l. 27, n.d.; GAKO f. R289, op. 7, d. 4, l. 10, November 28, 1946; d. 7, ll. 11–14, December 1946; GAKO f. R83, op. 1, d. 4, l. 10, May 1, 1947.

125. Clara M. Oberle, "Reconfiguring Postwar Antifascism: Reflections on the History of Ideology," *New German Critique* 117 (Fall 2012): 152; Felix Ackermann, "Autosovietization. Migration, Urbanization and Social Acculturation in Western Belarus," *Jahrbücher für Geschichte Osteuropas* 64, no. 3 (2016): 412.

126. Mark Edele, *Soviet Veterans of the Second World War: A Popular Movement in an Authoritarian Society*, 1941–1991 (New York: Oxford University Press, 2008), 185.

7. Slavic Soil

1. R. M. Douglas, *Orderly and Humane: The Expulsion of the Germans after the Second World War* (New Haven, CT: Yale University Press, 2012), 1.

2. Norman Naimark, *The Russians in Germany: A History of the Soviet Zone of Occupation, 1945–1949* (Cambridge, MA: Belknap Press of Harvard University Press, 1995), 10, 261–69; Krystyna Kersten, *The Establishment of Communist Rule in Poland, 1943–1948*, trans. and annotated by John Micgiel and Michael H. Bernhard (Berkeley: University of California Press, 1991), 38.

3. Antonia Grunenberg, *Antifaschismus—ein deutscher Mythos* (Hamburg: Rowoholt, 1993); Jeffrey Herf, *Divided Memory: The Nazi Past in the Two Germanies* (Cambridge, MA: Harvard University Press, 1997); Catherine Epstein, *The Last Revolutionaries: German Communists and Their Century* (Cambridge, MA: Harvard University Press, 2003).

4. José María Faraldo, "An Antifascist Political Identity? On the Cult of Antifascism in the Soviet Union and Post-Socialist Russia," in *Rethinking Antifascism: History, Memory, and Politics, 1922 to the Present*, ed. Hugo Garcia, et al. (New York: Berghahn Books, 2016); Nina Tumarkin, *The Living and the Dead: The Rise and Fall of the Cult of World War II in Russia* (New York: Basic Books, 1995); Mark Edele, *Soviet Veterans of the Second World War: A Popular Movement in an Authoritarian Society, 1941–1991* (New York: Oxford University Press, 2008).

5. GAKO f. R310, op. 1, d. 7, l. 8, April 18, 1947; GARF f. A259, op. 6, d. 3923, l. 6, n.d. [mid-1947]; GAKO f. R180, op. 1, d. 10, ll. 59–63, January 13, 1948.

6. GANIKO f. 2, op. 1, d. 22, l. 37, November 11, 1947.

7. GAKO f. R541, op. 1, d. 4, l. 8, December 27, 1947; GAKO f. R310, op. 1, d. 9, l. 1, 1948; GAKO f. R216, op. 1, d. 2, l. 85, February 14, 1948.

8. GANIKO f. 1, op. 1, d. 1, l. 74, December 2–4, 1947; GAKO f. R216, op. 1, d. 2, l. 410; GARF f. A259, op. 6, d. 3923, l. 6, n.d. [mid-1947]; GAKO f. 6, op. 4544, d. 26, n.d. [late 1946].

9. GAKO f. R180, op. 1, d. 10, ll. 59–63, January 13, 1948.

10. GAKO f. R297, op. 1, d. 102, ll. 68–79, May 16, 1947.

11. Iu. V. Kostiashov, "Obratnichestvo v protsesse zaseleniia Kaliningradskoi oblasti v poslevoennye gody," in *Baltiiskii region v istorii Rossii i Evropy*, ed. V. I. Galtsov (Kaliningrad, Russia: Izdatel'stvo Rossiiskogo Gosudarstvennogo Universita imeni Immanuila Kanta, 2005), 215–16; GAKO f. R310, op. 1, d. 7, l. 5, n.d. [early 1947]; GARF f. 327, op. 2, d. 623, l. 72; GAKO f. R293, op. 11, d. 9, l. 15; GAKO f. R141, op. 7, d. 8, l. 14 ob.; GAKO f. R141, op. 7, d. 10, ll. 8–8 ob.

12. GAKO f. R298, op. 1, d. 7, l. 71, September 30, 1946; Svetlana Galcova, "Die Neusiedler auf dem Gebiet Ostpreußens (Kaliningrader Oblast)," *Annaberger Annalen: Jahrbuch über Litauen und deutsch-litauische Beziehungen* 7 (1999): 107; Iu. V. Kostiashov, "Zaselenie Kaliningradskoi oblasti posle Vtoroi mirovoi voiny," in *Gumanitarnaia nauka v Rossii: sorosovskie lauriaty* (Moscow: Mezhdunarodnaia nauchnyi fond, 1996), 85; *Vostochnaia Prussiia glazami sovetskikh pereselentsev: Pervye gody Kaliningradskoi oblasti v vospominaniiakh i dokumentakh* (Kaliningrad: Izdatel'stvo Kaliningradskogo gosudarstvennogo universiteta, 2003), 75.

13. GAKO f. R216, op. 1, d. 2, l. 81, February 14, 1948.

14. *Kaliningradskaia pravda*, February 2, 1947.

15. GANIKO f. 2, op. 1, d. 22, l. 37, November 11, 1947; GAKO f. R216, op. 1, d. 2, l. 81, February 14, 1948.

16. GAKO f. R180, op. 1, d. 14, ll. 7–8; Kostiashov, "Obratnichestvo," 215; Galcova, "Die Neusiedler," 111.

17. GANIKO f. 2, op. 1, d. 42, l. 5, March 11, 1948.

18. Kostiashov, "Obratnichestvo," 211–13, 219; Galcova, "Die Neusiedler," 109.

19. GAKO f. R298, op. 1, d. 8, l. 67, October 15, 1946; GAKO f. R298, op. 1, d. 23, ll. 30–32, October 24, 1946.

20. Nicholas Ganson, *The Soviet Famine of 1946–47 in Global and Historical Perspective* (New York: Palgrave, 2009), xv.

21. GAKO f. R216, op. 1, d. 2, l. 217, June 10, 1948; GAKO f. R298, op. 1, d. 7, l. 71, September 30, 1946; Galcova, "Die Neusiedler," 107; Kostiashov, "Zaselenie," 85.

22. Galtsova and Kostiashov, eds., *Vostochnaia Prussiia*, 75.

23. Galtsova and Kostiashov, eds., *Vostochnaia Prussiia*, 75.

24. Galtsova and Kostiashov, eds., *Vostochnaia Prussiia*, 71.

25. GANIKO f. 1, op. 1, d. 1, ll. 77, December 2–4, 1947; GAKO f. R216, op. 1, d. 2, ll. 313–81, September 2, 1948; Galtsova and Kostiashov, eds., *Vostochnaia Prussiia*, 85.

26. Galtsova and Kostiashov, eds., *Vostochnaia Prussiia*, 71; Galcova, "Die Neusiedler," 107.

27. Matthes, *Als Russe*, 319, 324.

28. Matthes, *Als Russe*, 326–27, 350, 148.

29. GAKO f. R237, op. 1, d. 1, l. 9 n.d. [late February to early March 1947].

30. GAKO f. R332, op. 1 d. 1, ll. 25–26, February 15, 1946.

31. GANIKO f. 121, op. 1, d. 16, l. 13, July 10, 1946.

32. Tarik Cyril Amar, *The Paradox of Ukrainian Lviv: A Borderland City between Stalinists, Nazis, and Nationalists* (Ithaca, NY: Cornell University Press, 2015), 10, 16.

33. GAKO f. R181, op. 10, d. 22; Kostiashov, "Zaselenie," 82; RGASPI f. 17, op. 122, d. 143, ll. 78–80, June 1, 1946.

34. GAKO f. R298, op. 1, d. 3, l. 14, May 25, 1946; GANIKO f. 2, op. 1, d. 2, l. 20, November 15, 1947.

35. GANIKO f. 2, op. 1, d. 1, l. 82, December 5, 1946. While Polish and Czech governments similarly blamed supposed German sabotage for ongoing problems of settlement and reconstruction around this time, archival records in Kaliningrad give no indication that local officials were aware of the international dimension of this rhetoric until late in the summer of 1947.

36. J. V. Kostjašov [Iu. V. Kostiashov], "Russen und Deutschen in Ostpreußen nach 1945—Konfrontation oder Integration?" *Annaberger Annalen: Jahrbuch über Litauen und deutsch-litauische Beziehungen* 7 (1999): 163; GARF f. R9479, op. 1, d. 304, ll. 99, 208–9.

37. Kostiashov, "Obratnichestvo," 217; GAKO f. R293, op. 11, d. 9, l. 55.

38. Kostiashov, "Russen und Deutsche," 163; GARF f. R9479, op. 1, d. 304, l. 40.

39. GANIKO f. 1, op. 1, d. 58, l. 3.

40. Kostiashov, "Russen und Deutschen," 167; Ruth Kibelka, *Ostpreussens Schicksaljahre, 1944–1948* (Berlin: Aufbau, 2002), 189.

41. Kostiashov, "Russen und Deutschen," 167.

42. Matthes, *Als Russe*, 313.

43. Matthes, *Als Russe*, 315.

44. Kostiashov, "Russen und Deutschen," 165–66; GAKO f. R37, op. 1, d. 11; GAKO f. R361, op. 5, d. 1; GAKO f. R361, op. 5, d. 5; GAKO f. R361, op. 5, d. 7; Matthes, *Als Russe*, 315.

45. E. A. Maslov, "Religiozno-politicheskaia zhizn' v Kaliningradskoi oblasti vo vtoroi polovine 1940-kh–1950-kh godakh" (PhD diss., Kaliningradskii gosudarstvennyi universitet, 2004), 152–53.

46. Iurii Kostiashov, "Stalin i Kaliningradskaia oblast': Popytka istoricheskoi rekonstruktsii," *Acta Historica Universitatis Klaipedensis* 28 (2009): 60–61.

47. Kostiashov, "Stalin," 61.

48. GANIKO f. 1, op. 1, d. 26, ll. 38–39, March 25, 1947.

49. Arūnė Arbušauskaitė. "Das tragische Schicksal Ostpreussens nach 1945 im Lichte neuer Dokumente," *Annaberger Annalen: Jahrbuch über Litauen und deutsch-litauische Beziehungen*, 3 (1995): 16.

50. GARF f. A612, op. 1, d. 1, l. 1, February 1, 1947.

51. GARF f. A612, op. 1, d. 1, l. 26, n.d. [spring of 1947].

52. Quoted in Bert Hoppe, *Auf den Trümmern von Königsberg: Kaliningrad 1946–1970* (Munich: R. Oldenbourg Verlag, 2000), 29.

53. GANIKO f. 1, op. 1, d. 59, ll. 25–28, July 5, 1947.

54. GANIKO f. 1, op. 1, d. 59, ll. 25–28, July 5, 1947.

55. GARF f. 9401, op. 2, d. 172, l. 44, January 31, 1947; GARF f. 9401, op. 2, d. 172, ll. 303–04; GAKO f. R246, op. 2, d. 13, l. 12, n.d. [early to mid-1947]; GAKO f. R246, op. 2, d. 1, ll. 120–24.

56. Arbušauskaitė, "Das tragische Schicksal," 16.

57. Hoppe, *Auf den Trümmern*, 32; Iurii Kostiashov, "Vyselenie nemtsev iz Kaliningradskoi oblasti v poslevoennye gody," *Voprosy istorii* 6 (1994): 187.

58. GAKO f. R310, op. 1, d. 7, l. 8, April 18, 1947.

59. GAKO f. R310, op. 1, d. 7, l. 8–9, April 18, 1947.

60. GAKO f. R297, op. 1, d. 102, l. 68, May 16, 1947.

61. GANIKO f. 1, op. 1, d. 62, ll. 4–9, May 28, 1947.

62. GANIKO f. 1, op. 1, d. 62, ll. 4–9, May 28, 1947.

63. "Posetiteli kremlevskogo kabineta I.V. Stalina," *Istoricheskii arkhiv* 4 (1996): 14; Kostiashov, "Stalin," 62, 14.

64. Kostiashov, "Stalin," 62.

65. Kostiashov, "Stalin," 62.

66. Iu. V. Kostiashov, "Kaliningradskaia oblast' v 1947–1948 gg. i plany ee razvitiia," *Voprosy istorii* 5 (2008): 109–11.

67. Kostiashov, "Stalin," 63–64; Kostiashov, "Kaliningradskaia oblast'," 109–11. The most thorough paragraph of the plan outlined the secret seventh

point of the decree, which supplied extra rations and supplies specifically to Kaliningrad's administrative elite.

68. GAKO f. R19, op. 1, d. 6, ll. 94–96, August 15, 1947.

69. Kostiashov, "Stalin," 64.

70. Per Brodersen, *Die Stadt im Westen: wie Königsberg Kaliningrad wurde* (Göttingen: Vandenhoeck & Ruprecht, 2008), 80.

71. Kostiashov, "Vyselenie," 187.

72. Käthe Hielscher, *Als Ostpreußin in russischer Kriegsgefangenschaft* (Berlin: Frieling, 1998), 145–47.

73. Hielscher, *Als Ostpreußin*, 158.

74. GARF f. A259, op. 6, d. 3923, ll. 137–38, April 7, 1947.

75. GANIKO f. 1, op. 1, d. 101, l. 66, August 12, 1947; GANIKO f. 1, op. 1, d. 101, l. 75, September 30, 1947; GANIKO f. 1, op. 1, d. 101, l. 72, September 1947; GANIKO f. 1, op. 1, d. 101, l. 77, September 1947; GAKO f. R291, op. 1, d. 110, ll. 40–41, October 1, 1947.

76. GANIKO f. 1, op. 1, d. 101, l. 72, September 1947; GANIKO f. 1, op. 1, d. 59, ll. 53, 55, October 7, 1947.

77. Sergei Kruglov signed the formal expulsion order No. 001067 on October 14, 1947; GARF f. 9401c, op. 12, d. 229, ll. 104-6, October 14, 1947.

78. Kostiashov, "Vyselenie," 187.

79. Kostiashov, "Vyselenie," 188.

80. Amar, *The Paradox*, 15.

81. David Brandenberger, *National Bolshevism: Stalinist Mass Culture and the Formation of Modern Russian National Identity, 1931–1956* (Cambridge, MA: Harvard University Press, 2002), 95–112.

82. Alexander Statiev, *The Soviet Counterinsurgency in the Western Borderlands* (Cambridge: Cambridge University Press, 2010), 182–83, 194.

83. E. A. Rees, "The Sovietization of Eastern Europe," in *The Sovietization of Eastern Europe: New Perspectives on the Postwar Period*, ed. Balázs Apor, Péter Apor, and E. A. Rees (Washington, DC: New Academia Publishing, 2008), 10–11.

84. Kibelka, *Ostpreußens Schicksaljahre*, 104–5, 116--119; Vygantis Vareikis, "Klaipėda (Memel) in der Nachkriegszeit 1945-1953," *Annaberger Annalen: Jahrbuch über Litauen und deutsch-litauische Beziehungen* 3 (1995): 54.

85. Vareikis, "Klaipeda," 55, 56, 63.

86. Statiev, *The Counterinsurgency*, 172.

87. GANIKO f. 2, op. 1, d. 42, l. 3, January 23, 1948.

88. GAKO f. R216, op. 1, d. 2, ll. 5-13, December 30, 1947; GAKO f. R180, op. 1, d. 26 [entire folder], November 1, 1947.

89. Hoppe, *Auf den Trümmern*, 33; GAKO f. R180, op. 1, d. 26, November 1, 1947, GAKO f. R180, op. 1, d.10, l. 58, January 13, 1948. In January 1948, a report about the industrial output for 1947 to the Gosplan SSSR for Kaliningrad Oblast discussed various deficiencies in production by referring to the high number of workers who left the oblast in 1947, particularly those who left in November (a reference to the German population).

90. Kostiashov, "Vyselenie," 188; Arbušauskaitė, "Das Tragische Schicksal," 18; Bernhard Fisch und Marina Klemeševa, "Zum Schicksal der Deutschen in

Königsberg 1945–1948 (im Spiegel bisher unbekannter russischer Quellen)," *Zeitschrift für Ostmitteleuropa- Forschung* 44, 3 (1995): 399.

91. Andreas Kossert writes, for example, that 24,000 Germans were re-settled to Germany in 1947–48 and more than 100,000 died—75 percent from hunger, 2.6 percent from typhus, and 15 percent from murder. Andreas Kossert, *Damals in Ostpreußen: der Untergang einer deutschen Provinz* (Munich: Pantheon, 2010), 178.

92. Kostiashov, "Vyselenie," 188; Arbušauskaitė, "Das Tragische Schicksal," 18; Fisch and Klemeševa, "Zum Schicksal," 399.

93. This estimate is based on the periodic censuses and known deaths reported in official Soviet sources between 1945 and 1948: GARF f. 9401, op. 2, d. 96, ll. 255-6, May 30, 1945; GAKO f. R330, op. 2, d. 9, ll.1–32, October 1945; GAKO f. R330, op. 1, d. 5, ll. 61-3, November 12, 1945; GAKO f. R332 op. 2, d. 7, l. 3, 21, n.d. [after February 1, 1946]; GARF f. A259, op. 6, d. 3923, l. 179, n.d. [April 1946]; GAKO f. R330, op. 2, d. 5, ll. 23-8, April 26, 1946; GARF f. A259, op. 6, d. 3923, ll. 73-6, May 21, 1946; RGASPI f. 17, op. 122, d. 143, ll. 78-80, June 1, 1946; GARF f. A259, op. 6, d. 3923, l. 40, August 19, 1946; GAKO f. R310, op. 1, d. 7, l. 13, April 18, 1947; GARF f. A259, op. 6, d. 3923, l. 1, June 12, 1947.

94. Hans von Lehndorff, *East Prussian Diary: A Journal of Faith, 1945–1947*, trans. Violet M. Macdonald (London: Oswald Wolff, 1963), 95 [April 30, 1945].

95. Quoted in Galtsova and Kostiashov, eds., *Vostochnaia Prussiia*, 77.

96. GARF f. 9401, op. 2, d. 172, l. 44, January 31, 1947; GARF f. 9401, op. 2, d. 172, ll. 303-04; GAKO f. R246, op. 2, d. 13, l. 12, no date [early to mid-1947]; GAKO f. R246, op. 2, d. 1, ll. 120-24.

97. Hielscher, *Als Ostpreußin*, 144–45.

98. Hielscher, *Als Ostpreußin*, 164.

99. Brodersen, *Die Stadt*, 81. As Brodersen notes, a handful of direct petitions by German women in Kaliningrad to obtain Soviet citizenship caught Moscow officials unprepared, and no clear policy was in place to process them.

100. Interview with Nina Vavilova, in GAKO collection, *Interv'iu s pervimy pereselentsev, pribyvshimi v Kaliningradskuiu Oblast' v 1945–1950 gg,"* 1:101; Interview with Alekandra Kliukha in *Interv'iu*, 6:84; Interview with Aleksandr Furmanov in *Interv'iu*, 8:100-101.

101. Elena Zubkova, *Russia after the War: Hopes, Illusions, and Disappointments, 1945–1957* trans. and ed. Hugh Ragsdale (Abington, NY: Routledge, 1998), 83-86, 120-21; Geoffrey Roberts, *The Soviet Union in World Politics: Coexistence, Revolution and Cold War, 1945–1991* (New York: Routledge, 1999), 25-27.

102. GANIKO f. 1, op. 1, d. 58, l. 17, October 1947; GANIKO f. 2, op. 1, d. 12, l. 4, October 23, 1947; GANIKO f. 2, op. 1, d. 12, ll. 23-24, October 1947; GANIKO f. 2, op. 1, d. 2, ll. 69-71, November 15-16, 1947.

103. GANIKO f. 197, op. 1, d. 31, l. 171, September 16, 1947. Fears of Soviet citizens "going native" were common in newly acquired lands across the Soviet sphere. See Tarik Cyril Amar, "Sovietization as a Civilizing Mission in the West," in *The Sovietization of Eastern Europe: New Perspectives on the Postwar Period*, ed. Balázs Apor, Péter Apor, and E. A. Rees, 1-9 (Washington, DC: New Academia Publishing, 2008), 41-43.

104. GANIKO f. 197, op. 1, d. 31, l. 166, September 16, 1947.

105. Quoted in Brodersen, *Die Stadt*, 82.

106. GAKO f. R59, op. 1, d. 3, l. 27, n.d. [early 1948].

107. V. Velichko, "Padenie Kenigsberga," *Pravda*, April 13, 1945.

108. N. P. Gratsianskii, *Kenigsberg: Stenogramma publichnoi lektsii* (Moscow: All-Union Lecture Bureau of the Committee for Higher Education Affairs of the People's Commissariat of the USSR, 1945).

109. GAKO f. R310, op. 1, d. 1, ll. 1–14, November 23, 1945.

110. GARF f. A259, op. 6, d. 4544, ll. 22–23, 26, n.d. [late 1946]; d. 3923, l. 21, n.d. [mid-1947]; GAKO f. R310, op. 1, d. 7, l. 32, n.d. [before October 1947].

111. Violeta Davoliūtė, *The Making and Breaking of Soviet Lithuania: Memory and Modernity in the Wake of War* (New York: Routledge, 2013), 61.

112. GAKO f. R216, op. 1, d. 2, l. 410, November 18, 1948.

113. This trend was also present elsewhere in newly Sovietized parts of the USSR, including in Vilnius, a city newly incorporated into the Lithuanian SSR from Poland. Just as in Kaliningrad, architecture connected to the previous population's history in the region was dismissed as simultaneously bourgeois or fascist and deemed not worth preserving. Davoliūtė, *The Making and Breaking of Soviet Lithuania*, 62.

114. Dmitrii Tian, *Kaliningradskaia pravda*, May 1, 1948.

115. GAKO f. R520, op. 1, d. 12, l. 1f.

116. GAKO f. R520, op. 1, d. 12, l. 1f.

117. Hoppe, *Auf den Trümmern*, 55.

118. GANIKO f. 197, op. 1, d. 31, l. 171, September 16, 1947.

119. GAKO f. R216, op. 1, d. 2, l. 91, February 14, 1948.

120. GANIKO f. 1, op. 11, d. 17, l. 109f., May 30, 1952.

121. Hoppe, *Auf den Trümmern*, 49.

122. Rüdiger Ritter, "Prescribed Identity: The Role of History for the Legitimization of Soviet Rule in Lithuania," in *The Sovietization of the Baltic States, 1940–1956*, ed. Olaf Mertelsmann (Tartu, Estonia: Kleio Ajalookirjanduse Sihtasutus, 2003), 86; Robert Gerwarth, *The Vanquished: Why the First World War Failed to End* (New York: Farrar, Straus and Giroux, 2016), 214; Paul Robert Magocsi, *Historical Atlas of Central Europe*, 3rd. revised and expanded edition (Toronto: University of Toronto Press, 2018), 189.

123. See, for example, Michael Fleming, *Communism, Nationalism, and Ethnicity in Poland, 1944–50* (London: Routledge, 2010).

124. Richard J. Kirckus, *The Kaliningrad Question* (Lanham, MD: Rowman and Littlefield, 2002), 29; Fleming, *Communism*.

125. A. V. Filatov and V. N. Patserina, *Naselenie Severo-Vostochnoi Prussii posle II Mirovoi voiny. Pravovoi analiz. Chast' I: Pereselenie ili izgnanie? Pravovye predposylki i posledstviia* (Kaliningrad, Russia: Biznes-Kontakt, 2001), 9–25; Richard J. Kirckus, *The Kaliningrad Question* (Lanham, MD: Rowman and Littlefield, 2002), 29; Tony Sharp, "The Russian Annexation of the Königsberg Area 1941–45," *Survey: A Journal of East & West Studies* 23, no. 4 (1977): 156.

126. United States Department of State, *Foreign Relations of the United States Diplomatic Papers, The Conferences at Cairo and Tehran, 1943* (Washington, DC: U.S. Government Printing Office, 1943), 604.

127. Kostiashov, "Stalin," 58. "German aggression" referred to Germany in the First and Second World Wars and perhaps to Russia's participation in Napoleonic War battles in East Prussia (although not against "German aggressors" then) and also to the Rus' prince Alexander Nevskii's thirteenth-century victory over the Teutonic Knights.

128. *Sovetskii Soiuz na mezhdunarodnykh konferentsiiakh perioda Velikoi Otechestvennoi voiny 1941–1945 gg. Tom II. Tegeranskaia konferentsiia rukovoditelei trekh soiuznykh derzhav—SSSR, SShA i Velikobritanii (28 noiabria–1 dekabria 1943 g.)* (Moscow: Politizdat, 1984), 150.

129. GAKO f. R310, op. 1, d. 1, ll. 1–14, November 23, 1945.

130. GAKO f. R310, op. 1, d. 1, ll. 1–32, 94.

131. GARF f. A259, op. 6, d. 3923, l. 81, April 20, 1946.

132. GARF f. A259, op. 6, d. 3923, ll. 82–82b, May 3, 1946.

133. GARF f. A259, op. 6, d. 5950, l. 65, February 13, 1947.

134. GARF f. A259, op. 6, d. 4950. ll. 67–69, February 12, 1947; d. 5950, ll. 40–41, February 20, 1947.

135. GARF f. A259, op. 6, d. 5950, l. 65, February 13, 1947. Bagration was also the code name for the Soviet offensive during the initial invasion in 1944.

136. A. S. Erusalimskii, *Likvidatsiia prusskogo gosudarstva: Stenogramma publichnoi lektsii* (Moscow: Izdatel'stvo "Pravda," 1947).

137. Dmitrii Tian, "Sovetskii gorod Kaliningrad," *Kaliningradskaia pravda*, November 7, 1947.

138. GAKO f. R541, op. 1, d. 1, December 27, 1947.

139. Theodor Schieder, ed., *Documents on the Expulsion of the Germans from Eastern Central Europe, Volume 1: The Expulsions of the German Population from the Territories East of the Oder-Neisse Line* (Bonn: Federal Ministry for Expellees, Refugees, and War Victims, 1956); Kibelka, *Ostpreussens Schicksaljahre.*

140. Gerhild Luschnat, *Die Lage der Deutschen im Königsberger Gebiet, 1945–1948* (Frankfurt am Main: Peter Lang, 1996); Brodersen, *Die Stadt.*

141. *Samaia Zapadnaia: Sbornik dokumentov i materialov o stanovlenii i razvitii Kaliningradskoi oblasti: 1946–1952* (Kaliningrad: Knizhnoe izdatel'stvo, 1980).

142. Kostjašov, "Russen und Deutschen," 168.

143. Edele, *Soviet Veterans*, 185.

144. Terry Martin, "The Origins of Soviet Ethnic Cleansing," *Journal of Modern History* 70, no. 4 (December 1998): 860.

Conclusion

1. Constantine FitzGibbon, Introduction to Hans von Lehndorff, *East Prussian Diary: A Journal of Faith, 1945–1947*, trans. Violet M. Macdonald (London: Oswald Wolff, 1963), vii.

2. Yuri Buida, "The Prussian Bride," in *The Prussian Bride*, trans. Oliver Ready (Sawtry, UK: Dedalus, 2002), 13–17.

3. Ian Kershaw, "'Working toward the Führer': Reflections on the Nature of the Hitler Dictatorship," in *Stalinism and Nazism: Dictatorships in Comparison*, ed. Ian Kershaw and Moshe Lewin (Cambridge: Cambridge University Press, 1997) 100–103.

4. Jochen Hellbeck, "The Diaries of Fritzes and the Letters of Gretchens," in *Fascination and Enmity: Russia and Germany as Entangled Histories, 1914–1945*, ed. Michael David-Fox, Peter Holquist, and Alexander M. Martin (Pittsburgh: University of Pittsburgh Press, 2012), 127.

5. *Kaliningradskaia pravda*, November 17, 1948.

6. Yuri Slezkine, "The USSR as a Communal Apartment, or How a Socialist State Promoted Ethnic Particularism," *Slavic Review* 53, no. 2 (Summer 1994): 41–52; Martin, *The Affirmative Action Empire*; Francine Hirsch, *Empire of Nations: Ethnographic Knowledge and the Making of the Soviet Union* (Ithaca, NY: Cornell University Press, 2005); Ronald Grigor Suny and Terry Martin, eds., *A State of Nations: Empire and Nation-Making in the Age of Lenin and Stalin* (Oxford: Oxford University Press, 2001).

7. Michael Wieck, *A Childhood under Hitler and Stalin: Memoirs of a "Certified Jew,"* trans. Penny Milbouer (Madison, WI: University of Wisconsin Press, 2003), 166–67.

8. Deichelmann, *Ich sah Königsberg sterben: Tagebuch eines Arztes in Königsberg 1945 bis 1948* (Beltheim, Germany: Bublies, 1999), 211 [December 31, 1947].

9. Polina Kaganova, "Dorogoi na Berlin," *Zvezda* 2 (1972): 120.

10. Wieck, *A Childhood*, 32.

INDEX

Page numbers in *italics* refer to maps and figures.

www.ingramcontent.com/pod-product-compliance
Lightning Source LLC
Chambersburg PA
CBHW020339100426

42812CB00029B/3183/J